KU-536-263

# KEATS
## POETICAL WORKS

# KEATS

## POETICAL WORKS

———

EDITED BY

## H. W. GARROD

**OXFORD UNIVERSITY PRESS**
LONDON OXFORD NEW YORK

STOCKTON · BILLINGHAM

LIBRARY

TECHNICAL COLLEGE

821 KEA

39374

*Oxford University Press*

LONDON OXFORD NEW YORK
GLASGOW TORONTO MELBOURNE WELLINGTON
CAPE TOWN IBADAN NAIROBI DAR ES SALAAM LUSAKA ADDIS ABABA
DELHI BOMBAY CALCUTTA MADRAS KARACHI DACCA
KUALA LUMPUR SINGAPORE HONG KONG TOKYO

ISBN 0 19 281067 7

*This edition first published in the* OXFORD STANDARD
AUTHORS *series by Oxford University Press, London, 1956*
*First issued as an Oxford University Press paperback 1970*
*Reprinted 1973 and 1976*

*All rights reserved. No part of this publication may be reproduced,
stored in a retrieval system, or transmitted, in any form or by
any means, electronic, mechanical, photocopying, recording, or
otherwise, without the prior permission of Oxford University
Press*

*This book is sold subject to the condition that it shall not, by way
of trade or otherwise, be lent, re-sold, hired out, or otherwise
circulated without the publisher's prior consent in any form of
binding or cover other than that in which it is published and
without a similar condition including this condition being imposed
on the subsequent purchaser*

*Printed in Great Britain
at the University Press, Oxford
by Vivian Ridler
Printer to the University*

# PREFATORY NOTE

THE present volume replaces the volume prepared for the Oxford series of Standard Authors by H. Buxton Forman as long ago as 1906. The first section of the Introduction (*Early Printed Editions*) is taken over from Buxton Forman, with small changes and additions. For the second section, which deals generally with the relation of the printed texts to the manuscripts, I have drawn largely on the opening pages of my edition of Keats in the Oxford English Texts series. For a detailed account of the manuscripts, and for the variants which they offer, the reader is referred to that edition. Our printed texts of Keats are nearly everywhere good; affording small opportunity for textual criticism as ordinarily understood. The textual criticism of Keats studies, in fact, not so much to establish the text as to go behind it. Its primary concern is, not the poet's *ultima manus*, but his first fingerings and gropings. This edition does not help the reader to go behind the text. Yet to tempt him to do so, I have appended to it a sheaf of critical notes. They are few, and they are confined to passages notable and famous.

I have placed in an Appendix the fragment *Gripus*, which has not hitherto been included in any edition of Keats's Works. It is preserved in the Morgan Library Woodhouse Book. No author's name is added by Woodhouse. But the title-page advises the reader that all the poems that are not by Keats have the names of the authors added. The fragment was accepted as the composition of Keats by Miss Lowell, who printed it (not altogether accurately) in an Appendix to her *Life of Keats* (1924).

*July* 1956                                              H. W. G.

# CONTENTS

viii                     CONTENTS

CONTENTS

# INTRODUCTION

I N an edition of Keats intended to meet a popular demand among the educated classes, it seems worth while to record precisely how and in what forms the text has come through the nineteenth century and reached his lovers and admirers in the twentieth.

The volumes which Keats himself issued through the press are three. The contents of the first reappear in Keats's own order of arrangement as the text of the first 52 pages in the present edition. The book is a foolscap octavo. It was issued in drab boards, with a back-label reading 'Keats's | Poems', and consists of a blank leaf, fly-title 'Poems' in heavy black letter, with imprint on verso, 'Printed by C. Richards, | No. 18, Warwick Street, Golden Square, London'; title-page, in all known copies a cancel-leaf (Poems, | By | John Keats. | 'What more felicity can fall to creature, | Than to enjoy delight with liberty' | *Fate of the Butterfly.*—Spenser. | ⸤Vignette head of Spenser⸥ London: | Printed for | C. & J. Ollier, 3, Welbeck Street, Cavendish Square. | 1817); Dedication with a note on the verso, and pages 1 to 121 including the fly-titles to the Epistles, Sonnets, and *Sleep and Poetry*. The fly-titles give us a book in four sections with headlines in Roman capitals running throughout each section, recto and verso alike, (1) 'Poems', (2) 'Epistles', (3) 'Sonnets', and (4) 'Sleep and Poetry'. The note after the Dedication is as follows: '⸤The Short Pieces in the middle of the Book, as | well as some of the Sonnets, were written at an | earlier period than the rest of the Poems.⸥'

Keats's second venture was the far more ambitious work *Endymion*, forming pages 53 to 157 of the present volume. There was talk of making the poem a quarto, with a portrait of Keats by Haydon; but ultimately it appeared without a portrait, as a handsome octavo volume. It was done up in thick drab boards labelled at the back, 'Keats's | Endymion. | *Lond.* 1818', and consisted of (1) fly-title 'Endymion: | A Romance' with imprint at foot of verso, 'Printed by T. Miller, Noble street Cheapside', (2) title-page (with motto adapted from Shakespeare's seventeenth Sonnet), (3) the dedication reprinted on page 53 in the present edition, (4) the Preface (page 54), (5) an erratum leaf with sometimes one and sometimes five errata printed on the recto, and (6) 207 pages of text including the fly-titles to the four books. The headline throughout is 'Endymion' in Roman small capitals, the number of the Book being indicated in smaller letters at the inner corners, and the pages in Arabic figures as usual at the outer corners. The full page consists of twenty-two lines; and the lines are numbered in tens in the margin, not every ten lines of verse, but every ten lines of print, so that when a fresh paragraph begins with a portion of a verse, that particular verse counts for two lines. In numbering the lines for the present edition I have of course counted by lines of verse.

The poet's third and last book of poems, the contents of which, arranged in the order adopted by Keats, occupy pages 159 to 243 of this edition, was issued in 12mo in the summer of 1820, put up in stout drab boards like those of *Endymion*, with a back-label 'Lamia, Isabella, | &c. | — | 7s. 6d.' It consists of half-title, reading 'Lamia, Isabella, | &c.', with imprint on verso, 'London: | Printed by Thomas Davison, Whitefriars', title-page, as given (*post*) following that of *Endymion*, Advertisement, Contents, and pages 1 to 199 including the half-titles to *Lamia*, *Isabella*, *The Eve of St. Agnes*, the miscellaneous Poems, and *Hyperion*. There are headlines in Roman capitals running throughout each section, recto and verso alike : (1) 'Lamia', (2) 'Isabella', (3) 'Eve of St. Agnes', (4) 'Poems', and (5) 'Hyperion'. The pages are numbered in the usual way with Arabic figures; and in *Lamia* and *Hyperion* the Parts and Books are marked at the inner side of the headline in smaller Roman capitals. On the verso of page 199 the imprint of Davison is repeated; and there are eight pages of Taylor and Hessey's advertisements, beginning with one of *Endymion*. The Advertisement prefixed to the published volume (page 160 in this edition) appears to have been supplied by the publishers. In a copy belonging to the late Canon Ainger, Keats had drawn his pen through and through this advertisement, writing at the head, 'I had no part in this; I was ill at the time.' The statement about *Endymion* he had bracketed off from the rest; and beneath it he had written 'This is a lie!' In connexion with this unusual vehemence of expression, it is no more than fair to mention that the Woodhouse Common-place book, used by the publishers when considering which of Keats's unpublished poems they would issue in 1820, records a vote against *Hyperion*; and the inference is that they were induced by Keats's friends to publish the fragment after all.

We have not, however, yet completed the tale of the *editiones principes* of Keats's Poetry, seeing that his *posthuma* have from time to time been issued in substantive volumes as distinguished from the mere extension of editions of his works. The first in importance, as in date, of these posthumous *editiones principes* is Monckton Milnes's invaluable contribution of 1848. In 1833, at the villa of Walter Savage Landor 'on the beautiful hill-side of Fiesole', Monckton Milnes had met Charles Armitage Brown, whose name is now universally associated with that of Keats; he had previously learnt much about the poet from Joseph Severn, then still (as to the end) at Rome; and he now found that Brown, having carefully guarded the literary remains of Keats, intended to publish them in two or three years on returning to England. Brown returned, got forward with his preparations, wrote his biographical account of Keats, and had arranged for publication, when he suddenly decided to emigrate to New Zealand. This he did, leaving his material for Milnes to make use of, 'for the purpose of vindicating the character and advancing the fame' of Keats.

Charles Cowden Clarke, Edward Holmes, George Felton Mathew, and Henry Stephens helped the biographer and editor with their recollections; John Hamilton Reynolds 'contributed the rich store of his correspondence'; Charles Wentworth Dilke and William Haslam supported the undertaking with letters and reminiscences; to John Taylor and James Augustus Hessey, Keats's friendly and helpful publishers, and Charles Ollier, who in a less friendly and helpful manner had preceded them in that office, Milnes was 'indebted for willing co-operation'; and Mr. Jeffrey, who had married George Keats's widow, contributed, in a very slovenly and misleading way, a great mass of letters and *data* which, notwithstanding his lack of judgement, of experience, and of thoroughness, were of quite extraordinary value. The result founded on all these aids and communications was given to the world in the year 1848, in two of those handy and agreeable volumes which, printed by Messrs. Bradbury and Evans, issued in a steady stream for some years from the house of Edward Moxon of Dover Street—the volumes which we associate with the names of Shelley, Wordsworth, Landor, Hood, Tennyson, and the Brownings.

When the book made its appearance, one of the main literary supporters of the undertaking, who had known intimately both Keats and Brown, was amused as well as nettled at the role claimed for Brown as the 'generous protector' of Keats, and left a somewhat caustic note on the subject in his copy of Milnes's work, the title-page of which he decorated with the following couplet from *The Rosciad*:

> Appearances to save his only care;
> So things *seem* right, no matter what they are.

Charles Wentworth Dilke, in quoting thus epigrammatically from Churchill, did not of course mean to apply the couplet literally; but the inscription and other notes show how advanced his views of editorial obligation were; for Milnes can scarcely be said to have carried editorial licence beyond the limits then usual.

Milnes's first contribution to Keats literature, published in the best of company, may be bibliographically described as consisting of two volumes, foolscap octavo, bound in purple-brown cloth, upright-straight-grained, blind-blocked on the sides with the same severe floral-scroll design that appears on the fourth edition of Tennyson's Poems (two volumes, 1846), *The Princess* (1847), *In Memoriam* (1850), Landor's *Hellenics* (1847), and many others. The colour is the same as that of the cloth used for several editions of *In Memoriam*. The Keats volumes are gilt-lettered across the back, 'Life | Letters &c. | of Keats. | Vol. I. [II.]' The Title-pages are as follows:

LIFE,
## LETTERS, AND LITERARY REMAINS,

OF

# JOHN KEATS

EDITED BY

RICHARD MONCKTON MILNES.

IN TWO VOLUMES.

VOL. I. [II.]

LONDON:

EDWARD MOXON, DOVER STREET

1848.

The half-titles read 'Life, Letters, &c. | of | John Keats.' Their
versos are blank; but those of the titles have the central im-
print 'London: | Bradbury and Evans, Printers, Whitefriars.'
In volume I, pages v to vii contain a dedication to Francis
(afterwards Lord) Jeffrey, page viii is blank, the preface
extends from page ix to page xix, page xx is blank, and page 1
starts with a dropped head reading 'Life and Letters | of | John
Keats.' There are 288 pages of the text, with headlines read-
ing 'Life and Letters of' on the versos and 'John Keats' on the
rectos, save on page 288, where the legend appears in full:
the printers' imprint is repeated at the foot. The volume has
for frontispiece a print from a steel plate engraved by H.
Robinson after the well-known half-length portrait of Keats
by Severn, three-quarter face, seated behind a table with an
open book before him, the right hand resting on the book, the
left supporting the chin and cheek (fingers closed), while the
elbow rests on the table. An eight-page catalogue of Moxon's
publications is generally found in perfect copies, inserted
within the glazed primrose end-paper of the recto cover.

Of volume II the text also starts with a dropped head
worded as in volume I, with which it is uniform as to headlines
up to page 108. Then there is a half-title, 'Literary Remains',
dividing the posthumous poetry from the Life and Letters;
and the poetry itself occupies the remainder of the volume,
ending on page 306, and bearing distinctive headlines. At the
foot of page 306 the printers' imprint recurs; and facing it is
a list, headed 'Poetry,' of volumes sold by Moxon: the verso

of this is blank. The frontispiece to this second volume is a well-lithographed facsimile of a holograph manuscript,—the song 'Shed no tear—O shed no tear'.

These fascinating volumes have no index of any kind, or even so much as a table of contents; but besides the Literary Remains forming the bulk of the second volume, many poems and fragments are scattered through the first volume, some embodied in letters, and some appended at the close of the volume, after the Notes on Milton there reprinted from the scarce American periodical the *Dial*. A list of these poems is proper to this place. The page column indicates the position in Lord Houghton's volumes.

## POEMS IN VOLUME II

Moxon had already in 1846 reprinted, in his delightful paper-covered 24mo series of Poets, Smith's edition of Keats's *Poetical Works* (1841) with a trifling change of order in the contents; and he now proceeded to publish a reissue in foolscap octavo to accompany the *Life, Letters, and Literary Remains*. The 1851 issue of this book (' a new edition') has no biography, but contains the same portrait print as the *Life*, &c. Since that time no substantive volume of fresh poems by Keats has been published; but additions have been made in one issue after another until the mass has grown very considerably.

One more posthumous *editio princeps* remains to be dealt with. In the long journal-letter which Keats wrote to his brother and sister-in-law in America in December 1818 and January 1819, occurs the following passage, headed 'Friday' simply, but belonging probably to Christmas Day 1818:

> I think you knew before you left England, that my next subject would be 'the fall of Hyperion'. I went on a little with it last night, but it will take some time to get into the vein again. I will not give you any extracts because I wish the whole to make an impression. I have however a few Poems which you will like, and I will copy them out on the next sheet.

This no doubt relates to the fragment of *Hyperion* in direct narration, as ultimately published in 1820. The poem in that form, it will be remembered, was abandoned finally in August 1819; but by the end of the year he was at work on an attempt to recast it in a wholly different form. This took place at Wentworth Place: in the morning he sat with Brown and worked at *The Cap and Bells*: in the evening, *fide* Brown, he had a room to himself 'and was deeply engaged in re-modelling the fragment of *Hyperion* into the form of a vision'. This remarkable production (pages 401–16 of this edition) was mentioned in the *Life, Letters*, &c. (1848), as a recast, but remained in manuscript until Milnes contributed it to the third volume of the *Bibliographical and Historical Miscellanies* of the Philobiblon Society (1856–7), in doubt whether it was a recast or a draft. A few copies of it were also printed in pamphlet form apart from the *Miscellanies*. The fragment was afterwards published in the Appendix to Milnes's new edition of *The Life and Letters of John Keats* issued in 1867 by Moxon & Co. On that occasion it was said to be without doubt the first draft. But Lord Houghton must have failed to consult again his manuscript memoir by Charles Brown, wherein the 'Vision' is distinctly said to be a late reconstruction. It will be seen that, although a great deal of the 'Vision' is special to the new poem, there are large passages from the epic version of *Hyperion*. A comparison of passages which are substantially identical while varying in detail perhaps affords the most astounding instance on record of the loss of artistic power and perception under physical decay and mental agony. The conception of Moneta, though not artistically on Keats's highest level, has a touching grandeur of its own, and, apart from the detrimental treatment of the *Hyperion* fragment, is highly notable. As regards the holograph manuscript of the 'Vision', Lord Houghton stated in 1883 that a mystery attached to its fate: it was lent for some purposes of the 1867 reprint; and the owner failed to recover it.

The Philobiblon Society's separate print of course ranks among the *editiones principes* of Keats's writings; and it is perhaps the scarcest of all. It is a pott quarto pamphlet of twenty-four pages printed on Saunders's unbleached hand-made paper, water-marked '1856'. There is no title-page; but there is a half-title reading 'Another Version of Keats's "Hyperion".' Pages 3 and 4 are occupied by the following note:

Another Version of Keats's
'Hyperion.'

The MS. of the following Poem was given to me by Mr. Brown, the friend and protector of John Keats, together with the other *Literary Remains* which I published in 1848. Is it the original sketch out of which the earlier part of the printed poem was composed, or is it the commencement of a reconstruction of the whole? I have no external evidence to decide this question; but it seems to me that, in either case, this fragment well deserves preservation. If it is the first composition out of which a portion of the printed poem was selected, it is most remarkable, as showing the affluence and self-command of the genius that could afford to lay by passages of so much originality and splendour as, on this supposition, have here been cancelled. If, on the other hand, it is the beginning of a new version of the whole Poem, we may equally admire the imagination which was not content with what had been already accomplished, and, not satisfied with completing the work as it stood, desired to improve its scope and enlarge its proportions. There is, indeed, no lover of the writings of this wonderful youth who will not be glad to see this production for its own sake, and apart from all discussion as to its intention; but the problem of the priority of the two poems—both fragments, and both so beautiful—may afford a wide field for ingenious and critical conjecture.

R. M. MILNES.

The poem starts on page 5 with a dropped head reading 'Hyperion, a Vision'; but the headlines, from page 6 to page 24, read on the versos, 'Another version of', and on the rectos 'Keats's Hyperion'. Concerning the title of this reconstruction, I do not find much evidence properly so called. As we have seen, Brown is the authority for the now established fact that Keats attempted the task of 're-modelling the fragment of *Hyperion* into the form of a Vision'; but it does not appear that he called it 'Hyperion, a Vision'. Lord Houghton contributed it to the Philobiblon Society's Collections as 'Another Version' of the fragment, and used the description 'A Vision' on one page. The almost invariably accurate Woodhouse calls it 'The Fall of Hyperion, a Dream'—not casually or descriptively, but as the title of an unpublished work from which he inscribes some extracts in a collection of quotations from various authors prefixed to his interleaved copy of *Endymion*.

Many of Keats's poems appeared first in periodicals; and mention should here be made of the *Examiner* (in Leigh Hunt's time), *Annals of the Fine Arts* (1817–20), Hunt's *Literary Pocket-Book*, his *Indicator*, *The Gem, a Literary Annual*, edited by Thomas Hood, *Hood's Magazine, The Dial, The Athenaeum, Notes and Queries*, and *The Century Guild Hobby Horse*.

H. BUXTON FORMAN

## II. MANUSCRIPT SOURCES

FOR each of the longer poems of Keats, with the exception of *The Fall of Hyperion*, we have manuscripts in Keats's autograph. Three of these autograph manuscripts—those of *Endymion, Lamia, Isabella*—are fair copies; the two first are the manuscript actually sent to the printer. For *Hyperion, The Eve of St. Agnes, The Cap and Bells, Otho,* and the fragment of *King Stephen,* we have Keats's first draft. For *The Fall of Hyperion* we have, in lieu of the autograph, three manuscript transcripts (one of them incomplete). What manuscript of it Monckton Milnes gave to the printer in 1856, we have no means of knowing. Of the three extant transcripts, one—first brought to light in 1904—is in the hand of Keats's friend Woodhouse; another is written by one of Woodhouse's clerks. The fragmentary transcript was made by another friend of Keats, J. H. Reynolds. The text printed in this edition derives from Woodhouse's transcript.

For the shorter poems our wealth of manuscripts is less, but still great. It is least in the volume of 1817; where, even so, seventeen poems, out of a total of thirty-three, exist in Keats's autograph—for all of the seventeen we have, in addition, transcripts. For seven other poems we have, not Keats's autograph, but manuscript copies made from it; leaving nine pieces for which no manuscript is available. This was Keats's first book; Olliers, who published it, did not attach to Keats's autograph the religious importance which Taylor and Hessey felt for it later. Tom and George Keats were willing copyists, falling short, however, of the monkish diligence of Woodhouse and Brown.

The volume of 1820 contains nine short poems; for all of which, with the exception of the *Ode on a Grecian Urn,* we have Keats's autograph. For the *Grecian Urn* we have four transcripts.

Monckton Milnes's two volumes of 1848 added to the corpus of Keats's poetry seventy-one new short poems. For thirty-five of these, we still have Keats's autograph; for all the others, with the exception of the sonnet beginning 'This mortal body . . .', and the lines 'What can I do to drive away . . .', we have transcripts.

Since 1848 there have been brought to light forty-two additional pieces, of which thirty are in autograph and twelve in transcript.

Of the three volumes which were printed during Keats's lifetime the texts are in general good. If we leave aside punctuation and orthography, the *Poems* of 1817 have not more than three provable errors of the press;[1] in the 1820 volume there are none. *Endymion* is printed with less circumspection; the Errata leaf lists five misprints, and there are in fact something like twice as many—the most serious is the loss of a whole line after iii. 201. But the defects are for the most part trifling, and easily remediable. The three volumes represent fairly Keats's *ultima manus*. That phrase must, so far as the volume of 1820 goes, be interpreted generously—the book offers here and there readings to which Keats was, it seems likely, not more than a consenting party. Of the text of *The Eve of St. Agnes* Woodhouse says plainly: 'Keats left it to his Publishers to adopt which [of two variant readings] they pleased, & to revise the whole.' The printed text of the poem sometimes has readings for which there is no manuscript authority; they are mostly of a kind which studies 'propriety' —an effect for which Taylor and Woodhouse were over-zealous. In *Isabella*, again, notes made by Keats himself in the printer's copy show that he was not pedantically exigent. Against stanza vi he has scrawled 'Stop this as you please'; against xxii 'Please point this as you like'. Against the last line of xxv he has written 'You may use your judgment between your lines and mine' (a note addressed, apparently, to Taylor). Taylor and Hessey and Woodhouse took those liberties which Keats allowed them. But it is not, I think, proved, or probable, that they took any others.[2] The more I study Woodhouse's papers, the better is my opinion of his integrity—everywhere his fidelity appears equal to his diligence. It can hardly be accident that the poem which offers the greatest number of discrepancies between manuscript and printed text, *The Eve of St. Agnes*, is the poem in which the publishers were given liberty 'to revise the whole'. Monckton Milnes handled his manuscripts somewhat more freely: in particular, *The Fall of Hyperion* offers several patent interpolations. But in general he too, I think, must be accounted faithful. The volumes of 1848—where we can nearly always check him by his manuscripts—are, in the main, 'good texts'. Here and there he has stopped a gap with his

---

[1] *Induction* 46, *To some Ladies* 6, Sonnet xvi, 7.

[2] I confess to a doubt about 'She dwells with Beauty' in the *Ode on Melancholy*, iii. 1; where all our MSS., including Keats's autograph, agree in giving 'She lives in beauty'.

own plausible invention. A notable example is *Otho*, III. i. 8, where the printer misread *limbo* as *limbs*, and Milnes stopped the gap by writing *white limbs*. Occasionally, he has adopted a conjecture which he found pencilled in the margin of his text—an example is *shrouds* for *creeds* in the third line of the cancelled first stanza of the *Ode on Melancholy*. Once at least he has introduced order—or what has seemed order—by a violent emendation of his own (*Ode on Indolence*, v. 1).

In general, then, the manuscripts of Keats do not help us to resolve problems in the text of Keats. Our printed texts give us almost everywhere what Keats, sometimes after infinite writing and rewriting, wished us to have. The manuscripts do not help us to get at the true text. But they do help us to see the gropings, the strivings, the agonies, through which great poetry comes to truth. Of no other poet do we know so well both what he is and how he came to it.

H. W. GARROD

# KEATS'S LIFE

1795  John Keats's birth in Finsbury, 31 October.
1797  Birth of his brother George, 28 February.
1799  Birth of his brother Thomas, 18 November.
1803  Birth of his sister Frances Mary (Fanny), 3 June.
1804  Death of his father, 16 April.
      His mother marries William Rawlings, 27 June.
      Keats goes to live with his grandmother, Mrs. Jennings, at
        Edmonton.
1810  Death of his mother, March.
1803–11  Is educated at Mr. Clarke's school, Enfield.
      Begins translating THE AENEID.
1811  Apprenticed to Thomas Hammond, Surgeon.
      Finishes translating THE AENEID.
1812  Writes IMITATION OF SPENSER.
1813  Introduced to Severn.
1815  Writes ODE TO APOLLO ('In thy western halls . . .').
      Entered at Guy's Hospital, 1 October.
      Writes EPISTLE TO GEORGE FELTON MATHEW, November.
1816  First published poem (the sonnet 'O Solitude . . .') appears
        in the *Examiner*, 5 May
      Addresses a sonnet to Charles Wells, 29 June.
      Receives certificate qualifying him to practise as an apothe-
        cary, 26 July.
      Writes EPISTLE TO GEORGE KEATS, August.
      Writes EPISTLE TO CHARLES COWDEN CLARKE, September.
      Writes the Chapman's Homer Sonnet, October.
      Meeting with Leigh Hunt, October.
      Introduced to Haydon, November.
      Contemplates the subject of ENDYMION and writes 'I stood
        tip-toe upon a little hill', December.
1817  First volume of POEMS published, early.
      ENDYMION begun, spring.
      Stays in the Isle of Wight, April, and Margate, May.
      Visits Benjamin Bailey at Oxford, September.
      Visits Stratford-on-Avon with Bailey.
      Draft of ENDYMION finished at Burford Bridge, 28 November.
      Sees Kean's return to the public and criticizes him in the
        *Champion*, 1 December.
1817–18  Winters at Hampstead.
1818  Book I of ENDYMION sent to press, January.
      Seeing 'a good deal' of Wordsworth, January.

1818    Joins his brothers at Teignmouth, March.
Revision of ENDYMION finished, March.
ENDYMION published, April.
ISABELLA, OR THE POT OF BASIL, finished by 27 April.
FRAGMENT OF AN ODE TO MAY written, 1 May.
Returns to Hampstead, May.
Departure of George Keats and his bride for America, June
Visits the Lakes with Brown, June.
Scotch tour with Brown, July and August.
A fleeting visit to Ireland, July.
A violent cold caught in the Isle of Mull, July.
'Cockney School' attack in *Blackwood's Magazine* published
      August.
Returns to Hampstead, August.
Troubled by sore throat, September.
Attack in the *Quarterly Review* published, September.
At Well Walk, Hampstead, September to December.
First meeting with Fanny Brawne, September.
Thomas Keats dies, 1 December, and John moves to Went-
      worth Place to live with Brown, December.
Sore throat again, December.

1818–19  HYPERION begun, winter.

1819    Stays at Chichester and Bedhampton, January.
THE EVE OF ST. AGNES written, January.
Returns to Wentworth Place, February.
Persistent sore throat, February.
ODE TO PSYCHE and LA BELLE DAME SANS MERCI written,
      April–May.
ODE TO A NIGHTINGALE composed, May.
Throat still sore in June and July.
Visits the Isle of Wight with James Rice, July.
ODE TO A NIGHTINGALE published, July.
Writes LAMIA, Part I, and OTHO THE GREAT, Act I, July.
Removes with Brown to Winchester, August.
OTHO THE GREAT finished, HYPERION continued, August.
Fleeting visit to London and return to Winchester, September.
To AUTUMN composed, HYPERION abandoned, LAMIA finished,
      THE EVE OF ST. AGNES revised, September.
Resolves to work for periodicals, September.

1819    Returns to Hampstead to winter, October.
Leaves off animal food, October.
Throat in a threatening state again, December.

1820    ODE ON A GRECIAN URN published, January.
Fatal illness commences, 3 February.
Keats and Brown finally part at Gravesend, 7 May.

1820 LA BELLE DAME SANS MERCI published in the *Indicator*, 10 May.
Fragment of THE CAP AND BELLS written, June (?).
LAMIA, ISABELLA, &c., published, first week in July.
Stays at Kentish Town, near and with Hunt, June–July.
Attack of blood-spitting, 22 June.
Returns to Wentworth Place to be nursed by Mrs. and Miss Brawne, August.
THE CAP AND BELLS xxvi–xxx. 4 quoted by Hunt in the *Indicator*, 23 August.
Sails for Italy with Severn, September.
Final version of the Sonnet 'Bright Star . . .' written on board ship.
Writes his last letter from Rome, November.

1821 His death, 23 February, and burial near the tomb of Caius Cestius, 26 February.

# POEMS

## PUBLISHED IN 1817

E

DEDICATION

## TO LEIGH HUNT, ESQ.

GLORY and loveliness have pass'd away;
    For if we wander out in early morn,
    No wreathed incense do we see upborne
Into the east, to meet the smiling day:
No crowd of nymphs soft voic'd and young, and gay,
    In woven baskets bringing ears of corn,
    Roses, and pinks, and violets, to adorn
The shrine of Flora in her early May.
But there are left delights as high as these,
    And I shall ever bless my destiny,
That in a time, when under pleasant trees
    Pan is no longer sought, I feel a free,
A leafy luxury, seeing I could please
    With these poor offerings, a man like thee.

# POEMS

'Places of nestling green for Poets made.'

*Story of Rimini*

I STOOD tip-toe upon a little hill,
The air was cooling, and so very still,
That the sweet buds which with a modest pride
Pull droopingly, in slanting curve aside,
Their scantly leav'd, and finely tapering stems,
Had not yet lost those starry diadems
Caught from the early sobbing of the morn.
The clouds were pure and white as flocks new shorn,
And fresh from the clear brook; sweetly they slept
On the blue fields of heaven, and then there crept          10
A little noiseless noise among the leaves,
Born of the very sigh that silence heaves:
For not the faintest motion could be seen
Of all the shades that slanted o'er the green.
There was wide wand'ring for the greediest eye,
To peer about upon variety;
Far round the horizon's crystal air to skim,
And trace the dwindled edgings of its brim;
To picture out the quaint, and curious bending
Of a fresh woodland alley, never ending;          20
Or by the bowery clefts, and leafy shelves,
Guess where the jaunty streams refresh themselves.
I gazed awhile, and felt as light, and free
As though the fanning wings of Mercury
Had play'd upon my heels: I was light-hearted,
And many pleasures to my vision started;
So I straightway began to pluck a posey
Of luxuries bright, milky, soft and rosy.

A bush of May flowers with the bees about them;
Ah, sure no tasteful nook would be without them;          30
And let a lush laburnum oversweep them,
And let long grass grow round the roots to keep them
Moist, cool and green; and shade the violets,
That they may bind the moss in leafy nets.

A filbert hedge with wild briar overtwined,
And clumps of woodbine taking the soft wind
Upon their summer thrones; there too should be
The frequent chequer of a youngling tree,
That with a score of light green brethren shoots
From the quaint mossiness of aged roots:        40
Round which is heard a spring-head of clear waters
Babbling so wildly of its lovely daughters
The spreading blue-bells: it may haply mourn
That such fair clusters should be rudely torn
From their fresh beds, and scattered thoughtlessly
By infant hands, left on the path to die.

Open afresh your round of starry folds,
Ye ardent marigolds!
Dry up the moisture from your golden lids,
For great Apollo bids        50
That in these days your praises should be sung
On many harps, which he has lately strung;
And when again your dewiness he kisses,
Tell him, I have you in my world of blisses:
So haply when I rove in some far vale,
His mighty voice may come upon the gale.

Here are sweet peas, on tip-toe for a flight:
With wings of gentle flush o'er delicate white,
And taper fingers catching at all things,
To bind them all about with tiny rings.        60

Linger awhile upon some bending planks
That lean against a streamlet's rushy banks,
And watch intently Nature's gentle doings:
They will be found softer than ring-dove's cooings.
How silent comes the water round that bend;
Not the minutest whisper does it send
To the o'erhanging sallows: blades of grass
Slowly across the chequer'd shadows pass.
Why, you might read two sonnets, ere they reach
To where the hurrying freshnesses aye preach        70
A natural sermon o'er their pebbly beds;
Where swarms of minnows show their little heads,

Staying their wavy bodies 'gainst the streams,
To taste the luxury of sunny beams
Temper'd with coolness. How they ever wrestle
With their own sweet delight, and ever nestle
Their silver bellies on the pebbly sand.
If you but scantily hold out the hand,
That very instant not one will remain;
But turn your eye, and they are there again.                    80
The ripples seem right glad to reach those cresses,
And cool themselves among the em'rald tresses;
The while they cool themselves, they freshness give,
And moisture, that the bowery green may live:
So keeping up an interchange of favours,
Like good men in the truth of their behaviours.
Sometimes goldfinches one by one will drop
From low hung branches; little space they stop;
But sip, and twitter, and their feathers sleek;
Then off at once, as in a wanton freak:                        90
Or perhaps, to show their black, and golden wings,
Pausing upon their yellow flutterings.
Were I in such a place, I sure should pray
That naught less sweet, might call my thoughts away,
Than the soft rustle of a maiden's gown
Fanning away the dandelion's down;
Than the light music of her nimble toes
Patting against the sorrel as she goes.
How she would start, and blush, thus to be caught
Playing in all her innocence of thought.                       100
O let me lead her gently o'er the brook,
Watch her half-smiling lips, and downward look;
O let me for one moment touch her wrist;
Let me one moment to her breathing list;
And as she leaves me may she often turn
Her fair eyes looking through her locks auburne.
What next? A tuft of evening primroses,
O'er which the mind may hover till it dozes;
O'er which it well might take a pleasant sleep,
But that 'tis ever startled by the leap                        110
Of buds into ripe flowers; or by the flitting
Of diverse moths, that aye their rest are quitting;
Or by the moon lifting her silver rim

Above a cloud, and with a gradual swim
Coming into the blue with all her light.
O Maker of sweet poets, dear delight
Of this fair world, and all its gentle livers;
Spangler of clouds, halo of crystal rivers,
Mingler with leaves, and dew and tumbling streams,
Closer of lovely eyes to lovely dreams,                    120
Lover of loneliness, and wandering,
Of upcast eye, and tender pondering!
Thee must I praise above all other glories
That smile us on to tell delightful stories.
For what has made the sage or poet write
But the fair paradise of Nature's light?
In the calm grandeur of a sober line,
We see the waving of the mountain pine;
And when a tale is beautifully staid,
We feel the safety of a hawthorn glade:                    130
When it is moving on luxurious wings,
The soul is lost in pleasant smotherings:
Fair dewy roses brush against our faces,
And flowering laurels spring from diamond vases;
O'er head we see the jasmine and sweet briar,
And bloomy grapes laughing from green attire;
While at our feet, the voice of crystal bubbles
Charms us at once away from all our troubles:
So that we feel uplifted from the world,
Walking upon the white clouds wreath'd and curl'd.        140
So felt he, who first told, how Psyche went
On the smooth wind to realms of wonderment;
What Psyche felt, and Love, when their full lips
First touch'd; what amorous, and fondling nips
They gave each other's cheeks; with all their sighs,
And how they kist each other's tremulous eyes:
The silver lamp,—the ravishment,—the wonder—
The darkness,—loneliness,—the fearful thunder;
Their woes gone by, and both to heaven upflown,
To bow for gratitude before Jove's throne.                150
So did he feel, who pull'd the boughs aside,
That we might look into a forest wide,
To catch a glimpse of Fauns, and Dryades
Coming with softest rustle through the trees;

And garlands woven of flowers wild, and sweet,
Upheld on ivory wrists, or sporting feet:
Telling us how fair, trembling Syrinx fled
Arcadian Pan, with such a fearful dread.
Poor nymph,—poor Pan,—how he did weep to find,
Nought but a lovely sighing of the wind          160
Along the reedy stream; a half-heard strain,
Full of sweet desolation—balmy pain.

What first inspired a bard of old to sing
Narcissus pining o'er the untainted spring?
In some delicious ramble, he had found
A little space, with boughs all woven round;
And in the midst of all, a clearer pool
Than e'er reflected in its pleasant cool,
The blue sky here, and there, serenely peeping
Through tendril wreaths fantastically creeping.          170
And on the bank a lonely flower he spied,
A meek and forlorn flower, with naught of pride,
Drooping its beauty o'er the watery clearness,
To woo its own sad image into nearness:
Deaf to light Zephyrus it would not move;
But still would seem to droop, to pine, to love.
So while the poet stood in this sweet spot,
Some fainter gleamings o'er his fancy shot;
Nor was it long ere he had told the tale
Of young Narcissus, and sad Echo's bale.          180

Where had he been, from whose warm head out-flew
That sweetest of all songs, that ever new,
That aye refreshing, pure deliciousness,
Coming ever to bless
The wanderer by moonlight? to him bringing
Shapes from the invisible world, unearthly singing
From out the middle air, from flowery nests,
And from the pillowy silkiness that rests
Full in the speculation of the stars.
Ah! surely he had burst our mortal bars;          190
Into some wond'rous region he had gone,
To search for thee, divine Endymion!

He was a Poet, sure a lover too,
Who stood on Latmus' top, what time there blew
Soft breezes from the myrtle vale below;
And brought in faintness solemn, sweet, and slow
A hymn from Dian's temple; while upswelling,
The incense went to her own starry dwelling.
But though her face was clear as infant's eyes,
Though she stood smiling o'er the sacrifice,          200
The Poet wept at her so piteous fate,
Wept that such beauty should be desolate:
So in fine wrath some golden sounds he won,
And gave meek Cynthia her Endymion.

Queen of the wide air; thou most lovely queen
Of all the brightness that mine eyes have seen!
As thou exceedest all things in thy shine,
So every tale, does this sweet tale of thine.
O for three words of honey, that I might
Tell but one wonder of thy bridal night!          210

Where distant ships do seem to show their keels,
Phoebus awhile delay'd his mighty wheels,
And turn'd to smile upon thy bashful eyes,
Ere he his unseen pomp would solemnize.
The evening weather was so bright, and clear,
That men of health were of unusual cheer;
Stepping like Homer at the trumpet's call,
Or young Apollo on the pedestal:
And lovely women were as fair and warm,
As Venus looking sideways in alarm.          220
The breezes were ethereal, and pure,
And crept through half-closed lattices to cure
The languid sick; it cool'd their fever'd sleep,
And soothed them into slumbers full and deep.
Soon they awoke clear eyed: nor burnt with thirsting,
Nor with hot fingers, nor with temples bursting:
And springing up, they met the wond'ring sight
Of their dear friends, nigh foolish with delight;
Who feel their arms, and breasts, and kiss and stare,
And on their placid foreheads part the hair.          230
Young men, and maidens at each other gaz'd
With hands held back, and motionless, amaz'd

To see the brightness in each other's eyes;
And so they stood, fill'd with a sweet surprise,
Until their tongues were loos'd in poesy.
Therefore no lover did of anguish die:
But the soft numbers, in that moment spoken,
Made silken ties, that never may be broken.
Cynthia! I cannot tell the greater blisses,
That follow'd thine, and thy dear shepherd's kisses:    240
Was there a poet born?—but now no more,
My wand'ring spirit must no further soar.—

## SPECIMEN OF AN INDUCTION TO A POEM

Lo! I must tell a tale of chivalry;
For large white plumes are dancing in mine eye.
Not like the formal crest of latter days:
But bending in a thousand graceful ways;
So graceful, that it seems no mortal hand,
Or e'en the touch of Archimago's wand,
Could charm them into such an attitude.
We must think rather, that in playful mood,
Some mountain breeze had turn'd its chief delight,
To show this wonder of its gentle might.    10
Lo! I must tell a tale of chivalry;
For while I muse, the lance points slantingly
Athwart the morning air: some lady sweet,
Who cannot feel for cold her tender feet,
From the worn top of some old battlement
Hails it with tears, her stout defender sent:
And from her own pure self no joy dissembling,
Wraps round her ample robe with happy trembling.
Sometimes, when the good Knight his rest would take,
It is reflected, clearly, in a lake,    20
With the young ashen boughs, 'gainst which it rests,
And th' half seen mossiness of linnets' nests.
Ah! shall I ever tell its cruelty,
When the fire flashes from a warrior's eye,
And his tremendous hand is grasping it,
And his dark brow for very wrath is knit?
Or when his spirit, with more calm intent,
Leaps to the honors of a tournament,

And makes the gazers round about the ring
Stare at the grandeur of the ballancing?                    30
No, no! this is far off:—then how shall I
Revive the dying tones of minstrelsy,
Which linger yet about long gothic arches,
In dark green ivy, and among wild larches?
How sing the splendour of the revelries,
When butts of wine are drunk off to the lees?
And that bright lance, against the fretted wall,
Beneath the shade of stately banneral,
Is slung with shining cuirass, sword, and shield?
Where ye may see a spur in bloody field.                    40
Light-footed damsels move with gentle paces
Round the wide hall, and show their happy faces;
Or stand in courtly talk by fives and sevens:
Like those fair stars that twinkle in the heavens.
Yet must I tell a tale of chivalry:
Or wherefore comes that steed so proudly by?
Wherefore more proudly does the gentle knight
Rein in the swelling of his ample might?

Spenser! thy brows are arched, open, kind,
And come like a clear sun-rise to my mind;                  50
And always does my heart with pleasure dance,
When I think on thy noble countenance:
Where never yet was aught more earthly seen
Than the pure freshness of thy laurels green.
Therefore, great bard, I not so fearfully
Call on thy gentle spirit to hover nigh
My daring steps: or if thy tender care,
Thus startled unaware,
Be jealous that the foot of other wight
Should madly follow that bright path of light               60
Trac'd by thy lov'd Libertas; he will speak,
And tell thee that my prayer is very meek;
That I will follow with due reverence,
And start with awe at mine own strange pretence.
Him thou wilt hear; so I will rest in hope
To see wide plains, fair trees and lawny slope:
The morn, the eve, the light, the shade, the flowers;
Clear streams, smooth lakes, and overlooking towers.

# CALIDORE

A FRAGMENT

Young Calidore is paddling o'er the lake;
His healthful spirit eager and awake
To feel the beauty of a silent eve,
Which seem'd full loth this happy world to leave;
The light dwelt o'er the scene so lingeringly.
He bares his forehead to the cool blue sky,
And smiles at the far clearness all around,
Until his heart is well nigh over wound,
And turns for calmness to the pleasant green
Of easy slopes, and shadowy trees that lean          10
So elegantly o'er the waters' brim
And show their blossoms trim.
Scarce can his clear and nimble eye-sight follow
The freaks, and dartings of the black-wing'd swallow,
Delighting much, to see it half at rest,
Dip so refreshingly its wings, and breast
'Gainst the smooth surface, and to mark anon,
The widening circles into nothing gone.

And now the sharp keel of his little boat
Comes up with ripple, and with easy float,          20
And glides into a bed of water lillies:
Broad leav'd are they and their white canopies
Are upward turn'd to catch the heaven's dew.
Near to a little island's point they grew;
Whence Calidore might have the goodliest view
Of this sweet spot of earth. The bowery shore
Went off in gentle windings to the hoar
And light blue mountains: but no breathing man
With a warm heart, and eye prepared to scan
Nature's clear beauty, could pass lightly by          30
Objects that look'd out so invitingly
On either side. These, gentle Calidore
Greeted, as he had known them long before.

The sidelong view of swelling leafiness,
Which the glad setting sun, in gold doth dress;
Whence ever, and anon the jay outsprings,
And scales upon the beauty of its wings.

The lonely turret, shatter'd, and outworn,
Stands venerably proud; too proud to mourn
Its long lost grandeur: fir trees grow around,          40
Aye dropping their hard fruit upon the ground.

The little chapel with the cross above
Upholding wreaths of ivy; the white dove,
That on the window spreads his feathers light,
And seems from purple clouds to wing its flight.
Green tufted islands casting their soft shades
Across the lake; sequester'd leafy glades,
That through the dimness of their twilight show
Large dock leaves, spiral foxgloves, or the glow
Of the wild cat's eyes, or the silvery stems          50
Of delicate birch trees, or long grass which hems
A little brook. The youth had long been viewing
These pleasant things, and heaven was bedewing
The mountain flowers, when his glad senses caught
A trumpet's silver voice. Ah! it was fraught
With many joys for him: the warder's ken
Had found white coursers prancing in the glen:
Friends very dear to him he soon will see;
So pushes off his boat most eagerly,
And soon upon the lake he skims along,          60
Deaf to the nightingale's first under-song;
Nor minds he the white swans that dream so sweetly:
His spirit flies before him so completely.

And now he turns a jutting point of land,
Whence may be seen the castle gloomy, and grand:
Nor will a bee buzz round two swelling peaches,
Before the point of his light shallop reaches
Those marble steps that through the water dip:
Now over them he goes with hasty trip,
And scarcely stays to ope the folding doors:          70
Anon he leaps along the oaken floors
Of halls and corridors.
Delicious sounds! those little bright-eyed things
That float about the air on azure wings,
Had been less heartfelt by him than the clang
Of clattering hoofs; into the court he sprang,

Just as two noble steeds, and palfreys twain,
Were slanting out their necks with loosened rein;
While from beneath the threat'ning portcullis
They brought their happy burthens. What a kiss,                80
What gentle squeeze he gave each lady's hand!
How tremblingly their delicate ankles spann'd!
Into how sweet a trance his soul was gone,
While whisperings of affection
Made him delay to let their tender feet
Come to the earth; with an incline so sweet
From their low palfreys o'er his neck they bent:
And whether there were tears of languishment,
Or that the evening dew had pearl'd their tresses
He feels a moisture on his cheek, and blesses              90
With lips that tremble, and with glistening eye,
All the soft luxury
That nestled in his arms. A dimpled hand,
Fair as some wonder out of fairy land,
Hung from his shoulder like the drooping flowers
Of whitest Cassia, fresh from summer showers:
And this he fondled with his happy cheek
As if for joy he would no further seek;
When the kind voice of good Sir Clerimond
Came to his ear, like something from beyond                100
His present being; so he gently drew
His warm arms, thrilling now with pulses new,
From their sweet thrall, and forward meekly bending,
Thank'd heaven that his joy was never ending;
While 'gainst his forehead he devoutly press'd
A hand heaven made to succour the distress'd;
A hand that from the world's bleak promontory
Had lifted Calidore for deeds of Glory.

Amid the pages, and the torches' glare,
There stood a knight, patting the flowing hair             110
Of his proud horse's mane: he was withal
A man of elegance, and stature tall:
So that the waving of his plumes would be
High as the berries of a wild ash tree,
Or as the winged cap of Mercury.
His armour was so dexterously wrought

In shape, that sure no living man had thought
It hard, and heavy steel: but that indeed
It was some glorious form, some splendid weed,
In which a spirit new come from the skies            120
Might live, and show itself to human eyes.
'Tis the far-fam'd, the brave Sir Gondibert,
Said the good man to Calidore alert;
While the young warrior with a step of grace
Came up,—a courtly smile upon his face,
And mailed hand held out, ready to greet
The large-eyed wonder, and ambitious heat
Of the aspiring boy; who as he led
Those smiling ladies, often turn'd his head
To admire the visor arch'd so gracefully             130
Over a knightly brow; while they went by
The lamps that from the high roof'd hall were pendent,
And gave the steel a shining quite transcendent.

Soon in a pleasant chamber they are seated;
The sweet-lipp'd ladies have already greeted
All the green leaves that round the window clamber,
To show their purple stars, and bells of amber.
Sir Gondibert has doff'd his shining steel,
Gladdening in the free, and airy feel
Of a light mantle; and while Clerimond             140
Is looking round about him with a fond,
And placid eye, young Calidore is burning
To hear of knightly deeds, and gallant spurning
Of all unworthiness; and how the strong of arm
Kept off dismay, and terror, and alarm
From lovely woman: while brimful of this,
He gave each damsel's hand so warm a kiss,
And had such manly ardour in his eye,
That each at other look'd half staringly;
And then their features started into smiles          150
Sweet as blue heavens o'er enchanted isles.

Softly the breezes from the forest came,
Softly they blew aside the taper's flame;
Clear was the song from Philomel's far bower;
Grateful the incense from the lime-tree flower;

Mysterious, wild, the far heard trumpet's tone;
Lovely the moon in ether, all alone:
Sweet too the converse of these happy mortals,
As that of busy spirits when the portals
Are closing in the west; or that soft humming                160
We hear around when Hesperus is coming.
Sweet be their sleep. * * * * * * * *


## TO SOME LADIES

WHAT though while the wonders of nature exploring,
    I cannot your light, mazy footsteps attend;
Nor listen to accents, that almost adoring,
    Bless Cynthia's face, the enthusiast's friend:


Yet over the steep, whence the mountain stream rushes,
    With you, kindest friends, in idea I muse;
Mark the clear tumbling crystal, its passionate gushes,
    In spray that the wild flower kindly bedews.


Why linger you so, the wild labyrinth strolling?
    Why breathless, unable your bliss to declare?          10
Ah! you list to the nightingale's tender condoling,
    Responsive to sylphs, in the moon-beamy air.


'Tis morn, and the flowers with dew are yet drooping,
    I see you are treading the verge of the sea:
And now! ah, I see it—you just now are stooping
    To pick up the keep-sake intended for me.


If a cherub, on pinions of silver descending,
    Had brought me a gem from the fret-work of heaven;
And smiles, with his star-cheering voice sweetly blending,
    The blessing of Tighe had melodiously given;          20


It had not created a warmer emotion
    Than the present, fair nymphs, I was blest with from you,
Than the shell, from the bright golden sands of the ocean
    Which the emerald waves at your feet gladly threw.

For, indeed, 'tis a sweet and peculiar pleasure
  (And blissful is he who such happiness finds),
To possess but a span of the hour of leisure,
  In elegant, pure, and aerial minds.


## ON RECEIVING A CURIOUS SHELL, AND A COPY OF VERSES, FROM THE SAME LADIES

HAST thou from the caves of Golconda, a gem
  Pure as the ice-drop that froze on the mountain?
Bright as the humming-bird's green diadem,
  When it flutters in sun-beams that shine through a fountain?

Hast thou a goblet for dark sparkling wine?
  That goblet right heavy, and massy, and gold?
And splendidly mark'd with the story divine
  Of Armida the fair, and Rinaldo the bold?

Hast thou a steed with a mane richly flowing?
  Hast thou a sword that thine enemy's smart is?    10
Hast thou a trumpet rich melodies blowing?
  And wear'st thou the shield of the fam'd Britomartis?

What is it that hangs from thy shoulder, so brave,
  Embroider'd with many a spring peering flower?
Is it a scarf that thy fair lady gave?
  And hastest thou now to that fair lady's bower?

Ah! courteous Sir Knight, with large joy thou art crown'd;
  Full many the glories that brighten thy youth!
I will tell thee my blisses, which richly abound
  In magical powers to bless, and to sooth.    20

On this scroll thou seest written in characters fair
  A sun-beamy tale of a wreath, and a chain;
And, warrior, it nurtures the property rare
  Of charming my mind from the trammels of pain.

This canopy mark: 'tis the work of a fay;
   Beneath its rich shade did King Oberon languish,
When lovely Titania was far, far away,
   And cruelly left him to sorrow, and anguish.

There, oft would he bring from his soft sighing lute
   Wild strains to which, spell-bound, the nightingales
     listen'd;                                 30
The wondering spirits of heaven were mute,
   And tears 'mong the dewdrops of morning oft glisten'd.

In this little dome, all those melodies strange,
   Soft, plaintive, and melting, for ever will sigh;
Nor e'er will the notes from their tenderness change;
   Nor e'er will the music of Oberon die.

So, when I am in a voluptuous vein,
   I pillow my head on the sweets of the rose,
And list to the tale of the wreath, and the chain,
   Till its echoes depart; then I sink to repose.       40

Adieu, valiant Eric! with joy thou art crown'd;
   Full many the glories that brighten thy youth,
I too have my blisses, which richly abound
   In magical powers, to bless and to sooth.

## TO ****

H ADST thou liv'd in days of old,
O what wonders had been told
Of thy lively countenance,
And thy humid eyes that dance
In the midst of their own brightness;
In the very fane of lightness.
Over which thine eyebrows, leaning,
Picture out each lovely meaning:
In a dainty bend they lie,
Like to streaks across the sky,      10

Or the feathers from a crow,
Fallen on a bed of snow.
Of thy dark hair that extends
Into many graceful bends:
As the leaves of Hellebore
Turn to whence they sprung before
And behind each ample curl
Peeps the richness of a pearl.
Downward too flows many a tress
With a glossy waviness;                              20
Full, and round like globes that rise
From the censer to the skies
Through sunny air. Add too, the sweetness
Of thy honey'd voice; the neatness
Of thine ankle lightly turn'd:
With those beauties, scarce discern'd,
Kept with such sweet privacy,
That they seldom meet the eye
Of the little loves that fly
Round about with eager pry.                          30
Saving when, with freshening lave,
Thou dipp'st them in the taintless wave;
Like twin water lillies, born
In the coolness of the morn.
O, if thou hadst breathed then,
Now the Muses had been ten.
Couldst thou wish for lineage higher
Than twin sister of Thalia?
At least for ever, evermore,
Will I call the Graces four.                         40

Hadst thou liv'd when chivalry
Lifted up her lance on high,
Tell me what thou wouldst have been?
Ah! I see the silver sheen
Of thy broider'd, floating vest
Cov'ring half thine ivory breast;
Which, O heavens! I should see,
But that cruel destiny
Has placed a golden cuirass there;
Keeping secret what is fair.                         50

Like sunbeams in a cloudlet nested
Thy locks in knightly casque are rested:
O'er which bend four milky plumes
Like the gentle lilly's blooms
Springing from a costly vase.
See with what a stately pace
Comes thine alabaster steed;
Servant of heroic deed!
O'er his loins, his trappings glow
Like the northern lights on snow.                    60
Mount his back! thy sword unsheath!
Sign of the enchanter's death;
Bane of every wicked spell;
Silencer of dragon's yell.
Alas! thou this wilt never do:
Thou art an enchantress too,
And wilt surely never spill
Blood of those whose eyes can kill.


## TO HOPE

WHEN by my solitary hearth I sit,
  And hateful thoughts enwrap my soul in gloom;
When no fair dreams before my 'mind's eye' flit,
  And the bare heath of life presents no bloom;
    Sweet Hope, ethereal balm upon me shed,
    And wave thy silver pinions o'er my head.

Whene'er I wander, at the fall of night,
  Where woven boughs shut out the moon's bright ray,
Should sad Despondency my musings fright,
  And frown, to drive fair Cheerfulness away,            10
    Peep with the moon-beams through the leafy roof,
    And keep that fiend Despondence far aloof.

Should Disappointment, parent of Despair,
  Strive for her son to seize my careless heart;
When, like a cloud, he sits upon the air,
  Preparing on his spell-bound prey to dart:
    Chace him away, sweet Hope, with visage bright,
    And fright him as the morning frightens night!

Whene'er the fate of those I hold most dear
  Tells to my fearful breast a tale of sorrow,       20
O bright-eyed Hope, my morbid fancy cheer;
  Let me awhile thy sweetest comforts borrow:
    Thy heaven-born radiance around me shed,
    And wave thy silver pinions o'er my head!

Should e'er unhappy love my bosom pain,
  From cruel parents, or relentless fair;
O let me think it is not quite in vain
  To sigh out sonnets to the midnight air!
    Sweet Hope, ethereal balm upon me shed,
    And wave thy silver pinions o'er my head!  .    30

In the long vista of the years to roll,
  Let me not see our country's honour fade:
O let me see our land retain her soul,
  Her pride, her freedom; and not freedom's shade.
    From thy bright eyes unusual brightness shed—
    Beneath thy pinions canopy my head!

Let me not see the patriot's high bequest,
  Great liberty! how great in plain attire!
With the base purple of a court oppress'd,
  Bowing her head, and ready to expire:      40
    But let me see thee stoop from heaven on wings
    That fill the skies with silver glitterings!

And as, in sparkling majesty, a star
  Gilds the bright summit of some gloomy cloud;
Brightening the half veil'd face of heaven afar:
  So, when dark thoughts my boding spirit shroud,
    Sweet Hope, celestial influence round me shed,
    Waving thy silver pinions o'er my head.

*February, 1815*

## IMITATION OF SPENSER

\*   \*   \*   \*   \*   \*   \*

Now Morning from her orient chamber came,
And her first footsteps touch'd a verdant hill;
Crowning its lawny crest with amber flame,
Silv'ring the untainted gushes of its rill;

Which, pure from mossy beds, did down distill,
And after parting beds of simple flowers,
By many streams a little lake did fill,
Which round its marge reflected woven bowers,
And, in its middle space, a sky that never lowers.

There the king-fisher saw his plumage bright          10
Vieing with fish of brilliant dye below;
Whose silken fins, and golden scales' light
Cast upward, through the waves, a ruby glow:
There saw the swan his neck of arched snow,
And oar'd himself along with majesty;
Sparkled his jetty eyes; his feet did show
Beneath the waves like Afric's ebony,
And on his back a fay reclined voluptuously.

Ah! could I tell the wonders of an isle
That in that fairest lake had placed been,          20
I could e'en Dido of her grief beguile;
Or rob from aged Lear his bitter teen:
For sure so fair a place was never seen,
Of all that ever charm'd romantic eye:
It seem'd an emerald in the silver sheen
Of the bright waters; or as when on high,
Through clouds of fleecy white, laughs the cœrulean sky.

And all around it dipp'd luxuriously
Slopings of verdure through the glossy tide,
Which, as it were in gentle amity,          30
Rippled delighted up the flowery side;
As if to glean the ruddy tears, it tried,
Which fell profusely from the rose-tree stem!
Haply it was the workings of its pride,
In strife to throw upon the shore a gem
Outvieing all the buds in Flora's diadem.

\*    \*    \*    \*    \*    \*    \*

[EDMONTON]

WOMAN! when I behold thee flippant, vain,
    Inconstant, childish, proud, and full of fancies;
    Without that modest softening that enhances
The downcast eye, repentant of the pain

That its mild light creates to heal again:
  E'en then, elate, my spirit leaps, and prances,
  E'en then my soul with exultation dances
For that to love, so long, I've dormant lain:
But when I see thee meek, and kind, and tender,
  Heavens! how desperately do I adore                    10
Thy winning graces;—to be thy defender
  I hotly burn—to be a Calidore—
A very Red Cross Knight—a stout Leander—
  Might I be loved by thee like these of yore.

Light feet, dark violet eyes, and parted hair;
  Soft dimpled hands, white neck, and creamy breast,
  Are things on which the dazzled senses rest
Till the fond, fixed eyes, forget they stare.
From such fine pictures, heavens! I cannot dare
  To turn my admiration, though unpossess'd            20
  They be of what is worthy,—though not drest
In lovely modesty, and virtues rare.
Yet these I leave as thoughtless as a lark;
  These lures I straight forget,—e'en ere I dine,
Or thrice my palate moisten: but when I mark
  Such charms with mild intelligences shine,
My ear is open like a greedy shark,
  To catch the tunings of a voice divine.

Ah! who can e'er forget so fair a being?
  Who can forget her half retiring sweets?             30
  God! she is like a milk-white lamb that bleats
For man's protection. Surely the All-seeing,
Who joys to see us with his gifts agreeing,
  Will never give him pinions, who intreats
  Such innocence to ruin,—who vilely cheats
A dove-like bosom. In truth there is no freeing
One's thoughts from such a beauty; when I hear
  A lay that once I saw her hand awake,
Her form seems floating palpable, and near;
  Had I e'er seen her from an arbour take              40
A dewy flower, oft would that hand appear,
  And o'er my eyes the trembling moisture shake.

# EPISTLES

'Among the rest a shepheard (though but young
Yet hartned to his pipe) with all the skill
His few yeeres could, began to fit his quill.'
*Britannia's Pastorals.* BROWNE.

## TO GEORGE FELTON MATHEW

SWEET are the pleasures that to verse belong,
And doubly sweet a brotherhood in song;
Nor can remembrance, Mathew! bring to view
A fate more pleasing, a delight more true
Than that in which the brother Poets joy'd,
Who with combined powers, their wit employ'd
To raise a trophy to the drama's muses.
The thought of this great partnership diffuses
Over the genius-loving heart, a feeling
Of all that's high, and great, and good, and healing.   10

Too partial friend! fain would I follow thee
Past each horizon of fine poesy;
Fain would I echo back each pleasant note·
As o'er Sicilian seas, clear anthems float
'Mong the light skimming gondolas far parted,
Just when the sun his farewell beam has darted:
But 'tis impossible; far different cares
Beckon me sternly from soft 'Lydian airs,'
And hold my faculties so long in thrall,
That I am oft in doubt whether at all                   20
I shall again see Phœbus in the morning:
Or flush'd Aurora in the roseate dawning!
Or a white Naiad in a rippling stream;
Or a rapt seraph in a moonlight beam;
Or again witness what with thee I've seen,
The dew by fairy feet swept from the green,
After a night of some quaint jubilee
Which every elf and fay had come to see:
When bright processions took their airy march
Beneath the curved moon's triumphal arch.              30
But might I now each passing moment give
To the coy muse, with me she would not live

In this dark city, nor would condescend
'Mid contradictions her delights to lend.
Should e'er the fine-eyed maid to me be kind,
Ah! surely it must be whene'er I find
Some flowery spot, sequester'd, wild, romantic,
That often must have seen a poet frantic;
Where oaks, that erst the Druid knew, are growing,
And flowers, the glory of one day, are blowing;    40
Where the dark-leav'd laburnum's drooping clusters
Reflect athwart the stream their yellow lustres,
And intertwined the cassia's arms unite,
With its own drooping buds, but very white.
Where on one side are covert branches hung,
'Mong which the nightingales have always sung
In leafy quiet: where to pry, aloof,
Atween the pillars of the sylvan roof,
Would be to find where violet beds were nestling,
And where the bee with cowslip bells was wrestling.  50
There must be too a ruin dark, and gloomy,
To say 'joy not too much in all that's bloomy.'

Yet this is vain—O Mathew lend thy aid
To find a place where I may greet the maid—
Where we may soft humanity put on,
And sit, and rhyme and think on Chatterton;
And that warm-hearted Shakspeare sent to meet him
Four laurell'd spirits, heaven-ward to intreat him.
With reverence would we speak of all the sages
Who have left streaks of light athwart their ages:    60
And thou shouldst moralize on Milton's blindness,
And mourn the fearful dearth of human kindness
To those who strove with the bright golden wing
Of genius, to flap away each sting
Thrown by the pitiless world. We next could tell
Of those who in the cause of freedom fell;
Of our own Alfred, of Helvetian Tell;
Of him whose name to ev'ry heart's a solace,
High-minded and unbending William Wallace.
While to the rugged north our musing turns    70
We well might drop a tear for him, and Burns.
Felton! without incitements such as these,

How vain for me the niggard Muse to tease:
For thee, she will thy every dwelling grace,
And make 'a sun-shine in a shady place:'
For thou wast once a flowret blooming wild,
Close to the source, bright, pure, and undefil'd,
Whence gush the streams of song: in happy hour
Came chaste Diana from her shady bower,
Just as the sun was from the east uprising;        80
And, as for him some gift she was devising,
Beheld thee, pluck'd thee, cast thee in the stream
To meet her glorious brother's greeting beam.
I marvel much that thou hast never told
How, from a flower, into a fish of gold
Apollo chang'd thee; how thou next didst seem
A black-eyed swan upon the widening stream;
And when thou first didst in that mirror trace
The placid features of a human face:
That thou hast never told thy travels strange,        90
And all the wonders of the mazy range
O'er pebbly crystal, and o'er golden sands;
Kissing thy daily food from Naiad's pearly hands.

*November, 1815*


## TO MY BROTHER GEORGE

FULL many a dreary hour have I past,
My brain bewilder'd, and my mind o'ercast
With heaviness; in seasons when I've thought
No spherey strains by me could e'er be caught
From the blue dome, though I to dimness gaze
On the far depth where sheeted lightning plays;
Or, on the wavy grass outstretch'd supinely,
Pry 'mong the stars, to strive to think divinely:
That I should never hear Apollo's song,
Though feathery clouds were floating all along        10
The purple west, and, two bright streaks between,
The golden lyre itself were dimly seen:
That the still murmur of the honey bee
Would never teach a rural song to me:

That the bright glance from beauty's eyelids slanting
Would never make a lay of mine enchanting,
Or warm my breast with ardour to unfold
Some tale of love and arms in time of old.
But there are times, when those that love the bay,
Fly from all sorrowing far, far away;                          20
A sudden glow comes on them, naught they see
In water, earth, or air, but poesy.
It has been said, dear George, and true I hold it,
(For knightly Spenser to Libertas told it,)
That when a Poet is in such a trance,
In air he sees white coursers paw, and prance,
Bestridden of gay knights, in gay apparel,
Who at each other tilt in playful quarrel,
And what we, ignorantly, sheet-lightning call,
Is the swift opening of their wide portal,                     30
When the bright warder blows his trumpet clear,
Whose tones reach naught on earth but Poet's ear.
When these enchanted portals open wide,
And through the light the horsemen swiftly glide,
The Poet's eye can reach those golden halls,
And view the glory of their festivals:
Their ladies fair, that in the distance seem
Fit for the silv'ring of a seraph's dream;
Their rich brimm'd goblets, that incessant run
Like the bright spots that move about the sun;                 40
And, when upheld, the wine from each bright jar
Pours with the lustre of a falling star.
Yet further off, are dimly seen their bowers,
Of which, no mortal eye can reach the flowers;
And 'tis right just, for well Apollo knows
'Twould make the Poet quarrel with the rose.
All that's reveal'd from that far seat of blisses,
Is, the clear fountains' interchanging kisses,
As gracefully descending, light and thin,
Like silver streaks across a dolphin's fin,                    50
When he upswimmeth from the coral caves,
And sports with half his tail above the waves.

These wonders strange he sees, and many more,
Whose head is pregnant with poetic lore.

Should he upon an evening ramble fare
With forehead to the soothing breezes bare,
Would he naught see but the dark, silent blue
With all its diamonds trembling through and through?
Or the coy moon, when in the waviness
Of whitest clouds she does her beauty dress,          60
And staidly paces higher up, and higher,
Like a sweet nun in holy-day attire?
Ah, yes! much more would start into his sight—
The revelries, and mysteries of night:
And should I ever see them, I will tell you
Such tales as needs must with amazement spell you.

These are the living pleasures of the bard:
But richer far posterity's award.
What does he murmur with his latest breath,
While his proud eye looks through the film of death?  70
'What though I leave this dull, and earthly mould,
Yet shall my spirit lofty converse hold
With after times.—The patriot shall feel
My stern alarum, and unsheath his steel;
Or, in the senate thunder out my numbers
To startle princes from their easy slumbers.
The sage will mingle with each moral theme
My happy thoughts sententious; he will teem
With lofty periods when my verses fire him,
And then I'll stoop from heaven to inspire him.       80
Lays have I left of such a dear delight
That maids will sing them on their bridal night.
Gay villagers, upon a morn of May,
When they have tired their gentle limbs with play,
And form'd a snowy circle on the grass,
And plac'd in midst of all that lovely lass
Who chosen is their queen,—with her fine head
Crowned with flowers purple, white, and red:
For there the lilly, and the musk-rose, sighing,
Are emblems true of hapless lovers dying:             90
Between her breasts, that never yet felt trouble,
A bunch of violets full blown, and double,
Serenely sleep:—she from a casket takes
A little book,—and then a joy awakes

About each youthful heart,—with stifled cries,
And rubbing of white hands, and sparkling eyes:
For she's to read a tale of hopes, and fears;
One that I foster'd in my youthful years:
The pearls, that on each glist'ning circlet sleep,
Gush ever and anon with silent creep,                      100
Lured by the innocent dimples. To sweet rest
Shall the dear babe, upon its mother's breast,
Be lull'd with songs of mine. Fair world, adieu!
Thy dales, and hills, are fading from my view:
Swiftly I mount, upon wide spreading pinions,
Far from the narrow bounds of thy dominions.
Full joy I feel, while thus I cleave the air,
That my soft verse will charm thy daughters fair,
And warm thy sons!' Ah, my dear friend and brother,
Could I, at once, my mad ambition smother,                 110
For tasting joys like these, sure I should be
Happier, and dearer to society.
At times, 'tis true, I've felt relief from pain
When some bright thought has darted through my brain:
Through all that day I've felt a greater pleasure
Than if I'd brought to light a hidden treasure.
As to my sonnets, though none else should heed them,
I feel delighted, still, that you should read them.
Of late, too, I have had much calm enjoyment,
Stretch'd on the grass at my best lov'd employment        120
Of scribbling lines for you. These things I thought
While, in my face, the freshest breeze I caught.
E'en now I'm pillow'd on a bed of flowers
That crowns a lofty clift, which proudly towers
Above the ocean-waves. The stalks, and blades,
Chequer my tablet with their quivering shades.
On one side is a field of drooping oats,
Through which the poppies show their scarlet coats;
So pert and useless, that they bring to mind
The scarlet coats that pester human-kind.                  130
And on the other side, outspread, is seen
Ocean's blue mantle streak'd with purple, and green.
Now 'tis I see a canvass'd ship, and now
Mark the bright silver curling round her prow.
I see the lark down-dropping to his nest,

And the broad winged sea-gull never at rest;
For when no more he spreads his feathers free,
His breast is dancing on the restless sea.
Now I direct my eyes into the west,
Which at this moment is in sunbeams drest:        140
Why westward turn? 'Twas but to say adieu!
'Twas but to kiss my hand, dear George, to you!

[MARGATE] *August 1816*

## TO CHARLES COWDEN CLARKE

O FT have you seen a swan superbly frowning,
And with proud breast his own white shadow crowning;
He slants his neck beneath the waters bright
So silently, it seems a beam of light
Come from the galaxy: anon he sports,—
With outspread wings the Naiad Zephyr courts,
Or ruffles all the surface of the lake
In striving from its crystal face to take
Some diamond water drops, and them to treasure
In milky nest, and sip them off at leisure.        10
But not a moment can he there insure them,
Nor to such downy rest can he allure them;
For down they rush as though they would be free,
And drop like hours into eternity.
Just like that bird am I in loss of time,
Whene'er I venture on the stream of rhyme;
With shatter'd boat, oar snapt, and canvass rent
I slowly sail, scarce knowing my intent;
Still scooping up the water with my fingers,
In which a trembling diamond never lingers.        20
By this, friend Charles, you may full plainly see
Why I have never penn'd a line to thee:
Because my thoughts were never free, and clear,
And little fit to please a classic ear;
Because my wine was of too poor a savour
For one whose palate gladdens in the flavour
Of sparkling Helicon:—small good it were
To take him to a desert rude, and bare,
Who had on Baiæ's shore reclin'd at ease,
While Tasso's page was floating in a breeze        30

That gave soft music from Armida's bowers,
Mingled with fragrance from her rarest flowers:
Small good to one who had by Mulla's stream
Fondled the maidens with the breasts of cream;
Who had beheld Belphœbe in a brook,
And lovely Una in a leafy nook,
And Archimago leaning o'er his book:
Who had of all that's sweet tasted, and seen,
From silv'ry ripple, up to beauty's queen;
From the sequester'd haunts of gay Titania,                 40
To the blue dwelling of divine Urania:
One, who, of late, had ta'en sweet forest walks
With him who elegantly chats, and talks—
The wrong'd Libertas,—who has told you stories
Of laurel chaplets, and Apollo's glories;
Of troops chivalrous prancing through a city,
And tearful ladies made for love, and pity:
With many else which I have never known.
Thus have I thought; and days on days have flown
Slowly, or rapidly—unwilling still                          50
For you to try my dull, unlearned quill.
Nor should I now, but that I've known you long;
That you first taught me all the sweets of song:
The grand, the sweet, the terse, the free, the fine;
What swell'd with pathos, and what right divine:
Spenserian vowels that elope with ease,
And float along like birds o'er summer seas;
Miltonian storms, and more, Miltonian tenderness;
Michael in arms, and more, meek Eve's fair slenderness,
Who read for me the sonnet swelling loudly                  60
Up to its climax and then dying proudly?
Who found for me the grandeur of the ode,
Growing, like Atlas, stronger from its load?
Who let me taste that more than cordial dram,
The sharp, the rapier-pointed epigram?
Show'd me that epic was of all the king,
Round, vast, and spanning all like Saturn's ring?
You too upheld the veil from Clio's beauty,
And pointed out the patriot's stern duty;
The might of Alfred, and the shaft of Tell;                 70
The hand of Brutus, that so grandly fell

Upon a tyrant's head. Ah! had I never seen,
Or known your kindness, what might I have been?
What my enjoyments in my youthful years,
Bereft of all that now my life endears?
And can I e'er these benefits forget?
And can I e'er repay the friendly debt?
No, doubly no;—yet should these rhymings please,
I shall roll on the grass with two-fold ease:
For I have long time been my fancy feeding        80
With hopes that you would one day think the reading
Of my rough verses not an hour misspent;
Should it e'er be so, what a rich content!
Some weeks have pass'd since last I saw the spires
In lucent Thames reflected:—warm desires
To see the sun o'erpeep the eastern dimness,
And morning shadows, streaking into slimness
Across the lawny fields, and pebbly water;
To mark the time as they grow broad, and shorter;
To feel the air that plays about the hills,        90
And sips its freshness from the little rills;
To see high, golden corn wave in the light
When Cynthia smiles upon a summer's night,
And peers among the cloudlets jet and white,
As though she were reclining in a bed
Of bean blossoms, in heaven freshly shed.
No sooner had I stepp'd into these pleasures
Than I began to think of rhymes and measures:
The air that floated by me seem'd to say
'Write! thou wilt never have a better day.'        100
And so I did. When many lines I'd written,
Though with their grace I was not oversmitten,
Yet, as my hand was warm, I thought I'd better
Trust to my feelings, and write you a letter.
Such an attempt required an inspiration
Of a peculiar sort,—a consummation;—
Which, had I felt, these scribblings might have been
Verses from which the soul would never wean:
But many days have passed since last my heart
Was warm'd luxuriously by divine Mozart;        110
By Arne delighted, or by Handel madden'd;
Or by the song of Erin pierc'd and sadden'd:

What time you were before the music sitting,
And the rich notes to each sensation fitting.
Since I have walk'd with you through shady lanes
That freshly terminate in open plains,
And revel'd in a chat that ceased not
When at night-fall among your books we got:
No, nor when supper came, nor after that,—
Nor when reluctantly I took my hat;                    120
No, nor till cordially you shook my hand
Mid-way between our homes:—your accents bland
Still sounded in my ears, when I no more
Could hear your footsteps touch the grav'ly floor.
Sometimes I lost them, and then found again;
You chang'd the footpath for the grassy plain.
In those still moments I have wish'd you joys
That well you know to honour:—'Life's very toys
'With him,' said I, 'will take a pleasant charm;
'It cannot be that aught will work him harm.'         130
These thoughts now come o'er me with all their might:—
Again I shake your hand,—friend Charles, good night.

*September, 1816*

# SONNETS

I

## TO MY BROTHER GEORGE

MANY the wonders I this day have seen:
  The sun, when first he kist away the tears
  That fill'd the eyes of morn;—the laurell'd peers
Who from the feathery gold of evening lean;—
The ocean with its vastness, its blue green,
  Its ships, its rocks, its caves, its hopes, its fears,—
  Its voice mysterious, which whoso hears
Must think on what will be, and what has been.
E'en now, dear George, while this for you I write,
  Cynthia is from her silken curtains peeping     10
So scantly, that it seems her bridal night,
  And she her half-discover'd revels keeping.
But what, without the social thought of thee,
  Would be the wonders of the sky and sea?

II

## TO —

HAD I a man's fair form, then might my sighs
  Be echoed swiftly through that ivory shell
  Thine ear, and find thy gentle heart; so well
Would passion arm me for the enterprize:
But ah! I am no knight whose foeman dies;
  No cuirass glistens on my bosom's swell;
  I am no happy shepherd of the dell
Whose lips have trembled with a maiden's eyes.
Yet must I dote upon thee,—call thee sweet,
  Sweeter by far than Hybla's honied roses     10
    When steep'd in dew rich to intoxication.
Ah! I will taste that dew, for me 'tis meet,
  And when the moon her pallid face discloses,
    I'll gather some by spells, and incantation.

B 5432        C

### III

### WRITTEN ON THE DAY THAT MR. LEIGH HUNT LEFT PRISON

What though, for showing truth to flatter'd state,
  Kind Hunt was shut in prison, yet has he,
  In his immortal spirit, been as free
As the sky-searching lark, and as elate.
Minion of grandeur! think you he did wait?
  Think you he naught but prison walls did see,
  Till, so unwilling, thou unturn'dst the key?
Ah, no! far happier, nobler was his fate!
In Spenser's halls he stray'd, and bowers fair,
  Culling enchanted flowers; and he flew          10
With daring Milton through the fields of air:
  To regions of his own his genius true
Took happy flights. Who shall his fame impair
  When thou art dead, and all thy wretched crew?


### IV

How many bards gild the lapses of time!
  A few of them have ever been the food
  Of my delighted fancy,—I could brood
Over their beauties, earthly, or sublime:
And often, when I sit me down to rhyme,
  These will in throngs before my mind intrude:
  But no confusion, no disturbance rude
Do they occasion; 'tis a pleasing chime.
So the unnumber'd sounds that evening store;
The songs of birds—the whisp'ring of the leaves—   10
  The voice of waters—the great bell that heaves
With solemn sound,—and thousand others more,
  That distance of recognizance bereaves,
Make pleasing music, and not wild uproar.

V

## TO A FRIEND WHO SENT ME SOME ROSES

As late I rambled in the happy fields,
　　What time the sky-lark shakes the tremulous dew
　　From his lush clover covert;—when anew
Adventurous knights take up their dinted shields:
I saw the sweetest flower wild nature yields,
　　A fresh-blown musk-rose; 'twas the first that threw
　　Its sweets upon the summer: graceful it grew
As is the wand that queen Titania wields.
And, as I feasted on its fragrancy,
　　I thought the garden-rose it far excell'd:　　　　　10
But when, O Wells! thy roses came to me
　　My sense with their deliciousness was spell'd:
Soft voices had they, that with tender plea
　　Whisper'd of peace, and truth, and friendliness unquell'd.

[*June 29, 1816*]

VI

## TO G. A. W.

[GEORGIANA AUGUSTA WYLIE]

NYMPH of the downward smile and sidelong glance,
　　In what diviner moments of the day
　　Art thou most lovely?—when gone far astray
Into the labyrinths of sweet utterance,
Or when serenely wand'ring in a trance
　　Of sober thought?—or when starting away
　　With careless robe to meet the morning ray
Thou spar'st the flowers in thy mazy dance?
Haply 'tis when thy ruby lips part sweetly,
　　And so remain, because thou listenest:　　　　　10
But thou to please wert nurtured so completely
　　That I can never tell what mood is best.
I shall as soon pronounce which Grace more neatly
　　Trips it before Apollo than the rest.

VII

O Solitude! if I must with thee dwell,
  Let it not be among the jumbled heap
  Of murky buildings; climb with me the steep,—
Nature's observatory—whence the dell,
Its flowery slopes, its river's crystal swell,
  May seem a span; let me thy vigils keep
  'Mongst boughs pavillion'd, where the deer's swift leap
Startles the wild bee from the fox-glove bell.
But though I'll gladly trace these scenes with thee,
  Yet the sweet converse of an innocent mind,       10
  Whose words are images of thoughts refin'd,
Is my soul's pleasure; and it sure must be
  Almost the highest bliss of human-kind,
When to thy haunts two kindred spirits flee.


VIII

TO MY BROTHERS

Small, busy flames play through the fresh laid coals,
  And their faint cracklings o'er our silence creep
  Like whispers of the household gods that keep
A gentle empire o'er fraternal souls.
And while, for rhymes, I search around the poles,
  Your eyes are fix'd, as in poetic sleep,
  Upon the lore so voluble and deep,
That aye at fall of night our care condoles.
This is your birth-day Tom, and I rejoice
  That thus it passes smoothly, quietly.       10
Many such eves of gently whisp'ring noise
  May we together pass, and calmly try
What are this world's true joys,—ere the great voice,
  From its fair face, shall bid our spirits fly.

*November 18, 1816*

IX

KEEN, fitful gusts are whisp'ring here and there
 Among the bushes half leafless, and dry;
 The stars look very cold about the sky,
And I have many miles on foot to fare.
Yet feel I little of the cool bleak air,
 Or of the dead leaves rustling drearily,
 Or of those silver lamps that burn on high,
Or of the distance from home's pleasant lair:
For I am brimfull of the friendliness
 That in a little cottage I have found;   10
Of fair-hair'd Milton's eloquent distress,
 And all his love for gentle Lycid drown'd;
Of lovely Laura in her light green dress,
 And faithful Petrarch gloriously crown'd.

X

To one who has been long in city pent,
 'Tis very sweet to look into the fair
 And open face of heaven,—to breathe a prayer
Full in the smile of the blue firmament.
Who is more happy, when, with heart's content,
 Fatigued he sinks into some pleasant lair
 Of wavy grass, and reads a debonair
And gentle tale of love and languishment?
Returning home at evening, with an ear
 Catching the notes of Philomel,—an eye  10
Watching the sailing cloudlet's bright career,
 He mourns that day so soon has glided by:
E'en like the passage of an angel's tear
 That falls through the clear ether silently.

XI

## ON FIRST LOOKING INTO CHAPMAN'S HOMER

MUCH have I travell'd in the realms of gold,
  And many goodly states and kingdoms seen;
  Round many western islands have I been
Which bards in fealty to Apollo hold.
Oft of one wide expanse had I been told
  That deep-brow'd Homer ruled as his demesne;
  Yet did I never breathe its pure serene
Till I heard Chapman speak out loud and bold:
Then felt I like some watcher of the skies
  When a new planet swims into his ken;          10
Or like stout Cortez when with eagle eyes
  He star'd at the Pacific—and all his men
Look'd at each other with a wild surmise—
  Silent, upon a peak in Darien.


XII

## ON LEAVING SOME FRIENDS AT AN EARLY HOUR

GIVE me a golden pen, and let me lean
  On heap'd up flowers, in regions clear, and far;
  Bring me a tablet whiter than a star,
Or hand of hymning angel, when 'tis seen
The silver strings of heavenly harp atween:
  And let there glide by many a pearly car,
  Pink robes, and wavy hair, and diamond jar,
And half discovered wings, and glances keen.
The while let music wander round my ears,
  And as it reaches each delicious ending,          10
    Let me write down a line of glorious tone,
And full of many wonders of the spheres:
  For what a height my spirit is contending!
    'Tis not content so soon to be alone.

## XIII

## ADDRESSED TO HAYDON

HIGHMINDEDNESS, a jealousy for good,
  A loving-kindness for the great man's fame,
  Dwells here and there with people of no name,
In noisome alley, and in pathless wood:
And where we think the truth least understood,
  Oft may be found a 'singleness of aim,'
That ought to frighten into hooded shame
A money-mong'ring, pitiable brood.
How glorious this affection for the cause
  Of stedfast genius, toiling gallantly!                    10
What when a stout unbending champion awes
  Envy, and Malice to their native sty?
Unnumber'd souls breathe out a still applause,
  Proud to behold him in his country's eye.


## XIV

## ADDRESSED TO THE SAME

GREAT spirits now on earth are sojourning;
  He of the cloud, the cataract, the lake,
  Who on Helvellyn's summit, wide awake,
Catches his freshness from Archangel's wing:
He of the rose, the violet, the spring,
  The social smile, the chain for Freedom's sake:
  And lo!—whose stedfastness would never take
A meaner sound than Raphael's whispering.
And other spirits there are standing apart
  Upon the forehead of the age to come;                    10
These, these will give the world another heart,
  And other pulses. Hear ye not the hum
Of mighty workings?——
  Listen awhile ye nations, and be dumb.

XV

## ON THE GRASSHOPPER AND CRICKET

THE poetry of earth is never dead:
  When all the birds are faint with the hot sun,
  And hide in cooling trees, a voice will run
From hedge to hedge about the new-mown mead;
That is the Grasshopper's—he takes the lead
  In summer luxury,—he has never done
  With his delights; for when tired out with fun
He rests at ease beneath some pleasant weed.
The poetry of earth is ceasing never:
  On a lone winter evening, when the frost     10
    Has wrought a silence, from the stove there shrills
The Cricket's song, in warmth increasing ever,
  And seems to one in drowsiness half lost,
    The Grasshopper's among some grassy hills.

*December 30, 1816*


XVI

## TO KOSCIUSKO

GOOD Kosciusko, thy great name alone
  Is a full harvest whence to reap high feeling;
  It comes upon us like the glorious pealing
Of the wide spheres—an everlasting tone.
And now it tells me, that in worlds unknown,
  The names of heroes, burst from clouds concealing,
  And change to harmonies, for ever stealing
Through cloudless blue, and round each silver throne.
It tells me too, that on a happy day,
  When some good spirit walks upon the earth,     10
    Thy name with Alfred's, and the great of yore
  Gently commingling, gives tremendous birth
To a loud hymn, that sounds far, far away
    To where the great God lives for evermore.

*[December, 1816]*

## XVII

Happy is England! I could be content
  To see no other verdure than its own;
  To feel no other breezes than are blown
Through its tall woods with high romances blent:
Yet do I sometimes feel a languishment
  For skies Italian, and an inward groan
  To sit upon an Alp as on a throne,
And half forget what world or worldling meant.
Happy is England, sweet her artless daughters;
  Enough their simple loveliness for me,       10
    Enough their whitest arms in silence clinging:
  Yet do I often warmly burn to see
    Beauties of deeper glance, and hear their singing,
And float with them about the summer waters.

# SLEEP AND POETRY

As I lay in my bed slepe full unmete
Was unto me, but why that I ne might
Rest I ne wist, for there n'as erthly wight
[As I suppose] had more of hertis ese
Than I, for I n'ad sicknesse nor diese.

CHAUCER

WHAT is more gentle than a wind in summer?
What is more soothing than the pretty hummer
That stays one moment in an open flower,
And buzzes cheerily from bower to bower?
What is more tranquil than a musk-rose blowing
In a green island, far from all men's knowing?
More healthful than the leafiness of dales?
More secret than a nest of nightingales?
More serene than Cordelia's countenance?
More full of visions than a high romance?                10
What, but thee Sleep? Soft closer of our eyes!
Low murmurer of tender lullabies!
Light hoverer around our happy pillows!
Wreather of poppy buds, and weeping willows!
Silent entangler of a beauty's tresses!
Most happy listener! when the morning blesses
Thee for enlivening all the cheerful eyes
That glance so brightly at the new sun-rise.

But what is higher beyond thought than thee?
Fresher than berries of a mountain tree?                20
More strange, more beautiful, more smooth, more regal,
Than wings of swans, than doves, than dim-seen eagle?
What is it? And to what shall I compare it?
It has a glory, and naught else can share it:
The thought thereof is awful, sweet, and holy,
Chasing away all worldliness and folly;
Coming sometimes like fearful claps of thunder,
Or the low rumblings earth's regions under;
And sometimes like a gentle whispering
Of all the secrets of some wond'rous thing                30
That breathes about us in the vacant air;
So that we look around with prying stare,

Perhaps to see shapes of light, aerial limning,
And catch soft floatings from a faint-heard hymning;
To see the laurel wreath, on high suspended,
That is to crown our name when life is ended.
Sometimes it gives a glory to the voice,
And from the heart up-springs, 'Rejoice! rejoice!'
Sounds which will reach the Framer of all things,
And die away in ardent mutterings.                    40

No one who once the glorious sun has seen,
And all the clouds, and felt his bosom clean
For his great Maker's presence, but must know
What 'tis I mean, and feel his being glow:
Therefore no insult will I give his spirit,
By telling what he sees from native merit.

O Poesy! for thee I hold my pen
That am not yet a glorious denizen
Of thy wide heaven—Should I rather kneel
Upon some mountain-top until I feel                    50
A glowing splendour round about me hung,
And echo back the voice of thine own tongue?
O Poesy! for thee I grasp my pen
That am not yet a glorious denizen
Of thy wide heaven; yet, to my ardent prayer,
Yield from thy sanctuary some clear air,
Smooth'd for intoxication by the breath
Of flowering bays, that I may die a death
Of luxury, and my young spirit follow
The morning sun-beams to the great Apollo              60
Like a fresh sacrifice; or, if I can bear
The o'erwhelming sweets, 'twill bring to me the fair
Visions of all places: a bowery nook
Will be elysium—an eternal book
Whence I may copy many a lovely saying
About the leaves, and flowers—about the playing
Of nymphs in woods, and fountains; and the shade
Keeping a silence round a sleeping maid;
And many a verse from so strange influence
That we must ever wonder how, and whence               70
It came. Also imaginings will hover
Round my fire-side, and haply there discover

Vistas of solemn beauty, where I'd wander
In happy silence, like the clear Meander
Through its lone vales; and where I found a spot
Of awfuller shade, or an enchanted grot,
Or a green hill o'erspread with chequer'd dress
Of flowers, and fearful from its loveliness,
Write on my tablets all that was permitted,
All that was for our human senses fitted.                    80
Then the events of this wide world I'd seize
Like a strong giant, and my spirit teaze
Till at its shoulders it should proudly see
Wings to find out an immortality.

Stop and consider! life is but a day;
A fragile dew-drop on its perilous way
From a tree's summit; a poor Indian's sleep
While his boat hastens to the monstrous steep
Of Montmorenci. Why so sad a moan?
Life is the rose's hope while yet unblown;                    90
The reading of an ever-changing tale;
The light uplifting of a maiden's veil;
A pigeon tumbling in clear summer air;
A laughing school-boy, without grief or care,
Riding the springy branches of an elm.

O for ten years, that I may overwhelm
Myself in poesy; so I may do the deed
That my own soul has to itself decreed.
Then will I pass the countries that I see
In long perspective, and continually                        100
Taste their pure fountains. First the realm I'll pass
Of Flora, and old Pan: sleep in the grass,
Feed upon apples red, and strawberries,
And choose each pleasure that my fancy sees;
Catch the white-handed nymphs in shady places,
To woo sweet kisses from averted faces,—
Play with their fingers, touch their shoulders white
Into a pretty shrinking with a bite
As hard as lips can make it: till agreed,
A lovely tale of human life we'll read.                      110
And one will teach a tame dove how it best
May fan the cool air gently o'er my rest;

Another, bending o'er her nimble tread,
Will set a green robe floating round her head,
And still will dance with ever varied ease,
Smiling upon the flowers and the trees:
Another will entice me on, and on
Through almond blossoms and rich cinnamon;
Till in the bosom of a leafy world
We rest in silence, like two gems upcurl'd          120
In the recesses of a pearly shell.

And can I ever bid these joys farewell?
Yes, I must pass them for a nobler life,
Where I may find the agonies, the strife
Of human hearts: for lo! I see afar,
O'ersailing the blue cragginess, a car
And steeds with streamy manes—the charioteer
Looks out upon the winds with glorious fear:
And now the numerous tramplings quiver lightly
Along a huge cloud's ridge; and now with sprightly          130
Wheel downward come they into fresher skies,
Tipt round with silver from the sun's bright eyes.
Still downward with capacious whirl they glide;
And now I see them on the green-hill's side
In breezy rest among the nodding stalks.
The charioteer with wond'rous gesture talks
To the trees and mountains; and there soon appear
Shapes of delight, of mystery, and fear,
Passing along before a dusky space
Made by some mighty oaks: as they would chase          140
Some ever-fleeting music on they sweep.
Lo! how they murmur, laugh, and smile, and weep:
Some with upholden hand and mouth severe;
Some with their faces muffled to the ear
Between their arms; some, clear in youthful bloom,
Go glad and smilingly athwart the gloom;
Some looking back, and some with upward gaze;
Yes, thousands in a thousand different ways
Flit onward—now a lovely wreath of girls
Dancing their sleek hair into tangled curls;          150
And now broad wings. Most awfully intent
The driver of those steeds is forward bent,

And seems to listen: O that I might know
All that he writes with such a hurrying glow.

The visions all are fled—the car is fled
Into the light of heaven, and in their stead
A sense of real things comes doubly strong,
And, like a muddy stream, would bear along
My soul to nothingness: but I will strive
Against all doubtings, and will keep alive     160
The thought of that same chariot, and the strange
Journey it went.
                    Is there so small a range
In the present strength of manhood, that the high
Imagination cannot freely fly
As she was wont of old? prepare her steeds,
Paw up against the light, and do strange deeds
Upon the clouds? Has she not shown us all?
From the clear space of ether, to the small
Breath of new buds unfolding? From the meaning
Of Jove's large eye-brow, to the tender greening     170
Of April meadows? Here her altar shone,
E'en in this isle; and who could paragon
The fervid choir that lifted up a noise
Of harmony, to where it aye will poise
Its mighty self of convoluting sound,
Huge as a planet, and like that roll round,
Eternally around a dizzy void?
Ay, in those days the Muses were nigh cloy'd
With honors; nor had any other care
Than to sing out and sooth their wavy hair.     180

Could all this be forgotten? Yes, a schism
Nurtured by foppery and barbarism,
Made great Apollo blush for this his land.
Men were thought wise who could not understand
His glories: with a puling infant's force
They sway'd about upon a rocking horse,
And thought it Pegasus. Ah dismal soul'd!
The winds of heaven blew, the ocean roll'd
Its gathering waves—ye felt it not. The blue
Bared its eternal bosom, and the dew     190

Of summer nights collected still to make
The morning precious: beauty was awake!
Why were ye not awake? But ye were dead
To things ye knew not of,—were closely wed
To musty laws lined out with wretched rule
And compass vile: so that ye taught a school
Of dolts to smooth, inlay, and clip, and fit,
Till, like the certain wands of Jacob's wit,
Their verses tallied. Easy was the task:
A thousand handicraftsmen wore the mask            200
Of Poesy. Ill-fated, impious race!
That blasphemed the bright Lyrist to his face,
And did not know it,—no, they went about,
Holding a poor, decrepid standard out
Mark'd with most flimsy mottos, and in large
The name of one Boileau!

                         O ye whose charge
It is to hover round our pleasant hills!
Whose congregated majesty so fills
My boundly reverence, that I cannot trace
Your hallowed names, in this unholy place,            210
So near those common folk; did not their shames
Affright you? Did our old lamenting Thames
Delight you? Did ye never cluster round
Delicious Avon, with a mournful sound,
And weep? Or did ye wholly bid adieu
To regions where no more the laurel grew?
Or did ye stay to give a welcoming
To some lone spirits who could proudly sing
Their youth away, and die? 'Twas even so:
But let me think away those times of woe:            220
Now 'tis a fairer season; ye have breathed
Rich benedictions o'er us; ye have wreathed
Fresh garlands: for sweet music has been heard
In many places;—some has been upstirr'd
From out its crystal dwelling in a lake,
By a swan's ebon bill; from a thick brake,
Nested and quiet in a valley mild,
Bubbles a pipe; fine sounds are floating wild
About the earth: happy are ye and glad.

These things are doubtless: yet in truth we've had    230
Strange thunders from the potency of song;
Mingled indeed with what is sweet and strong,
From majesty: but in clear truth the themes
Are ugly clubs, the Poets' Polyphemes
Disturbing the grand sea. A drainless shower
Of light is poesy; 'tis the supreme of power;
'Tis might half slumb'ring on its own right arm.
The very archings of her eye-lids charm
A thousand willing agents to obey,
And still she governs with the mildest sway:    240
But strength alone though of the Muses born
Is like a fallen angel: trees uptorn,
Darkness, and worms, and shrouds, and sepulchres
Delight it; for it feeds upon the burrs,
And thorns of life; forgetting the great end
Of poesy, that it should be a friend
To sooth the cares, and lift the thoughts of man.

    Yet I rejoice: a myrtle fairer than
E'er grew in Paphos, from the bitter weeds
Lifts its sweet head into the air, and feeds    250
A silent space with ever sprouting green.
All tenderest birds there find a pleasant screen,
Creep through the shade with jaunty fluttering,
Nibble the little cupped flowers and sing.
Then let us clear away the choking thorns
From round its gentle stem; let the young fawns,
Yeaned in after times, when we are flown,
Find a fresh sward beneath it, overgrown
With simple flowers: let there nothing be
More boisterous than a lover's bended knee;    260
Nought more ungentle than the placid look
Of one who leans upon a closed book;
Nought more untranquil than the grassy slopes
Between two hills. All hail delightful hopes!
As she was wont, th' imagination
Into most lovely labyrinths will be gone,
And they shall be accounted poet kings
Who simply tell the most heart-easing things.
O may these joys be ripe before I die.

Will not some say that I presumptuously                    270
Have spoken? that from hastening disgrace
'Twere better far to hide my foolish face?
That whining boyhood should with reverence bow
Ere the dread thunderbolt could reach? How!
If I do hide myself, it sure shall be
In the very fane, the light of Poesy:
If I do fall, at least I will be laid
Beneath the silence of a poplar shade;
And over me the grass shall be smooth shaven;
And there shall be a kind memorial graven.                    280
But off Despondence! miserable bane!
They should not know thee, who athirst to gain
A noble end, are thirsty every hour.
What though I am not wealthy in the dower
Of spanning wisdom; though I do not know
The shiftings of the mighty winds that blow
Hither and thither all the changing thoughts
Of man: though no great minist'ring reason sorts
Out the dark mysteries of human souls
To clear conceiving: yet there ever rolls                    290
A vast idea before me, and I glean
Therefrom my liberty; thence too I've seen
The end and aim of Poesy. 'Tis clear
As anything most true; as that the year
Is made of the four seasons—manifest
As a large cross, some old cathedral's crest,
Lifted to the white clouds. Therefore should I
Be but the essence of deformity,
A coward, did my very eye-lids wink
At speaking out what I have dared to think.                    300
Ah! rather let me like a madman run
Over some precipice; let the hot sun
Melt my Dedalian wings, and drive me down
Convuls'd and headlong! Stay! an inward frown
Of conscience bids me be more calm awhile.
An ocean dim, sprinkled with many an isle,
Spreads awfully before me. How much toil!
How many days! what desperate turmoil!
Ere I can have explored its widenesses.
Ah, what a task! upon my bended knees,                    310

I could unsay those—no, impossible!
Impossible!
            For sweet relief I'll dwell
On humbler thoughts, and let this strange assay
Begun in gentleness die so away.
E'en now all tumult from my bosom fades:
I turn full hearted to the friendly aids
That smooth the path of honour; brotherhood,
And friendliness the nurse of mutual good.
The hearty grasp that sends a pleasant sonnet
Into the brain ere one can think upon it;                    320
The silence when some rhymes are coming out;
And when they're come, the very pleasant rout:
The message certain to be done to-morrow.
'Tis perhaps as well that it should be to borrow
Some precious book from out its snug retreat,
To cluster round it when we next shall meet.
Scarce can I scribble on; for lovely airs
Are fluttering round the room like doves in pairs;
Many delights of that glad day recalling,
When first my senses caught their tender falling.             330
And with these airs come forms of elegance
Stooping their shoulders o'er a horse's prance,
Careless, and grand—fingers soft and round
Parting luxuriant curls;—and the swift bound
Of Bacchus from his chariot, when his eye
Made Ariadne's cheek look blushingly.
Thus I remember all the pleasant flow
Of words at opening a portfolio.

Things such as these are ever harbingers
To trains of peaceful images: the stirs                      340
Of a swan's neck unseen among the rushes:
A linnet starting all about the bushes:
A butterfly, with golden wings broad parted,
Nestling a rose, convuls'd as though it smarted
With over pleasure—many, many more,
Might I indulge at large in all my store
Of luxuries: yet I must not forget
Sleep, quiet with his poppy coronet:
For what there may be worthy in these rhymes

I partly owe to him: and thus, the chimes    350
Of friendly voices had just given place
To as sweet a silence, when I 'gan retrace
The pleasant day, upon a couch at ease.
It was a poet's house who keeps the keys
Of pleasure's temple. Round about were hung
The glorious features of the bards who sung
In other ages—cold and sacred busts
Smiled at each other. Happy he who trusts
To clear Futurity his darling fame!
Then there were fauns and satyrs taking aim    360
At swelling apples with a frisky leap
And reaching fingers, 'mid a luscious heap
Of vine-leaves. Then there rose to view a fane
Of liny marble, and thereto a train
Of nymphs approaching fairly o'er the sward:
One, loveliest, holding her white hand toward
The dazzling sun-rise: two sisters sweet
Bending their graceful figures till they meet
Over the trippings of a little child:
And some are hearing, eagerly, the wild    370
Thrilling liquidity of dewy piping.
See, in another picture, nymphs are wiping
Cherishingly Diana's timorous limbs;—
A fold of lawny mantle dabbling swims
At the bath's edge, and keeps a gentle motion
With the subsiding crystal: as when ocean
Heaves calmly its broad swelling smoothness o'er
Its rocky marge, and balances once more
The patient weeds; that now unshent by foam
Feel all about their undulating home.    380

Sappho's meek head was there half smiling down
At nothing; just as though the earnest frown
Of over thinking had that moment gone
From off her brow, and left her all alone.

Great Alfred's too, with anxious, pitying eyes,
As if he always listened to the sighs
Of the goaded world; and Kosciusko's worn
By horrid suffrance—mightily forlorn.

Petrarch, outstepping from the shady green,
Starts at the sight of Laura; nor can wean                    390
His eyes from her sweet face. Most happy they!
For over them was seen a free display
Of out-spread wings, and from between them shone
The face of Poesy: from off her throne
She overlook'd things that I scarce could tell.
The very sense of where I was might well
Keep Sleep aloof: but more than that there came
Thought after thought to nourish up the flame
Within my breast; so that the morning light
Surprised me even from a sleepless night;                    400
And up I rose refresh'd, and glad, and gay,
Resolving to begin that very day
These lines; and howsoever they be done,
I leave them as a father does his son.

# ENDYMION:

## A POETIC ROMANCE

'The stretched metre of an antique song'

INSCRIBED TO THE MEMORY OF

## THOMAS CHATTERTON

# PREFACE

KNOWING within myself the manner in which this Poem has been produced, it is not without a feeling of regret that I make it public.

What manner I mean, will be quite clear to the reader, who must soon perceive great inexperience, immaturity, and every error denoting a feverish attempt, rather than a deed accomplished. The two first books, and indeed the two last, I feel sensible are not of such completion as to warrant their passing the press; nor should they if I thought a year's castigation would do them any good;—it will not: the foundations are too sandy. It is just that this youngster should die away: a sad thought for me, if I had not some hope that while it is dwindling I may be plotting, and fitting myself for verses fit to live.

This may be speaking too presumptuously, and may deserve a punishment: but no feeling man will be forward to inflict it: he will leave me alone, with the conviction that there is not a fiercer hell than the failure in a great object. This is not written with the least atom of purpose to forestall criticisms of course, but from the desire I have to conciliate men who are competent to look, and who do look with a zealous eye, to the honour of English literature.

The imagination of a boy is healthy, and the mature imagination of a man is healthy; but there is a space of life between, in which the soul is in a ferment, the character undecided, the way of life uncertain, the ambition thick-sighted: thence proceeds mawkishness, and all the thousand bitters which those men I speak of must necessarily taste in going over the following pages.

I hope I have not in too late a day touched the beautiful mythology of Greece, and dulied its brightness: for I wish to try once more, before I bid it farewell.

TEIGNMOUTH, *April 10, 1818*

# ENDYMION

## BOOK I

A THING of beauty is a joy for ever:
Its loveliness increases; it will never
Pass into nothingness; but still will keep
A bower quiet for us, and a sleep
Full of sweet dreams, and health, and quiet breathing.
Therefore, on every morrow, are we wreathing
A flowery band to bind us to the earth,
Spite of despondence, of the inhuman dearth
Of noble natures, of the gloomy days,
Of all the unhealthy and o'er-darkened ways            10
Made for our searching: yes, in spite of all,
Some shape of beauty moves away the pall
From our dark spirits. Such the sun, the moon,
Trees old, and young, sprouting a shady boon
For simple sheep; and such are daffodils
With the green world they live in; and clear rills
That for themselves a cooling covert make
'Gainst the hot season; the mid forest brake,
Rich with a sprinkling of fair musk-rose blooms:
And such too is the grandeur of the dooms            20
We have imagined for the mighty dead;
All lovely tales that we have heard or read:
An endless fountain of immortal drink,
Pouring unto us from the heaven's brink.

  Nor do we merely feel these essences
For one short hour; no, even as the trees
That whisper round a temple become soon
Dear as the temple's self, so does the moon,
The passion poesy, glories infinite,
Haunt us till they become a cheering light            30
Unto our souls, and bound to us so fast,
That, whether there be shine, or gloom o'ercast,
They alway must be with us, or we die.

TO17040

Therefore, 'tis with full happiness that I
Will trace the story of Endymion.
The very music of the name has gone
Into my being, and each pleasant scene
Is growing fresh before me as the green
Of our own vallies: so I will begin
Now while I cannot hear the city's din;                    40
Now while the early budders are just new,
And run in mazes of the youngest hue
About old forests; while the willow trails
Its delicate amber; and the dairy pails
Bring home increase of milk. And, as the year
Grows lush in juicy stalks, I'll smoothly steer
My little boat, for many quiet hours,
With streams that deepen freshly into bowers.
Many and many a verse I hope to write,
Before the daisies, vermeil rimm'd and white,              50
Hide in deep herbage; and ere yet the bees
Hum about globes of clover and sweet peas,
I must be near the middle of my story.
O may no wintry season, bare and hoary,
See it half finish'd: but let Autumn bold,
With universal tinge of sober gold,
Be all about me when I make an end.
And now at once, adventuresome, I send
My herald thought into a wilderness:
There let its trumpet blow, and quickly dress              60
My uncertain path with green, that I may speed
Easily onward, thorough flowers and weed.

    Upon the sides of Latmos was outspread
A mighty forest; for the moist earth fed
So plenteously all weed-hidden roots
Into o'er-hanging boughs, and precious fruits.
And it had gloomy shades, sequestered deep,
Where no man went; and if from shepherd's keep
A lamb stray'd far a-down those inmost glens,
Never again saw he the happy pens                          70
Whither his brethren, bleating with content,
Over the hills at every nightfall went.
Among the shepherds, 'twas believed ever,
That not one fleecy lamb which thus did sever

From the white flock, but pass'd unworried
By angry wolf, or pard with prying head,
Until it came to some unfooted plains
Where fed the herds of Pan: aye great his gains
Who thus one lamb did lose. Paths there were many,
Winding through palmy fern, and rushes fenny,          80
And ivy banks; all leading pleasantly
To a wide lawn, whence one could only see
Stems thronging all around between the swell
Of turf and slanting branches: who could tell
The freshness of the space of heaven above,
Edg'd round with dark tree tops? through which a dove
Would often beat its wings, and often too
A little cloud would move across the blue.

    Full in the middle of this pleasantness
There stood a marble altar, with a tress              90
Of flowers budded newly; and the dew
Had taken fairy phantasies to strew
Daisies upon the sacred sward last eve,
And so the dawned light in pomp receive.
For 'twas the morn: Apollo's upward fire
Made every eastern cloud a silvery pyre
Of brightness so unsullied, that therein
A melancholy spirit well might win
Oblivion, and melt out his essence fine
Into the winds: rain-scented eglantine               100
Gave temperate sweets to that well-wooing sun;
The lark was lost in him; cold springs had run
To warm their chilliest bubbles in the grass;
Man's voice was on the mountains; and the mass
Of nature's lives and wonders puls'd tenfold,
To feel this sun-rise and its glories old.

    Now while the silent workings of the dawn
Were busiest, into that self-same lawn
All suddenly, with joyful cries, there sped
A troop of little children garlanded;                110
Who gathering round the altar, seem'd to pry
Earnestly round as wishing to espy
Some folk of holiday: nor had they waited
For many moments, ere their ears were sated

With a faint breath of music, which ev'n then
Fill'd out its voice, and died away again.
Within a little space again it gave
Its airy swellings, with a gentle wave,
To light-hung leaves, in smoothest echoes breaking
Through copse-clad vallies,—ere their death, o'ertaking   120
The surgy murmurs of the lonely sea.

    And now, as deep into the wood as we
Might mark a lynx's eye, there glimmered light
Fair faces and a rush of garments white,
Plainer and plainer showing, till at last
Into the widest alley they all past,
Making directly for the woodland altar.
O kindly muse! let not my weak tongue faulter
In telling of this goodly company,
Of their old piety, and of their glee:                   130
But let a portion of ethereal dew
Fall on my head, and presently unmew
My soul; that I may dare, in wayfaring,
To stammer where old Chaucer us'd to sing.

    Leading the way, young damsels danced along,
Bearing the burden of a shepherd song;
Each having a white wicker over brimm'd
With April's tender younglings: next, well trimm'd,
A crowd of shepherds with as sunburnt looks
As may be read of in Arcadian books;                     140
Such as sat listening round Apollo's pipe,
When the great deity, for earth too ripe,
Let his divinity o'erflowing die
In music, through the vales of Thessaly:
Some idly trail'd their sheep-hooks on the ground,
And some kept up a shrilly mellow sound
With ebon-tipped flutes: close after these,
Now coming from beneath the forest trees,
A venerable priest full soberly,
Begirt with ministring looks: alway his eye              150
Stedfast upon the matted turf he kept,
And after him his sacred vestments swept.
From his right hand there swung a vase, milk-white,
Of mingled wine, out-sparkling generous light;

And in his left he held a basket full
Of all sweet herbs that searching eye could cull:
Wild thyme, and valley-lillies whiter still
Than Leda's love, and cresses from the rill.
His aged head, crowned with beechen wreath,
Seem'd like a poll of ivy in the teeth                    160
Of winter hoar. Then came another crowd
Of shepherds, lifting in due time aloud
Their share of the ditty. After them appear'd,
Up-followed by a multitude that rear'd
Their voices to the clouds, a fair wrought car,
Easily rolling so as scarce to mar
The freedom of three steeds of dapple brown:
Who stood therein did seem of great renown
Among the throng. His youth was fully blown,
Showing like Ganymede to manhood grown;                    170
And, for those simple times, his garments were
A chieftain king's: beneath his breast, half bare,
Was hung a silver bugle, and between
His nervy knees there lay a boar-spear keen.
A smile was on his countenance; he seem'd,
To common lookers on, like one who dream'd
Of idleness in groves Elysian:
But there were some who feelingly could scan
A lurking trouble in his nether lip,
And see that oftentimes the reins would slip                    180
Through his forgotten hands: then would they sigh,
And think of yellow leaves, of owlets' cry,
Of logs piled solemnly.—Ah, well-a-day,
Why should our young Endymion pine away!

　　Soon the assembly, in a circle rang'd,
Stood silent round the shrine: each look was chang'd
To sudden veneration: women meek
Beckon'd their sons to silence; while each cheek
Of virgin bloom paled gently for slight fear.
Endymion too, without a forest peer,                    190
Stood, wan, and pale, and with an awed face,
Among his brothers of the mountain chace.
In midst of all, the venerable priest
Eyed them with joy from greatest to the least,

And, after lifting up his aged hands,
Thus spake he: 'Men of Latmos! shepherd bands!
Whose care it is to guard a thousand flocks:
Whether descended from beneath the rocks
That overtop your mountains; whether come
From vallies where the pipe is never dumb;          200
Or from your swelling downs, where sweet air stirs
Blue hare-bells lightly, and where prickly furze
Buds lavish gold; or ye, whose precious charge
Nibble their fill at ocean's very marge,
Whose mellow reeds are touch'd with sounds forlorn
By the dim echoes of old Triton's horn:
Mothers and wives! who day by day prepare
The scrip, with needments, for the mountain air;
And all ye gentle girls who foster up
Udderless lambs, and in a little cup          210
Will put choice honey for a favoured youth:
Yea, every one attend! for in good truth
Our vows are wanting to our great god Pan.
Are not our lowing heifers sleeker than
Night-swollen mushrooms? Are not our wide plains
Speckled with countless fleeces? Have not rains
Green'd over April's lap? No howling sad
Sickens our fearful ewes; and we have had
Great bounty from Endymion our lord.
The earth is glad: the merry lark has pour'd          220
His early song against yon breezy sky,
That spreads so clear o'er our solemnity.'

    Thus ending, on the shrine he heap'd a spire
Of teeming sweets, enkindling sacred fire;
Anon he stain'd the thick and spongy sod
With wine, in honour of the shepherd-god.
Now while the earth was drinking it, and while
Bay leaves were crackling in the fragrant pile,
And gummy frankincense was sparkling bright
'Neath smothering parsley, and a hazy light          230
Spread greyly eastward, thus a chorus sang:

    'O THOU, whose mighty palace roof doth hang
From jagged trunks, and overshadoweth
Eternal whispers, glooms, the birth, life, death

Of unseen flowers in heavy peacefulness;
Who lov'st to see the hamadryads dress
Their ruffled locks where meeting hazels darken;
And through whole solemn hours dost sit, and hearken
The dreary melody of bedded reeds—
In desolate places, where dank moisture breeds          240
The pipy hemlock to strange overgrowth;
Bethinking thee, how melancholy loth
Thou wast to lose fair Syrinx—do thou now,
By thy love's milky brow!
By all the trembling mazes that she ran,
Hear us, great Pan!

    'O thou, for whose soul-soothing quiet, turtles
Passion their voices cooingly 'mong myrtles,
What time thou wanderest at eventide
Through sunny meadows, that outskirt the side          25c
Of thine enmossed realms: O thou, to whom
Broad leaved fig trees even now foredoom
Their ripen'd fruitage; yellow girted bees
Their golden honeycombs; our village leas
Their fairest blossom'd beans and poppied corn;
The chuckling linnet its five young unborn,
To sing for thee; low creeping strawberries
Their summer coolness; pent up butterflies
Their freckled wings; yea, the fresh budding year
All its completions—be quickly near,                   260
By every wind that nods the mountain pine,
O forester divine!

    'Thou, to whom every faun and satyr flies
For willing service; whether to surprise
The squatted hare while in half sleeping fit;
Or upward ragged precipices flit
To save poor lambkins from the eagle's maw;
Or by mysterious enticement draw
Bewildered shepherds to their path again;
Or to tread breathless round the frothy main,          270
And gather up all fancifullest shells
For thee to tumble into Naiads' cells,
And, being hidden, laugh at their out-peeping;
Or to delight thee with fantastic leaping,

The while they pelt each other on the crown
With silvery oak apples, and fir cones brown—
By all the echoes that about thee ring,
Hear us, O satyr king!

'O Hearkener to the loud clapping shears
While ever and anon to his shorn peers                    280
A ram goes bleating: Winder of the horn,
When snouted wild-boars routing tender corn
Anger our huntsmen: Breather round our farms,
To keep off mildews, and all weather harms:
Strange ministrant of undescribed sounds,
That come a swooning over hollow grounds,
And wither drearily on barren moors:
Dread opener of the mysterious doors
Leading to universal knowledge—see,
Great son of Dryope,                                      290
The many that are come to pay their vows
With leaves about their brows!

'Be still the unimaginable lodge
For solitary thinkings; such as dodge
Conception to the very bourne of heaven,
Then leave the naked brain: be still the leaven,
That spreading in this dull and clodded earth
Gives it a touch ethereal—a new birth:
Be still a symbol of immensity;
A firmament reflected in a sea;                           300
An element filling the space between;
An unknown—but no more: we humbly screen
With uplift hands our foreheads, lowly bending,
And giving out a shout most heaven rending,
Conjure thee to receive our humble Pæan,
Upon thy Mount Lycean!'

Even while they brought the burden to a close,
A shout from the whole multitude arose,
That lingered in the air like dying rolls
Of abrupt thunder, when Ionian shoals                     310
Of dolphins bob their noses through the brine.
Meantime, on shady levels, mossy fine,
Young companies nimbly began dancing

To the swift treble pipe, and humming string.
Aye, those fair living forms swam heavenly
To tunes forgotten—out of memory:
Fair creatures! whose young children's children bred
Thermopylæ its heroes—not yet dead,
But in old marbles ever beautiful.
High genitors, unconscious did they cull                    320
Time's sweet first-fruits—they danc'd to weariness,
And then in quiet circles did they press
The hillock turf, and caught the latter end
Of some strange history, potent to send
A young mind from its bodily tenement.
Or they might watch the quoit-pitchers, intent
On either side; pitying the sad death
Of Hyacinthus, when the cruel breath
Of Zephyr slew him,—Zephyr penitent,
Who now, ere Phœbus mounts the firmament,                   330
Fondles the flower amid the sobbing rain.
The archers too, upon a wider plain,
Beside the feathery whizzing of the shaft,
And the dull twanging bowstring, and the raft
Branch down sweeping from a tall ash top,
Call'd up a thousand thoughts to envelope
Those who would watch. Perhaps, the trembling knee
And frantic gape of lonely Niobe,
Poor, lonely Niobe! when her lovely young
Were dead and gone, and her caressing tongue                340
Lay a lost thing upon her paly lip,
And very, very deadliness did nip
Her motherly cheeks. Arous'd from this sad mood
By one, who at a distance loud halloo'd,
Uplifting his strong bow into the air,
Many might after brighter visions stare:
After the Argonauts, in blind amaze
Tossing about on Neptune's restless ways,
Until, from the horizon's vaulted side,
There shot a golden splendour far and wide,                 350
Spangling those million poutings of the brine
With quivering ore: 'twas even an awful shine
From the exaltation of Apollo's bow;
A heavenly beacon in their dreary woe.

Who thus were ripe for high contemplating,
Might turn their steps towards the sober ring
Where sat Endymion and the aged priest
'Mong shepherds gone in eld, whose looks increas'd
The silvery setting of their mortal star.
There they discours'd upon the fragile bar       360
That keeps us from our homes ethereal;
And what our duties there: to nightly call
Vesper, the beauty-crest of summer weather;
To summon all the downiest clouds together
For the sun's purple couch; to emulate
In ministring the potent rule of fate
With speed of fire-tail'd exhalations;
To tint her pallid cheek with bloom, who cons
Sweet poesy by moonlight: besides these,
A world of other unguess'd offices.       370
Anon they wander'd, by divine converse,
Into Elysium; vieing to rehearse
Each one his own anticipated bliss.
One felt heart-certain that he could not miss
His quick gone love, among fair blossom'd boughs,
Where every zephyr-sigh pouts, and endows
Her lips with music for the welcoming.
Another wish'd, mid that eternal spring,
To meet his rosy child, with feathery sails,
Sweeping, eye-earnestly, through almond vales:       380
Who, suddenly, should stoop through the smooth wind,
And with the balmiest leaves his temples bind;
And, ever after, through those regions be
His messenger, his little Mercury.
Some were athirst in soul to see again
Their fellow huntsmen o'er the wide champaign
In times long past; to sit with them, and talk
Of all the chances in their earthly walk;
Comparing, joyfully, their plenteous stores
Of happiness, to when upon the moors,       390
Benighted, close they huddled from the cold,
And shar'd their famish'd scrips. Thus all out-told
Their fond imaginations,—saving him
Whose eyelids curtain'd up their jewels dim,
Endymion: yet hourly had he striven

To hide the cankering venom, that had riven
His fainting recollections. Now indeed
His senses had swoon'd off: he did not heed
The sudden silence, or the whispers low,
Or the old eyes dissolving at his woe,                                    400
Or anxious calls, or close of trembling palms,
Or maiden's sigh, that grief itself embalms:
But in the self-same fixed trance he kept,
Like one who on the earth had never stept.
Aye, even as dead still as a marble man,
Frozen in that old tale Arabian.

Who whispers him so pantingly and close?
Peona, his sweet sister: of all those,
His friends, the dearest. Hushing signs she made,
And breath'd a sister's sorrow to persuade                                410
A yielding up, a cradling on her care.
Her eloquence did breathe away the curse:
She led him, like some midnight spirit nurse
Of happy changes in emphatic dreams,
Along a path between two little streams,—
Guarding his forehead, with her round elbow,
From low-grown branches, and his footsteps slow
From stumbling over stumps and hillocks small;
Until they came to where these streamlets fall,
With mingled bubblings and a gentle rush,                                 420
Into a river, clear, brimful, and flush
With crystal mocking of the trees and sky.
A little shallop, floating there hard by,
Pointed its beak over the fringed bank;
And soon it lightly dipt, and rose, and sank,
And dipt again, with the young couple's weight,—
Peona guiding, through the water straight,
Towards a bowery island opposite;
Which gaining presently, she steered light
Into a shady, fresh, and ripply cove,                                     430
Where nested was an arbour, overwove
By many a summer's silent fingering;
To whose cool bosom she was used to bring
Her playmates, with their needle broidery,
And minstrel memories of times gone by.

So she was gently glad to see him laid
Under her favourite bower's quiet shade,
On her own couch, new made of flower leaves,
Dried carefully on the cooler side of sheaves
When last the sun his autumn tresses shook,      440
And the tann'd harvesters rich armfuls took.
Soon was he quieted to slumbrous rest:
But, ere it crept upon him, he had prest
Peona's busy hand against his lips,
And still, a sleeping, held her finger-tips
In tender pressure. And as a willow keeps
A patient watch over the stream that creeps
Windingly by it, so the quiet maid
Held her in peace: so that a whispering blade
Of grass, a wailful gnat, a bee bustling      450
Down in the blue-bells, or a wren light rustling
Among sere leaves and twigs, might all be heard.

O magic sleep! O comfortable bird,
That broodest o'er the troubled sea of the mind
Till it is hush'd and smooth! O unconfin'd
Restraint! imprisoned liberty! great key
To golden palaces, strange minstrelsy,
Fountains grotesque, new trees, bespangled caves,
Echoing grottos, full of tumbling waves
And moonlight; aye, to all the mazy world      460
Of silvery enchantment!—who, upfurl'd
Beneath thy drowsy wing a triple hour,
But renovates and lives?—Thus, in the bower,
Endymion was calm'd to life again.
Opening his eyelids with a healthier brain,
He said: 'I feel this thine endearing love
All through my bosom: thou art as a dove
Trembling its closed eyes and sleeked wings
About me; and the pearliest dew not brings
Such morning incense from the fields of May,      470
As do those brighter drops that twinkling stray
From those kind eyes,—the very home and haunt
Of sisterly affection. Can I want
Aught else, aught nearer heaven, than such tears?
Yet dry them up, in bidding hence all fears

That, any longer, I will pass my days
Alone and sad. No, I will once more raise
My voice upon the mountain-heights; once more
Make my horn parley from their foreheads hoar:
Again my trooping hounds their tongues shall loll          480
Around the breathed boar: again I'll poll
The fair-grown yew tree, for a chosen bow:
And, when the pleasant sun is getting low,
Again I'll linger in a sloping mead
To hear the speckled thrushes, and see feed
Our idle sheep. So be thou cheered, sweet,
And, if thy lute is here, softly intreat
My soul to keep in its resolved course.'

    Hereat Peona, in their silver source,
Shut her pure sorrow drops with glad exclaim,          490
And took a lute, from which there pulsing came
A lively prelude, fashioning the way
In which her voice should wander. 'Twas a lay
More subtle cadenced, more forest wild
Than Dryope's lone lulling of her child;
And nothing since has floated in the air
So mournful strange. Surely some influence rare
Went, spiritual, through the damsel's hand;
For still, with Delphic emphasis, she spann'd
The quick invisible strings, even though she saw          500
Endymion's spirit melt away and thaw
Before the deep intoxication.
But soon she came, with sudden burst, upon
Her self-possession—swung the lute aside,
And earnestly said: 'Brother, 'tis vain to hide
That thou dost know of things mysterious,
Immortal, starry; such alone could thus
Weigh down thy nature. Hast thou sinn'd in aught
Offensive to the heavenly power? Caught
A Paphian dove upon a message sent?          510
Thy deathful bow against some deer-herd bent
Sacred to Dian? Haply, thou hast seen
Her naked limbs among the alders green;
And that, alas! is death. No, I can trace
Something more high-perplexing in thy face!'

Endymion look'd at her, and press'd her hand,
And said, 'Art thou so pale, who wast so bland
And merry in our meadows? How is this?
Tell me thine ailment: tell me all amiss!—
Ah! thou hast been unhappy at the change      520
Wrought suddenly in me. What indeed more strange?
Or more complete to overwhelm surmise?
Ambition is no sluggard: 'tis no prize,
That toiling years would put within my grasp,
That I have sighed for: with so deadly gasp
No man e'er panted for a mortal love.
So all have set my heavier grief above
These things which happen. Rightly have they done:
I, who still saw the horizontal sun
Heave his broad shoulder o'er the edge of the world,      530
Out-facing Lucifer, and then had hurl'd
My spear aloft, as signal for the chace—
I, who, for very sport of heart, would race
With my own steed from Araby; pluck down
A vulture from his towery perching; frown
A lion into growling, loth retire—
To lose, at once, all my toil-breeding fire,
And sink thus low! but I will ease my breast
Of secret grief, here in this bowery nest.

'This river does not see the naked sky,      540
Till it begins to progress silverly
Around the western border of the wood,
Whence, from a certain spot, its winding flood
Seems at the distance like a crescent moon:
And in that nook, the very pride of June,
Had I been used to pass my weary eves;
The rather for the sun unwilling leaves
So dear a picture of his sovereign power,
And I could witness his most kingly hour,
When he doth tighten up the golden reins,      550
And paces leisurely down amber plains
His snorting four. Now when his chariot last
Its beams against the zodiac-lion cast,
There blossom'd suddenly a magic bed
Of sacred ditamy, and poppies red:

At which I wondered greatly, knowing well
That but one night had wrought this flowery spell;
And, sitting down close by, began to muse
What it might mean. Perhaps, thought I, Morpheus,
In passing here, his owlet pinions shook; 560
Or, it may be, ere matron Night uptook
Her ebon urn, young Mercury, by stealth,
Had dipt his rod in it: such garland wealth
Came not by common growth. Thus on I thought,
Until my head was dizzy and distraught.
Moreover, through the dancing poppies stole
A breeze, most softly lulling to my soul;
And shaping visions all about my sight
Of colours, wings, and bursts of spangly light:
The which became more strange, and strange, and dim, 570
And then were gulph'd in a tumultuous swim:
And then I fell asleep. Ah, can I tell
The enchantment that afterwards befel?
Yet it was but a dream: yet such a dream
That never tongue, although it overteem
With mellow utterance, like a cavern spring,
Could figure out and to conception bring
All I beheld and felt. Methought I lay
Watching the zenith, where the milky way
Among the stars in virgin splendour pours; 580
And travelling my eye, until the doors
Of heaven appear'd to open for my flight,
I became loth and fearful to alight
From such high soaring by a downward glance:
So kept me stedfast in that airy trance,
Spreading imaginary pinions wide.
When, presently, the stars began to glide,
And faint away, before my eager view:
At which I sigh'd that I could not pursue,
And dropt my vision to the horizon's verge; 590
And lo! from opening clouds, I saw emerge
The loveliest moon, that ever silver'd o'er
A shell for Neptune's goblet: she did soar
So passionately bright, my dazzled soul
Commingling with her argent spheres did roll
Through clear and cloudy, even when she went

At last into a dark and vapoury tent—
Whereat, methought, the lidless-eyed train
Of planets all were in the blue again.
To commune with those orbs, once more I rais'd          600
My sight right upward: but it was quite dazed
By a bright something, sailing down apace,
Making me quickly veil my eyes and face:
Again I look'd, and, O ye deities,
Who from Olympus watch our destinies!
Whence that completed form of all completeness?
Whence came that high perfection of all sweetness?
Speak, stubborn earth, and tell me where, O where
Hast thou a symbol of her golden hair?
Not oat-sheaves drooping in the western sun;          610
Not—thy soft hand, fair sister! let me shun
Such follying before thee—yet she had,
Indeed, locks bright enough to make me mad;
And they were simply gordian'd up and braided,
Leaving, in naked comeliness, unshaded,
Her pearl round ears, white neck, and orbed brow;
The which were blended in, I know not how,
With such a paradise of lips and eyes,
Blush-tinted cheeks, half smiles, and faintest sighs,
That, when I think thereon, my spirit clings          620
And plays about its fancy, till the stings
Of human neighbourhood envenom all.
Unto what awful power shall I call?
To what high fane?—Ah! see her hovering feet,
More bluely vein'd, more soft, more whitely sweet
Than those of sea-born Venus, when she rose
From out her cradle shell. The wind out-blows
Her scarf into a fluttering pavillion;
'Tis blue, and over-spangled with a million
Of little eyes, as though thou wert to shed,          630
Over the darkest, lushest blue-bell bed,
Handfuls of daisies.'—'Endymion, how strange!
Dream within dream!'—'She took an airy range,
And then, towards me, like a very maid,
Came blushing, waning, willing, and afraid,
And press'd me by the hand: Ah! 'twas too much;
Methought I fainted at the charmed touch,

Yet held my recollection, even as one
Who dives three fathoms where the waters run
Gurgling in beds of coral: for anon,                     640
I felt upmounted in that region
Where falling stars dart their artillery forth,
And eagles struggle with the buffeting north
That balances the heavy meteor-stone;—
Felt too, I was not fearful, nor alone,
But lapp'd and lull'd along the dangerous sky.
Soon, as it seem'd, we left our journeying high,
And straightway into frightful eddies swoop'd;
Such as aye muster where grey time has scoop'd
Huge dens and caverns in a mountain's side;               650
There hollow sounds arous'd me, and I sigh'd
To faint once more by looking on my bliss—
I was distracted; madly did I kiss
The wooing arms which held me, and did give
My eyes at once to death: but 'twas to live,
To take in draughts of life from the gold fount
Of kind and passionate looks; to count, and count
The moments, by some greedy help that seem'd
A second self, that each might be redeem'd
And plunder'd of its load of blessedness.                 660
Ah, desperate mortal! I e'en dar'd to press
Her very cheek against my crowned lip,
And, at that moment, felt my body dip
Into a warmer air: a moment more,
Our feet were soft in flowers. There was store
Of newest joys upon that alp. Sometimes
A scent of violets, and blossoming limes,
Loiter'd around us; then of honey cells,
Made delicate from all white-flower bells;
And once, above the edges of our nest,                    670
An arch face peep'd,—an Oread as I guess'd.


'Why did I dream that sleep o'er-power'd me
In midst of all this heaven? Why not see,
Far off, the shadows of his pinions dark,
And stare them from me? But no, like a spark
That needs must die, although its little beam
Reflects upon a diamond, my sweet dream

Fell into nothing—into stupid sleep.
And so it was, until a gentle creep,
A careful moving caught my waking ears,                    680
And up I started: Ah! my sighs, my tears,
My clenched hands:—for lo! the poppies hung
Dew-dabbled on their stalks, the ouzel sung
A heavy ditty, and the sullen day
Had chidden herald Hesperus away,
With leaden looks: the solitary breeze
Bluster'd, and slept, and its wild self did teaze
With wayward melancholy; and I thought,
Mark me, Peona! that sometimes it brought
Faint fare-thee-wells, and sigh-shrilled adieus!—          690
Away I wander'd—all the pleasant hues
Of heaven and earth had faded: deepest shades
Were deepest dungeons; heaths and sunny glades
Were full of pestilent light; our taintless rills
Seem'd sooty, and o'er-spread with upturn'd gills
Of dying fish; the vermeil rose had blown
In frightful scarlet, and its thorns out-grown
Like spiked aloe. If an innocent bird
Before my heedless footsteps stirr'd, and stirr'd
In little journeys, I beheld in it                         700
A disguis'd demon, missioned to knit
My soul with under darkness; to entice
My stumblings down some monstrous precipice:
Therefore I eager followed, and did curse
The disappointment. Time, that aged nurse,
Rock'd me to patience. Now, thank gentle heaven!
These things, with all their comfortings, are given
To my down-sunken hours, and with thee,
Sweet sister, help to stem the ebbing sea
Of weary life.'
                    Thus ended he, and both                710
Sat silent: for the maid was very loth
To answer; feeling well that breathed words
Would all be lost, unheard, and vain as swords
Against the enchased crocodile, or leaps
Of grasshoppers against the sun. She weeps
And wonders; struggles to devise some blame;
To put on such a look as would say, *Shame*

*On this poor weakness!* but, for all her strife,
She could as soon have crush'd away the life
From a sick dove. At length, to break the pause,            720
She said with trembling chance: 'Is this the cause?
This all? Yet it is strange, and sad, alas!
That one who through this middle earth should pass
Most like a sojourning demi-god, and leave
His name upon the harp-string, should achieve
No higher bard than simple maidenhood,
Singing alone, and fearfully,—how the blood
Left his young cheek; and how he used to stray
He knew not where; and how he would say, *nay,*
If any said 'twas love: and yet 'twas love;              730
What could it be but love? How a ring-dove
Let fall a sprig of yew tree in his path;
And how he died: and then, that love doth scathe
The gentle heart, as northern blasts do roses;
And then the ballad of his sad life closes
With sighs, and an alas!—Endymion!
Be rather in the trumpet's mouth,—anon
Among the winds at large—that all may hearken!
Although, before the crystal heavens darken,
I watch and dote upon the silver lakes              740
Pictur'd in western cloudiness, that takes
The semblance of gold rocks and bright gold sands,
Islands, and creeks, and amber-fretted strands
With horses prancing o'er them, palaces
And towers of amethyst,—would I so teaze
My pleasant days, because I could not mount
Into those regions? The Morphean fount
Of that fine element that visions, dreams,
And fitful whims of sleep are made of, streams
Into its airy channels with so subtle,              750
So thin a breathing, not the spider's shuttle,
Circled a million times within the space
Of a swallow's nest-door, could delay a trace,
A tinting of its quality: how light
Must dreams themselves be; seeing they're more slight
Than the mere nothing that engenders them!
Then wherefore sully the entrusted gem
Of high and noble life with thoughts so sick?

Why pierce high-fronted honour to the quick
For nothing but a dream?' Hereat the youth          760
Look'd up: a conflicting of shame and ruth
Was in his plaited brow: yet, his eyelids
Widened a little, as when Zephyr bids
A little breeze to creep between the fans
Of careless butterflies: amid his pains
He seem'd to taste a drop of manna-dew,
Full palatable; and a colour grew
Upon his cheek, while thus he lifeful spake.

   'Peona! ever have I long'd to slake
My thirst for the world's praises: nothing base,          770
No merely slumberous phantasm, could unlace
The stubborn canvas for my voyage prepar'd—
Though now 'tis tatter'd; leaving my bark bar'd
And sullenly drifting: yet my higher hope
Is of too wide, too rainbow-large a scope,
To fret at myriads of earthly wrecks.
Wherein lies happiness? In that which becks
Our ready minds to fellowship divine,
A fellowship with essence; till we shine,
Full alchemiz'd, and free of space. Behold          780
The clear religion of heaven! Fold
A rose leaf round thy finger's taperness,
And soothe thy lips: hist, when the airy stress
Of music's kiss impregnates the free winds,
And with a sympathetic touch unbinds
Æolian magic from their lucid wombs:
Then old songs waken from enclouded tombs;
Old ditties sigh above their father's grave;
Ghosts of melodious prophecyings rave
Round every spot where trod Apollo's foot;          790
Bronze clarions awake, and faintly bruit,
Where long ago a giant battle was;
And, from the turf, a lullaby doth pass
In every place where infant Orpheus slept.
Feel we these things?—that moment have we stept
Into a sort of oneness, and our state
Is like a floating spirit's. But there are
Richer entanglements, enthralments far

More self-destroying, leading, by degrees,
To the chief intensity: the crown of these            800
Is made of love and friendship, and sits high
Upon the forehead of humanity.
All its more ponderous and bulky worth
Is friendship, whence there ever issues forth
A steady splendour; but at the tip-top,
There hangs by unseen film, an orbed drop
Of light, and that is love: its influence,
Thrown in our eyes, genders a novel sense,
At which we start and fret; till in the end,
Melting into its radiance, we blend,                  810
Mingle, and so become a part of it,—
Nor with aught else can our souls interknit
So wingedly: when we combine therewith,
Life's self is nourish'd by its proper pith,
And we are nurtured like a pelican brood.
Aye, so delicious is the unsating food,
That men, who might have tower'd in the van
Of all the congregated world, to fan
And winnow from the coming step of time
All chaff of custom, wipe away all slime               820
Left by men-slugs and human serpentry,
Have been content to let occasion die,
Whilst they did sleep in love's elysium.
And, truly, I would rather be struck dumb,
Than speak against this ardent listlessness:
For I have ever thought that it might bless
The world with benefits unknowingly;
As does the nightingale, upperched high,
And cloister'd among cool and bunched leaves—
She sings but to her love, nor e'er conceives          830
How tiptoe Night holds back her dark-grey hood.
Just so may love, although 'tis understood
The mere commingling of passionate breath,
Produce more than our searching witnesseth:
What I know not: but who, of men, can tell
That flowers would bloom, or that green fruit would swell
To melting pulp, that fish would have bright mail,
The earth its dower of river, wood, and vale,
The meadows runnels, runnels pebble-stones,

The seed its harvest, or the lute its tones,          840
Tones ravishment, or ravishment its sweet,
If human souls did never kiss and greet?

   'Now, if this earthly love has power to make
Men's being mortal, immortal; to shake
Ambition from their memories, and brim
Their measure of content: what merest whim,
Seems all this poor endeavour after fame,
To one, who keeps within his stedfast aim
A love immortal, an immortal too.
Look not so wilder'd; for these things are true,    850
And never can be born of atomies
That buzz about our slumbers, like brain-flies,
Leaving us fancy-sick. No, no, I'm sure,
My restless spirit never could endure
To brood so long upon one luxury,
Unless it did, though fearfully, espy
A hope beyond the shadow of a dream.
My sayings will the less obscured seem,
When I have told thee how my waking sight
Has made me scruple whether that same night   860
Was pass'd in dreaming. Hearken, sweet Peona!
Beyond the matron-temple of Latona,
Which we should see but for these darkening boughs,
Lies a deep hollow, from whose ragged brows
Bushes and trees do lean all round athwart
And meet so nearly, that with wings outraught,
And spreaded tail, a vulture could not glide
Past them, but he must brush on every side.
Some moulder'd steps lead into this cool cell,
Far as the slabbed margin of a well,         870
Whose patient level peeps its crystal eye
Right upward, through the bushes, to the sky.
Oft have I brought thee flowers, on their stalks set
Like vestal primroses, but dark velvet
Edges them round, and they have golden pits:
'Twas there I got them, from the gaps and slits
In a mossy stone, that sometimes was my seat,
When all above was faint with mid-day heat.
And there in strife no burning thoughts to heed,

I'd bubble up the water through a reed;                    880
So reaching back to boy-hood: make me ships
Of moulted feathers, touchwood, alder chips,
With leaves stuck in them; and the Neptune be
Of their petty ocean. Oftener, heavily,
When love-lorn hours had left me less a child,
I sat contemplating the figures wild
Of o'er-head clouds melting the mirror through.
Upon a day, while thus I watch'd, by flew
A cloudy Cupid, with his bow and quiver;
So plainly character'd, no breeze would shiver                    890
The happy chance: so happy, I was fain
To follow it upon the open plain,
And, therefore, was just going; when, behold!
A wonder, fair as any I have told—
The same bright face I tasted in my sleep,
Smiling in the clear well. My heart did leap
Through the cool depth.—It moved as if to flee—
I started up, when lo! refreshfully
There came upon my face in plenteous showers
Dew-drops, and dewy buds, and leaves, and flowers,                    900
Wrapping all objects from my smothered sight,
Bathing my spirit in a new delight.
Aye, such a breathless honey-feel of bliss
Alone preserved me from the drear abyss
Of death, for the fair form had gone again.
Pleasure is oft a visitant; but pain
Clings cruelly to us, like the gnawing sloth
On the deer's tender haunches: late, and loth,
'Tis scar'd away by slow returning pleasure.
How sickening, how dark the dreadful leisure                    910
Of weary days, made deeper exquisite,
By a fore-knowledge of unslumbrous night!
Like sorrow came upon me, heavier still,
Than when I wander'd from the poppy hill:
And a whole age of lingering moments crept
Sluggishly by, ere more contentment swept
Away at once the deadly yellow spleen.
Yes, thrice have I this fair enchantment seen;
Once more been tortured with renewed life.
When last the wintry gusts gave over strife                    920

With the conquering sun of spring, and left the skies
Warm and serene, but yet with moistened eyes
In pity of the shatter'd infant buds,—
That time thou didst adorn, with amber studs,
My hunting cap, because I laugh'd and smil'd,
Chatted with thee, and many days exil'd
All torment from my breast;—'twas even then,
Straying about, yet, coop'd up in the den
Of helpless discontent,—hurling my lance
From place to place, and following at chance,        930
At last, by hap, through some young trees it struck,
And, plashing among bedded pebbles, stuck
In the middle of a brook,—whose silver ramble
Down twenty little falls, through reeds and bramble,
Tracing along, it brought me to a cave,
Whence it ran brightly forth, and white did lave
The nether sides of mossy stones and rock,—
'Mong which it gurgled blythe adieus, to mock
Its own sweet grief at parting. Overhead,
Hung a lush screen of drooping weeds, and spread        940
Thick, as to curtain up some wood-nymph's home.
"Ah! impious mortal, whither do I roam?"
Said I, low voic'd: "Ah, whither! 'Tis the grot
"Of Proserpine, when Hell, obscure and hot,
"Doth her resign; and where her tender hands
"She dabbles, on the cool and sluicy sands:
"Or 'tis the cell of Echo, where she sits,
"And babbles thorough silence, till her wits
"Are gone in tender madness, and anon,
"Faints into sleep, with many a dying tone        950
"Of sadness. O that she would take my vows,
"And breathe them sighingly among the boughs,
"To sue her gentle ears for whose fair head,
"Daily, I pluck sweet flowerets from their bed,
"And weave them dyingly—send honey-whispers
"Round every leaf, that all those gentle lispers
"May sigh my love unto her pitying!
"O charitable Echo! hear, and sing
"This ditty to her!—tell her"—so I stay'd
My foolish tongue, and listening, half afraid,        960
Stood stupefied with my own empty folly,

And blushing for the freaks of melancholy.
Salt tears were coming, when I heard my name
Most fondly lipp'd, and then these accents came:
"Endymion! the cave is secreter
"Than the isle of Delos. Echo hence shall stir
"No sighs but sigh-warm kisses, or light noise
"Of thy combing hand, the while it travelling cloys
"And trembles through my labyrinthine hair."
At that oppress'd I hurried in.—Ah! where          970
Are those swift moments? Whither are they fled?
I'll smile no more, Peona; nor will wed
Sorrow the way to death; but patiently
Bear up against it: so farewell, sad sigh;
And come instead demurest meditation,
To occupy me wholly, and to fashion
My pilgrimage for the world's dusky brink.
No more will I count over, link by link,
My chain of grief: no longer strive to find
A half-forgetfulness in mountain wind          980
Blustering about my ears: aye, thou shalt see,
Dearest of sisters, what my life shall be;
What a calm round of hours shall make my days.
There is a paly flame of hope that plays
Where'er I look: but yet, I'll say 'tis naught—
And here I bid it die. Have not I caught,
Already, a more healthy countenance?
By this the sun is setting; we may chance
Meet some of our near-dwellers with my car.'

    This said, he rose, faint-smiling like a star          990
Through autumn mists, and took Peona's hand:
They stept into the boat, and launch'd from land.


## BOOK II

O SOVEREIGN power of love! O grief! O balm!
All records, saving thine, come cool, and calm,
And shadowy, through the mist of passed years:
For others, good or bad, hatred and tears
Have become indolent; but touching thine,
One sigh doth echo, one poor sob doth pine,

One kiss brings honey-dew from buried days.
The woes of Troy, towers smothering o'er their blaze,
Stiff-holden shields, far-piercing spears, keen blades,
Struggling, and blood, and shrieks—all dimly fades          10
Into some backward corner of the brain:
Yet, in our very souls, we feel amain
The close of Troilus and Cressid sweet.
Hence, pageant history! hence, gilded cheat!
Swart planet in the universe of deeds!
Wide sea, that one continuous murmur breeds
Along the pebbled shore of memory!
Many old rotten-timber'd boats there be
Upon thy vaporous bosom, magnified
To goodly vessels; many a sail of pride,                    20
And golden keel'd, is left unlaunch'd and dry.
But wherefore this? What care, though owl did fly
About the great Athenian admiral's mast?
What care, though striding Alexander past
The Indus with his Macedonian numbers?
Though old Ulysses tortured from his slumbers
The glutted Cyclops, what care?—Juliet leaning
Amid her window-flowers,—sighing,—weaning
Tenderly her fancy from its maiden snow,
Doth more avail than these: the silver flow                 30
Of Hero's tears, the swoon of Imogen,
Fair Pastorella in the bandit's den,
Are things to brood on with more ardency
Than the death-day of empires. Fearfully
Must such conviction come upon his head,
Who, thus far, discontent, has dared to tread,
Without one muse's smile, or kind behest,
The path of love and poesy. But rest,
In chafing restlessness, is yet more drear
Than to be crush'd, in striving to uprear                   40
Love's standard on the battlements of song.
So once more days and nights aid me along,
Like legion'd soldiers.

                        Brain-sick shepherd prince,
What promise hast thou faithful guarded since
The day of sacrifice? Or, have new sorrows

Come with the constant dawn upon thy morrows?
Alas! 'tis his old grief. For many days,
Has he been wandering in uncertain ways:
Through wilderness, and woods of mossed oaks;
Counting his woe-worn minutes, by the strokes     50
Of the lone woodcutter; and listening still,
Hour after hour, to each lush-leav'd rill.
Now he is sitting by a shady spring,
And elbow-deep with feverous fingering
Stems the upbursting cold: a wild rose tree
Pavillions him in bloom, and he doth see
A bud which snares his fancy: lo! but now
He plucks it, dips its stalk in the water: how!
It swells, it buds, it flowers beneath his sight;
And, in the middle, there is softly pight     60
A golden butterfly; upon whose wings
There must be surely character'd strange things,
For with wide eye he wonders, and smiles oft.

    Lightly this little herald flew aloft,
Follow'd by glad Endymion's clasped hands:
Onward it flies. From languor's sullen bands
His limbs are loos'd, and eager, on he hies
Dazzled to trace it in the sunny skies.
It seem'd he flew, the way so easy was;
And like a new-born spirit did he pass     70
Through the green evening quiet in the sun,
O'er many a heath, through many a woodland dun,
Through buried paths, where sleepy twilight dreams
The summer time away. One track unseams
A wooded cleft, and, far away, the blue
Of ocean fades upon him; then, anew,
He sinks adown a solitary glen,
Where there was never sound of mortal men,
Saving, perhaps, some snow-light cadences
Melting to silence, when upon the breeze     80
Some holy bark let forth an anthem sweet,
To cheer itself to Delphi. Still his feet
Went swift beneath the merry-winged guide,
Until it reach'd a splashing fountain's side
That, near a cavern's mouth, for ever pour'd

Unto the temperate air: then high it soar'd,
And, downward, suddenly began to dip,
As if, athirst with so much toil, 'twould sip
The crystal spout-head: so it did, with touch
Most delicate, as though afraid to smutch          90
Even with mealy gold the waters clear.
But, at that very touch, to disappear
So fairy-quick, was strange! Bewildered,
Endymion sought around, and shook each bed
Of covert flowers in vain; and then he flung
Himself along the grass. What gentle tongue,
What whisperer disturb'd his gloomy rest?
It was a nymph uprisen to the breast
In the fountain's pebbly margin, and she stood
'Mong lilies, like the youngest of the brood.          100
To him her dripping hand she softly kist,
And anxiously began to plait and twist
Her ringlets round her fingers, saying: 'Youth!
Too long, alas, hast thou starv'd on the ruth,
The bitterness of love: too long indeed,
Seeing thou art so gentle. Could I weed
Thy soul of care, by heavens, I would offer
All the bright riches of my crystal coffer
To Amphitrite; all my clear-eyed fish,
Golden, or rainbow-sided, or purplish,          110
Vermilion-tail'd, or finn'd with silvery gauze;
Yea, or my veined pebble-floor, that draws
A virgin light to the deep; my grotto-sands
Tawny and gold, ooz'd slowly from far lands
By my diligent springs; my level lilies, shells,
My charming rod, my potent river spells;
Yes, every thing, even to the pearly cup
Meander gave me,—for I bubbled up
To fainting creatures in a desert wild.
But woe is me, I am but as a child          120
To gladden thee; and all I dare to say,
Is, that I pity thee; that on this day
I've been thy guide; that thou must wander far
In other regions, past the scanty bar
To mortal steps, before thou cans't be ta'en
From every wasting sigh, from every pain,

Into the gentle bosom of thy love.
Why it is thus, one knows in heaven above:
But, a poor Naiad, I guess not. Farewell!
I have a ditty for my hollow cell.'                        130

    Hereat, she vanished from Endymion's gaze,
Who brooded o'er the water in amaze:
The dashing fount pour'd on, and where its pool
Lay, half asleep, in grass and rushes cool,
Quick waterflies and gnats were sporting still,
And fish were dimpling, as if good nor ill
Had fallen out that hour. The wanderer,
Holding his forehead, to keep off the burr
Of smothering fancies, patiently sat down;
And, while beneath the evening's sleepy frown         140
Glow-worms began to trim their starry lamps,
Thus breath'd he to himself: 'Whoso encamps
To take a fancied city of delight,
O what a wretch is he! and when 'tis his,
After long toil and travelling, to miss
The kernel of his hopes, how more than vile:
Yet, for him there's refreshment even in toil;
Another city doth he set about,
Free from the smallest pebble-bead of doubt
That he will seize on trickling honey-combs:         150
Alas, he finds them dry; and then he foams,
And onward to another city speeds.
But this is human life: the war, the deeds,
The disappointment, the anxiety,
Imagination's struggles, far and nigh,
All human; bearing in themselves this good,
That they are still the air, the subtle food,
To make us feel existence, and to show
How quiet death is. Where soil is men grow,
Whether to weeds or flowers; but for me,              160
There is no depth to strike in: I can see
Naught earthly worth my compassing; so stand
Upon a misty, jutting head of land—
Alone? No, no; and by the Orphean lute,
When mad Eurydice is listening to't;
I'd rather stand upon this misty peak,

With not a thing to sigh for, or to seek,
But the soft shadow of my thrice-seen love,
Than be—I care not what. O meekest dove
Of heaven! O Cynthia, ten-times bright and fair!          170
From thy blue throne, now filling all the air,
Glance but one little beam of temper'd light
Into my bosom, that the dreadful might
And tyranny of love be somewhat scar'd!
Yet do not so, sweet queen; one torment spar'd,
Would give a pang to jealous misery,
Worse than the torment's self: but rather tie
Large wings upon my shoulders, and point out
My love's far dwelling. Though the playful rout
Of Cupids shun thee, too divine art thou,          180
Too keen in beauty, for thy silver prow
Not to have dipp'd in love's most gentle stream.
O be propitious, nor severely deem
My madness impious; for, by all the stars
That tend thy bidding, I do think the bars
That kept my spirit in are burst—that I
Am sailing with thee through the dizzy sky!
How beautiful thou art! The world how deep!
How tremulous-dazzlingly the wheels sweep
Around their axle! Then these gleaming reins,          190
How lithe! When this thy chariot attains
Its airy goal, haply some bower veils
Those twilight eyes? Those eyes!—my spirit fails—
Dear goddess, help! or the wide-gaping air
Will gulph me—help!'—At this with madden'd stare,
And lifted hands, and trembling lips he stood;
Like old Deucalion mountain'd o'er the flood,
Or blind Orion hungry for the morn.
And, but from the deep cavern there was borne
A voice, he had been froze to senseless stone;          200
Nor sigh of his, nor plaint, nor passion'd moan
Had more been heard. Thus swell'd it forth: 'Descend,
Young mountaineer! descend where alleys bend
Into the sparry hollows of the world!
Oft hast thou seen bolts of the thunder hurl'd
As from thy threshold; day by day hast been
A little lower than the chilly sheen

Of icy pinnacles, and dipp'dst thine arms
Into the deadening ether that still charms
Their marble being: now, as deep profound          210
As those are high, descend! He ne'er is crown'd
With immortality, who fears to follow
Where airy voices lead: so through the hollow,
The silent mysteries of earth, descend!'


    He heard but the last words, nor could contend
One moment in reflection: for he fled
Into the fearful deep, to hide his head
From the clear moon, the trees, and coming madness.


    'Twas far too strange, and wonderful for sadness;
Sharpening, by degrees, his appetite          220
To dive into the deepest. Dark, nor light,
The region; nor bright, nor sombre wholly,
But mingled up; a gleaming melancholy;
A dusky empire and its diadems;
One faint eternal eventide of gems.
Aye, millions sparkled on a vein of gold,
Along whose track the prince quick footsteps told,
With all its lines abrupt and angular:
Out-shooting sometimes, like a meteor-star,
Through a vast antre; then the metal woof,          230
Like Vulcan's rainbow, with some monstrous roof
Curves hugely: now, far in the deep abyss,
It seems an angry lightning, and doth hiss
Fancy into belief: anon it leads
Through winding passages, where sameness breeds
Vexing conceptions of some sudden change;
Whether to silver grots, or giant range
Of sapphire columns, or fantastic bridge
Athwart a flood of crystal. On a ridge
Now fareth he, that o'er the vast beneath          240
Towers like an ocean-cliff, and whence he seeth
A hundred waterfalls, whose voices come
But as the murmuring surge. Chilly and numb
His bosom grew, when first he, far away
Descried an orbed diamond, set to fray

Old darkness from his throne: 'twas like the sun
Uprisen o'er chaos: and with such a stun
Came the amazement, that, absorb'd in it,
He saw not fiercer wonders—past the wit
Of any spirit to tell, but one of those          250
Who, when this planet's sphering time doth close,
Will be its high remembrancers: who they?
The mighty ones who have made eternal day
For Greece and England. While astonishment
With deep-drawn sighs was quieting, he went
Into a marble gallery, passing through
A mimic temple, so complete and true
In sacred custom, that he well nigh fear'd
To search it inwards; whence far off appear'd,
Through a long pillar'd vista, a fair shrine,          260
And just beyond, on light tiptoe divine,
A quiver'd Dian. Stepping awfully,
The youth approach'd; oft turning his veil'd eye
Down sidelong aisles, and into niches old.
And when, more near against the marble cold
He had touch'd his forehead, he began to thread
All courts and passages, where silence dead
Rous'd by his whispering footsteps murmured faint:
And long he travers'd to and fro, to acquaint
Himself with every mystery, and awe;          270
Till, weary, he sat down before the maw
Of a wide outlet, fathomless and dim,
To wild uncertainty and shadows grim.
There, when new wonders ceas'd to float before,
And thoughts of self came on, how crude and sore
The journey homeward to habitual self!
A mad-pursuing of the fog-born elf,
Whose flitting lantern, through rude nettle-briar,
Cheats us into a swamp, into a fire,
Into the bosom of a hated thing.          280

    What misery most drowningly doth sing
In lone Endymion's ear, now he has raught
The goal of consciousness? Ah, 'tis the thought,
The deadly feel of solitude: for lo!
He cannot see the heavens, nor the flow

Of rivers, nor hill-flowers running wild
In pink and purple chequer, nor, up-pil'd,
The cloudy rack slow journeying in the west,
Like herded elephants; nor felt, nor prest
Cool grass, nor tasted the fresh slumberous air;            290
But far from such companionship to wear
An unknown time, surcharg'd with grief, away,
Was now his lot. And must he patient stay,
Tracing fantastic figures with his spear?
'No!' exclaim'd he, 'why should I tarry here?'
No! loudly echoed times innumerable.
At which he straightway started, and 'gan tell
His paces back into the temple's chief;
Warming and glowing strong in the belief
Of help from Dian: so that when again            300
He caught her airy form, thus did he plain,
Moving more near the while: 'O Haunter chaste
Of river sides, and woods, and heathy waste,
Where with thy silver bow and arrows keen
Art thou now forested? O woodland Queen,
What smoothest air thy smoother forehead woos?
Where dost thou listen to the wide halloos
Of thy disparted nymphs? Through what dark tree
Glimmers thy crescent? Wheresoe'er it be,
'Tis in the breath of heaven: thou dost taste            310
Freedom as none can taste it, nor dost waste
Thy loveliness in dismal elements;
But, finding in our green earth sweet contents,
There livest blissfully. Ah, if to thee
It feels Elysian, how rich to me,
An exil'd mortal, sounds its pleasant name!
Within my breast there lives a choking flame—
O let me cool't the zephyr-boughs among!
A homeward fever parches up my tongue—
O let me slake it at the running springs!            320
Upon my ear a noisy nothing rings—
O let me once more hear the linnet's note!
Before mine eyes thick films and shadows float—
O let me 'noint them with the heaven's light!
Dost thou now lave thy feet and ankles white?
O think how sweet to me the freshening sluice!

Dost thou now please thy thirst with berry-juice?
O think how this dry palate would rejoice!
If in soft slumber thou dost hear my voice,
O think how I should love a bed of flowers!—        330
Young goddess! let me see my native bowers!
Deliver me from this rapacious deep!'

　　Thus ending loudly, as he would o'erleap
His destiny, alert he stood: but when
Obstinate silence came heavily again,
Feeling about for its old couch of space
And airy cradle, lowly bow'd his face
Desponding, o'er the marble floor's cold thrill.
But 'twas not long; for, sweeter than the rill
To its old channel, or a swollen tide                340
To margin sallows, were the leaves he spied,
And flowers, and wreaths, and ready myrtle crowns
Up heaping through the slab: refreshment drowns
Itself, and strives its own delights to hide—
Nor in one spot alone; the floral pride
In a long whispering birth enchanted grew
Before his footsteps; as when heav'd anew
Old ocean rolls a lengthened wave to the shore,
Down whose green back the short-liv'd foam, all hoar,
Bursts gradual, with a wayward indolence.            350

　　Increasing still in heart, and pleasant sense,
Upon his fairy journey on he hastes;
So anxious for the end, he scarcely wastes
One moment with his hand among the sweets:
Onward he goes—he stops—his bosom beats
As plainly in his ear, as the faint charm
Of which the throbs were born. This still alarm,
This sleepy music, forc'd him walk tiptoe:
For it came more softly than the east could blow
Arion's magic to the Atlantic isles;                 360
Or than the west, made jealous by the smiles
Of thron'd Apollo, could breathe back the lyre
To seas Ionian and Tyrian.

　　O did he ever live, that lonely man,
Who lov'd—and music slew not? 'Tis the pest

Of love, that fairest joys give most unrest;
That things of delicate and tenderest worth
Are swallow'd all, and made a seared dearth,
By one consuming flame: it doth immerse
And suffocate true blessings in a curse.                    370
Half-happy, by comparison of bliss,
Is miserable. 'Twas even so with this
Dew-dropping melody, in the Carian's ear;
First heaven, then hell, and then forgotten clear,
Vanish'd in elemental passion.

And down some swart abysm he had gone,
Had not a heavenly guide benignant led
To where thick myrtle branches, 'gainst his head
Brushing, awakened: then the sounds again
Went noiseless as a passing noontide rain                    380
Over a bower, where little space he stood;
For as the sunset peeps into a wood
So saw he panting light, and towards it went
Through winding alleys; and lo, wonderment!
Upon soft verdure saw, one here, one there,
Cupids a slumbering on their pinions fair.

After a thousand mazes overgone,
At last, with sudden step, he came upon
A chamber, myrtle wall'd, embowered high,
Full of light, incense, tender minstrelsy,                    390
And more of beautiful and strange beside:
For on a silken couch of rosy pride,
In midst of all, there lay a sleeping youth
Of fondest beauty; fonder, in fair sooth,
Than sighs could fathom, or contentment reach:
And coverlids gold-tinted like the peach,
Or ripe October's faded marigolds,
Fell sleek about him in a thousand folds—
Not hiding up an Apollonian curve
Of neck and shoulder, nor the tenting swerve                    400
Of knee from knee, nor ankles pointing light;
But rather, giving them to the filled sight
Officiously. Sideway his face repos'd
On one white arm, and tenderly unclos'd,
By tenderest pressure, a faint damask mouth

To slumbery pout; just as the morning south
Disparts a dew-lipp'd rose.  Above his head,
Four lilly stalks did their white honours wed
To make a coronal; and round him grew
All tendrils green, of every bloom and hue,                    410
Together intertwin'd and trammel'd fresh:
The vine of glossy sprout; the ivy mesh,
Shading its Ethiop berries; and woodbine,
Of velvet leaves and bugle-blooms divine;
Convolvulus in streaked vases flush;
The creeper, mellowing for an autumn blush;
And virgin's bower, trailing airily;
With others of the sisterhood. Hard by,
Stood serene Cupids watching silently.
One, kneeling to a lyre, touch'd the strings,                  420
Muffling to death the pathos with his wings;
And, ever and anon, uprose to look
At the youth's slumber; while another took
A willow-bough, distilling odorous dew,
And shook it on his hair; another flew
In through the woven roof, and fluttering-wise
Rain'd violets upon his sleeping eyes.

    At these enchantments, and yet many more,
The breathless Latmian wonder'd o'er and o'er;
Until, impatient in embarrassment,                             430
He forthright pass'd, and lightly treading went
To that same feather'd lyrist, who straightway,
Smiling, thus whisper'd: 'Though from upper day
Thou art a wanderer, and thy presence here
Might seem unholy, be of happy cheer!
For 'tis the nicest touch of human honour,
When some ethereal and high-favouring donor
Presents immortal bowers to mortal sense;
As now 'tis done to thee, Endymion. Hence
Was I in no wise startled. So recline                          440
Upon these living flowers. Here is wine,
Alive with sparkles—never, I aver,
Since Ariadne was a vintager,
So cool a purple: taste these juicy pears,
Sent me by sad Vertumnus, when his fears

Were high about Pomona: here is cream,
Deepening to richness from a snowy gleam;
Sweeter than that nurse Amalthea skimm'd
For the boy Jupiter: and here, undimm'd
By any touch, a bunch of blooming plums 450
Ready to melt between an infant's gums:
And here is manna pick'd from Syrian trees,
In starlight, by the three Hesperides.
Feast on, and meanwhile I will let thee know
Of all these things around us.' He did so,
Still brooding o'er the cadence of his lyre;
And thus: 'I need not any hearing tire
By telling how the sea-born goddess pin'd
For a mortal youth, and how she strove to bind
Him all in all unto her doting self. 460
Who would not be so prison'd? but, fond elf,
He was content to let her amorous plea
Faint through his careless arms; content to see
An unseiz'd heaven dying at his feet;
Content, O fool! to make a cold retreat,
When on the pleasant grass such love, lovelorn,
Lay sorrowing; when every tear was born
Of diverse passion; when her lips and eyes
Were clos'd in sullen moisture, and quick sighs
Came vex'd and pettish through her nostrils small. 470
Hush! no exclaim—yet, justly mightst thou call
Curses upon his head.—I was half glad,
But my poor mistress went distract and mad,
When the boar tusk'd him: so away she flew
To Jove's high throne, and by her plainings drew
Immortal tear-drops down the thunderer's beard;
Whereon, it was decreed he should be rear'd
Each summer time to life. Lo! this is he,
That same Adonis, safe in the privacy
Of this still region all his winter-sleep. 480
Aye, sleep; for when our love-sick queen did weep
Over his waned corse, the tremulous shower
Heal'd up the wound, and, with a balmy power,
Medicined death to a lengthened drowsiness:
The which she fills with visions, and doth dress
In all this quiet luxury; and hath set

Us young immortals, without any let,
To watch his slumber through. 'Tis well nigh pass'd,
Even to a moment's filling up, and fast
She scuds with summer breezes, to pant through          490
The first long kiss, warm firstling, to renew
Embower'd sports in Cytherea's isle.
Look! how those winged listeners all this while
Stand anxious: see! behold!'—This clamant word
Broke through the careful silence; for they heard
A rustling noise of leaves, and out there flutter'd
Pigeons and doves: Adonis something mutter'd
The while one hand, that erst upon his thigh
Lay dormant, mov'd convuls'd and gradually
Up to his forehead. Then there was a hum          500
Of sudden voices, echoing, 'Come! come!
Arise! awake! Clear summer has forth walk'd
Unto the clover-sward, and she has talk'd
Full soothingly to every nested finch:
Rise, Cupids! or we'll give the blue-bell pinch
To your dimpled arms. Once more sweet life begin!'
At this, from every side they hurried in,
Rubbing their sleepy eyes with lazy wrists,
And doubling over head their little fists
In backward yawns. But all were soon alive:          510
For as delicious wine doth, sparkling, dive
In nectar'd clouds and curls through water fair,
So from the arbour roof down swell'd an air
Odorous and enlivening; making all
To laugh, and play, and sing, and loudly call
For their sweet queen: when lo! the wreathed green
Disparted, and far upward could be seen
Blue heaven, and a silver car, air-borne,
Whose silent wheels, fresh wet from clouds of morn,
Spun off a drizzling dew,—which falling chill          520
On soft Adonis' shoulders, made him still
Nestle and turn uneasily about.
Soon were the white doves plain, with neck stretch'd out,
And silken traces lighten'd in descent;
And soon, returning from love's banishment,
Queen Venus leaning downward open arm'd:
Her shadow fell upon his breast, and charm'd

A tumult to his heart, and a new life
Into his eyes. Ah, miserable strife,
But for her comforting! unhappy sight,                    530
But meeting her blue orbs! Who, who can write
Of these first minutes? The unchariest muse
To embracements warm as theirs makes coy excuse.

   O it has ruffled every spirit there,
Saving Love's self, who stands superb to share
The general gladness: awfully he stands;
A sovereign quell is in his waving hands;
No sight can bear the lightning of his bow;
His quiver is mysterious, none can know
What themselves think of it; from forth his eyes        540
There darts strange light of varied hues and dyes:
A scowl is sometimes on his brow, but who
Look full upon it feel anon the blue
Of his fair eyes run liquid through their souls.
Endymion feels it, and no more controls
The burning prayer within him; so, bent low,
He had begun a plaining of his woe.
But Venus, bending forward, said: 'My child,
Favour this gentle youth; his days are wild
With love—he—but alas! too well I see                   550
Thou know'st the deepness of his misery.
Ah, smile not so, my son: I tell thee true,
That when through heavy hours I used to rue
The endless sleep of this new-born Adon',
This stranger aye I pitied. For upon
A dreary morning once I fled away
Into the breezy clouds, to weep and pray
For this my love: for vexing Mars had teaz'd
Me even to tears: thence, when a little eas'd,
Down-looking, vacant, through a hazy wood,              560
I saw this youth as he despairing stood:
Those same dark curls blown vagrant in the wind;
Those same full fringed lids a constant blind
Over his sullen eyes: I saw him throw
Himself on wither'd leaves, even as though
Death had come sudden; for no jot he mov'd,
Yet mutter'd wildly. I could hear he lov'd

Some fair immortal, and that his embrace
Had zoned her through the night. There is no trace
Of this in heaven: I have mark'd each cheek,        570
And find it is the vainest thing to seek;
And that of all things 'tis kept secretest.
Endymion! one day thou wilt be blest:
So still obey the guiding hand that fends
Thee safely through these wonders for sweet ends.
'Tis a concealment needful in extreme;
And if I guess'd not so, the sunny beam
Thou shouldst mount up to with me. Now adieu!
Here must we leave thee.'—At these words upflew
The impatient doves, uprose the floating car,        580
Up went the hum celestial. High afar
The Latmian saw them minish into naught;
And, when all were clear vanish'd, still he caught
A vivid lightning from that dreadful bow.
When all was darkened, with Ætnean throe
The earth clos'd—gave a solitary moan—
And left him once again in twilight lone.

He did not rave, he did not stare aghast,
For all those visions were o'ergone, and past,
And he in loneliness: he felt assur'd        590
Of happy times, when all he had endur'd
Would seem a feather to the mighty prize.
So, with unusual gladness, on he hies
Through caves, and palaces of mottled ore,
Gold dome, and crystal wall, and turquois floor,
Black polish'd porticos of awful shade,
And, at the last, a diamond balustrade,
Leading afar past wild magnificence,
Spiral through ruggedest loopholes, and thence
Stretching across a void, then guiding o'er        600
Enormous chasms, where, all foam and roar,
Streams subterranean teaze their granite beds;
Then heighten'd just above the silvery heads
Of a thousand fountains, so that he could dash
The waters with his spear; but at the splash,
Done heedlessly, those spouting columns rose
Sudden a poplar's height, and 'gan to enclose

His diamond path with fretwork, streaming round
Alive, and dazzling cool, and with a sound,
Haply, like dolphin tumults, when sweet shells          610
Welcome the float of Thetis. Long he dwells
On this delight; for, every minute's space,
The streams with changed magic interlace:
Sometimes like delicatest lattices,
Cover'd with crystal vines; then weeping trees.
Moving about as in a gentle wind,
Which, in a wink, to watery gauze refin'd,
Pour'd into shapes of curtain'd canopies,
Spangled, and rich with liquid broideries
Of flowers, peacocks, swans, and naiads fair.          620
Swifter than lightning went these wonders rare;
And then the water, into stubborn streams
Collecting, mimick'd the wrought oaken beams,
Pillars, and frieze, and high fantastic roof,
Of those dusk places in times far aloof
Cathedrals call'd. He bade a loth farewell
To these founts Protean, passing gulph, and dell,
And torrent, and ten thousand jutting shapes,
Half seen through deepest gloom, and griesly gapes,
Blackening on every side, and overhead                 630
A vaulted dome like Heaven's, far bespread
With starlight gems: aye, all so huge and strange,
The solitary felt a hurried change
Working within him into something dreary,—
Vex'd like a morning eagle, lost, and weary,
And purblind amid foggy, midnight wolds.
But he revives at once: for who beholds
New sudden things, nor casts his mental slough?
Forth from a rugged arch, in the dusk below,
Came mother Cybele! alone—alone—                       640
In sombre chariot; dark foldings thrown
About her majesty, and front death-pale,
With turrets crown'd. Four maned lions hale
The sluggish wheels; solemn their toothed maws,
Their surly eyes brow-hidden, heavy paws
Uplifted drowsily, and nervy tails
Cowering their tawny brushes. Silent sails
This shadowy queen athwart, and faints away

In another gloomy arch.
                   Wherefore delay,
Young traveller, in such a mournful place?          650
Art thou wayworn, or canst not further trace
The diamond path? And does it indeed end
Abrupt in middle air? Yet earthward bend
Thy forehead, and to Jupiter cloud-borne
Call ardently! He was indeed wayworn;
Abrupt, in middle air, his way was lost;
To cloud-borne Jove he bowed, and there crost
Towards him a large eagle, 'twixt whose wings,
Without one impious word, himself he flings,
Committed to the darkness and the gloom:        660
Down, down, uncertain to what pleasant doom,
Swift as a fathoming plummet down he fell
Through unknown things; till exhaled asphodel,
And rose, with spicy fannings interbreath'd,
Came swelling forth where little caves were wreath'd
So thick with leaves and mosses, that they seem'd
Large honey-combs of green, and freshly teem'd
With airs delicious. In the greenest nook
The eagle landed him, and farewell took.

    It was a jasmine bower, all bestrown        670
With golden moss. His every sense had grown
Ethereal for pleasure; 'bove his head
Flew a delight half-graspable; his tread
Was Hesperean; to his capable ears
Silence was music from the holy spheres;
A dewy luxury was in his eyes;
The little flowers felt his pleasant sighs
And stirr'd them faintly. Verdant cave and cell
He wander'd through, oft wondering at such swell
Of sudden exaltation: but, 'Alas!'        680
Said he, 'will all this gush of feeling pass
Away in solitude? And must they wane,
Like melodies upon a sandy plain,
Without an echo? Then shall I be left
So sad, so melancholy, so bereft!
Yet still I feel immortal! O my love,
My breath of life, where art thou? High above,

Dancing before the morning gates of heaven?
Or keeping watch among those starry seven,
Old Atlas' children? Art a maid of the waters,          690
One of shell-winding Triton's bright-hair'd daughters?
Or art, impossible! a nymph of Dian's,
Weaving a coronal of tender scions
For very idleness? Where'er thou art,
Methinks it now is at my will to start
Into thine arms; to scare Aurora's train,
And snatch thee from the morning; o'er the main
To scud like a wild bird, and take thee off
From thy sea-foamy cradle; or to doff
Thy shepherd vest, and woo thee mid fresh leaves.          700
No, no, too eagerly my soul deceives
Its powerless self: I know this cannot be.
O let me then by some sweet dreaming flee
To her entrancements: hither, Sleep, awhile!
Hither, most gentle Sleep! and soothing foil
For some few hours the coming solitude.'

    Thus spake he, and that moment felt endued
With power to dream deliciously; so wound
Through a dim passage, searching till he found
The smoothest mossy bed and deepest, where          710
He threw himself, and just into the air
Stretching his indolent arms, he took, O bliss!
A naked waist: 'Fair Cupid, whence is this?'
A well-known voice sigh'd, 'Sweetest, here am I!'
At which soft ravishment, with doting cry
They trembled to each other.—Helicon!
O fountain'd hill! Old Homer's Helicon!
That thou wouldst spout a little streamlet o'er
These sorry pages; then the verse would soar
And sing above this gentle pair, like lark          720
Over his nested young: but all is dark
Around thine aged top, and thy clear fount
Exhales in mists to heaven. Aye, the count
Of mighty Poets is made up; the scroll
Is folded by the Muses; the bright roll
Is in Apollo's hand: our dazed eyes
Have seen a new tinge in the western skies:

The world has done its duty. Yet, oh yet,
Although the sun of poesy is set,
These lovers did embrace, and we must weep          730
That there is no old power left to steep
A quill immortal in their joyous tears.
Long time in silence did their anxious fears
Question that thus it was; long time they lay
Fondling and kissing every doubt away;
Long time ere soft caressing sobs began
To mellow into words, and then there ran
Two bubbling springs of talk from their sweet lips.
'O known Unknown! from whom my being sips
Such darling essence, wherefore may I not          740
Be ever in these arms? in this sweet spot
Pillow my chin for ever? ever press
These toying hands and kiss their smooth excess?
Why not for ever and for ever feel
That breath about my eyes? Ah, thou wilt steal
Away from me again, indeed, indeed—
Thou wilt be gone away, and wilt not heed
My lonely madness. Speak, delicious fair!
Is—is it to be so? No! Who will dare
To pluck thee from me? And, of thine own will,          750
Full well I feel thou wouldst not leave me. Still
Let me entwine thee surer, surer—now
How can we part? Elysium! who art thou?
Who, that thou canst not be for ever here,
Or lift me with thee to some starry sphere?
Enchantress! tell me by this soft embrace,
By the most soft completion of thy face,
Those lips, O slippery blisses, twinkling eyes
And by these tenderest, milky sovereignties—
These tenderest, and by the nectar-wine,          760
The passion'————'O dov'd Ida the divine!
Endymion! dearest! Ah, unhappy me!
His soul will 'scape us—O felicity!
How he does love me! His poor temples beat
To the very tune of love—how sweet, sweet, sweet.
Revive, dear youth, or I shall faint and die;
Revive, or these soft hours will hurry by
In tranced dulness; speak, and let that spell

Affright this lethargy! I cannot quell
Its heavy pressure, and will press at least          770
My lips to thine, that they may richly feast
Until we taste the life of love again.
What! dost thou move? dost kiss? O bliss! O pain!
I love thee, youth, more than I can conceive;
And so long absence from thee doth bereave
My soul of any rest: yet must I hence:
Yet, can I not to starry eminence
Uplift thee; nor for very shame can own
Myself to thee: Ah, dearest, do not groan
Or thou wilt force me from this secrecy,               780
And I must blush in heaven. O that I
Had done 't already; that the dreadful smiles
At my lost brightness, my impassion'd wiles,
Had waned from Olympus' solemn height,
And from all serious Gods; that our delight
Was quite forgotten, save of us alone!
And wherefore so ashamed? 'Tis but to atone
For endless pleasure, by some coward blushes:
Yet must I be a coward!—Horror rushes
Too palpable before me—the sad look                   790
Of Jove—Minerva's start—no bosom shook
With awe of purity—no Cupid pinion
In reverence vailed—my crystalline dominion
Half lost, and all old hymns made nullity!
But what is this to love? O I could fly
With thee into the ken of heavenly powers,
So thou wouldst thus, for many sequent hours,
Press me so sweetly. Now I swear at once
That I am wise, that Pallas is a dunce—
Perhaps her love like mine is but unknown—             800
O I do think that I have been alone
In chastity: yes, Pallas has been sighing,
While every eve saw me my hair uptying
With fingers cool as aspen leaves. Sweet love,
I was as vague as solitary dove,
Nor knew that nests were built. Now a soft kiss-
Aye, by that kiss, I vow an endless bliss,
An immortality of passion's thine:
Ere long I will exalt thee to the shine

Of heaven ambrosial; and we will shade                              810
Ourselves whole summers by a river glade;
And I will tell thee stories of the sky,
And breathe thee whispers of its minstrelsy.
My happy love will overwing all bounds!
O let me melt into thee; let the sounds
Of our close voices marry at their birth;
Let us entwine hoveringly—O dearth
Of human words! roughness of mortal speech!
Lispings empyrean will I sometime teach
Thine honied tongue—lute-breathings, which I gasp       820
To have thee understand, now while I clasp
Thee thus, and weep for fondness—I am pain'd,
Endymion: woe! woe! is grief contain'd
In the very deeps of pleasure, my sole life?'—
Hereat, with many sobs, her gentle strife
Melted into a languor. He return'd
Entranced vows and tears.

                              Ye who have yearn'd
With too much passion, will here stay and pity,
For the mere sake of truth; as 'tis a ditty
Not of these days, but long ago 'twas told           830
By a cavern wind unto a forest old;
And then the forest told it in a dream
To a sleeping lake, whose cool and level gleam
A poet caught as he was journeying
To Phœbus' shrine; and in it he did fling
His weary limbs, bathing an hour's space,
And after, straight in that inspired place
He sang the story up into the air,
Giving it universal freedom. There
Has it been ever sounding for those ears             840
Whose tips are glowing hot. The legend cheers
Yon centinel stars; and he who listens to it
Must surely be self-doom'd or he will rue it:
For quenchless burnings come upon the heart,
Made fiercer by a fear lest any part
Should be engulphed in the eddying wind.
As much as here is penn'd doth always find

A resting place, thus much comes clear and plain;
Anon the strange voice is upon the wane—
And 'tis but echo'd from departing sound,                    850
That the fair visitant at last unwound
Her gentle limbs, and left the youth asleep.—
Thus the tradition of the gusty deep.

Now turn we to our former chroniclers.—
Endymion awoke, that grief of hers
Sweet paining on his ear: he sickly guess'd
How lone he was once more, and sadly press'd
His empty arms together, hung his head,
And most forlorn upon that widow'd bed
Sat silently. Love's madness he had known:                    860
Often with more than tortured lion's groan
Moanings had burst from him; but now that rage
Had pass'd away: no longer did he wage
A rough-voic'd war against the dooming stars.
No, he had felt too much for such harsh jars:
The lyre of his soul Æolian tun'd
Forgot all violence, and but commun'd
With melancholy thought: O he had swoon'd
Drunken from pleasure's nipple; and his love
Henceforth was dove-like.—Loth was he to move                    870
From the imprinted couch, and when he did,
'Twas with slow, languid paces, and face hid
In muffling hands. So temper'd, out he stray'd
Half seeing visions that might have dismay'd
Alecto's serpents; ravishments more keen
Than Hermes' pipe, when anxious he did lean
Over eclipsing eyes: and at the last
It was a sounding grotto, vaulted, vast,
O'er studded with a thousand, thousand pearls,
And crimson mouthed shells with stubborn curls,                    880
Of every shape and size, even to the bulk
In which whales arbour close, to brood and sulk
Against an endless storm. Moreover too,
Fish-semblances, of green and azure hue,
Ready to snort their streams. In this cool wonder
Endymion sat down, and 'gan to ponder
On all his life: his youth, up to the day

When 'mid acclaim, and feasts, and garlands gay,
He stept upon his shepherd throne: the look
Of his white palace in wild forest nook,                       890
And all the revels he had lorded there:
Each tender maiden whom he once thought fair,
With every friend and fellow-woodlander—
Pass'd like a dream before him. Then the spur
Of the old bards to mighty deeds: his plans
To nurse the golden age 'mong shepherd clans:
That wondrous night: the great Pan-festival:
His sister's sorrow; and his wanderings all,
Until into the earth's deep maw he rush'd:
Then all its buried magic, till it flush'd                      900
High with excessive love. 'And now', thought he,
'How long must I remain in jeopardy
Of blank amazements that amaze no more?
Now I have tasted her sweet soul to the core
All other depths are shallow: essences,
Once spiritual, are like muddy lees,
Meant but to fertilize my earthly root,
And make my branches lift a golden fruit
Into the bloom of heaven: other light,
Though it be quick and sharp enough to blight                  910
The Olympian eagle's vision, is dark,
Dark as the parentage of chaos. Hark!
My silent thoughts are echoing from these shells;
Or they are but the ghosts, the dying swells
Of noises far away?—list!'—Hereupon
He kept an anxious ear. The humming tone
Came louder, and behold, there as he lay,
On either side outgush'd, with misty spray,
A copious spring; and both together dash'd
Swift, mad, fantastic round the rocks and lash'd              920
Among the conchs and shells of the lofty grot,
Leaving a trickling dew. At last they shot
Down from the ceiling's height, pouring a noise
As of some breathless racers whose hopes poize
Upon the last few steps, and with spent force
Along the ground they took a winding course.
Endymion follow'd—for it seem'd that one
Ever pursued, the other strove to shun—

Follow'd their languid mazes, till well nigh
He had left thinking of the mystery,—                    930
And was now rapt in tender hoverings
Over the vanish'd bliss. Ah! what is it sings
His dream away? What melodies are these?
They sound as through the whispering of trees,
Not native in such barren vaults. Give ear!

   'O Arethusa, peerless nymph! why fear
Such tenderness as mine? Great Dian, why,
Why didst thou hear her prayer? O that I
Were rippling round her dainty fairness now,
Circling about her waist, and striving how         940
To entice her to a dive! then stealing in
Between her luscious lips and eyelids thin.
O that her shining hair was in the sun,
And I distilling from it thence to run
In amorous rillets down her shrinking form!
To linger on her lilly shoulders, warm
Between her kissing breasts, and every charm
Touch raptur'd!—See how painfully I flow:
Fair maid, be pitiful to my great woe.
Stay, stay thy weary course, and let me lead,        950
A happy wooer, to the flowery mead
Where all that beauty snar'd me.'—'Cruel god,
Desist! or my offended mistress' nod
Will stagnate all thy fountains:—teaze me not
With syren words—Ah, have I really got
Such power to madden thee? And is it true—
Away, away, or I shall dearly rue
My very thoughts: in mercy then away,
Kindest Alpheus, for should I obey
My own dear will, 'twould be a deadly bane.          960
O, Oread-Queen! would that thou hadst a pain
Like this of mine, then would I fearless turn
And be a criminal. Alas, I burn,
I shudder—gentle river, get thee hence.
Alpheus! thou enchanter! every sense
Of mine was once made perfect in these woods.
Fresh breezes, bowery lawns, and innocent floods,
Ripe fruits, and lonely couch, contentment gave;

But ever since I heedlessly did lave
In thy deceitful stream, a panting glow　　　　　970
Grew strong within me: wherefore serve me so,
And call it love? Alas, 'twas cruelty.
Not once more did I close my happy eye
Amid the thrushes' song. Away! Avaunt!
O 'twas a cruel thing.'—'Now thou dost taunt
So softly, Arethusa, that I think
If thou wast playing on my shady brink,
Thou wouldst bathe once again. Innocent maid!
Stifle thine heart no more; nor be afraid
Of angry powers: there are deities　　　　　980
Will shade us with their wings. Those fitful sighs
'Tis almost death to hear: O let me pour
A dewy balm upon them!—fear no more,
Sweet Arethusa! Dian's self must feel
Sometime these very pangs. Dear maiden, steal
Blushing into my soul, and let us fly
These dreary caverns for the open sky.
I will delight thee all my winding course,
From the green sea up to my hidden source
About Arcadian forests; and will show　　　　　990
The channels where my coolest waters flow
Through mossy rocks; where, 'mid exuberant green,
I roam in pleasant darkness, more unseen
Than Saturn in his exile; where I brim
Round flowery islands, and take thence a skim
Of mealy sweets, which myriads of bees
Buzz from their honey'd wings: and thou shouldst please
Thyself to choose the richest, where we might
Be incense-pillow'd every summer night.
Doff all sad fears, thou white deliciousness,　　　　　1000
And let us be thus comforted; unless
Thou couldst rejoice to see my hopeless stream
Hurry distracted from Sol's temperate beam,
And pour to death along some hungry sands.'—
'What can I do, Alpheus? Dian stands
Severe before me: persecuting fate!
Unhappy Arethusa! thou wast late
A huntress free in'—At this, sudden fell
Those two sad streams adown a fearful dell.

The Latmian listen'd, but he heard no more,                1010
Save echo, faint repeating o'er and o'er
The name of Arethusa. On the verge
Of that dark gulph he wept, and said: 'I urge
Thee, gentle Goddess of my pilgrimage,
By our eternal hopes, to soothe, to assuage,
If thou art powerful, these lovers' pains;
And make them happy in some happy plains.'

He turn'd—there was a whelming sound—he stept,
There was a cooler light; and so he kept
Towards it by a sandy path, and lo!                        1020
More suddenly than doth a moment go,
The visions of the earth were gone and fled—
He saw the giant sea above his head.


## BOOK III

THERE are who lord it o'er their fellow-men
With most prevailing tinsel: who unpen
Their baaing vanities, to browse away
The comfortable green and juicy hay
From human pastures; or, O torturing fact!
Who, through an idiot blink, will see unpack'd
Fire-branded foxes to sear up and singe
Our gold and ripe-ear'd hopes. With not one tinge
Of sanctuary splendour, not a sight
Able to face an owl's, they still are dight                10
By the blear-eyed nations in empurpled vests,
And crowns, and turbans. With unladen breasts,
Save of blown self-applause, they proudly mount
To their spirit's perch, their being's high account,
Their tiptop nothings, their dull skies, their thrones—
Amid the fierce intoxicating tones
Of trumpets, shoutings, and belabour'd drums,
And sudden cannon. Ah! how all this hums,
In wakeful ears, like uproar past and gone—
Like thunder clouds that spake to Babylon,                 20
And set those old Chaldeans to their tasks.—
Are then regalities all gilded masks?

No, there are throned seats unscalable
But by a patient wing, a constant spell,
Or by ethereal things that, unconfin'd,
Can make a ladder of the eternal wind,
And poize about in cloudy thunder-tents
To watch the abysm-birth of elements.
Aye, 'bove the withering of old-lipp'd Fate
A thousand Powers keep religious state,                    30
In water, fiery realm, and airy bourne;
And, silent as a consecrated urn,
Hold sphery sessions for a season due.
Yet few of these far majesties, ah, few!
Have bared their operations to this globe—
Few, who with gorgeous pageantry enrobe
Our piece of heaven—whose benevolence
Shakes hand with our own Ceres; every sense
Filling with spiritual sweets to plenitude,
As bees gorge full their cells. And, by the feud       40
'Twixt Nothing and Creation, I here swear,
Eterne Apollo! that thy Sister fair
Is of all these the gentlier-mightiest.
When thy gold breath is misting in the west,
She unobserved steals unto her throne,
And there she sits most meek and most alone;
As if she had not pomp subservient;
As if thine eye, high Poet! was not bent
Towards her with the Muses in thine heart;
As if the ministring stars kept not apart,              50
Waiting for silver-footed messages.
O Moon! the oldest shades 'mong oldest trees
Feel palpitations when thou lookest in:
O Moon! old boughs lisp forth a holier din
The while they feel thine airy fellowship.
Thou dost bless every where, with silver lip
Kissing dead things to life. The sleeping kine,
Couch'd in thy brightness, dream of fields divine:
Innumerable mountains rise, and rise,
Ambitious for the hallowing of thine eyes;             60
And yet thy benediction passeth not
One obscure hiding-place, one little spot
Where pleasure may be sent: the nested wren

Has thy fair face within its tranquil ken,
And from beneath a sheltering ivy leaf
Takes glimpses of thee; thou art a relief
To the poor patient oyster, where it sleeps
Within its pearly house.—The mighty deeps,
The monstrous sea is thine—the myriad sea!
O Moon! far-spooming Ocean bows to thee,            70
And Tellus feels his forehead's cumbrous load.

    Cynthia! where art thou now? What far abode
Of green or silvery bower doth enshrine
Such utmost beauty? Alas, thou dost pine
For one as sorrowful: thy cheek is pale
For one whose cheek is pale: thou dost bewail
His tears, who weeps for thee. Where dost thou sigh?
Ah! surely that light peeps from Vesper's eye,
Or what a thing is love! 'Tis She, but lo!
How chang'd, how full of ache, how gone in woe!    80
She dies at the thinnest cloud; her loveliness
Is wan on Neptune's blue: yet there's a stress
Of love-spangles, just off yon cape of trees,
Dancing upon the waves, as if to please
The curly foam with amorous influence.
O, not so idle: for down-glancing thence
She fathoms eddies, and runs wild about
O'erwhelming water-courses; scaring out
The thorny sharks from hiding-holes, and fright'ning
Their savage eyes with unaccustom'd lightning.     90
Where will the splendour be content to reach?
O love! how potent hast thou been to teach
Strange journeyings! Wherever beauty dwells,
In gulph or aerie, mountains or deep dells,
In light, in gloom, in star or blazing sun,
Thou pointest out the way, and straight 'tis won.
Amid his toil thou gav'st Leander breath;
Thou leddest Orpheus through the gleams of death;
Thou madest Pluto bear thin element;
And now, O winged Chieftain! thou has sent          100
A moon-beam to the deep, deep water-world,
To find Endymion.

           On gold sand impearl'd

With lilly shells, and pebbles milky white,
Poor Cynthia greeted him, and sooth'd her light
Against his pallid face: he felt the charm
To breathlessness, and suddenly a warm
Of his heart's blood: 'twas very sweet; he stay'd
His wandering steps, and half-entranced laid
His head upon a tuft of straggling weeds,
To taste the gentle moon, and freshening beads,          110
Lash'd from the crystal roof by fishes' tails.
And so he kept, until the rosy veils
Mantling the east, by Aurora's peering hand
Were lifted from the water's breast, and fann'd
Into sweet air; and sober'd morning came
Meekly through billows:—when like taper-flame
Left sudden by a dallying breath of air,
He rose in silence, and once more 'gan fare
Along his fated way.

                    Far had he roam'd,
With nothing save the hollow vast, that foam'd,          120
Above, around, and at his feet; save things
More dead than Morpheus' imaginings:
Old rusted anchors, helmets, breast-plates large
Of gone sea-warriors; brazen beaks and targe;
Rudders that for a hundred years had lost
The sway of human hand; gold vase emboss'd
With long-forgotten story, and wherein
No reveller had ever dipp'd a chin
But those of Saturn's vintage; mouldering scrolls,
Writ in the tongue of heaven, by those souls          130
Who first were on the earth; and sculptures rude
In ponderous stone, developing the mood
Of ancient Nox;—then skeletons of man,
Of beast, behemoth, and leviathan,
And elephant, and eagle, and huge jaw
Of nameless monster. A cold leaden awe
These secrets struck into him; and unless
Dian had chaced away that heaviness,
He might have died: but now, with cheered feel,
He onward kept; wooing these thoughts to steal          140
About the labyrinth in his soul of love.

'What is there in thee, Moon! that thou shouldst move
My heart so potently? When yet a child
I oft have dried my tears when thou hast smil'd.
Thou seem'dst my sister: hand in hand we went
From eve to morn across the firmament.
No apples would I gather from the tree,
Till thou hadst cool'd their cheeks deliciously:
No tumbling water ever spake romance,
But when my eyes with thine thereon could dance:          150
No woods were green enough, no bower divine,
Until thou liftedst up thine eyelids fine:
In sowing time ne'er would I dibble take,
Or drop a seed, till thou wast wide awake;
And, in the summer tide of blossoming,
No one but thee hath heard me blithly sing
And mesh my dewy flowers all the night.
No melody was like a passing spright
If it went not to solemnize thy reign.
Yes, in my boyhood, every joy and pain          160
By thee were fashion'd to the self-same end;
And as I grew in years, still didst thou blend
With all my ardours: thou wast the deep glen;
Thou wast the mountain-top—the sage's pen—
The poet's harp—the voice of friends—the sun;
Thou wast the river—thou wast glory won;
Thou wast my clarion's blast—thou wast my steed—
My goblet full of wine—my topmost deed:—
Thou wast the charm of women, lovely Moon!
O what a wild and harmonized tune          170
My spirit struck from all the beautiful!
On some bright essence could I lean, and lull
Myself to immortality: I prest
Nature's soft pillow in a wakeful rest.
But, gentle Orb! there came a nearer bliss—
My strange love came—Felicity's abyss!
She came, and thou didst fade, and fade away—
Yet not entirely; no, thy starry sway
Has been an under-passion to this hour.
Now I begin to feel thine orby power          180
Is coming fresh upon me: O be kind,
Keep back thine influence, and do not blind

My sovereign vision.—Dearest love, forgive
That I can think away from thee and live!—
Pardon me, airy planet, that I prize
One thought beyond thine argent luxuries!
How far beyond!' At this a surpris'd start
Frosted the springing verdure of his heart;
For as he lifted up his eyes to swear
How his own goddess was past all things fair,          190
He saw far in the concave green of the sea
An old man sitting calm and peacefully.
Upon a weeded rock this old man sat,
And his white hair was awful, and a mat
Of weeds were cold beneath his cold thin feet;
And, ample as the largest winding-sheet,
A cloak of blue wrapp'd up his aged bones,
O'erwrought with symbols by the deepest groans
Of ambitious magic: every ocean-form
Was woven in with black distinctness; storm,          200
And calm, and whispering, and hideous roar,
Quicksand, and whirlpool, and deserted shore,
Were emblem'd in the woof; with every shape
That skims, or dives, or sleeps, 'twixt cape and cape.
The gulphing whale was like a dot in the spell,
Yet look upon it, and 'twould size and swell
To its huge self; and the minutest fish
Would pass the very hardest gazer's wish,
And show his little eye's anatomy.
Then there was pictur'd the regality          210
Of Neptune; and the sea nymphs round his state,
In beauteous vassalage, look up and wait.
Beside this old man lay a pearly wand,
And in his lap a book, the which he conn'd
So stedfastly, that the new denizen
Had time to keep him in amazed ken,
To mark these shadowings, and stand in awe.

   The old man rais'd his hoary head and saw
The wilder'd stranger—seeming not to see,
His features were so lifeless. Suddenly          220
He woke as from a trance; his snow-white brows
Went arching up, and like two magic ploughs

Furrow'd deep wrinkles in his forehead large,
Which kept as fixedly as rocky marge,
Till round his wither'd lips had gone a smile.
Then up he rose, like one whose tedious toil
Had watch'd for years in forlorn hermitage,
Who had not from mid-life to utmost age
Eas'd in one accent his o'er-burden'd soul,
Even to the trees. He rose: he grasp'd his stole,          230
With convuls'd clenches waving it abroad,
And in a voice of solemn joy, that aw'd
Echo into oblivion, he said:—

   'Thou art the man! Now shall I lay my head
In peace upon my watery pillow: now
Sleep will come smoothly to my weary brow.
O Jove! I shall be young again, be young!
O shell-borne Neptune, I am pierc'd and stung
With new-born life! What shall I do? Where go,
When I have cast this serpent-skin of woe?—                240
I'll swim to the syrens, and one moment listen
Their melodies, and see their long hair glisten;
Anon upon that giant's arm I'll be,
That writhes about the roots of Sicily:
To northern seas I'll in a twinkling sail,
And mount upon the snortings of a whale
To some black cloud; thence down I'll madly sweep
On forked lightning, to the deepest deep,
Where through some sucking pool I will be hurl'd
With rapture to the other side of the world!              250
O, I am full of gladness! Sisters three,
I bow full hearted to your old decree!
Yes, every god be thank'd, and power benign,
For I no more shall wither, droop, and pine.
Thou art the man!' Endymion started back
Dismay'd; and, like a wretch from whom the rack
Tortures hot breath, and speech of agony,
Mutter'd: 'What lonely death am I to die
In this cold region? Will he let me freeze,
And float my brittle limbs o'er polar seas?               260
Or will he touch me with his searing hand,
And leave a black memorial on the sand?

Or tear me piece-meal with a bony saw,
And keep me as a chosen food to draw
His magian fish through hated fire and flame?
O misery of hell! resistless, tame,
Am I to be burnt up? No, I will shout,
Until the gods through heaven's blue look out!—
O Tartarus! but some few days agone
Her soft arms were entwining me, and on          270
Her voice I hung like fruit among green leaves:
Her lips were all my own, and—ah, ripe sheaves
Of happiness! ye on the stubble droop,
But never may be garner'd. I must stoop
My head, and kiss death's foot. Love! love, farewell!
Is there no hope from thee? This horrid spell
Would melt at thy sweet breath.—By Dian's hind
Feeding from her white fingers, on the wind
I see thy streaming hair! and now, by Pan,
I care not for this old mysterious man!'          280

He spake, and walking to that aged form,
Look'd high defiance. Lo! his heart 'gan warm
With pity, for the grey-hair'd creature wept.
Had he then wrong'd a heart where sorrow kept?
Had he, though blindly contumelious, brought
Rheum to kind eyes, a sting to humane thought,
Convulsion to a mouth of many years?
He had in truth; and he was ripe for tears.
The penitent shower fell, as down he knelt
Before that care-worn sage, who trembling felt          290
About his large dark locks, and faultering spake:

'Arise, good youth, for sacred Phœbus' sake!
I know thine inmost bosom, and I feel
A very brother's yearning for thee steal
Into mine own: for why? thou openest
The prison gates that have so long opprest
My weary watching. Though thou know'st it not,
Thou art commission'd to this fated spot
For great enfranchisement. O weep no more;
I am a friend to love, to loves of yore:          300
Aye, hadst thou never lov'd an unknown power,

I had been grieving at this joyous hour.
But even now most miserable old,
I saw thee, and my blood no longer cold
Gave mighty pulses: in this tottering case
Grew a new heart, which at this moment plays
As dancingly as thine. Be not afraid,
For thou shalt hear this secret all display'd,
Now as we speed towards our joyous task.'

So saying, this young soul in age's mask          310
Went forward with the Carian side by side:
Resuming quickly thus: while ocean's tide
Hung swollen at their backs, and jewel'd sands
Took silently their foot-prints.

                          'My soul stands
Now past the midway from mortality,
And so I can prepare without a sigh
To tell thee briefly all my joy and pain.
I was a fisher once, upon this main,
And my boat danc'd in every creek and bay;
Rough billows were my home by night and day,—          320
The sea-gulls not more constant; for I had
No housing from the storm and tempests mad,
But hollow rocks,—and they were palaces
Of silent happiness, of slumberous ease:
Long years of misery have told me so.
Aye, thus it was one thousand years ago.
One thousand years!—Is it then possible
To look so plainly through them? to dispel
A thousand years with backward glance sublime?
To breathe away as 'twere all scummy slime          330
From off a crystal pool, to see its deep,
And one's own image from the bottom peep?
Yes: now I am no longer wretched thrall,
My long captivity and moanings all
Are but a slime, a thin-pervading scum,
The which I breathe away, and thronging come
Like things of yesterday my youthful pleasures.

'I touch'd no lute, I sang not, trod no measures:
I was a lonely youth on desert shores.

My sports were lonely, 'mid continuous roars,                    340
And craggy isles, and sea-mew's plaintive cry
Plaining discrepant between sea and sky.
Dolphins were still my playmates; shapes unseen
Would let me feel their scales of gold and green,
Nor be my desolation; and, full oft,
When a dread waterspout had rear'd aloft
Its hungry hugeness, seeming ready ripe
To burst with hoarsest thunderings, and wipe
My life away like a vast sponge of fate,
Some friendly monster, pitying my sad state,                     350
Has dived to its foundations, gulph'd it down,
And left me tossing safely. But the crown
Of all my life was utmost quietude:
More did I love to lie in cavern rude,
Keeping in wait whole days for Neptune's voice,
And if it came at last, hark, and rejoice!
There blush'd no summer eve but I would steer
My skiff along green shelving coasts, to hear
The shepherd's pipe come clear from aery steep,
Mingled with ceaseless bleatings of his sheep:                   360
And never was a day of summer shine,
But I beheld its birth upon the brine:
For I would watch all night to see unfold
Heaven's gates, and Æthon snort his morning gold
Wide o'er the swelling streams: and constantly
At brim of day-tide, on some grassy lea,
My nets would be spread out, and I at rest.
The poor folk of the sea-country I blest
With daily boon of fish most delicate:
They knew not whence this bounty, and elate                      370
Would strew sweet flowers on a sterile beach.

'Why was I not contented? Wherefore reach
At things which, but for thee, O Latmian!
Had been my dreary death? Fool! I began
To feel distemper'd longings: to desire
The utmost privilege that ocean's sire
Could grant in benediction: to be free
Of all his kingdom. Long in misery
I wasted, ere in one extremest fit

I plung'd for life or death. To interknit                    380
One's senses with so dense a breathing stuff
Might seem a work of pain; so not enough
Can I admire how crystal-smooth it felt,
And buoyant round my limbs. At first I dwelt
Whole days and days in sheer astonishment;
Forgetful utterly of self-intent;
Moving but with the mighty ebb and flow.
Then, like a new fledg'd bird that first doth show
His spreaded feathers to the morrow chill,
I tried in fear the pinions of my will.                      390
'Twas freedom! and at once I visited
The ceaseless wonders of this ocean-bed.
No need to tell thee of them, for I see
That thou hast been a witness—it must be—
For these I know thou canst not feel a drouth,
By the melancholy corners of that mouth.
So I will in my story straightway pass
To more immediate matter. Woe, alas!
That love should be my bane! Ah, Scylla fair!
Why did poor Glaucus ever—ever dare                          400
To sue thee to his heart? Kind stranger-youth!
I lov'd her to the very white of truth,
And she would not conceive it. Timid thing!
She fled me swift as sea-bird on the wing,
Round every isle, and point, and promontory,
From where large Hercules wound up his story
Far as Egyptian Nile. My passion grew
The more, the more I saw her dainty hue
Gleam delicately through the azure clear:
Until 'twas too fierce agony to bear;                        410
And in that agony, across my grief
It flash'd, that Circe might find some relief—
Cruel enchantress! So above the water
I rear'd my head, and look'd for Phœbus' daughter.
Æææ's isle was wondering at the moon:—
It seem'd to whirl around me, and a swoon
Left me dead-drifting to that fatal power.

    'When I awoke, 'twas in a twilight bower;
Just when the light of morn, with hum of bees,

Stole through its verdurous matting of fresh trees.          420
How sweet, and sweeter! for I heard a lyre,
And over it a sighing voice expire.
It ceased—I caught light footsteps; and anon
The fairest face that morn e'er look'd upon
Push'd through a screen of roses. Starry Jove!
With tears, and smiles, and honey-words she wove
A net whose thraldom was more bliss than all
The range of flower'd Elysium. Thus did fall
The dew of her rich speech: "Ah! Art awake?
"O let me hear thee speak, for Cupid's sake!          430
"I am so oppress'd with joy! Why, I have shed
"An urn of tears, as though thou wert cold dead;
"And now I find thee living, I will pour
"From these devoted eyes their silver store,
"Until exhausted of the latest drop,
"So it will pleasure thee, and force thee stop
"Here, that I too may live: but if beyond
"Such cool and sorrowful offerings, thou art fond
"Of soothing warmth, of dalliance supreme;
"If thou art ripe to taste a long love dream;          440
"If smiles, if dimples, tongues for ardour mute,
"Hang in thy vision like a tempting fruit,
"O let me pluck it for thee." Thus she link'd
Her charming syllables, till indistinct
Their music came to my o'er-sweeten'd soul;
And then she hover'd over me, and stole
So near, that if no nearer it had been
This furrow'd visage thou hadst never seen.

'Young man of Latmos! thus particular
Am I, that thou may'st plainly see how far          450
This fierce temptation went: and thou may'st not
Exclaim, How then, was Scylla quite forgot?

'Who could resist? Who in this universe?
She did so breathe ambrosia; so immerse
My fine existence in a golden clime.
She took me like a child of suckling time,
And cradled me in roses. Thus condemn'd,
The current of my former life was stemm'd,

And to this arbitrary queen of sense
I bow'd a tranced vassal: nor would thence                    460
Have mov'd, even though Amphion's harp had woo'd
Me back to Scylla o'er the billows rude.
For as Apollo each eve doth devise
A new appareling for western skies;
So every eve, nay every spendthrift hour
Shed balmy consciousness within that bower.
And I was free of haunts umbrageous;
Could wander in the mazy forest-house
Of squirrels, foxes shy, and antler'd deer,
And birds from coverts innermost and drear                    470
Warbling for very joy mellifluous sorrow—
To me new born delights!

                                    'Now let me borrow,
For moments few, a temperament as stern
As Pluto's sceptre, that my words not burn
These uttering lips, while I in calm speech tell
How specious heaven was changed to real hell.

    'One morn she left me sleeping: half awake
I sought for her smooth arms and lips, to slake
My greedy thirst with nectarous camel-draughts;
But she was gone. Whereat the barbed shafts                    480
Of disappointment stuck in me so sore,
That out I ran and search'd the forest o'er.
Wandering about in pine and cedar gloom
Damp awe assail'd me; for there 'gan to boom
A sound of moan, an agony of sound,
Sepulchral from the distance all around.
Then came a conquering earth-thunder, and rumbled
That fierce complain to silence: while I stumbled
Down a precipitous path, as if impell'd.
I came to a dark valley.—Groanings swell'd                    490
Poisonous about my ears, and louder grew,
The nearer I approach'd a flame's gaunt blue,
That glar'd before me through a thorny brake
This fire, like the eye of gordian snake,
Bewitch'd me towards; and I soon was near
A sight too fearful for the feel of fear:
    thicket hid I curs'd the haggard scene—

The banquet of my arms, my arbour queen,
Seated upon an uptorn forest root;
And all around her shapes, wizard and brute,                    500
Laughing, and wailing, groveling, serpenting,
Showing tooth, tusk, and venom-bag, and sting!
O such deformities! Old Charon's self,
Should he give up awhile his penny pelf,
And take a dream 'mong rushes Stygian,
It could not be so phantasied. Fierce, wan,
And tyrannizing was the lady's look,
As over them a gnarled staff she shook.
Oft-times upon the sudden she laugh'd out,
And from a basket emptied to the rout                           510
Clusters of grapes, the which they raven'd quick
And roar'd for more; with many a hungry lick
About their shaggy jaws. Avenging, slow,
Anon she took a branch of mistletoe,
And emptied on't a black dull-gurgling phial:
Groan'd one and all, as if some piercing trial
Was sharpening for their pitiable bones.
She lifted up the charm: appealing groans
From their poor breasts went sueing to her ear
In vain; remorseless as an infant's bier                        520
She whisk'd against their eyes the sooty oil.
Whereat was heard a noise of painful toil,
Increasing gradual to a tempest rage,
Shrieks, yells, and groans of torture-pilgrimage;
Until their grieved bodies 'gan to bloat
And puff from the tail's end to stifled throat:
Then was appalling silence: then a sight
More wildering than all that hoarse affright;
For the whole herd, as by a whirlwind writhen,
Went through the dismal air like one huge Python                530
Antagonizing Boreas,—and so vanish'd.
Yet there was not a breath of wind: she banish'd
These phantoms with a nod. Lo! from the dark
Came waggish fauns, and nymphs, and satyrs stark,
With dancing and loud revelry,—and went
Swifter than centaurs after rapine bent.—
Sighing an elephant appear'd and bow'd
Before the fierce witch, speaking thus aloud

In human accent: "Potent goddess! chief
"Of pains resistless! make my being brief,     540
"Or let me from this heavy prison fly:
"Or give me to the air, or let me die!
"I sue not for my happy crown again;
"I sue not for my phalanx on the plain;
"I sue not for my lone, my widow'd wife;
"I sue not for my ruddy drops of life,
"My children fair, my lovely girls and boys!
"I will forget them; I will pass these joys;
"Ask nought so heavenward, so too—too high:
"Only I pray, as fairest boon, to die,     550
"Or be deliver'd from this cumbrous flesh,
"From this gross, detestable, filthy mesh,
"And merely given to the cold bleak air.
"Have mercy, Goddess! Circe, feel my prayer!"

   'That curst magician's name fell icy numb
Upon my wild conjecturing: truth had come
Naked and sabre-like against my heart.
I saw a fury whetting a death-dart;
And my slain spirit, overwrought with fright,
Fainted away in that dark lair of night.     560
Think, my deliverer, how desolate
My waking must have been! disgust, and hate,
And terrors manifold divided me
A spoil amongst them. I prepar'd to flee
Into the dungeon core of that wild wood:
I fled three days—when lo! before me stood
Glaring the angry witch. O Dis, even now,
A clammy dew is beading on my brow,
At mere remembering her pale laugh, and curse.
"Ha! ha! Sir Dainty! there must be a nurse     570
"Made of rose leaves and thistledown, express,
"To cradle thee my sweet, and lull thee: yes,
"I am too flinty-hard for thy nice touch:
"My tenderest squeeze is but a giant's clutch.
"So, fairy-thing, it shall have lullabies
"Unheard of yet: and it shall still its cries
"Upon some breast more lilly-feminine.
"Oh, no—it shall not pine, and pine, and pine

"More than one pretty, trifling thousand years;
"And then 'twere pity, but fate's gentle shears          580
"Cut short its immortality. Sea-flirt!
"Young dove of the waters! truly I'll not hurt
"One hair of thine: see how I weep and sigh,
"That our heart-broken parting is so nigh.
"And must we part? Ah, yes, it must be so.
"Yet ere thou leavest me in utter woe,
"Let me sob over thee my last adieus,
"And speak a blessing: Mark me! Thou hast thews
"Immortal, for thou art of heavenly race:
"But such a love is mine, that here I chace          590
"Eternally away from thee all bloom
"Of youth, and destine thee towards a tomb.
"Hence shalt thou quickly to the watery vast;
"And there, ere many days be overpast,
"Disabled age shall seize thee; and even then
"Thou shalt not go the way of aged men;
"But live and wither, cripple and still breathe
"Ten hundred years: which gone, I then bequeath
"Thy fragile bones to unknown burial.
"Adieu, sweet love, adieu!"—As shot stars fall,          600
She fled ere I could groan for mercy. Stung
And poison'd was my spirit: despair sung
A war-song of defiance 'gainst all hell.
A hand was at my shoulder to compel
My sullen steps; another 'fore my eyes
Moved on with pointed finger. In this guise
Enforced, at the last by ocean's foam
I found me; by my fresh, my native home.
Its tempering coolness, to my life akin,
Came salutary as I waded in;          610
And, with a blind voluptuous rage, I gave
Battle to the swollen billow-ridge, and drave
Large froth before me, while there yet remain'd
Hale strength, nor from my bones all marrow drain'd.

  'Young lover, I must weep—such hellish spite
With dry cheek who can tell? While thus my might
Proving upon this element, dismay'd,
Upon a dead thing's face my hand I laid;

I look'd—'twas Scylla! Cursed, cursed Circe!
O vulture-witch, hast never heard of mercy?                    620
Could not thy harshest vengeance be content,
But thou must nip this tender innocent
Because I lov'd her?—Cold, O cold indeed
Were her fair limbs, and like a common weed
The sea-swell took her hair. Dead as she was
I clung about her waist, nor ceas'd to pass
Fleet as an arrow through unfathom'd brine,
Until there shone a fabric crystalline,
Ribb'd and inlaid with coral, pebble, and pearl.
Headlong I darted; at one eager swirl                    630
Gain'd its bright portal, enter'd, and behold!
'Twas vast, and desolate, and icy-cold;
And all around—But wherefore this to thee
Who in few minutes more thyself shalt see?—
I left poor Scylla in a niche and fled.
My fever'd parchings up, my scathing dread
Met palsy half way: soon these limbs became
Gaunt, wither'd, sapless, feeble, cramp'd, and lame.

   'Now let me pass a cruel, cruel space,
Without one hope, without one faintest trace                    640
Of mitigation, or redeeming bubble
Of colour'd phantasy; for I fear 'twould trouble
Thy brain to loss of reason: and next tell
How a restoring chance came down to quell
One half of the witch in me.

                                   'On a day,
Sitting upon a rock above the spray,
I saw grow up from the horizon's brink
A gallant vessel: soon she seem'd to sink
Away from me again, as though her course
Had been resum'd in spite of hindering force—                    650
So vanish'd: and not long, before arose
Dark clouds, and muttering of winds morose.
Old Æolus would stifle his mad spleen,
But could not: therefore all the billows green
Toss'd up the silver spume against the clouds.
The tempest came: I saw that vessel's shrouds

In perilous bustle; while upon the deck
Stood trembling creatures. I beheld the wreck;
The final gulphing; the poor struggling souls:
I heard their cries amid loud thunder-rolls.            660
O they had all been sav'd but crazed eld
Annull'd my vigorous cravings: and thus quell'd
And curb'd, think on't, O Latmian! did I sit
Writhing with pity, and a cursing fit
Against that hell-born Circe. The crew had gone,
By one and one, to pale oblivion;
And I was gazing on the surges prone,
With many a scalding tear and many a groan,
When at my feet emerg'd an old man's hand,
Grasping this scroll, and this same slender wand.      670
I knelt with pain—reach'd out my hand—had grasp'd
These treasures—touch'd the knuckles—they unclasp'd—
I caught a finger: but the downward weight
O'erpowered me—it sank. Then 'gan abate
The storm, and through chill aguish gloom outburst
The comfortable sun. I was athirst
To search the book, and in the warming air
Parted its dripping leaves with eager care.
Strange matters did it treat of, and drew on
My soul page after page, till well-nigh won           680
Into forgetfulness; when, stupefied,
I read these words, and read again, and tried
My eyes against the heavens, and read again.
O what a load of misery and pain
Each Atlas-line bore off!—a shine of hope
Came gold around me, cheering me to cope
Strenuous with hellish tyranny. Attend!
For thou hast brought their promise to an end.

  'In the wide sea there lives a forlorn wretch,
Doom'd with enfeebled carcase to outstretch           690
His loath'd existence through ten centuries,
And then to die alone. Who can devise
A total opposition? No one. So
One million times ocean must ebb and flow,
And he oppressed. Yet he shall not die,
These things accomplish'd:—If he utterly

*Scans all the depths of magic, and expounds*
*The meanings of all motions, shapes and sounds;*
*If he explores all forms and substances*
*Straight homeward to their symbol-essences;*                    700
*He shall not die. Moreover, and in chief,*
*He must pursue this task of joy and grief*
*Most piously;—all lovers tempest-tost,*
*And in the savage overwhelming lost,*
*He shall deposit side by side, until*
*Time's creeping shall the dreary space fulfil:*
*Which done, and all these labours ripened,*
*A youth, by heavenly power lov'd and led,*
*Shall stand before him; whom he shall direct*
*How to consummate all. The youth elect*                    710
*Must do the thing, or both will be destroy'd.'—*

'Then,' cried the young Endymion, overjoy'd,
'We are twin brothers in this destiny!
Say, I intreat thee, what achievement high
Is, in this restless world, for me reserv'd.
What! if from thee my wandering feet had swerv'd,
Had we both perish'd?'—'Look!' the sage replied,
'Dost thou not mark a gleaming through the tide,
Of diverse brilliances? 'tis the edifice
I told thee of, where lovely Scylla lies;                    720
And where I have enshrined piously
All lovers, whom fell storms have doom'd to die
Throughout my bondage.' Thus discoursing, on
They went till unobscur'd the porches shone;
Which hurryingly they gain'd, and enter'd straight.
Sure never since king Neptune held his state
Was seen such wonder underneath the stars.
Turn to some level plain where haughty Mars
Has legion'd all his battle; and behold
How every soldier, with firm foot, doth hold                    730
His even breast: see, many steeled squares,
And rigid ranks of iron—whence who dares
One step? Imagine further, line by line,
These warrior thousands on the field supine:—
So in that crystal place, in silent rows,
Poor lovers lay at rest from joys and woes.—

The stranger from the mountains, breathless, trac'd
Such thousands of shut eyes in order plac'd;
Such ranges of white feet, and patient lips
All ruddy,—for here death no blossom nips.            740
He mark'd their brows and foreheads; saw their hair·
Put sleekly on one side with nicest care;
And each one's gentle wrists, with reverence,
Put cross-wise to its heart.

                          'Let us commence,'
Whisper'd the guide, stuttering with joy, 'even now.'
He spake, and, trembling like an aspen-bough,
Began to tear his scroll in pieces small,
Uttering the while some mumblings funeral.
He tore it into pieces small as snow
That drifts unfeather'd when bleak northerns blow;   750
And having done it, took his dark blue cloak
And bound it round Endymion: then struck
His wand against the empty air times nine.—
'What more there is to do, young man, is thine:
But first a little patience; first undo
This tangled thread, and wind it to a clue.
Ah, gentle! 'tis as weak as spider's skein;
And shouldst thou break it—What, is it done so clean?
A power overshadows thee! O, brave!
The spite of hell is tumbling to its grave.          760
Here is a shell; 'tis pearly blank to me,
Nor mark'd with any sign or charactery—
Canst thou read aught? O read for pity's sake!
Olympus! we are safe! Now, Carian, break
This wand against yon lyre on the pedestal.'

   'Twas done: and straight with sudden swell and fall
Sweet music breath'd her soul away, and sigh'd
A lullaby to silence.—'Youth! now strew
These minced leaves on me, and passing through
Those files of dead, scatter the same around,        770
And thou wilt see the issue.'—'Mid the sound
Of flutes and viols, ravishing his heart,
Endymion from Glaucus stood apart,
And scatter'd in his face some fragments light.

How lightning-swift the change! a youthful wight
Smiling beneath a coral diadem,
Out-sparkling sudden like an upturn'd gem,
Appear'd, and, stepping to a beauteous corse,
Kneel'd down beside it, and with tenderest force
Press'd its cold hand, and wept,—and Scylla sigh'd!        780
Endymion, with quick hand, the charm applied—
The nymph arose: he left them to their joy,
And onward went upon his high employ,
Showering those powerful fragments on the dead.
And, as he pass'd, each lifted up its head,
As doth a flower at Apollo's touch.
Death felt it to his inwards: 'twas too much:
Death fell a weeping in his charnel-house.
The Latmian persever'd along, and thus
All were re-animated. There arose                         790
A noise of harmony, pulses and throes
Of gladness in the air—while many, who
Had died in mutual arms devout and true,
Sprang to each other madly; and the rest
Felt a high certainty of being blest.
They gaz'd upon Endymion. Enchantment
Grew drunken, and would have its head and bent.
Delicious symphonies, like airy flowers,
Budded, and swell'd, and, full-blown, shed full showers
Of light, soft, unseen leaves of sounds divine.           800
The two deliverers tasted a pure wine
Of happiness, from fairy-press ooz'd out.
Speechless they eyed each other, and about
The fair assembly wander'd to and fro,
Distracted with the richest overflow
Of joy that ever pour'd from heaven.

                                  ——'Away!'
Shouted the new born god; 'Follow, and pay
Our piety to Neptunus supreme!'—
Then Scylla, blushing sweetly from her dream,
They led on first, bent to her meek surprise,             810
Through portal columns of a giant size,
Into the vaulted, boundless emerald.
Joyous all follow'd as the leader call'd,

Down marble steps; pouring as easily
As hour-glass sand,—and fast, as you might see
Swallows obeying the south summer's call,
Or swans upon a gentle waterfall.

Thus went that beautiful multitude, nor far,
Ere from among some rocks of glittering spar,
Just within ken, they saw descending thick          820
Another multitude. Whereat more quick
Moved either host. On a wide sand they met,
And of those numbers every eye was wet;
For each their old love found. A murmuring rose,
Like what was never heard in all the throes
Of wind and waters: 'tis past human wit
To tell; 'tis dizziness to think of it.

This mighty consummation made, the host
Mov'd on for many a league; and gain'd, and lost
Huge sea-marks; vanward swelling in array,          830
And from the rear diminishing away,—
Till a faint dawn surpris'd them. Glaucus cried,
'Behold! behold, the palace of his pride!
God Neptune's palaces!' With noise increas'd,
They shoulder'd on towards that brightening east.
At every onward step proud domes arose
In prospect,—diamond gleams, and golden glows
Of amber 'gainst their faces levelling.
Joyous, and many as the leaves in spring,
Still onward; still the splendour gradual swell'd.   840
Rich opal domes were seen, on high upheld
By jasper pillars, letting through their shafts
A blush of coral. Copious wonder-draughts
Each gazer drank; and deeper drank more near.
For what poor mortals fragment up, as mere
As marble was there lavish, to the vast
Of one fair palace, that far far surpass'd,
Even for common bulk, those olden three,
Memphis, and Babylon, and Nineveh.

As large, as bright, as colour'd as the bow          850
Of Iris, when unfading it doth show

Beyond a silvery shower, was the arch
Through which this Paphian army took its march,
Into the outer courts of Neptune's state:
Whence could be seen, direct, a golden gate,
To which the leaders sped; but not half raught
Ere it burst open swift as fairy thought,
And made those dazzled thousands veil their eyes
Like callow eagles at the first sunrise.
Soon with an eagle nativeness their gaze                    860
Ripe from hue-golden swoons took all the blaze,
And then, behold! large Neptune on his throne
Of emerald deep: yet not exalt alone;
At his right hand stood winged Love, and on
His left sat smiling Beauty's paragon.

    Far as the mariner on highest mast
Can see all round upon the calmed vast,
So wide was Neptune's hall: and as the blue
Doth vault the waters, so the waters drew
Their doming curtains, high, magnificent,                   870
Aw'd from the throne aloof;—and when storm-rent
Disclos'd the thunder-gloomings in Jove's air;
But sooth'd as now, flash'd sudden everywhere,
Noiseless, sub-marine cloudlets, glittering
Death to a human eye: for there did spring
From natural west, and east, and south, and north,
A light as of four sunsets, blazing forth
A gold-green zenith 'bove the Sea-God's head.
Of lucid depth the floor, and far outspread
As breezeless lake, on which the slim canoe                 880
Of feather'd Indian darts about, as through
The delicatest air: air verily,
But for the portraiture of clouds and sky:
This palace floor breath-air,—but for the amaze
Of deep-seen wonders motionless,—and blaze
Of the dome pomp, reflected in extremes,
Globing a golden sphere.

                              They stood in dreams
Till Triton blew his horn. The palace rang;
The Nereids danc'd; the Syrens faintly sang;

And the great Sea-King bow'd his dripping head.        890
Then Love took wing, and from his pinions shed
On all the multitude a nectarous dew.
The ooze-born Goddess beckoned and drew
Fair Scylla and her guides to conference;
And when they reach'd the throned eminence
She kist the sea-nymph's cheek,—who sat her down
A toying with the doves. Then,—'Mighty crown
And sceptre of this kingdom!' Venus said,
'Thy vows were on a time to Nais paid:
Behold!'—Two copious tear-drops instant fell        900
From the God's large eyes; he smil'd delectable,
And over Glaucus held his blessing hands.—
'Endymion! Ah! still wandering in the bands
Of love? Now this is cruel. Since the hour
I met thee in earth's bosom, all my power
Have I put forth to serve thee. What, not yet
Escap'd from dull mortality's harsh net?
A little patience, youth! 'twill not be long,
Or I am skilless quite: an idle tongue,
A humid eye, and steps luxurious,        910
Where these are new and strange, are ominous.
Aye, I have seen these signs in one of heaven,
When others were all blind: and were I given
To utter secrets, haply I might say
Some pleasant words:—but Love will have his day.
So wait awhile expectant. Pr'ythee soon,
Even in the passing of thine honey-moon,
Visit thou my Cythera: thou wilt find
Cupid well-natured, my Adonis kind;
And pray persuade with thee—Ah, I have done,        920
All blisses be upon thee, my sweet son!'—
Thus the fair goddess: While Endymion
Knelt to receive those accents halcyon.

    Meantime a glorious revelry began
Before the Water-Monarch. Nectar ran
In courteous fountains to all cups outreach'd;
And plunder'd vines, teeming exhaustless, pleach'd
New growth about each shell and pendent lyre;
The which, in disentangling for their fire,

Pull'd down fresh foliage and coverture                     930
For dainty toying. Cupid, empire-sure,
Flutter'd and laugh'd, and oft-times through the throng
Made a delighted way. Then dance, and song,
And garlanding grew wild; and pleasure reign'd.
In harmless tendril they each other chain'd,
And strove who should be smother'd deepest in
Fresh crush of leaves.

                        O 'tis a very sin
For one so weak to venture his poor verse
In such a place as this. O do not curse,
High Muses! let him hurry to the ending.             940

    All suddenly were silent. A soft blending
Of dulcet instruments came charmingly;
And then a hymn.

                    'KING of the stormy sea!
Brother of Jove, and co-inheritor
Of elements! Eternally before
Thee the waves awful bow. Fast, stubborn rock,
At thy fear'd trident shrinking, doth unlock
Its deep foundations, hissing into foam.
All mountain-rivers, lost in the wide home
Of thy capacious bosom, ever flow.                    950
Thou frownest, and old Æolus thy foe
Skulks to his cavern, 'mid the gruff complaint
Of all his rebels tempests. Dark clouds faint
When, from thy diadem, a silver gleam
Slants over blue dominion. Thy bright team
Gulphs in the morning light, and scuds along
To bring thee nearer to that golden song
Apollo singeth, while his chariot
Waits at the doors of heaven. Thou art not
For scenes like this: an empire stern hast thou;     960
And it hath furrow'd that large front: yet now,
As newly come of heaven, dost thou sit
To blend and interknit
Subdued majesty with this glad time.
O shell-borne King sublime!

We lay our hearts before thee evermore—
We sing, and we adore!

   'Breathe softly, flutes;
Be tender of your strings, ye soothing lutes;
Nor be the trumpet heard! O vain, O vain;      970
Not flowers budding in an April rain,
Nor breath of sleeping dove, nor river's flow,—
No, nor the Æolian twang of Love's own bow,
Can mingle music fit for the soft ear
Of goddess Cytherea!
Yet deign, white Queen of Beauty, thy fair eyes
On our souls' sacrifice.

   'Bright-winged Child!
Who has another care when thou hast smil'd?
Unfortunates on earth, we see at last      980
All death-shadows, and glooms that overcast
Our spirits, fann'd away by thy light pinions.
O sweetest essence  sweetest of all minions!
God of warm pulses, and dishevell'd hair,
And panting bosoms bare!
Dear unseen light in darkness! eclipser
Of light in light! delicious poisoner!
Thy venom'd goblet will we quaff until
We fill—we fill!
And by thy Mother's lips——'

                Was heard no more      990
For clamour, when the golden palace door
Opened again, and from without, in shone
A new magnificence. On oozy throne
Smooth-moving came Oceanus the old,
To take a latest glimpse at his sheep-fold,
Before he went into his quiet cave
To muse for ever—Then a lucid wave,
Scoop'd from its trembling sisters of mid-sea,
Afloat, and pillowing up the majesty
Of Doris, and the Ægean seer, her spouse—      1000
Next, on a dolphin, clad in laurel boughs,
Theban Amphion leaning on his lute:
His fingers went across it—All were mute

To gaze on Amphitrite, queen of pearls,
And Thetis pearly too.—
                              The palace whirls
Around giddy Endymion; seeing he
Was there far strayed from mortality.
He could not bear it—shut his eyes in vain;
Imagination gave a dizzier pain.
'O I shall die! sweet Venus, be my stay!                    1010
Where is my lovely mistress? Well-away!
I die—I hear her voice—I feel my wing—'
At Neptune's feet he sank. A sudden ring
Of Nereids were about him, in kind strife
To usher back his spirit into life:
But still he slept. At last they interwove
Their cradling arms, and purpos'd to convey
Towards a crystal bower far away.

   Lo! while slow carried through the pitying crowd,
To his inward senses these words spake aloud;            1020
Written in star-light on the dark above:
*Dearest Endymion! my entire love!*
*How have I dwelt in fear of fate: 'tis done—*
*Immortal bliss for me too hast thou won.*
*Arise then! for the hen-dove shall not hatch*
*Her ready eggs, before I'll kissing snatch*
*Thee into endless heaven. Awake! awake!*

   The youth at once arose: a placid lake
Came quiet to his eyes; and forest green,
Cooler than all the wonders he had seen,                    1030
Lull'd with its simple song his fluttering breast.
How happy once again in grassy nest!


## BOOK IV

MUSE of my native land! loftiest Muse!
O first-born on the mountains! by the hues
Of heaven on the spiritual air begot:
Long didst thou sit alone in northern grot,
While yet our England was a wolfish den;
Before our forests heard the talk of men;

Before the first of Druids was a child;—
Long didst thou sit amid our regions wild
Rapt in a deep prophetic solitude.
There came an eastern voice of solemn mood:—                    10
Yet wast thou patient. Then sang forth the Nine,
Apollo's garland:—yet didst thou divine
Such home-bred glory, that they cry'd in vain,
'Come hither, Sister of the Island!' Plain
Spake fair Ausonia; and once more she spake
A higher summons:—still didst thou betake
Thee to thy native hopes. O thou hast won
A full accomplishment! The thing is done,
Which undone, these our latter days had risen
On barren souls. Great Muse, thou know'st what prison,
Of flesh and bone, curbs, and confines, and frets          21
Our spirit's wings: despondency besets
Our pillows; and the fresh to-morrow morn
Seems to give forth its light in very scorn
Of our dull, uninspired, snail-paced lives.
Long have I said, how happy he who shrives
To thee! But then I thought on poets gone,
And could not pray:—nor could I now—so on
I move to the end in lowliness of heart.——

      'Ah, woe is me! that I should fondly part          30
From my dear native land! Ah, foolish maid!
Glad was the hour, when, with thee, myriads bade
Adieu to Ganges and their pleasant fields!
To one so friendless the clear freshet yields
A bitter coolness; the ripe grape is sour:
Yet I would have, great gods! but one short hour
Of native air—let me but die at home.'

      Endymion to heaven's airy dome
Was offering up a hecatomb of vows,
When these words reach'd him. Whereupon he bows          40
His head through thorny-green entanglement
Of underwood, and to the sound is bent,
Anxious as hind towards her hidden fawn.

      'Is no one near to help me? No fair dawn
Of life from charitable voice? No sweet saying

To set my dull and sadden'd spirit playing?
No hand to toy with mine? No lips so sweet
That I may worship them? No eyelids meet
To twinkle on my bosom? No one dies
Before me, till from these enslaving eyes                    50
Redemption sparkles!—I am sad and lost.'

　　Thou, Carian lord, hadst better have been tost
Into a whirlpool. Vanish into air,
Warm mountaineer! for canst thou only bear
A woman's sigh alone and in distress?
See not her charms! Is Phœbe passionless?
Phœbe is fairer far—O gaze no more:—
Yet if thou wilt behold all beauty's store,
Behold her panting in the forest grass!
Do not those curls of glossy jet surpass                    60
For tenderness the arms so idly lain
Amongst them? Feelest not a kindred pain,
To see such lovely eyes in swimming search
After some warm delight, that seems to perch
Dovelike in the dim cell lying beyond
Their upper lids?—Hist!

　　　　　　　　　　'O for Hermes' wand,
To touch this flower into human shape!
That woodland Hyacinthus could escape
From his green prison, and here kneeling down
Call me his queen, his second life's fair crown!                    70
Ah me, how I could love!—My soul doth melt
For the unhappy youth—Love! I have felt
So faint a kindness, such a meek surrender
To what my own full thoughts had made too tender,
That but for tears my life had fled away!—
Ye deaf and senseless minutes of the day,
And thou, old forest, hold ye this for true,
There is no lightning, no authentic dew
But in the eye of love: there's not a sound,
Melodious howsoever, can confound                    80
The heavens and earth in one to such a death
As doth the voice of love: there's not a breath
Will mingle kindly with the meadow air,

Till it has panted round, and stolen a share
Of passion from the heart!'—

                            Upon a bough
He leant, wretched. He surely cannot now
Thirst for another love: O impious,
That he can ever dream upon it thus!—
Thought he, 'Why am I not as are the dead,
Since to a woe like this I have been led         90
Through the dark earth, and through the wondrous sea?
Goddess! I love thee not the less: from thee
By Juno's smile I turn not—no, no, no—
While the great waters are at ebb and flow.—
I have a triple soul! O fond pretence—
For both, for both my love is so immense,
I feel my heart is cut for them in twain.'

    And so he groan'd, as one by beauty slain.
The lady's heart beat quick, and he could see
Her gentle bosom heave tumultuously.         100
He sprang from his green covert: there she lay,
Sweet as a muskrose upon new-made hay;
With all her limbs on tremble, and her eyes
Shut softly up alive. To speak he tries.
'Fair damsel, pity me! forgive that I
Thus violate thy bower's sanctity!
O pardon me, for I am full of grief—
Grief born of thee, young angel! fairest thief!
Who stolen hast away the wings wherewith
I was to top the heavens. Dear maid, sith         110
Thou art my executioner, and I feel
Loving and hatred, misery and weal,
Will in a few short hours be nothing to me,
And all my story that much passion slew me;
Do smile upon the evening of my days:
And, for my tortur'd brain begins to craze,
Be thou my nurse; and let me understand
How dying I shall kiss that lilly hand.—
Dost weep for me? Then should I be content.
Scowl on, ye fates! until the firmament         120
Outblackens Erebus, and the full-cavern'd earth
Crumbles into itself. By the cloud girth

Of Jove, those tears have given me a thirst
To meet oblivion.'—As her heart would burst
The maiden sobb'd awhile, and then replied:
'Why must such desolation betide
As that thou speak'st of? Are not these green nooks
Empty of all misfortune? Do the brooks
Utter a gorgon voice? Does yonder thrush,
Schooling its half-fledg'd little ones to brush          130
About the dewy forest, whisper tales?—
Speak not of grief, young stranger, or cold snails
Will slime the rose to night. Though if thou wilt,
Methinks 'twould be a guilt—a very guilt—
Not to companion thee, and sigh away
The light—the dusk—the dark—till break of day!'
'Dear lady,' said Endymion, ''tis past:
I love thee! and my days can never last.
That I may pass in patience still speak:
Let me have music dying, and I seek                     140
No more delight—I bid adieu to all.
Didst thou not after other climates call,
And murmur about Indian streams?'—Then she,
Sitting beneath the midmost forest tree,
For pity sang this roundelay——

          'O Sorrow,
          Why dost borrow
The natural hue of health, from vermeil lips?—
          To give maiden blushes
          To the white rose bushes?                      150
Or is't thy dewy hand the daisy tips?

          'O Sorrow,
          Why dost borrow
The lustrous passion from a falcon-eye?—
          To give the glow-worm light?
          Or, on a moonless night,
To tinge, on syren shores, the salt sea-spry?

          'O Sorrow,
          Why dost borrow
The mellow ditties from a mourning tongue?—             160

To give at evening pale
Unto the nightingale,
That thou mayst listen the cold dews among?

'O Sorrow,
Why dost borrow
Heart's lightness from the merriment of May?—
A lover would not tread
A cowslip on the head,
Though he should dance from eve till peep of day—
Nor any drooping flower                     170
Held sacred for thy bower,
Wherever he may sport himself and play.

'To Sorrow,
I bade good-morrow,
And thought to leave her far away behind;
But cheerly, cheerly,
She loves me dearly;
She is so constant to me, and so kind:
I would deceive her
And so leave her,                            180
But ah! she is so constant and so kind.

'Beneath my palm trees, by the river side,
I sat a weeping: in the whole world wide
There was no one to ask me why I wept,—
And so I kept
Brimming the water-lilly cups with tears
Cold as my fears.

'Beneath my palm trees, by the river side,
I sat a weeping: what enamour'd bride,
Cheated by shadowy wooer from the clouds,       190
But hides and shrouds
Beneath dark palm trees by a river side?

'And as I sat, over the light blue hills
There came a noise of revellers: the rills
Into the wide stream came of purple hue—
'Twas Bacchus and his crew!
The earnest trumpet spake, and silver thrills

From kissing cymbals made a merry din—
    'Twas Bacchus and his kin!
Like to a moving vintage down they came,    200
Crown'd with green leaves, and faces all on flame;
All madly dancing through the pleasant valley,
    To scare thee, Melancholy!
O then, O then, thou wast a simple name!
And I forgot thee, as the berried holly
By shepherds is forgotten, when, in June,
Tall chesnuts keep away the sun and moon:—
    I rush'd into the folly!

'Within his car, aloft, young Bacchus stood,
Trifling his ivy-dart, in dancing mood,    210
    With sidelong laughing;
And little rills of crimson wine imbrued
His plump white arms, and shoulders, enough white
    For Venus' pearly bite:
And near him rode Silenus on his ass,
Pelted with flowers as he on did pass
    Tipsily quaffing.

'Whence came ye, merry Damsels! whence came ye!
So many, and so many, and such glee?
Why have ye left your bowers desolate,    220
    Your lutes and gentler fate?—
"We follow Bacchus! Bacchus on the wing,
    A conquering!
Bacchus, young Bacchus! good or ill betide,
We dance before him thorough kingdoms wide:—
Come hither, lady fair, and joined be
    To our wild minstrelsy!"

'Whence came ye, jolly Satyrs! whence came ye!
So many, and so many, and such glee?
Why have ye left your forest haunts, why left    230
    Your nuts in oak-tree cleft?—
"For wine, for wine we left our kernel tree;
For wine we left our heath, and yellow brooms,
    And cold mushrooms;
For wine we follow Bacchus through the earth;

Great God of breathless cups and chirping mirth!—
Come hither, lady fair, and joined be
          To our mad minstrelsy!''


'Over wide streams and mountains great we went,
And, save when Bacchus kept his ivy tent,          240
Onward the tiger and the leopard pants,
          With Asian elephants:
Onward these myriads—with song and dance,
With zebras striped, and sleek Arabians' prance,
Web-footed alligators, crocodiles,
Bearing upon their scaly backs, in files,
Plump infant laughers mimicking the coil
Of seamen, and stout galley-rowers' toil:
With toying oars and silken sails they glide,
          Nor care for wind and tide.          250


'Mounted on panthers' furs and lions' manes,
From rear to van they scour about the plains;
A three days' journey in a moment done:
And always, at the rising of the sun,
About the wilds they hunt with spear and horn,
          On spleenful unicorn.


'I saw Osirian Egypt kneel adown
          Before the vine-wreath crown!
I saw parch'd Abyssinia rouse and sing
          To the silver cymbals' ring!          260
I saw the whelming vintage hotly pierce
          Old Tartary the fierce!
The kings of Inde their jewel-sceptres vail,
And from their treasures scatter pearled hail;
Great Brahma from his mystic heaven groans,
          And all his priesthood moans;
Before young Bacchus' eye-wink turning pale.—
Into these regions came I following him,
Sick hearted, weary—so I took a whim
To stray away into these forests drear          270
          Alone, without a peer:
And I have told thee all thou mayest hear.

'Young stranger!
    I've been a ranger
In search of pleasure throughout every clime:
    Alas, 'tis not for me!
    Bewitch'd I sure must be,
To lose in grieving all my maiden prime.

    'Come then, Sorrow!
    Sweetest Sorrow!                                      280
Like an own babe I nurse thee on my breast:
    I thought to leave thee
    And deceive thee,
But now of all the world I love thee best.

    'There is not one,
    No, no, not one
But thee to comfort a poor lonely maid;
    Thou art her mother,
    And her brother,
Her playmate, and her wooer in the shade.'            290

O what a sigh she gave in finishing,
And look, quite dead to every worldly thing!
Endymion could not speak, but gazed on her;
And listened to the wind that now did stir
About the crisped oaks full drearily,
Yet with as sweet a softness as might be
Remember'd from its velvet summer song.
At last he said: 'Poor lady, how thus long
Have I been able to endure that voice?
Fair Melody! kind Syren! I've no choice;             300
I must be thy sad servant evermore:
I cannot choose but kneel here and adore.
Alas, I must not think—by Phœbe, no!
Let me not think, soft Angel! shall it be so?
Say, beautifullest, shall I never think?
O thou could'st foster me beyond the brink
Of recollection! make my watchful care
Close up its bloodshot eyes, nor see despair!
Do gently murder half my soul, and I
Shall feel the other half so utterly!—              310
I'm giddy at that cheek so fair and smooth;
O let it blush so ever! let it soothe

My madness! let it mantle rosy-warm
With the tinge of love, panting in safe alarm.—
This cannot be thy hand, and yet it is;
And this is sure thine other softling—this
Thine own fair bosom, and I am so near!
Wilt fall asleep? O let me sip that tear!
And whisper one sweet word that I may know
This is this world—sweet dewy blossom!'—*Woe!*                320
*Woe! Woe to that Endymion! Where is he?*—
Even these words went echoing dismally
Through the wide forest—a most fearful tone,
Like one repenting in his latest moan;
And while it died away a shade pass'd by,
As of a thunder cloud. When arrows fly
Through the thick branches, poor ring-doves sleek forth
Their timid necks and tremble; so these both
Leant to each other trembling, and sat so
Waiting for some destruction—when lo,                          330
Foot-feather'd Mercury appear'd sublime
Beyond the tall tree tops; and in less time
Than shoots the slanted hail-storm, down he dropt
Towards the ground; but rested not, nor stopt
One moment from his home: only the sward
He with his wand light touch'd, and heavenward
Swifter than sight was gone—even before
The teeming earth a sudden witness bore
Of his swift magic. Diving swans appear
Above the crystal circlings white and clear;                   340
And catch the cheated eye in wide surprise,
How they can dive in sight and unseen rise—
So from the turf outsprang two steeds jet-black,
Each with large dark blue wings upon his back.
The youth of Caria plac'd the lovely dame
On one, and felt himself in spleen to tame
The other's fierceness. Through the air they flew,
High as the eagles. Like two drops of dew
Exhal'd to Phœbus' lips, away they are gone,
Far from the earth away—unseen, alone,                         350
Among cool clouds and winds, but that the free,
The buoyant life of song can floating be
Above their heads, and follow them untir'd.—

Muse of my native land, am I inspir'd?
This is the giddy air, and I must spread
Wide pinions to keep here; nor do I dread
Or height, or depth, or width, or any chance
Precipitous: I have beneath my glance
Those towering horses and their mournful freight.
Could I thus sail, and see, and thus await                    360
Fearless for power of thought, without thine aid?—

   There is a sleepy dusk, an odorous shade
From some approaching wonder, and behold
Those winged steeds, with snorting nostrils bold
Snuff at its faint extreme, and seem to tire,
Dying to embers from their native fire!

   There curl'd a purple mist around them; soon,
It seem'd as when around the pale new moon
Sad Zephyr droops the clouds like weeping willow:
'Twas Sleep slow journeying with head on pillow.               370
For the first time, since he came nigh dead born
From the old womb of night, his cave forlorn
Had he left more forlorn; for the first time,
He felt aloof the day and morning's prime—
Because into his depth Cimmerian
There came a dream, showing how a young man,
Ere a lean bat could plump its wintery skin,
Would at high Jove's empyreal footstool win
An immortality, and how espouse
Jove's daughter, and be reckon'd of his house.                380
Now was he slumbering towards heaven's gate,
That he might at the threshold one hour wait
To hear the marriage melodies, and then
Sink downward to his dusky cave again.
His litter of smooth semilucent mist,
Diversely ting'd with rose and amethyst,
Puzzled those eyes that for the centre sought;
And scarcely for one moment could be caught
His sluggish form reposing motionless.
Those two on winged steeds, with all the stress               390
Of vision search'd for him, as one would look
Athwart the sallows of a river nook

To catch a glance at silver-throated eels,—
Or from old Skiddaw's top, when fog conceals
His rugged forehead in a mantle pale,
With an eye-guess towards some pleasant vale
Descry a favourite hamlet faint and far.

These raven horses, though they foster'd are
Of earth's splenetic fire, dully drop
Their full-vein'd ears, nostrils blood wide, and stop;          400
Upon the spiritless mist have they outspread
Their ample feathers, are in slumber dead,—
And on those pinions, level in mid air,
Endymion sleepeth and the lady fair.
Slowly they sail, slowly as icy isle
Upon a calm sea drifting: and meanwhile
The mournful wanderer dreams. Behold! he walks
On heaven's pavement; brotherly he talks
To divine powers: from his hand full fain
Juno's proud birds are pecking pearly grain:          410
He tries the nerve of Phœbus' golden bow,
And asketh where the golden apples grow:
Upon his arm he braces Pallas' shield,
And strives in vain to unsettle and wield
A Jovian thunderbolt: arch Hebe brings
A full-brimm'd goblet, dances lightly, sings
And tantalizes long; at last he drinks,
And lost in pleasure at her feet he sinks,
Touching with dazzled lips her starlight hand.
He blows a bugle,—an ethereal band          420
Are visible above: the Seasons four,—
Green-kyrtled Spring, flush Summer, golden store
In Autumn's sickle, Winter frosty hoar,
Join dance with shadowy Hours; while still the blast
In swells unmitigated, still doth last
To sway their floating morris. 'Whose is this?
Whose bugle?' he inquires; they smile—'O Dis!
Why is this mortal here? Dost thou not know
Its mistress' lips? Not thou?—'Tis Dian's: lo!
She rises crescented!' He looks, 'tis she,          430
His very goddess: good-bye earth, and sea,
And air, and pains, and care, and suffering;

Good-bye to all but love! Then doth he spring
Towards her, and awakes—and, strange, o'erhead,
Of those same fragrant exhalations bred,
Beheld awake his very dream: the gods
Stood smiling; merry Hebe laughs and nods;
And Phœbe bends towards him crescented.
O state perplexing! On the pinion bed,
Too well awake, he feels the panting side          440
Of his delicious lady. He who died
For soaring too audacious in the sun,
When that same treacherous wax began to run,
Felt not more tongue-tied than Endymion.
His heart leapt up as to its rightful throne,
To that fair shadow'd passion puls'd its way—
Ah, what perplexity! Ah, well a day!
So fond, so beauteous was his bed-fellow,
He could not help but kiss her: then he grew
Awhile forgetful of all beauty save             450
Young Phœbe's, golden hair'd; and so 'gan crave
Forgiveness: yet he turn'd once more to look
At the sweet sleeper,—all his soul was shook,—
She press'd his hand in slumber; so once more
He could not help but kiss her and adore.
At this the shadow wept, melting away.
The Latmian started up: 'Bright goddess, stay!
Search my most hidden breast! By truth's own tongue,
I have no dædale heart: why is it wrung
To desperation? Is there nought for me,          460
Upon the bourne of bliss, but misery?'

    These words awoke the stranger of dark tresses:
Her dawning love-look rapt Endymion blesses
With 'haviour soft. Sleep yawn'd from underneath.
'Thou swan of Ganges, let us no more breathe
This murky phantasm! thou contented seem'st
Pillow'd in lovely idleness, nor dream'st
What horrors may discomfort thee and me.
Ah, shouldst thou die from my heart-treachery!—
Yet did she merely weep—her gentle soul          470
Hath no revenge in it: as it is whole
In tenderness, would I were whole in love!

Can I prize thee, fair maid, all price above,
Even when I feel as true as innocence?
I do, I do.—What is this soul then? Whence
Came it? It does not seem my own, and I
Have no self-passion or identity.
Some fearful end must be: where, where is it?
By Nemesis, I see my spirit flit
Alone about the dark—Forgive me, sweet:          480
Shall we away?' He rous'd the steeds: they beat
Their wings chivalrous into the clear air,
Leaving old Sleep within his vapoury lair.

   The good-night blush of eve was waning slow,
And Vesper, risen star, began to throe
In the dusk heavens silverly, when they
Thus sprang direct towards the Galaxy.
Nor did speed hinder converse soft and strange—
Eternal oaths and vows they interchange,
In such wise, in such temper, so aloof          490
Up in the winds, beneath a starry roof,
So witless of their doom, that verily
'Tis well nigh past man's search their hearts to see;
Whether they wept, or laugh'd, or griev'd, or toy'd—
Most like with joy gone mad, with sorrow cloy'd.

   Full facing their swift flight, from ebon streak,
The moon put forth a little diamond peak,
No bigger than an unobserved star,
Or tiny point of fairy scymetar;
Bright signal that she only stoop'd to tie         500
Her silver sandals, ere deliciously
She bow'd into the heavens her timid head.
Slowly she rose, as though she would have fled,
While to his lady meek the Carian turn'd,
To mark if her dark eyes had yet discern'd
This beauty in its birth—Despair! despair!
He saw her body fading gaunt and spare
In the cold moonshine. Straight he seiz'd her wrist;
It melted from his grasp: her hand he kiss'd,
And, horror! kiss'd his own—he was alone.         510
Her steed a little higher soar'd, and then
Dropt hawkwise to the earth.

                                    There lies a den,
Beyond the seeming confines of the space
Made for the soul to wander in and trace
Its own existence, of remotest glooms.
Dark regions are around it, where the tombs
Of buried griefs the spirit sees, but scarce
One hour doth linger weeping, for the pierce
Of new-born woe it feels more inly smart:
And in these regions many a venom'd dart          520
At random flies; they are the proper home
Of every ill: the man is yet to come
Who hath not journeyed in this native hell.
But few have ever felt how calm and well
Sleep may be had in that deep den of all.
There anguish does not sting; nor pleasure pall:
Woe-hurricanes beat ever at the gate,
Yet all is still within and desolate.
Beset with plainful gusts, within ye hear
No sound so loud as when on curtain'd bier        530
The death-watch tick is stifled. Enter none
Who strive therefore: on the sudden it is won.
Just when the sufferer begins to burn,
Then it is free to him; and from an urn,
Still fed by melting ice, he takes a draught—
Young Semele such richness never quaft
In her maternal longing! Happy gloom!
Dark Paradise! where pale becomes the bloom
Of health by due; where silence dreariest
Is most articulate; where hopes infest;           540
Where those eyes are the brightest far that keep
Their lids shut longest in a dreamless sleep.
O happy spirit-home! O wondrous soul!
Pregnant with such a den to save the whole
In thine own depth. Hail, gentle Carian!
For, never since thy griefs and woes began,
Hast thou felt so content: a grievous feud
Hath led thee to this Cave of Quietude.
Aye, his lull'd soul was there, although upborne
With dangerous speed: and so he did not mourn     550
Because he knew not whither he was going.
So happy was he, not the aerial blowing

Of trumpets at clear parley from the east
Could rouse from that fine relish, that high feast.
They stung the feather'd horse: with fierce alarm
He flapp'd towards the sound. Alas, no charm
Could lift Endymion's head, or he had view'd
A skyey mask, a pinion'd multitude,—
And silvery was its passing: voices sweet
Warbling the while as if to lull and greet          560
The wanderer in his path. Thus warbled they,
While past the vision went in bright array.

   'Who, who from Dian's feast would be away?
For all the golden bowers of the day
Are empty left? Who, who away would be
From Cynthia's wedding and festivity?
Not Hesperus: lo! upon his silver wings
He leans away for highest heaven and sings,
Snapping his lucid fingers merrily!—
Ah, Zephyrus! art here, and Flora too!          570
Ye tender bibbers of the rain and dew,
Young playmates of the rose and daffodil,
Be careful, ere ye enter in, to fill
       Your baskets high
With fennel green, and balm, and golden pines,
Savory, latter-mint, and columbines,
Cool parsley, basil sweet, and sunny thyme;
Yea, every flower and leaf of every clime,
All gather'd in the dewy morning: hie
       Away! fly, fly!—          580
Crystalline brother of the belt of heaven,
Aquarius! to whom king Jove has given
Two liquid pulse streams 'stead of feather'd wings,
Two fan-like fountains,—thine illuminings
       For Dian play:
Dissolve the frozen purity of air;
Let thy white shoulders silvery and bare
Show cold through watery pinions; make more bright
The Star-Queen's crescent on her marriage night:
       Haste, haste away!—          590
Castor has tamed the planet Lion, see!
And of the Bear has Pollux mastery:

A third is in the race! who is the third
Speeding away swift as the eagle bird?
  The ramping Centaur!
The Lion's mane's on end: the Bear how fierce!
The Centaur's arrow ready seems to pierce
Some enemy: far forth his bow is bent
Into the blue of heaven. He'll be shent,
  Pale unrelentor,      600
When he shall hear the wedding lutes a playing.—
Andromeda! sweet woman! why delaying
So timidly among the stars: come hither!
Join this bright throng, and nimbly follow whither
  They all are going.
Danae's Son, before Jove newly bow'd,
Has wept for thee, calling to Jove aloud.
Thee, gentle lady, did he disenthral:
Ye shall for ever live and love, for all
  Thy tears are flowing.—     610
By Daphne's fright, behold Apollo!—'
           More
Endymion heard not: down his steed him bore,
Prone to the green head of a misty hill.

 His first touch of the earth went nigh to kill.
'Alas!' said he, 'were I but always borne
Through dangerous winds, had but my footsteps worn
A path in hell, for ever would I bless
Horrors which nourish an uneasiness
For my own sullen conquering: to him
Who lives beyond earth's boundary, grief is dim, 620
Sorrow is but a shadow: now I see
The grass; I feel the solid ground—Ah, me!
It is thy voice—divinest! Where?—who? who
Left thee so quiet on this bed of dew?
Behold upon this happy earth we are;
Let us aye love each other; let us fare
On forest-fruits, and never, never go
Among the abodes of mortals here below,
Or be by phantoms duped. O destiny!
Into a labyrinth now my soul would fly,  630
But with thy beauty will I deaden it.

Where didst thou melt to? By thee will I sit
For ever: let our fate stop here—a kid
I on this spot will offer: Pan will bid
Us live in peace, in love and peace among
His forest wildernesses. I have clung
To nothing, lov'd a nothing, nothing seen
Or felt but a great dream! O I have been
Presumptuous against love, against the sky,
Against all elements, against the tie            640
Of mortals each to each, against the blooms
Of flowers, rush of rivers, and the tombs
Of heroes gone! Against his proper glory
Has my own soul conspired: so my story
Will I to children utter, and repent.
There never liv'd a mortal man, who bent
His appetite beyond his natural sphere,
But starv'd and died. My sweetest Indian, here,
Here will I kneel, for thou redeemed hast
My life from too thin breathing: gone and past   650
Are cloudy phantasms. Caverns lone, farewell!
And air of visions, and the monstrous swell
Of visionary seas! No, never more
Shall airy voices cheat me to the shore
Of tangled wonder, breathless and aghast.
Adieu, my daintiest Dream! although so vast
My love is still for thee. The hour may come
When we shall meet in pure elysium.
On earth I may not love thee; and therefore
Doves will I offer up, and sweetest store        660
All through the teeming year: so thou wilt shine
On me, and on this damsel fair of mine,
And bless our simple lives. My Indian bliss!
My river-lilly bud! one human kiss!
One sigh of real breath—one gentle squeeze,
Warm as a dove's nest among summer trees,
And warm with dew at ooze from living blood!
Whither didst melt? Ah, what of that!—all good
We'll talk about—no more of dreaming.—Now,
Where shall our dwelling be? Under the brow      670
Of some steep mossy hill, where ivy dun
Would hide us up, although spring leaves were none;

And where dark yew trees, as we rustle through,
Will drop their scarlet berry cups of dew?
O thou wouldst joy to live in such a place;
Dusk for our loves, yet light enough to grace
Those gentle limbs on mossy bed reclin'd:
For by one step the blue sky shouldst thou find,
And by another, in deep dell below,
See, through the trees, a little river go                   680
All in its mid-day gold and glimmering.
Honey from out the gnarled hive I'll bring,
And apples, wan with sweetness, gather thee,—
Cresses that grow where no man may them see,
And sorrel untorn by the dew-claw'd stag:
Pipes will I fashion of the syrinx flag,
That thou mayst always know whither I roam,
When it shall please thee in our quiet home
To listen and think of love. Still let me speak;
Still let me dive into the joy I seek,—                     690
For yet the past doth prison me. The rill,
Thou haply mayst delight in, will I fill
With fairy fishes from the mountain tarn,
And thou shalt feed them from the squirrel's barn.
Its bottom will I strew with amber shells,
And pebbles blue from deep enchanted wells.
Its sides I'll plant with dew-sweet eglantine,
And honeysuckles full of clear bee-wine.
I will entice this crystal rill to trace
Love's silver name upon the meadow's face.                  700
I'll kneel to Vesta, for a flame of fire;
And to god Phœbus, for a golden lyre;
To Empress Dian, for a hunting spear;
To Vesper, for a taper silver-clear,
That I may see thy beauty through the night;
To Flora, and a nightingale shall light
Tame on thy finger; to the River-gods,
And they shall bring thee taper fishing-rods
Of gold, and lines of Naiads' long bright tress.
Heaven shield thee for thine utter loveliness!             710
Thy mossy footstool shall the altar be
'Fore which I'll bend, bending, dear love, to thee:
Those lips shall be my Delphos, and shall speak

Laws to my footsteps, colour to my cheek,
Trembling or stedfastness to this same voice,
And of three sweetest pleasurings the choice:
And that affectionate light, those diamond things,
Those eyes, those passions, those supreme pearl springs,
Shall be my grief, or twinkle me to pleasure.
Say, is not bliss within our perfect seisure?                    720
O that I could not doubt!'
                              The mountaineer
Thus strove by fancies vain and crude to clear
His briar'd path to some tranquillity.
It gave bright gladness to his lady's eye,
And yet the tears she wept were tears of sorrow;
Answering thus, just as the golden morrow
Beam'd upward from the vallies of the east:
'O that the flutter of this heart had ceas'd,
Or the sweet name of love had pass'd away.
Young feather'd tyrant! by a swift decay                         730
Wilt thou devote this body to the earth:
And I do think that at my very birth
I lisp'd thy blooming titles inwardly;
For at the first, first dawn and thought of thee,
With uplift hands I blest the stars of heaven.
Art thou not cruel? Ever have I striven
To think thee kind, but ah, it will not do!
When yet a child, I heard that kisses drew
Favour from thee, and so I kisses gave
To the void air, bidding them find out love:                     740
But when I came to feel how far above
All fancy, pride, and fickle maidenhood,
All earthly pleasure, all imagin'd good,
Was the warm tremble of a devout kiss,—
Even then, that moment, at the thought of this,
Fainting I fell into a bed of flowers,
And languish'd there three days. Ye milder powers,
Am I not cruelly wrong'd? Believe, believe
Me, dear Endymion, were I to weave
With my own fancies garlands of sweet life,                      750
Thou shouldst be one of all. Ah, bitter strife!
I may not be thy love: I am forbidden—
Indeed I am—thwarted, affrighted, chidden,

By things I trembled at, and gorgon wrath.
Twice hast thou ask'd whither I went: henceforth
Ask me no more! I may not utter it,
Nor may I be thy love. We might commit
Ourselves at once to vengeance; we might die;
We might embrace and die: voluptuous thought!
Enlarge not to my hunger, or I'm caught          760
In trammels of perverse deliciousness.
No, no, that shall not be: thee will I bless,
And bid a long adieu.'

                    The Carian
No word return'd: both lovelorn, silent, wan,
Into the vallies green together went.
Far wandering, they were perforce content
To sit beneath a fair lone beechen tree;
Nor at each other gaz'd, but heavily
Por'd on its hazle cirque of shedded leaves.

    Endymion! unhappy! it nigh grieves          770
Me to behold thee thus in last extreme:
Ensky'd ere this, but truly that I deem
Truth the best music in a first-born song.
Thy lute-voic'd brother will I sing ere long,
And thou shalt aid—hast thou not aided me?
Yes, moonlight Emperor! felicity
Has been thy meed for many thousand years;
Yet often have I, on the brink of tears,
Mourn'd as if yet thou wert a forester;—
Forgetting the old tale.

                    He did not stir          780
His eyes from the dead leaves, or one small pulse
Of joy he might have felt. The spirit culls
Unfaded amaranth, when wild it strays
Through the old garden-ground of boyish days.
A little onward ran the very stream
By which he took his first soft poppy dream;
And on the very bark 'gainst which he leant
A crescent he had carv'd, and round it spent
His skill in little stars. The teeming tree
Had swollen and green'd the pious charactery,          790

But not ta'en out. Why, there was not a slope
Up which he had not fear'd the antelope;
And not a tree, beneath whose rooty shade
He had not with his tamed leopards play'd:
Nor could an arrow light, or javelin,
Fly in the air where his had never been—
And yet he knew it not.

              O treachery!
Why does his lady smile, pleasing her eye
With all his sorrowing? He sees her not.
But who so stares on him? His sister sure!       **800**
Peona of the woods!—Can she endure—
Impossible—how dearly they embrace!
His lady smiles; delight is in her face;
It is no treachery.

           'Dear brother mine!
Endymion, weep not so! Why shouldst thou pine
When all great Latmos so exalt will be?
Thank the great gods, and look not bitterly;
And speak not one pale word, and sigh no more.
Sure I will not believe thou hast such store
Of grief, to last thee to my kiss again.       **810**
Thou surely canst not bear a mind in pain,
Come hand in hand with one so beautiful.
Be happy both of you! for I will pull
The flowers of autumn for your coronals.
Pan's holy priest for young Endymion calls;
And when he is restor'd, thou, fairest dame,
Shalt be our queen. Now, is it not a shame
To see ye thus,—not very, very sad?
Perhaps ye are too happy to be glad:
O feel as if it were a common day;       **820**
Free-voic'd as one who never was away.
No tongue shall ask, whence come ye? but ye shall
Be gods of your own rest imperial.
Not even I, for one whole month, will pry
Into the hours that have pass'd us by,
Since in my arbour I did sing to thee.
O Hermes! on this very night will be

A hymning up to Cynthia, queen of light;
For the soothsayers old saw yesternight
Good visions in the air,—whence will befal,                    830
As say these sages, health perpetual
To shepherds and their flocks; and furthermore,
In Dian's face they read the gentle lore:
Therefore for her these vesper-carols are.
Our friends will all be there from nigh and far.
Many upon thy death have ditties made;
And many, even now, their foreheads shade
With cypress, on a day of sacrifice.
New singing for our maids shalt thou devise,
And pluck the sorrow from our huntsmen's brows.                840
Tell me, my lady-queen, how to espouse
This wayward brother to his rightful joys!
His eyes are on thee bent, as thou didst poize
His fate most goddess-like. Help me, I pray,
To lure—Endymion, dear brother, say
What ails thee?' He could bear no more, and so
Bent his soul fiercely like a spiritual bow,
And twang'd it inwardly, and calmly said:
'I would have thee my only friend, sweet maid!
My only visitor! not ignorant though,                          850
That those deceptions which for pleasure go
'Mong men, are pleasures real as real may be:
But there are higher ones I may not see,
If impiously an earthly realm I take.
Since I saw thee, I have been wide awake
Night after night, and day by day, until
Of the empyrean I have drunk my fill.
Let it content thee, Sister, seeing me
More happy than betides mortality.
A hermit young, I'll live in mossy cave,                       860
Where thou alone shalt come to me, and lave
Thy spirit in the wonders I shall tell.
Through me the shepherd realm shall prosper well;
For to thy tongue will I all health confide.
And, for my sake, let this young maid abide
With thee as a dear sister. Thou alone,
Peona, mayst return to me. I own
This may sound strangely: but when, dearest girl,

Thou seest it for my happiness, no pearl
Will trespass down those cheeks. Companion fair!          870
Wilt be content to dwell with her, to share
This sister's love with me?' Like one resign'd
And bent by circumstance, and thereby blind
In self-commitment, thus that meek unknown:
'Aye, but a buzzing by my ears has flown,
Of jubilee to Dian:—truth I heard?
Well then, I see there is no little bird,
Tender soever, but is Jove's own care,
Long have I sought for rest, and, unaware,
Behold I find it! so exalted too!          880
So after my own heart! I knew, I knew
There was a place untenanted in it:
In that same void white Chastity shall sit,
And monitor me nightly to lone slumber.
With sanest lips I vow me to the number
Of Dian's sisterhood; and, kind lady,
With thy good help, this very night shall see
My future days to her fane consecrate.'

    As feels a dreamer what doth most create
His own particular fright, so these three felt:          890
Or like one who, in after ages, knelt
To Lucifer or Baal, when he'd pine
After a little sleep: or when in mine
Far under-ground, a sleeper meets his friends
Who know him not. Each diligently bends
Towards common thoughts and things for very fear;
Striving their ghastly malady to cheer,
By thinking it a thing of yes and no,
That housewives talk of. But the spirit-blow
Was struck, and all were dreamers. At the last          900
Endymion said: 'Are not our fates all cast?
Why stand we here? Adieu, ye tender pair!
Adieu!' Whereat those maidens, with wild stare,
Walk'd dizzily away. Pained and hot
His eyes went after them, until they got
Near to a cypress grove, whose deadly maw,
In one swift moment, would what then he saw
Engulph for ever. 'Stay!' he cried, 'ah, stay!

Turn, damsels! hist! one word I have to say.
Sweet Indian, I would see thee once again.                    910
It is a thing I dote on: so I'd fain,
Peona, ye should hand in hand repair
Into those holy groves, that silent are
Behind great Dian's temple. I'll be yon,
At vesper's earliest twinkle—they are gone—
But once, once, once again—' At this he press'd
His hands against his face, and then did rest
His head upon a mossy hillock green,
And so remain'd as he a corpse had been
All the long day; save when he scantly lifted                    920
His eyes abroad, to see how shadows shifted
With the slow move of time,—sluggish and weary
Until the poplar tops, in journey dreary,
Had reach'd the river's brim. Then up he rose,
And, slowly as that very river flows,
Walk'd towards the temple grove with this lament:
'Why such a golden eve? The breeze is sent
Careful and soft, that not a leaf may fall
Before the serene father of them all
Bows down his summer head below the west.                    930
Now am I of breath, speech, and speed possest,
But at the setting I must bid adieu
To her for the last time. Night will strew
On the damp grass myriads of lingering leaves,
And with them shall I die; nor much it grieves
To die, when summer dies on the cold sward.
Why, I have been a butterfly, a lord
Of flowers, garlands, love-knots, silly posies,
Groves, meadows, melodies, and arbour roses;
My kingdom's at its death, and just it is                    940
That I should die with it: so in all this
We miscall grief, bale, sorrow, heartbreak, woe,
What is there to plain of? By Titan's foe
I am but rightly serv'd.' So saying, he
Tripp'd lightly on, in sort of deathful glee;
Laughing at the clear stream and setting sun,
As though they jests had been: nor had he done
His laugh at nature's holy countenance,
Until that grove appear'd, as if perchance,

And then his tongue with sober seemlihed          950
Gave utterance as he enter'd: 'Ha! I said,
King of the butterflies; but by this gloom,
And by old Rhadamanthus' tongue of doom,
This dusk religion, pomp of solitude,
And the Promethean clay by thief endued,
By old Saturnus' forelock, by his head
Shook with eternal palsy, I did wed
Myself to things of light from infancy;
And thus to be cast out, thus lorn to die,
Is sure enough to make a mortal man          960
Grow impious.' So he inwardly began
On things for which no wording can be found;
Deeper and deeper sinking, until drown'd
Beyond the reach of music: for the choir
Of Cynthia he heard not, though rough briar
Nor muffling thicket interpos'd to dull
The vesper hymn, far swollen, soft and full,
Through the dark pillars of those sylvan aisles.
He saw not the two maidens, nor their smiles,
Wan as primroses gather'd at midnight          970
By chilly finger'd spring. 'Unhappy wight!
Endymion!' said Peona, 'we are here!
What wouldst thou ere we all are laid on bier?'
Then he embrac'd her, and his lady's hand
Press'd, saying: 'Sister, I would have command,
If it were heaven's will, on our sad fate.'
At which that dark-eyed stranger stood elate
And said, in a new voice, but sweet as love,
To Endymion's amaze: 'By Cupid's dove,
And so thou shalt! and by the lilly truth          980
Of my own breast thou shalt, beloved youth!'
And as she spake, into her face there came
Light, as reflected from a silver flame:
Her long black hair swell'd ampler, in display
Full golden; in her eyes a brighter day
Dawn'd blue and full of love. Aye, he beheld
Phœbe, his passion! joyous she upheld
Her lucid bow, continuing thus: 'Drear, drear
Has our delaying been; but foolish fear
Withheld me first; and then decrees of fate;          990

And then 'twas fit that from this mortal state
Thou shouldst, my love, by some unlook'd for change
Be spiritualiz'd. Peona, we shall range
These forests, and to thee they safe shall be
As was thy cradle; hither shalt thou flee
To meet us many a time.' Next Cynthia bright
Peona kiss'd, and bless'd with fair good night:
Her brother kiss'd her too, and knelt adown
Before his goddess, in a blissful swoon.
She gave her fair hands to him, and behold,                    1000
Before three swiftest kisses he had told,
They vanish'd far away!—Peona went
Home through the gloomy wood in wonderment.

THE END

# LAMIA

## ISABELLA

## THE EVE OF ST. AGNES

### AND OTHER POEMS

1820

## ADVERTISEMENT.

I F any apology be thought necessary for the appearance of the un-
finished poem of HYPERION, the publishers beg to state that they alone
are responsible, as it was printed at their particular request, and con-
trary to the wish of the author. The poem was intended to have been
o f equal length with ENDYMION, but the reception given to that work
discouraged the author from proceeding.

FLEET STREET, *June 26, 1820.*

# LAMIA

## PART I

Upon a time, before the faery broods
Drove Nymph and Satyr from the prosperous woods,
Before king Oberon's bright diadem,
Sceptre, and mantle, clasp'd with dewy gem,
Frighted away the Dryads and the Fauns
From rushes green, and brakes, and cowslip'd lawns,
The ever-smitten Hermes empty left
His golden throne, bent warm on amorous theft:
From high Olympus had he stolen light,
On this side of Jove's clouds, to escape the sight          10
Of his great summoner, and made retreat
Into a forest on the shores of Crete.
For somewhere in that sacred island dwelt
A nymph, to whom all hoofed Satyrs knelt;
At whose white feet the languid Tritons poured
Pearls, while on land they wither'd and adored.
Fast by the springs where she to bathe was wont,
And in those meads where sometime she might haunt,
Were strewn rich gifts, unknown to any Muse,
Though Fancy's casket were unlock'd to choose.          20
Ah, what a world of love was at her feet!
So Hermes thought, and a celestial heat
Burnt from his winged heels to either ear,
That from a whiteness, as the lilly clear,
Blush'd into roses 'mid his golden hair,
Fallen in jealous curls about his shoulders bare.

From vale to vale, from wood to wood, he flew,
Breathing upon the flowers his passion new,
And wound with many a river to its head,
To find where this sweet nymph prepar'd her secret bed:   30
In vain; the sweet nymph might nowhere be found,
And so he rested, on the lonely ground,
Pensive, and full of painful jealousies
Of the Wood-Gods, and even the very trees.

There as he stood, he heard a mournful voice,
Such as once heard, in gentle heart, destroys
All pain but pity: thus the lone voice spake:
'When from this wreathed tomb shall I awake!
'When move in a sweet body fit for life,
'And love, and pleasure, and the ruddy strife      40
'Of hearts and lips! Ah, miserable me!'
The God, dove-footed, glided silently
Round bush and tree, soft-brushing, in his speed,
The taller grasses and full-flowering weed,
Until he found a palpitating snake,
Bright, and cirque-couchant in a dusky brake.

   She was a gordian shape of dazzling hue,
Vermilion-spotted, golden, green, and blue;
Striped like a zebra, freckled like a pard,
Eyed like a peacock, and all crimson barr'd;      50
And full of silver moons, that, as she breathed,
Dissolv'd, or brighter shone, or interwreathed
Their lustres with the gloomier tapestries—
So rainbow-sided, touch'd with miseries,
She seem'd, at once, some penanced lady elf,
Some demon's mistress, or the demon's self.
Upon her crest she wore a wannish fire
Sprinkled with stars, like Ariadne's tiar:
Her head was serpent, but ah, bitter-sweet!
She had a woman's mouth with all its pearls complete:      60
And for her eyes: what could such eyes do there
But weep, and weep, that they were born so fair?
As Proserpine still weeps for her Sicilian air.
Her throat was serpent, but the words she spake
Came, as through bubbling honey, for Love's sake,
And thus; while Hermes on his pinions lay,
Like a stoop'd falcon ere he takes his prey.

   'Fair Hermes, crown'd with feathers, fluttering light,
'I had a splendid dream of thee last night:
'I saw thee sitting, on a throne of gold,      70
'Among the Gods, upon Olympus old,
The only sad one; for thou didst not hear
'The soft, lute-finger'd Muses chaunting clear,

'Nor even Apollo when he sang alone,
'Deaf to his throbbing throat's long, long melodious moan.
'I dreamt I saw thee, robed in purple flakes,
'Break amorous through the clouds, as morning breaks,
'And, swiftly as a bright Phœbean dart,
'Strike for the Cretan isle; and here thou art!
'Too gentle Hermes, hast thou found the maid?'    80
Whereat the star of Lethe not delay'd
His rosy eloquence, and thus inquired:
'Thou smooth-lipp'd serpent, surely high inspired!
'Thou beauteous wreath, with melancholy eyes,
'Possess whatever bliss thou canst devise,
'Telling me only where my nymph is fled,—
'Where she doth breathe!' 'Bright planet, thou hast said,'
Return'd the snake, 'but seal with oaths, fair God!'
'I swear,' said Hermes, 'by my serpent rod,
'And by thine eyes, and by thy starry crown!'    90
Light flew his earnest words, among the blossoms blown.
Then thus again the brilliance feminine:
'Too frail of heart! for this lost nymph of thine,
'Free as the air, invisibly, she strays
'About these thornless wilds; her pleasant days
'She tastes unseen; unseen her nimble feet
'Leave traces in the grass and flowers sweet;
'From weary tendrils, and bow'd branches green,
'She plucks the fruit unseen, she bathes unseen:
'And by my power is her beauty veil'd    100
'To keep it unaffronted, unassail'd
'By the love-glances of unlovely eyes,
'Of Satyrs, Fauns, and blear'd Silenus' sighs.
'Pale grew her immortality, for woe
'Of all these lovers, and she grieved so
'I took compassion on her, bade her steep
'Her hair in weïrd syrops, that would keep
'Her loveliness invisible, yet free
'To wander as she loves, in liberty.
'Thou shalt behold her, Hermes, thou alone,    110
'If thou wilt, as thou swearest, grant my boon!'
Then, once again, the charmed God began
An oath, and through the serpent's ears it ran
Warm, tremulous, devout, psalterian.

Ravish'd, she lifted her Circean head,
Blush'd a live damask, and swift-lisping said,
'I was a woman, let me have once more
'A woman's shape, and charming as before.
'I love a youth of Corinth—O the bliss!
'Give me my woman's form, and place me where he is.    120
'Stoop, Hermes, let me breathe upon thy brow,
'And thou shalt see thy sweet nymph even now.'
The God on half-shut feathers sank serene,
She breath'd upon his eyes, and swift was seen
Of both the guarded nymph near-smiling on the green.
It was no dream; or say a dream it was,
Real are the dreams of Gods, and smoothly pass
Their pleasures in a long immortal dream.
One warm, flush'd moment, hovering, it might seem
Dash'd by the wood-nymph's beauty, so he burn'd;    130
Then, lighting on the printless verdure, turn'd
To the swoon'd serpent, and with languid arm,
Delicate, put to proof the lythe Caducean charm.
So done, upon the nymph his eyes he bent
Full of adoring tears and blandishment,
And towards her stept: she, like a moon in wane,
Faded before him, cower'd, nor could restrain
Her fearful sobs, self-folding like a flower
That faints into itself at evening hour:
But the God fostering her chilled hand,    140
She felt the warmth, her eyelids open'd bland,
And, like new flowers at morning song of bees,
Bloom'd, and gave up her honey to the lees.
Into the green-recessed woods they flew;
Nor grew they pale, as mortal lovers do.

   Left to herself, the serpent now began
To change; her elfin blood in madness ran,
Her mouth foam'd, and the grass, therewith besprent,
Wither'd at dew so sweet and virulent;
Her eyes in torture fix'd, and anguish drear,    150
Hot, glaz'd, and wide, with lid-lashes all sear,
Flash'd phosphor and sharp sparks, without one cooling tear.
The colours all inflam'd throughout her train,
She writh'd about, convuls'd with scarlet pain:

A deep volcanian yellow took the place
Of all her milder-mooned body's grace;
And, as the lava ravishes the mead,
Spoilt all her silver mail, and golden brede;
Made gloom of all her frecklings, streaks and bars.
Eclips'd her crescents, and lick'd up her stars:            160
So that, in moments few, she was undrest
Of all her sapphires, greens, and amethyst,
And rubious-argent: of all these bereft,
Nothing but pain and ugliness were left.
Still shone her crown; that vanish'd, also she
Melted and disappear'd as suddenly;
And in the air, her new voice luting soft,
Cried, 'Lycius! gentle Lycius!'—Borne aloft
With the bright mists about the mountains hoar
These words dissolv'd: Crete's forests heard no more.        170

　　Whither fled Lamia, now a lady bright,
A full-born beauty new and exquisite?
She fled into that valley they pass o'er
Who go to Corinth from Cenchreas' shore;
And rested at the foot of those wild hills,
The rugged founts of the Peræan rills,
And of that other ridge whose barren back
Stretches, with all its mist and cloudy rack,
South-westward to Cleone. There she stood
About a young bird's flutter from a wood,                    180
Fair, on a sloping green of mossy tread,
By a clear pool, wherein she passioned
To see herself escap'd from so sore ills,
While her robes flaunted with the daffodils.

　　Ah, happy Lycius!—for she was a maid
More beautiful than ever twisted braid,
Or sigh'd, or blush'd, or on spring-flowered lea
Spread a green kirtle to the minstrelsy:
A virgin purest lipp'd, yet in the lore
Of love deep learned to the red heart's core:              190
Not one hour old, yet of sciential brain
To unperplex bliss from its neighbour pain;
Define their pettish limits, and estrange

Their points of contact, and swift counterchange;
Intrigue with the specious chaos, and dispart
Its most ambiguous atoms with sure art;
As though in Cupid's college she had spent
Sweet days a lovely graduate, still unshent,
And kept his rosy terms in idle languishment.

Why this fair creature chose so faerily                200
By the wayside to linger, we shall see;
But first 'tis fit to tell how she could muse
And dream, when in the serpent prison-house,
Of all she list, strange or magnificent:
How, ever, where she will'd, her spirit went;
Whether to faint Elysium, or where
Down through tress-lifting waves the Nereids fair
Wind into Thetis' bower by many a pearly stair;
Or where God Bacchus drains his cups divine,
Stretch'd out, at ease, beneath a glutinous pine;      210
Or where in Pluto's gardens palatine
Mulciber's columns gleam in far piazzian line.
And sometimes into cities she would send
Her dream, with feast and rioting to blend;
And once, while among mortals dreaming thus,
She saw the young Corinthian Lycius
Charioting foremost in the envious race,
Like a young Jove with calm uneager face,
And fell into a swooning love of him.
Now on the moth-time of that evening dim               220
He would return that way, as well she knew,
To Corinth from the shore; for freshly blew
The eastern soft wind, and his galley now
Grated the quaystones with her brazen prow
In port Cenchreas, from Egina isle
Fresh anchor'd; whither he had been awhile
To sacrifice to Jove, whose temple there
Waits with high marble doors for blood and incense rare.
Jove heard his vows, and better'd his desire;
For by some freakful chance he made retire             230
From his companions, and set forth to walk,
Perhaps grown wearied of their Corinth talk:
Over the solitary hills he fared,

Thoughtless at first, but ere eve's star appeared
His phantasy was lost, where reason fades,
In the calm'd twilight of Platonic shades.
Lamia beheld him coming, near, more near—
Close to her passing, in indifference drear,
His silent sandals swept the mossy green;
So neighbour'd to him, and yet so unseen                240
She stood: he pass'd, shut up in mysteries,
His mind wrapp'd like his mantle, while her eyes
Follow'd his steps, and her neck regal white
Turn'd—syllabling thus, 'Ah, Lycius bright,
'And will you leave me on the hills alone?
'Lycius, look back! and be some pity shown.'
He did; not with cold wonder fearingly,
But Orpheus-like at an Eurydice;
For so delicious were the words she sung,
It seem'd he had lov'd them a whole summer long:       250
And soon his eyes had drunk her beauty up,
Leaving no drop in the bewildering cup,
And still the cup was full,—while he, afraid
Lest she should vanish ere his lip had paid
Due adoration, thus began to adore;
Her soft look growing coy, she saw his chain so sure:
'Leave thee alone! Look back! Ah, Goddess, see
'Whether my eyes can ever turn from thee!
'For pity do not this sad heart belie—
'Even as thou vanishest so shall I die.                260
'Stay! though a Naiad of the rivers, stay!
'To thy far wishes will thy streams obey:
'Stay! though the greenest woods be thy domain,
'Alone they can drink up the morning rain:
'Though a descended Pleiad, will not one
'Of thine harmonious sisters keep in tune
'Thy spheres, and as thy silver proxy shine?
'So sweetly to these ravish'd ears of mine
'Came thy sweet greeting, that if thou shouldst fade
'Thy memory will waste me to a shade:—                270
'For pity do not melt!'—'If I should stay,'
Said Lamia, 'here, upon this floor of clay,
'And pain my steps upon these flowers too rough,
'What canst thou say or do of charm enough

'To dull the nice remembrance of my home?
'Thou canst not ask me with thee here to roam
'Over these hills and vales, where no joy is,—
'Empty of immortality and bliss!
'Thou art a scholar, Lycius, and must know
'That finer spirits cannot breathe below                    280
'In human climes, and live: Alas! poor youth,
'What taste of purer air hast thou to soothe
'My essence? What serener palaces,
'Where I may all my many senses please,
'And by mysterious sleights a hundred thirsts appease?
'It cannot be—Adieu!' So said, she rose
Tiptoe with white arms spread. He, sick to lose
The amorous promise of her lone complain,
Swoon'd, murmuring of love, and pale with pain.
The cruel lady, without any show                            290
Of sorrow for her tender favourite's woe,
But rather, if her eyes could brighter be,
With brighter eyes and slow amenity,
Put her new lips to his, and gave afresh
The life she had so tangled in her mesh:
And as he from one trance was wakening
Into another, she began to sing,
Happy in beauty, life, and love, and every thing,
A song of love, too sweet for earthly lyres,
While, like held breath, the stars drew in their panting
      fires.                                                300
And then she whisper'd in such trembling tone,
As those who, safe together met alone
For the first time through many anguish'd days,
Use other speech than looks; bidding him raise
His drooping head, and clear his soul of doubt,
For that she was a woman, and without
Any more subtle fluid in her veins
Than throbbing blood, and that the self-same pains
Inhabited her frail-strung heart as his.
And next she wonder'd how his eyes could miss              310
Her face so long in Corinth, where, she said,
She dwelt but half retir'd, and there had led
Days happy as the gold coin could invent
Without the aid of love; yet in content

Till she saw him, as once she pass'd him by,
Where 'gainst a column he lent thoughtfully
At Venus' temple porch, 'mid baskets heap'd
Of amorous herbs and flowers, newly reap'd
Late on that eve, as 'twas the night before
The Adonian feast; whereof she saw no more,                320
But wept alone those days, for why should she adore?
Lycius from death awoke into amaze,
To see her still, and singing so sweet lays;
Then from amaze into delight he fell
To hear her whisper woman's lore so well;
And every word she spake entic'd him on
To unperplex'd delight and pleasure known.
Let the mad poets say whate'er they please
Of the sweets of Faeries, Peris, Goddesses,
There is not such a treat among them all,                  330
Haunters of cavern, lake, and waterfall,
As a real woman, lineal indeed
From Pyrrha's pebbles or old Adam's seed.
Thus gentle Lamia judg'd, and judg'd aright,
That Lycius could not love in half a fright,
So threw the goddess off, and won his heart
More pleasantly by playing woman's part,
With no more awe than what her beauty gave,
That, while it smote, still guaranteed to save.
Lycius to all made eloquent reply,                         340
Marrying to every word a twinborn sigh;
And last, pointing to Corinth, ask'd her sweet,
If 'twas too far that night for her soft feet.
The way was short, for Lamia's eagerness
Made, by a spell, the triple league decrease
To a few paces; not at all surmised
By blinded Lycius, so in her comprized.
They pass'd the city gates, he knew not how,
So noiseless, and he never thought to know.

    As men talk in a dream, so Corinth all,                350
Throughout her palaces imperial,
And all her populous streets and temples lewd,
Mutter'd, like tempest in the distance brew'd,
To the wide-spreaded night above her towers.

Men, women, rich and poor, in the cool hours,
Shuffled their sandals o'er the pavement white
Companion'd or alone; while many a light
Flared, here and there, from wealthy festivals,
And threw their moving shadows on the walls,
Or found them cluster'd in the corniced shade          360
Of some arch'd temple door, or dusky colonade.

     Muffling his face, of greeting friends in fear,
Her fingers he press'd hard, as one came near
With curl'd gray beard, sharp eyes, and smooth bald crown,
Slow-stepp'd, and robed in philosophic gown:
Lycius shrank closer, as they met and past,
Into his mantle, adding wings to haste,
While hurried Lamia trembled: 'Ah,' said he,
'Why do you shudder, love, so ruefully?
'Why does your tender palm dissolve in dew?'—          370
'I'm wearied,' said fair Lamia: 'tell me who
'Is that old man? I cannot bring to mind
'His features:—Lycius! wherefore did you blind
'Yourself from his quick eyes?' Lycius replied,
''Tis Apollonius sage, my trusty guide
'And good instructor; but to-night he seems
'The ghost of folly haunting my sweet dreams.'

     While yet he spake they had arrived before
A pillar'd porch, with lofty portal door,
Where hung a silver lamp, whose phosphor glow          380
Reflected in the slabbed steps below,
Mild as a star in water; for so new,
And so unsullied was the marble's hue,
So through the crystal polish, liquid fine,
Ran the dark veins, that none but feet divine
Could e'er have touch'd there. Sounds Æolian
Breath'd from the hinges, as the ample span
Of the wide doors disclos'd a place unknown
Some time to any, but those two alone,
And a few Persian mutes, who that same year          390
Were seen about the markets: none knew where
They could inhabit; the most curious
Were foil'd, who watch'd to trace them to their house:

And but the flitter-winged verse must tell,
For truth's sake, what woe afterwards befel,
'Twould humour many a heart to leave them thus,
Shut from the busy world of more incredulous.


PART II

Love in a hut, with water and a crust,
Is—Love, forgive us!—cinders, ashes, dust;
Love in a palace is perhaps at last
More grievous torment than a hermit's fast:—
That is a doubtful tale from faery land,
Hard for the non-elect to understand.
Had Lycius liv'd to hand his story down,
He might have given the moral a fresh frown,
Or clench'd it quite: but too short was their bliss
To breed distrust and hate, that make the soft voice hiss.  10
Beside, there, nightly, with terrific glare,
Love, jealous grown of so complete a pair,
Hover'd and buzz'd his wings, with fearful roar,
Above the lintel of their chamber door,
And down the passage cast a glow upon the floor.

     For all this came a ruin: side by side
They were enthroned, in the even tide,
Upon a couch, near to a curtaining
Whose airy texture, from a golden string,
Floated into the room, and let appear                    20
Unveil'd the summer heaven, blue and clear,
Betwixt two marble shafts:—there they reposed,
Where use had made it sweet, with eyelids closed,
Saving a tythe which love still open kept,
That they might see each other while they almost slept;
When from the slope side of a suburb hill,
Deafening the swallow's twitter, came a thrill
Of trumpets—Lycius started—the sounds fled,
But left a thought a-buzzing in his head.
For the first time, since first he harbour'd in          30
That purple-lined palace of sweet sin,
His spirit pass'd beyond its golden bourn
Into the noisy world almost forsworn.

The lady, ever watchful, penetrant,
Saw this with pain, so arguing a want
Of something more, more than her empery
Of joys; and she began to moan and sigh
Because he mused beyond her, knowing well
That but a moment's thought is passion's passing bell.
'Why do you sigh, fair creature?' whisper'd he:             40
'Why do you think?' return'd she tenderly:
'You have deserted me;—where am I now?
'Not in your heart while care weighs on your brow:
'No, no, you have dismiss'd me; and I go
'From your breast houseless: aye, it must be so.'
He answer'd, bending to her open eyes,
Where he was mirror'd small in paradise,
'My silver planet, both of eve and morn!
'Why will you plead yourself so sad forlorn,
'While I am striving how to fill my heart             50
'With deeper crimson, and a double smart?
'How to entangle, trammel up and snare
'Your soul in mine, and labyrinth you there
'Like the hid scent in an unbudded rose?
'Aye, a sweet kiss—you see your mighty woes.
'My thoughts! shall I unveil them? Listen then!
'What mortal hath a prize, that other men
'May be confounded and abash'd withal,
'But lets it sometimes pace abroad majestical,
'And triumph, as in thee I should rejoice             60
'Amid the hoarse alarm of Corinth's voice.
'Let my foes choke, and my friends shout afar,
'While through the thronged streets your bridal car
'Wheels round its dazzling spokes.'—The lady's cheek
Trembled; she nothing said, but, pale and meek,
Arose and knelt before him, wept a rain
Of sorrows at his words; at last with pain
Beseeching him, the while his hand she wrung,
To change his purpose. He thereat was stung,
Perverse, with stronger fancy to reclaim             70
Her wild and timid nature to his aim:
Beside, for all his love, in self despite,
Against his better self, he took delight
Luxurious in her sorrows, soft and new.

His passion, cruel grown, took on a hue
Fierce and sanguineous as 'twas possible
In one whose brow had no dark veins to swell.
Fine was the mitigated fury, like
Apollo's presence when in act to strike
The serpent—Ha, the serpent! certes, she                80
Was none. She burnt, she lov'd the tyranny,
And, all subdued, consented to the hour
When to the bridal he should lead his paramour.
Whispering in midnight silence, said the youth,
'Sure some sweet name thou hast, though, by my truth,
'I have not ask'd it, ever thinking thee
'Not mortal, but of heavenly progeny,
'As still I do. Hast any mortal name,
'Fit appellation for this dazzling frame?
'Or friends or kinsfolk on the citied earth,             90
'To share our marriage feast and nuptial mirth?'
'I have no friends,' said Lamia, 'no, not one;
'My presence in wide Corinth hardly known:
'My parents' bones are in their dusty urns
'Sepulchred, where no kindled incense burns,
'Seeing all their luckless race are dead, save me,
'And I neglect the holy rite for thee.
'Even as you list invite your many guests;
'But if, as now it seems, your vision rests
'With any pleasure on me, do not bid                     100
'Old Apollonius—from him keep me hid.'
Lycius, perplex'd at words so blind and blank,
Made close inquiry; from whose touch she shrank,
Feigning a sleep; and he to the dull shade
Of deep sleep in a moment was betray'd.

    It was the custom then to bring away
The bride from home at blushing shut of day,
Veil'd, in a chariot, heralded along
By strewn flowers, torches, and a marriage song,
With other pageants: but this fair unknown               110
Had not a friend. So being left alone,
(Lycius was gone to summon all his kin)
And knowing surely she could never win
His foolish heart from its mad pompousness,

She set herself, high-thoughted, how to dress
The misery in fit magnificence.
She did so, but 'tis doubtful how and whence
Came, and who were her subtle servitors.
About the halls, and to and from the doors,
There was a noise of wings till in short space          120
The glowing banquet-room shone with wide-arched grace.
A haunting music, sole perhaps and lone
Supportress of the faery-roof, made moan
Throughout, as fearful the whole charm might fade.
Fresh carved cedar, mimicking a glade
Of palm and plantain, met from either side,
High in the midst, in honour of the bride:
Two palms and then two plantains, and so on,
From either side their stems branch'd one to one
All down the aisled place; and beneath all          130
There ran a stream of lamps straight on from wall to wall.
So canopied, lay an untasted feast
Teeming with odours. Lamia, regal drest,
Silently paced about, and as she went,
In pale contented sort of discontent,
Mission'd her viewless servants to enrich
The fretted splendour of each nook and niche.
Between the tree-stems, marbled plain at first,
Came jasper pannels; then anon, there burst
Forth creeping imagery of slighter trees,          140
And with the larger wove in small intricacies.
Approving all, she faded at self-will,
And shut the chamber up, close, hush'd and still,
Complete and ready for the revels rude,
When dreadful guests would come to spoil her solitude.

The day appear'd, and all the gossip rout.
O senseless Lycius! Madman! wherefore flout
The silent-blessing fate, warm cloister'd hours,
And show to common eyes these secret bowers?
The herd approach'd; each guest, with busy brain,          150
Arriving at the portal, gaz'd amain,
And enter'd marveling: for they knew the street,
Remember'd it from childhood all complete
Without a gap, yet ne'er before had seen

That royal porch, that high-built fair demesne;
So in they hurried all, maz'd, curious and keen:
Save one, who look'd thereon with eye severe,
And with calm-planted steps walk'd in austere;
'Twas Apollonius: something too he laugh'd,
As though some knotty problem, that had daft          160
His patient thought, had now begun to thaw,
And solve and melt:—'twas just as he foresaw.

    He met within the murmurous vestibule
His young disciple. "'Tis no common rule,
Lycius,' said he, 'for uninvited guest
'To force himself upon you, and infest
'With an unbidden presence the bright throng
'Of younger friends; yet must I do this wrong,
'And you forgive me.' Lycius blush'd, and led
The old man through the inner doors broad-spread;      170
With reconciling words and courteous mien
Turning into sweet milk the sophist's spleen.

    Of wealthy lustre was the banquet-room,
Fill'd with pervading brilliance and perfume:
Before each lucid pannel fuming stood
A censer fed with myrrh and spiced wood,
Each by a sacred tripod held aloft,
Whose slender feet wide-swerv'd upon the soft
Wool-woofed carpets: fifty wreaths of smoke
From fifty censers their light voyage took          180
To the high roof, still mimick'd as they rose
Along the mirror'd walls by twin-clouds odorous.
Twelve sphered tables, by silk seats insphered,
High as the level of a man's breast rear'd
On libbard's paws, upheld the heavy gold
Of cups and goblets, and the store thrice told
Of Ceres' horn, and, in huge vessels, wine
Come from the gloomy tun with merry shine.
Thus loaded with a feast the tables stood,
Each shrining in the midst the image of a God.      190

    When in an antichamber every guest
Had felt the cold full sponge to pleasure press'd,
By minist'ring slaves, upon his hands and feet,

And fragrant oils with ceremony meet
Pour'd on his hair, they all mov'd to the feast
In white robes, and themselves in order placed
Around the silken couches, wondering
Whence all this mighty cost and blaze of wealth could spring.

   Soft went the music the soft air along,
While fluent Greek a vowel'd undersong          200
Kept up among the guests, discoursing low
At first, for scarcely was the wine at flow;
But when the happy vintage touch'd their brains,
Louder they talk, and louder come the strains
Of powerful instruments:—the gorgeous dyes,
The space, the splendour of the draperies,
The roof of awful richness, nectarous cheer,
Beautiful slaves, and Lamia's self, appear,
Now, when the wine has done its rosy deed,
And every soul from human trammels freed,        210
No more so strange; for merry wine, sweet wine,
Will make Elysian shades not too fair, too divine.
Soon was God Bacchus at meridian height;
Flush'd were their cheeks, and bright eyes double bright:
Garlands of every green, and every scent
From vales deflower'd, or forest-trees branch-rent,
In baskets of bright osier'd gold were brought
High as the handles heap'd, to suit the thought
Of every guest; that each, as he did please,
Might fancy-fit his brows, silk-pillow'd at his ease.    220

   What wreath for Lamia? What for Lycius?
What for the sage, old Apollonius?
Upon her aching forehead be there hung
The leaves of willow and of adder's tongue;
And for the youth, quick, let us strip for him
The thyrsus, that his watching eyes may swim
Into forgetfulness; and, for the sage,
Let spear-grass and the spiteful thistle wage
War on his temples. Do not all charms fly
At the mere touch of cold philosophy?        230
There was an awful rainbow once in heaven:
We know her woof, her texture; she is given

In the dull catalogue of common things.
Philosophy will clip an Angel's wings,
Conquer all mysteries by rule and line,
Empty the haunted air, and gnomed mine—
Unweave a rainbow, as it erewhile made
The tender-person'd Lamia melt into a shade.

By her glad Lycius sitting, in chief place,
Scarce saw in all the room another face,                    240
Till, checking his love trance, a cup he took
Full brimm'd, and opposite sent forth a look
'Cross the broad table, to beseech a glance
From his old teacher's wrinkled countenance,
And pledge him. The bald-head philosopher
Had fix'd his eye, without a twinkle or stir
Full on the alarmed beauty of the bride,
Brow-beating her fair form, and troubling her sweet pride.
Lycius then press'd her hand, with devout touch,
As pale it lay upon the rosy couch:                         250
'Twas icy, and the cold ran through his veins;
Then sudden it grew hot, and all the pains
Of an unnatural heat shot to his heart.
'Lamia, what means this? Wherefore dost thou start?
'Know'st thou that man?' Poor Lamia answer'd not.
He gaz'd into her eyes, and not a jot
Own'd they the lovelorn piteous appeal:
More, more he gaz'd: his human senses reel:
Some hungry spell that loveliness absorbs;
There was no recognition in those orbs.                     260
'Lamia!' he cried—and no soft-toned reply.
The many heard, and the loud revelry
Grew hush; the stately music no more breathes;
The myrtle sicken'd in a thousand wreaths.
By faint degrees, voice, lute, and pleasure ceased;
A deadly silence step by step increased,
Until it seem'd a horrid presence there,
And not a man but felt the terror in his hair.
'Lamia!' he shriek'd; and nothing but the shriek
With its sad echo did the silence break.                    270
'Begone, foul dream!' he cried, gazing again
In the bride's face, where now no azure vein

Wander'd on fair-spaced temples; no soft bloom
Misted the cheek; no passion to illume
The deep-recessed vision:—all was blight;
Lamia, no longer fair, there sat a deadly white.
'Shut, shut those juggling eyes, thou ruthless man!
'Turn them aside, wretch! or the righteous ban
'Of all the Gods, whose dreadful images
'Here represent their shadowy presences,                    280
'May pierce them on the sudden with the thorn
'Of painful blindness; leaving thee forlorn,
'In trembling dotage to the feeblest fright
'Of conscience, for their long offended might,
'For all thine impious proud-heart sophistries,
'Unlawful magic, and enticing lies.
'Corinthians! look upon that grey-beard wretch!
'Mark how, possess'd, his lashless eyelids stretch
'Around his demon eyes! Corinthians, see!
'My sweet bride withers at their potency.'                   290
'Fool!' said the sophist, in an under-tone
Gruff with contempt; which a death-nighing moan
From Lycius answer'd, as heart-struck and lost,
He sank supine beside the aching ghost.
'Fool! Fool!' repeated he, while his eyes still
Relented not, nor mov'd; 'from every ill
'Of life have I preserv'd thee to this day,
'And shall I see thee made a serpent's prey?'
Then Lamia breath'd death breath; the sophist's eye,
Like a sharp spear, went through her utterly,              300
Keen, cruel, perceant, stinging: she, as well
As her weak hand could any meaning tell,
Motion'd him to be silent; vainly so,
He look'd and look'd again a level—No!
'A serpent!' echoed he; no sooner said,
Than with a frightful scream she vanished:
And Lycius' arms were empty of delight,
As were his limbs of life, from that same night.
On the high couch he lay!—his friends came round—
Supported him—no pulse, or breath they found,            310
And, in its marriage robe, the heavy body wound.

# ISABELLA;

OR,

## THE POT OF BASIL

*A Story from Boccaccio*

I

FAIR Isabel, poor simple Isabel!
  Lorenzo, a young palmer in Love's eye!
They could not in the self-same mansion dwell
  Without some stir of heart, some malady;
They could not sit at meals but feel how well
  It soothed each to be the other by;
They could not, sure, beneath the same roof sleep
But to each other dream, and nightly weep.

II

With every morn their love grew tenderer,
  With every eve deeper and tenderer still;
He might not in house, field, or garden stir,
  But her full shape would all his seeing fill;
And his continual voice was pleasanter
  To her, than noise of trees or hidden rill;
Her lute-string gave an echo of his name,
She spoilt her half-done broidery with the same.

III

He knew whose gentle hand was at the latch
  Before the door had given her to his eyes;
And from her chamber-window he would catch
  Her beauty farther than the falcon spies;
And constant as her vespers would he watch,
  Because her face was turn'd to the same skies;
And with sick longing all the night outwear,
To hear her morning-step upon the stair.

IV

A whole long month of May in this sad plight
   Made their cheeks paler by the break of June:
'To-morrow will I bow to my delight,
   'To-morrow will I ask my lady's boon.'—
'O may I never see another night,
   'Lorenzo, if thy lips breathe not love's tune.'—
So spake they to their pillows; but, alas,
Honeyless days and days did he let pass;


V

Until sweet Isabella's untouch'd cheek
   Fell sick within the rose's just domain,
Fell thin as a young mother's, who doth seek
   By every lull to cool her infant's pain:
'How ill she is,' said he, 'I may not speak,
   'And yet I will, and tell my love all plain:
'If looks speak love-laws, I will drink her tears,
'And at the least 'twill startle off her cares.'


VI

So said he one fair morning, and all day
   His heart beat awfully against his side;
And to his heart he inwardly did pray
   For power to speak; but still the ruddy tide
Stifled his voice, and puls'd resolve away—
   Fever'd his high conceit of such a bride,
Yet brought him to the meekness of a child:
Alas! when passion is both meek and wild!


VII

So once more he had wak'd and anguished
   A dreary night of love and misery,
If Isabel's quick eye had not been wed
   To every symbol on his forehead high;
She saw it waxing very pale and dead,
   And straight all flush'd; so, lisped tenderly,
'Lorenzo!'—here she ceas'd her timid quest,
But in her tone and look he read the rest.

### VIII

'O Isabella, I can half perceive
  'That I may speak my grief into thine ear;
'If thou didst ever anything believe,
  'Believe how I love thee, believe how near
'My soul is to its doom: I would not grieve
  'Thy hand by unwelcome pressing, would not fear
'Thine eyes by gazing; but I cannot live
'Another night, and not my passion shrive.

### IX

'Love! thou art leading me from wintry cold,
  'Lady! thou leadest me to summer clime,
'And I must taste the blossoms that unfold
  'In its ripe warmth this gracious morning time.'
So said, his erewhile timid lips grew bold,
  And poesied with hers in dewy rhyme:
Great bliss was with them, and great happiness
Grew, like a lusty flower in June's caress.

### X

Parting they seem'd to tread upon the air,
  Twin roses by the zephyr blown apart
Only to meet again more close, and share
  The inward fragrance of each other's heart.
She, to her chamber gone, a ditty fair
  Sang, of delicious love and honey'd dart;
He with light steps went up a western hill,
And bade the sun farewell, and joy'd his fill.

### XI

All close they met again, before the dusk
  Had taken from the stars its pleasant veil,
All close they met, all eves, before the dusk
  Had taken from the stars its pleasant veil,
Close in a bower of hyacinth and musk,
  Unknown of any, free from whispering tale.
Ah! better had it been for ever so,
Than idle ears should pleasure in their woe.

XII

Were they unhappy then?—It cannot be—
 Too many tears for lovers have been shed,
Too many sighs give we to them in fee,
 Too much of pity after they are dead,
Too many doleful stories do we see,
 Whose matter in bright gold were best be read;
Except in such a page where Theseus' spouse
Over the pathless waves towards him bows.


XIII

But, for the general award of love,
 The little sweet doth kill much bitterness;
Though Dido silent is in under-grove,
 And Isabella's was a great distress,
Though young Lorenzo in warm Indian clove
 Was not embalm'd, this truth is not the less—
Even bees, the little almsmen of spring-bowers,
Know there is richest juice in poison-flowers.


XIV

With her two brothers this fair lady dwelt,
 Enriched from ancestral merchandize,
And for them many a weary hand did swelt
 In torched mines and noisy factories,
And many once proud-quiver'd loins did melt
 In blood from stinging whip;—with hollow eyes
Many all day in dazzling river stood,
To take the rich-ored driftings of the flood.


XV

For them the Ceylon diver held his breath,
 And went all naked to the hungry shark;
For them his ears gush'd blood; for them in death
 The seal on the cold ice with piteous bark
Lay full of darts; for them alone did seethe
 A thousand men in troubles wide and dark:
Half-ignorant, they turn'd an easy wheel,
That set sharp racks at work, to pinch and peel.

### XVI

Why were they proud? Because their marble founts
   Gush'd with more pride than do a wretch's tears?—
Why were they proud? Because fair orange-mounts
   Were of more soft ascent than lazar stairs?—
Why were they proud? Because red-lin'd accounts
   Were richer than the songs of Grecian years?—
Why were they proud? again we ask aloud,
Why in the name of Glory were they proud?

### XVII

Yet were these Florentines as self-retired
   In hungry pride and gainful cowardice,
As two close Hebrews in that land inspired,
   Paled in and vineyarded from beggar-spies;
The hawks of ship-mast forests—the untired
   And pannier'd mules for ducats and old lies—
Quick cat's-paws on the generous stray-away,—
Great wits in Spanish, Tuscan, and Malay.

### XVIII

How was it these same ledger-men could spy
   Fair Isabella in her downy nest?
How could they find out in Lorenzo's eye
   A straying from his toil? Hot Egypt's pest
Into their vision covetous and sly!
   How could these money-bags see east and west?—
Yet so they did—and every dealer fair
Must see behind, as doth the hunted hare.

### XIX

O eloquent and famed Boccaccio!
   Of thee we now should ask forgiving boon,
And of thy spicy myrtles as they blow,
   And of thy roses amorous of the moon,
And of thy lillies, that do paler grow
   Now they can no more hear thy ghittern's tune,
For venturing syllables that ill beseem
The quiet glooms of such a piteous theme.

XX

Grant thou a pardon here, and then the tale
    Shall move on soberly, as it is meet;
There is no other crime, no mad assail
    To make old prose in modern rhyme more sweet:
But it is done—succeed the verse or fail—
    To honour thee, and thy gone spirit greet;
To stead thee as a verse in English tongue,
An echo of thee in the north-wind sung.


XXI

These brethren having found by many signs
    What love Lorenzo for their sister had,
And how she lov'd him too, each unconfines
    His bitter thoughts to other, well nigh mad
That he, the servant of their trade designs,
    Should in their sister's love be blithe and glad,
When 'twas their plan to coax her by degrees
To some high noble and his olive-trees.


XXII

And many a jealous conference had they,
    And many times they bit their lips alone,
Before they fix'd upon a surest way
    To make the youngster for his crime atone;
And at the last, these men of cruel clay
    Cut Mercy with a sharp knife to the bone;
For they resolved in some forest dim
To kill Lorenzo, and there bury him.


XXIII

So on a pleasant morning, as he leant
    Into the sun-rise, o'er the balustrade
Of the garden-terrace, towards him they bent
    Their footing through the dews; and to him said,
'You seem there in the quiet of content,
    'Lorenzo, and we are most loth to invade
'Calm speculation; but if you are wise,
    'Bestride your steed while cold is in the skies.

XXIV

'To-day we purpose, aye, this hour we mount
  'To spur three leagues towards the Apennine;
'Come down, we pray thee, ere the hot sun count
  'His dewy rosary on the eglantine.'
Lorenzo, courteously as he was wont,
  Bow'd a fair greeting to these serpents' whine;
And went in haste, to get in readiness,
With belt, and spur, and bracing huntsman's dress.


XXV

And as he to the court-yard pass'd along,
  Each third step did he pause, and listen'd oft
If he could hear his lady's matin-song,
  Or the light whisper of her footstep soft;
And as he thus over his passion hung,
  He heard a laugh full musical aloft;
When, looking up, he saw her features bright
Smile through an in-door lattice, all delight.


XXVI

'Love, Isabel!' said he, 'I was in pain
  'Lest I should miss to bid thee a good morrow:
'Ah! what if I should lose thee, when so fain
  'I am to stifle all the heavy sorrow
'Of a poor three hours' absence? but we'll gain
  'Out of the amorous dark what day doth borrow.
'Good bye! I'll soon be back.'—'Good bye!' said she:—
And as he went she chanted merrily.


XXVII

So the two brothers and their murder'd man
  Rode past fair Florence, to where Arno's stream
Gurgles through straiten'd banks, and still doth fan
  Itself with dancing bulrush, and the bream
Keeps head against the freshets. Sick and wan
  The brothers' faces in the ford did seem,
Lorenzo's flush with love.—They pass'd the water
Into a forest quiet for the slaughter.

XXVIII

There was Lorenzo slain and buried in,
　　There in that forest did his great love cease;
Ah! when a soul doth thus its freedom win,
　　It aches in loneliness—is ill at peace
As the break-covert blood-hounds of such sin:
　　They dipp'd their swords in the water, and did tease
Their horses homeward, with convulsed spur,
Each richer by his being a murderer.


XXIX

They told their sister how, with sudden speed,
　　Lorenzo had ta'en ship for foreign lands,
Because of some great urgency and need
　　In their affairs, requiring trusty hands.
Poor Girl! put on thy stifling widow's weed,
　　And 'scape at once from Hope's accursed bands;
To-day thou wilt not see him, nor to-morrow,
And the next day will be a day of sorrow.


XXX

She weeps alone for pleasures not to be;
　　Sorely she wept until the night came on.
And then, instead of love, O misery!
　　She brooded o'er the luxury alone:
His image in the dusk she seem'd to see,
　　And to the silence made a gentle moan,
Spreading her perfect arms upon the air,
And on her couch low murmuring 'Where? O where?'


XXXI

But Selfishness, Love's cousin, held not long
　　Its fiery vigil in her single breast;
She fretted for the golden hour, and hung
　　Upon the time with feverish unrest—
Not long—for soon into her heart a throng
　　Of higher occupants, a richer zest,
Came tragic; passion not to be subdued,
And sorrow for her love in travels rude.

### XXXII

In the mid days of autumn, on their eves
   The breath of Winter comes from far away,
And the sick west continually bereaves
   Of some gold tinge, and plays a roundelay
Of death among the bushes and the leaves,
   To make all bare before he dares to stray
From his north cavern. So sweet Isabel
By gradual decay from beauty fell,

### XXXIII

Because Lorenzo came not. Oftentimes
   She ask'd her brothers, with an eye all pale,
Striving to be itself, what dungeon climes
   Could keep him off so long? They spake a tale
Time after time, to quiet her. Their crimes
   Came on them, like a smoke from Hinnom's vale;
And every night in dreams they groan'd aloud,
To see their sister in her snowy shroud.

### XXXIV

And she had died in drowsy ignorance,
   But for a thing more deadly dark than all;
It came like a fierce potion, drunk by chance,
   Which saves a sick man from the feather'd pall
For some few gasping moments; like a lance,
   Waking an Indian from his cloudy hall
With cruel pierce, and bringing him again
Sense of the gnawing fire at heart and brain.

### XXXV

It was a vision.—In the drowsy gloom,
   The dull of midnight, at her couch's foot
Lorenzo stood, and wept: the forest tomb
   Had marr'd his glossy hair which once could shoot
Lustre into the sun, and put cold doom
   Upon his lips, and taken the soft lute
From his lorn voice, and past his loamed ears
Had made a miry channel for his tears.

### XXXVI

Strange sound it was, when the pale shadow spake;
  For there was striving, in its piteous tongue,
To speak as when on earth it was awake,
  And Isabella on its music hung:
Languor there was in it, and tremulous shake,
  As in a palsied Druid's harp unstrung;
And through it moan'd a ghostly under-song,
Like hoarse night-gusts sepulchral briars among.

### XXXVII

Its eyes, though wild, were still all dewy bright
  With love, and kept all phantom fear aloof
From the poor girl by magic of their light,
  The while it did unthread the horrid woof
Of the late darken'd time,—the murderous spite
  Of pride and avarice,—the dark pine roof
In the forest,—and the sodden turfed dell,
Where, without any word, from stabs he fell.

### XXXVIII

Saying moreover, 'Isabel, my sweet!
  'Red whortle-berries droop above my head,
'And a large flint-stone weighs upon my feet;
  'Around me beeches and high chestnuts shed
'Their leaves and prickly nuts; a sheep-fold bleat
  'Comes from beyond the river to my bed:
'Go, shed one tear upon my heather-bloom,
'And it shall comfort me within the tomb.

### XXXIX

'I am a shadow now, alas! alas!
  'Upon the skirts of human-nature dwelling
'Alone: I chant alone the holy mass,
  'While little sounds of life are round me knelling,
'And glossy bees at noon do fieldward pass,
  'And many a chapel bell the hour is telling,
'Paining me through: those sounds grow strange to me,
'And thou art distant in Humanity.

XL

'I know what was, I feel full well what is,
  'And I should rage, if spirits could go mad;
'Though I forget the taste of earthly bliss,
  'That paleness warms my grave, as though I had
'A Seraph chosen from the bright abyss
  'To be my spouse: thy paleness makes me glad;
'Thy beauty grows upon me, and I feel
'A greater love through all my essence steal.'


XLI

The Spirit mourn'd 'Adieu!'—dissolv'd and left
  The atom darkness in a slow turmoil;
As when of healthful midnight sleep bereft,
  Thinking on rugged hours and fruitless toil,
We put our eyes into a pillowy cleft,
  And see the spangly gloom froth up and boil:
It made sad Isabella's eyelids ache,
And in the dawn she started up awake;


XLII

'Ha! ha!' said she, 'I knew not this hard life,
  'I thought the worst was simple misery;
'I thought some Fate with pleasure or with strife
  'Portion'd us—happy days, or else to die;
'But there is crime—a brother's bloody knife!
  'Sweet Spirit, thou hast school'd my infancy:
'I'll visit thee for this, and kiss thine eyes,
'And greet thee morn and even in the skies.'


XLIII

When the full morning came, she had devised
  How she might secret to the forest hie;
How she might find the clay, so dearly prized,
  And sing to it one latest lullaby;
How her short absence might be unsurmised,
  While she the inmost of the dream would try.
Resolv'd, she took with her an aged nurse,
And went into that dismal forest-hearse.

XLIV

See, as they creep along the river side,
  How she doth whisper to that aged Dame,
And, after looking round the champaign wide,
  Shows her a knife.—'What feverous hectic flame
'Burns in thee, child?—What good can thee betide,
  'That thou should'st smile again?'—The evening came,
And they had found Lorenzo's earthy bed;
The flint was there, the berries at his head.


XLV

Who hath not loiter'd in a green church-yard,
  And let his spirit, like a demon-mole,
Work through the clayey soil and gravel hard,
  To see scull, coffin'd bones, and funeral stole;
Pitying each form that hungry Death hath marr'd
  And filling it once more with human soul?
Ah! this is holiday to what was felt
When Isabella by Lorenzo knelt.


XLVI

She gaz'd into the fresh-thrown mould, as though
  One glance did fully all its secrets tell;
Clearly she saw, as other eyes would know
  Pale limbs at bottom of a crystal well;
Upon the murderous spot she seem'd to grow,
  Like to a native lilly of the dell:
Then with her knife, all sudden, she began
To dig more fervently than misers can.


XLVII

Soon she turn'd up a soiled glove, whereon
  Her silk had play'd in purple phantasies,
She kiss'd it with a lip more chill than stone,
  And put it in her bosom, where it dries
And freezes utterly unto the bone
  Those dainties made to still an infant's cries:
Then 'gan she work again; nor stay'd her care,
But to throw back at times her veiling hair.

### XLVIII

That old nurse stood beside her wondering,
   Until her heart felt pity to the core
At sight of such a dismal labouring,
   And so she kneeled, with her locks all hoar,
And put her lean hands to the horrid thing:
   Three hours they labour'd at this travail sore;
At last they felt the kernel of the grave,
And Isabella did not stamp and rave.

### XLIX

Ah! wherefore all this wormy circumstance?
   Why linger at the yawning tomb so long?
O for the gentleness of old Romance,
   The simple plaining of a minstrel's song!
Fair reader, at the old tale take a glance,
   For here, in truth, it doth not well belong
To speak:—O turn thee to the very tale,
And taste the music of that vision pale.

### L

With duller steel than the Perséan sword
   They cut away no formless monster's head,
But one, whose gentleness did well accord
   With death, as life. The ancient harps have said,
Love never dies, but lives, immortal Lord:
   If Love impersonate was ever dead,
Pale Isabella kiss'd it, and low moan'd.
'Twas love; cold,—dead indeed, but not dethroned.

### LI

In anxious secrecy they took it home,
   And then the prize was all for Isabel:
She calm'd its wild hair with a golden comb,
   And all around each eye's sepulchral cell
Pointed each fringed lash; the smeared loam
   With tears, as chilly as a dripping well,
She drench'd away:—and still she comb'd, and kept
Sighing all day—and still she kiss'd, and wept.

LII

Then in a silken scarf,—sweet with the dews
  Of precious flowers pluck'd in Araby,
And divine liquids come with odorous ooze
  Through the cold serpent-pipe refreshfully,—
She wrapp'd it up; and for its tomb did choose
  A garden-pot, wherein she laid it by,
And cover'd it with mould, and o'er it set
Sweet Basil, which her tears kept ever wet.

LIII

And she forgot the stars, the moon, and sun,
  And she forgot the blue above the trees,
And she forgot the dells where waters run,
  And she forgot the chilly autumn breeze;
She had no knowledge when the day was done,
  And the new morn she saw not: but in peace
Hung over her sweet Basil evermore,
And moisten'd it with tears unto the core.

LIV

And so she ever fed it with thin tears,
  Whence thick, and green, and beautiful it grew,
So that it smelt more balmy than its peers
  Of Basil-tufts in Florence; for it drew
Nurture besides, and life, from human fears,
  From the fast mouldering head there shut from view:
So that the jewel, safely casketed,
Came forth, and in perfumed leafits spread.

LV

O Melancholy, linger here awhile!
  O Music, Music, breathe despondingly!
O Echo, Echo, from some sombre isle,
  Unknown, Lethean, sigh to us—O sigh!
Spirits in grief, lift up your heads, and smile;
  Lift up your heads, sweet Spirits, heavily,
And make a pale light in your cypress glooms,
Tinting with silver wan your marble tombs.

### LVI

Moan hither, all ye syllables of woe,
  From the deep throat of sad Melpomene!
Through bronzed lyre in tragic order go,
  And touch the strings into a mystery;
Sound mournfully upon the winds and low;
  For simple Isabel is soon to be
Among the dead: She withers, like a palm
Cut by an Indian for its juicy balm.

### LVII

O leave the palm to wither by itself;
  Let not quick Winter chill its dying hour!—
It may not be—those Baälites of pelf,
  Her brethren, noted the continual shower
From her dead eyes; and many a curious elf,
  Among her kindred, wonder'd that such dower
Of youth and beauty should be thrown aside
By one mark'd out to be a Noble's bride.

### LVIII

And, furthermore, her brethren wonder'd much
  Why she sat drooping by the Basil green,
And why it flourish'd, as by magic touch;
  Greatly they wonder'd what the thing might mean:
They could not surely give belief, that such
  A very nothing would have power to wean
Her from her own fair youth, and pleasures gay,
And even remembrance of her love's delay.

### LIX

Therefore they watch'd a time when they might sift
  This hidden whim; and long they watch'd in vain:
For seldom did she go to chapel-shrift,
  And seldom felt she any hunger-pain;
And when she left, she hurried back, as swift
  As bird on wing to breast its eggs again;
And, patient as a hen-bird, sat her there
Beside her Basil, weeping through her hair.

LX

Yet they contriv'd to steal the Basil-pot,
    And to examine it in secret place;
The thing was vile with green and livid spot,
    And yet they knew it was Lorenzo's face:
The guerdon of their murder they had got,
    And so left Florence in a moment's space,
Never to turn again.—Away they went,
With blood upon their heads, to banishment.


LXI

O Melancholy, turn thine eyes away!
    O Music, Music, breathe despondingly!
O Echo, Echo, on some other day,
    From isles Lethean, sigh to us—O sigh!
Spirits of grief, sing not your 'Well-a-way!'
    For Isabel, sweet Isabel, will die;
Will die a death too lone and incomplete,
Now they have ta'en away her Basil sweet.


LXII

Piteous she look'd on dead and senseless things,
    Asking for her lost Basil amorously;
And with melodious chuckle in the strings
    Of her lorn voice, she oftentimes would cry
After the Pilgrim in his wanderings,
    To ask him where her Basil was; and why
'Twas hid from her: 'For cruel 'tis,' said she,
'To steal my Basil-pot away from me.'


LXIII

And so she pined, and so she died forlorn,
    Imploring for her Basil to the last.
No heart was there in Florence but did mourn
    In pity of her love, so overcast.
And a sad ditty of this story born
    From mouth to mouth through all the country pass'd:
Still is the burthen sung—'O cruelty,
'To steal my Basil-pot away from me!'

# THE EVE OF ST. AGNES

### I

Sᴛ. Aɢɴᴇs' Eve—Ah, bitter chill it was!
The owl, for all his feathers, was a-cold;
The hare limp'd trembling through the frozen grass,
And silent was the flock in woolly fold:
Numb were the Beadsman's fingers, while he told
His rosary, and while his frosted breath,
Like pious incense from a censer old,
Seem'd taking flight for heaven, without a death,
Past the sweet Virgin's picture, while his prayer he saith.

### II

His prayer he saith, this patient, holy man;
Then takes his lamp, and riseth from his knees,
And back returneth, meagre, barefoot, wan,
Along the chapel aisle by slow degrees:
The sculptur'd dead, on each side, seem to freeze,
Emprison'd in black, purgatorial rails:
Knights, ladies, praying in dumb orat'ries,
He passeth by; and his weak spirit fails
To think how they may ache in icy hoods and mails.

### III

Northward he turneth through a little door,
And scarce three steps, ere Music's golden tongue
Flatter'd to tears this aged man and poor;
But no—already had his deathbell rung:
The joys of all his life were said and sung:
His was harsh penance on St. Agnes' Eve:
Another way he went, and soon among
Rough ashes sat he for his soul's reprieve,
And all night kept awake, for sinners' sake to grieve.

### IV

That ancient Beadsman heard the prelude soft;
And so it chanc'd, for many a door was wide,
From hurry to and fro. Soon, up aloft,
The silver, snarling trumpets 'gan to chide:

The level chambers, ready with their pride,
Were glowing to receive a thousand guests:
The carved angels, ever eager-eyed,
Star'd, where upon their heads the cornice rests,
With hair blown back, and wings put cross-wise on their
    breasts.


V

At length burst in the argent revelry,
With plume, tiara, and all rich array,
Numerous as shadows haunting faerily
The brain, new stuff'd, in youth, with triumphs gay
Of old romance. These let us wish away,
And turn, sole-thoughted, to one Lady there,
Whose heart had brooded, all that wintry day,
On love, and wing'd St. Agnes' saintly care,
As she had heard old dames full many times declare.


VI

They told her how, upon St. Agnes' Eve,
Young virgins might have visions of delight,
And soft adorings from their loves receive
Upon the honey'd middle of the night,
If ceremonies due they did aright;
As, supperless to bed they must retire,
And couch supine their beauties, lilly white;
Nor look behind, nor sideways, but require
Of Heaven with upward eyes for all that they desire.


VII

Full of this whim was thoughtful Madeline:
The music, yearning like a God in pain,
She scarcely heard: her maiden eyes divine,
Fix'd on the floor, saw many a sweeping train
Pass by—she heeded not at all: in vain
Came many a tiptoe, amorous cavalier,
And back retir'd; not cool'd by high disdain,
But she saw not: her heart was otherwhere:
She sigh'd for Agnes' dreams, the sweetest of the year.

VIII

She danc'd along with vague, regardless eyes,
Anxious her lips, her breathing quick and short:
The hallow'd hour was near at hand: she sighs
Amid the timbrels, and the throng'd resort
Of whisperers in anger, or in sport;
'Mid looks of love, defiance, hate, and scorn,
Hoodwink'd with faery fancy; all amort,
Save to St. Agnes and her lambs unshorn,
And all the bliss to be before to-morrow morn.

IX

So, purposing each moment to retire,
She linger'd still. Meantime, across the moors,
Had come young Porphyro, with heart on fire
For Madeline. Beside the portal doors,
Buttress'd from moonlight, stands he, and implores
All saints to give him sight of Madeline,
But for one moment in the tedious hours,
That he might gaze and worship all unseen;
Perchance speak, kneel, touch, kiss—in sooth such things
    have been.

X

He ventures in: let no buzz'd whisper tell:
All eyes be muffled, or a hundred swords
Will storm his heart, Love's fev'rous citadel:
For him, those chambers held barbarian hordes,
Hyena foemen, and hot-blooded lords,
Whose very dogs would execrations howl
Against his lineage: not one breast affords
Him any mercy, in that mansion foul,
Save one old beldame, weak in body and in soul.

XI

Ah, happy chance! the aged creature came,
Shuffling along with ivory-headed wand,
To where he stood, hid from the torch's flame,
Behind a broad hall-pillar, far beyond

The sound of merriment and chorus bland:
He startled her; but soon she knew his face,
And grasp'd his fingers in her palsied hand,
Saying, 'Mercy, Porphyro! hie thee from this place:
'They are all here to-night, the whole blood-thirsty race!


XII

'Get hence! get hence! there's dwarfish Hildebrand;
'He had a fever late, and in the fit
'He cursed thee and thine, both house and land:
'Then there's that old Lord Maurice, not a whit
'More tame for his gray hairs—Alas me! flit!
'Flit like a ghost away.'—'Ah, Gossip dear,
'We're safe enough; here in this arm-chair sit,
'And tell me how'—'Good Saints! not here, not here;
'Follow me, child, or else these stones will be thy bier.'


XIII

He follow'd through a lowly arched way,
Brushing the cobwebs with his lofty plume,
And as she mutter'd 'Well-a—well-a-day!'
He found him in a little moonlight room,
Pale, lattic'd, chill, and silent as a tomb.
'Now tell me where is Madeline,' said he,
'O tell me, Angela, by the holy loom
'Which none but secret sisterhood may see,
'When they St. Agnes' wool are weaving piously.'


XIV

'St. Agnes! Ah! it is St. Agnes' Eve—
'Yet men will murder upon holy days:
'Thou must hold water in a witch's sieve,
'And be liege-lord of all the Elves and Fays,
'To venture so: it fills me with amaze
'To see thee, Porphyro!—St. Agnes' Eve!
'God's help! my lady fair the conjuror plays
'This very night: good angels her deceive!
'But let me laugh awhile, I've mickle time to grieve.'

### XV

Feebly she laugheth in the languid moon,
While Porphyro upon her face doth look,
Like puzzled urchin on an aged crone
Who keepeth clos'd a wond'rous riddle-book,
As spectacled she sits in chimney nook.
But soon his eyes grew brilliant, when she told
His lady's purpose; and he scarce could brook
Tears, at the thought of those enchantments cold,
And Madeline asleep in lap of legends old.

### XVI

Sudden a thought came like a full-blown rose,
Flushing his brow, and in his pained heart
Made purple riot: then doth he propose
A stratagem, that makes the beldame start:
'A cruel man and impious thou art:
'Sweet lady, let her pray, and sleep, and dream
'Alone with her good angels, far apart
'From wicked men like thee. Go, go!—I deem
'Thou canst not surely be the same that thou didst seem.'

### XVII

'I will not harm her, by all saints I swear,'
Quoth Porphyro: 'O may I ne'er find grace
'When my weak voice shall whisper its last prayer,
'If one of her soft ringlets I displace,
'Or look with ruffian passion in her face:
'Good Angela, believe me by these tears;
'Or I will, even in a moment's space,
'Awake, with horrid shout, my foemen's ears,
'And beard them, though they be more fang'd than wolves
      and bears.'

### XVIII

'Ah! why wilt thou affright a feeble soul?
'A poor, weak, palsy-stricken, churchyard thing,
'Whose passing-bell may ere the midnight toll;
'Whose prayers for thee, each morn and evening,

'Were never miss'd.'—Thus plaining, doth she bring
A gentler speech from burning Porphyro;
So woful, and of such deep sorrowing,
That Angela gives promise she will do
Whatever he shall wish, betide her weal or woe.


### XIX

Which was, to lead him, in close secrecy,
Even to Madeline's chamber, and there hide
Him in a closet, of such privacy
That he might see her beauty unespied,
And win perhaps that night a peerless bride,
While legion'd faeries pac'd the coverlet,
And pale enchantment held her sleepy-eyed.
Never on such a night have lovers met,
Since Merlin paid his Demon all the monstrous debt.


### XX

'It shall be as thou wishest,' said the Dame:
'All cates and dainties shall be stored there
'Quickly on this feast-night: by the tambour frame
'Her own lute thou wilt see: no time to spare,
'For I am slow and feeble, and scarce dare
'On such a catering trust my dizzy head.
'Wait here, my child, with patience; kneel in prayer
'The while: Ah! thou must needs the lady wed,
'Or may I never leave my grave among the dead.'


### XXI

So saying, she hobbled off with busy fear.
The lover's endless minutes slowly pass'd;
The dame return'd, and whisper'd in his ear
To follow her; with aged eyes aghast
From fright of dim espial. Safe at last,
Through many a dusky gallery, they gain
The maiden's chamber, silken, hush'd, and chaste;
Where Porphyro took covert, pleas'd amain.
His poor guide hurried back with agues in her brain.

### XXII

Her falt'ring hand upon the balustrade,
Old Angela was feeling for the stair,
When Madeline, St. Agnes' charmed maid,
Rose, like a mission'd spirit, unaware:
With silver taper's light, and pious care,
She turn'd, and down the aged gossip led
To a safe level matting. Now prepare,
Young Porphyro, for gazing on that bed;
She comes, she comes again, like ring-dove fray'd and fled.

### XXIII

Out went the taper as she hurried in;
Its little smoke, in pallid moonshine, died:
She clos'd the door, she panted, all akin
To spirits of the air, and visions wide:
No uttered syllable, or, woe betide!
But to her heart, her heart was voluble,
Paining with eloquence her balmy side;
As though a tongueless nightingale should swell
Her throat in vain, and die, heart-stifled, in her dell.

### XXIV

A casement high and triple-arch'd there was,
All garlanded with carven imag'ries
Of fruits, and flowers, and bunches of knot-grass,
And diamonded with panes of quaint device,
Innumerable of stains and splendid dyes,
As are the tiger-moth's deep-damask'd wings;
And in the midst, 'mong thousand heraldries,
And twilight saints, and dim emblazonings,
A shielded scutcheon blush'd with blood of queens and kings.

### XXV

Full on this casement shone the wintry moon,
And threw warm gules on Madeline's fair breast,
As down she knelt for heaven's grace and boon;
Rose-bloom fell on her hands, together prest,
And on her silver cross soft amethyst,

And on her hair a glory, like a saint:
She seem'd a splendid angel, newly drest,
Save wings, for heaven:—Porphyro grew faint:
She knelt, so pure a thing, so free from mortal taint.


XXVI

Anon his heart revives: her vespers done,
Of all its wreathed pearls her hair she frees;
Unclasps her warmed jewels one by one;
Loosens her fragrant boddice; by degrees
Her rich attire creeps rustling to her knees:
Half-hidden, like a mermaid in sea-weed,
Pensive awhile she dreams awake, and sees,
In fancy, fair St. Agnes in her bed,
But dares not look behind, or all the charm is fled.


XXVII

Soon, trembling in her soft and chilly nest,
In sort of wakeful swoon, perplex'd she lay,
Until the poppied warmth of sleep oppress'd
Her soothed limbs, and soul fatigued away;
Flown, like a thought, until the morrow-day;
Blissfully haven'd both from joy and pain;
Clasp'd like a missal where swart Paynims pray;
Blinded alike from sunshine and from rain,
As though a rose should shut, and be a bud again.


XXVIII

Stol'n to this paradise, and so entranced,
Porphyro gazed upon her empty dress,
And listen'd to her breathing, if it chanced
To wake into a slumberous tenderness;
Which when he heard, that minute did he bless,
And breath'd himself: then from the closet crept,
Noiseless as fear in a wide wilderness,
And over the hush'd carpet, silent, stept,
And 'tween the curtains peep'd, where, lo!—how fast she
    slept.

### XXIX

Then by the bed-side, where the faded moon
Made a dim, silver twilight, soft he set
A table, and, half anguish'd, threw thereon
A cloth of woven crimson, gold, and jet:—
O for some drowsy Morphean amulet!
The boisterous, midnight, festive clarion,
The kettle-drum, and far-heard clarinet,
Affray his ears, though but in dying tone:—
The hall door shuts again, and all the noise is gone.

### XXX

And still she slept an azure-lidded sleep,
In blanched linen, smooth, and lavender'd,
While he from forth the closet brought a heap
Of candied apple, quince, and plum, and gourd;
With jellies soother than the creamy curd,
And lucent syrops, tinct with cinnamon;
Manna and dates, in argosy transferr'd
From Fez; and spiced dainties, every one,
From silken Samarcand to cedar'd Lebanon.

### XXXI

These delicates he heap'd with glowing hand
On golden dishes and in baskets bright
Of wreathed silver: sumptuous they stand
In the retired quiet of the night,
Filling the chilly room with perfume light.—
'And now, my love, my seraph fair, awake!
'Thou art my heaven, and I thine eremite:
'Open thine eyes, for meek St. Agnes' sake,
'Or I shall drowse beside thee, so my soul doth ache.'

### XXXII

Thus whispering, his warm, unnerved arm
Sank in her pillow. Shaded was her dream
By the dusk curtains:—'twas a midnight charm
Impossible to melt as iced stream:

The lustrous salvers in the moonlight gleam;
Broad golden fringe upon the carpet lies:
It seem'd he never, never could redeem
From such a stedfast spell his lady's eyes;
So mus'd awhile, entoil'd in woofed phantasies.


### XXXIII

Awakening up, he took her hollow lute,—
Tumultuous,—and, in chords that tenderest be,
He play'd an ancient ditty, long since mute,
In Provence call'd, 'La belle dame sans mercy:'
Close to her ear touching the melody;—
Wherewith disturb'd, she utter'd a soft moan:
He ceased—she panted quick—and suddenly
Her blue affrayed eyes wide open shone:
Upon his knees he sank, pale as smooth-sculptured stone.


### XXXIV

Her eyes were open, but she still beheld,
Now wide awake, the vision of her sleep:
There was a painful change, that nigh expell'd
The blisses of her dream so pure and deep
At which fair Madeline began to weep,
And moan forth witless words with many a sigh;
While still her gaze on Porphyro would keep;
Who knelt, with joined hands and piteous eye,
Fearing to move or speak, she look'd so dreamingly.


### XXXV

'Ah, Porphyro!' said she, 'but even now
'Thy voice was at sweet tremble in mine ear,
'Made tuneable with every sweetest vow;
'And those sad eyes were spiritual and clear:
'How chang'd thou art! how pallid, chill, and drear!
'Give me that voice again, my Porphyro,
'Those looks immortal, those complainings dear!
'Oh leave me not in this eternal woe,
'For if thou diest, my Love, I know not where to go.'

XXXVI

Beyond a mortal man impassion'd far
At these voluptuous accents, he arose,
Ethereal, flush'd, and like a throbbing star
Seen mid the sapphire heaven's deep repose;
Into her dream he melted, as the rose
Blendeth its odour with the violet,—
Solution sweet: meantime the frost-wind blows
Like Love's alarum pattering the sharp sleet
Against the window-panes; St. Agnes' moon hath set.


XXXVII

'Tis dark: quick pattereth the flaw-blown sleet:
'This is no dream, my bride, my Madeline!'
'Tis dark: the iced gusts still rave and beat:
'No dream, alas! alas! and woe is mine!
'Porphyro will leave me here to fade and pine.—
'Cruel! what traitor could thee hither bring?
'I curse not, for my heart is lost in thine,
'Though thou forsakest a deceived thing;—
'A dove forlorn and lost with sick unpruned wing.'


XXXVIII

'My Madeline! sweet dreamer! lovely bride!
'Say, may I be for aye thy vassal blest?
'Thy beauty's shield, heart-shap'd and vermeil dyed?
'Ah, silver shrine, here will I take my rest
'After so many hours of toil and quest,
'A famish'd pilgrim,—sav'd by miracle.
'Though I have found, I will not rob thy nest
'Saving of thy sweet self; if thou think'st well
'To trust, fair Madeline, to no rude infidel.


XXXIX

'Hark! 'tis an elfin-storm from faery land,
'Of haggard seeming, but a boon indeed:
'Arise—arise! the morning is at hand;—
'The bloated wassaillers will never heed:—

'Let us away, my love, with happy speed;
'There are no ears to hear, or eyes to see,—
'Drown'd all in Rhenish and the sleepy mead:
'Awake! arise! my love, and fearless be,
'For o'er the southern moors I have a home for thee.'


### XL

She hurried at his words, beset with fears,
For there were sleeping dragons all around,
At glaring watch, perhaps, with ready spears—
Down the wide stairs a darkling way they found.—
In all the house was heard no human sound.
A chain-droop'd lamp was flickering by each door;
The arras, rich with horseman, hawk, and hound,
Flutter'd in the besieging wind's uproar;
And the long carpets rose along the gusty floor.


### XLI

They glide, like phantoms, into the wide hall;
Like phantoms, to the iron porch, they glide;
Where lay the Porter, in uneasy sprawl,
With a huge empty flaggon by his side:
The wakeful bloodhound rose, and shook his hide,
But his sagacious eye an inmate owns:
By one, and one, the bolts full easy slide:—
The chains lie silent on the footworn stones;—
The key turns, and the door upon its hinges groans.


### XLII

And they are gone: aye, ages long ago
These lovers fled away into the storm.
That night the Baron dreamt of many a woe,
And all his warrior-guests, with shade and form
Of witch, and demon, and large coffin-worm,
Were long be-nightmar'd. Angela the old
Died palsy-twitch'd, with meagre face deform;
The Beadsman, after thousand aves told,
For aye unsought for slept among his ashes cold.

# POEMS

## ODE TO A NIGHTINGALE

### I

My heart aches, and a drowsy numbness pains
  My sense, as though of hemlock I had drunk,
Or emptied some dull opiate to the drains
  One minute past, and Lethe-wards had sunk:
'Tis not through envy of thy happy lot,
  But being too happy in thine happiness,—
    That thou, light-winged Dryad of the trees,
      In some melodious plot
  Of beechen green, and shadows numberless,
    Singest of summer in full-throated ease.

### II

O, for a draught of vintage! that hath been
  Cool'd a long age in the deep-delved earth,
Tasting of Flora and the country green,
  Dance, and Provençal song, and sunburnt mirth!
O for a beaker full of the warm South,
  Full of the true, the blushful Hippocrene,
    With beaded bubbles winking at the brim,
      And purple-stained mouth;
  That I might drink, and leave the world unseen,
    And with thee fade away into the forest dim:

### III

Fade far away, dissolve, and quite forget
  What thou among the leaves hast never known,
The weariness, the fever, and the fret
  Here, where men sit and hear each other groan;
Where palsy shakes a few, sad, last gray hairs,
  Where youth grows pale, and spectre-thin, and dies;
    Where but to think is to be full of sorrow
      And leaden-eyed despairs,
    Where Beauty cannot keep her lustrous eyes,
      Or new Love pine at them beyond to-morrow.

IV

Away! away! for I will fly to thee,
 Not charioted by Bacchus and his pards,
But on the viewless wings of Poesy,
 Though the dull brain perplexes and retards:
Already with thee! tender is the night,
 And haply the Queen-Moon is on her throne,
  Cluster'd around by all her starry Fays;
   But here there is no light,
 Save what from heaven is with the breezes blown
  Through verdurous glooms and winding mossy ways.


V

I cannot see what flowers are at my feet,
 Nor what soft incense hangs upon the boughs,
But, in embalmed darkness, guess each sweet
 Wherewith the seasonable month endows
The grass, the thicket, and the fruit-tree wild;
 White hawthorn, and the pastoral eglantine;
  Fast fading violets cover'd up in leaves;
   And mid-May's eldest child,
 The coming musk-rose, full of dewy wine,
  The murmurous haunt of flies on summer eves.


VI

Darkling I listen; and, for many a time
 I have been half in love with easeful Death,
Call'd him soft names in many a mused rhyme,
 To take into the air my quiet breath;
Now more than ever seems it rich to die,
 To cease upon the midnight with no pain,
  While thou art pouring forth thy soul abroad
   In such an ecstasy!
 Still wouldst thou sing, and I have ears in vain—
  To thy high requiem become a sod.


VII

Thou wast not born for death, immortal Bird!
 No hungry generations tread thee down;
The voice I hear this passing night was heard
 In ancient days by emperor and clown:

Perhaps the self-same song that found a path
　　Through the sad heart of Ruth, when, sick for home,
　　　She stood in tears amid the alien corn;
　　　　The same that oft-times hath
　　Charm'd magic casements, opening on the foam
　　Of perilous seas, in faery lands forlorn.


### VIII

Forlorn! the very word is like a bell
　　To toll me back from thee to my sole self!
Adieu! the fancy cannot cheat so well
　　As she is fam'd to do, deceiving elf.
Adieu! adieu! thy plaintive anthem fades
　　Past the near meadows, over the still stream,
　　　Up the hill-side; and now 'tis buried deep
　　　　In the next valley-glades:
　　Was it a vision, or a waking dream?
　　Fled is that music:—Do I wake or sleep?


## ODE ON A GRECIAN URN

### I

Thou still unravish'd bride of quietness,
　　Thou foster-child of silence and slow time,
Sylvan historian, who canst thus express
　　A flowery tale more sweetly than our rhyme:
What leaf-fring'd legend haunts about thy shape
　　Of deities or mortals, or of both,
　　　In Tempe or the dales of Arcady?
　　What men or gods are these? What maidens loth?
What mad pursuit? What struggle to escape?
　　　What pipes and timbrels? What wild ecstasy?


### II

Heard melodies are sweet, but those unheard
　　Are sweeter; therefore, ye soft pipes, play on;
Not to the sensual ear, but, more endear'd,
　　Pipe to the spirit ditties of no tone:

Fair youth, beneath the trees, thou canst not leave
    Thy song, nor ever can those trees be bare;
        Bold Lover, never, never canst thou kiss,
Though winning near the goal—yet, do not grieve;
    She cannot fade, though thou hast not thy bliss,
        For ever wilt thou love, and she be fair!

### III

Ah, happy, happy boughs! that cannot shed
    Your leaves, nor ever bid the Spring adieu;
And, happy melodist, unwearied,
    For ever piping songs for ever new;
More happy love! more happy, happy love!
    For ever warm and still to be enjoy'd,
        For ever panting, and for ever young;
All breathing human passion far above,
    That leaves a heart high-sorrowful and cloy'd,
        A burning forehead, and a parching tongue.

### IV

Who are these coming to the sacrifice?
    To what green altar, O mysterious priest,
Lead'st thou that heifer lowing at the skies,
    And all her silken flanks with garlands drest?
What little town by river or sea shore,
    Or mountain-built with peaceful citadel,
        Is emptied of this folk, this pious morn?
And, little town, thy streets for evermore
    Will silent be; and not a soul to tell
        Why thou art desolate, can e'er return.

### V

O Attic shape! Fair attitude! with brede
    Of marble men and maidens overwrought,
With forest branches and the trodden weed;
    Thou, silent form, dost tease us out of thought
As doth eternity: Cold Pastoral!
    When old age shall this generation waste,
        Thou shalt remain, in midst of other woe
Than ours, a friend to man, to whom thou say'st,
    'Beauty is truth, truth beauty,'—that is all
        Ye know on earth, and all ye need to know.

## ODE TO PSYCHE

O GODDESS! hear these tuneless numbers, wrung
  By sweet enforcement and remembrance dear,
And pardon that thy secrets should be sung
  Even into thine own soft-conched ear:
Surely I dreamt to-day, or did I see
  The winged Psyche with awaken'd eyes?
I wander'd in a forest thoughtlessly,
  And, on the sudden, fainting with surprise,
Saw two fair creatures, couched side by side
    In deepest grass, beneath the whisp'ring roof     10
    Of leaves and trembled blossoms, where there ran
        A brooklet, scarce espied:


'Mid hush'd, cool-rooted flowers, fragrant-eyed,
  Blue, silver-white, and budded Tyrian,
They lay calm-breathing on the bedded grass;
  Their arms embraced, and their pinions too;
  Their lips touch'd not, but had not bade adieu,
As if disjoined by soft-handed slumber,
And ready still past kisses to outnumber
    At tender eye-dawn of aurorean love:     20
        The winged boy I knew;
  But who wast thou, O happy, happy dove?
        His Psyche true!


O latest born and loveliest vision far
  Of all Olympus' faded hierarchy!
Fairer than Phœbe's sapphire-region'd star,
  Or Vesper, amorous glow-worm of the sky;
Fairer than these, though temple thou hast none,
    Nor altar heap'd with flowers;
Nor virgin-choir to make delicious moan     30
    Upon the midnight hours;
No voice, no lute, no pipe, no incense sweet
  From chain-swung censer teeming;
No shrine, no grove, no oracle, no heat
  Of pale-mouth'd prophet dreaming.

O brightest! though too late for antique vows,
   Too, too late for the fond believing lyre,
When holy were the haunted forest boughs,
   Holy the air, the water, and the fire;
Yet even in these days so far retir'd          40
   From happy pieties, thy lucent fans,
     Fluttering among the faint Olympians,
I see, and sing, by my own eyes inspir'd.
So let me be thy choir, and make a moan
        Upon the midnight hours;
Thy voice, thy lute, thy pipe, thy incense sweet
   From swinged censer teeming;
Thy shrine, thy grove, thy oracle, thy heat
   Of pale-mouth'd prophet dreaming.


Yes, I will be thy priest, and build a fane     50
   In some untrodden region of my mind,
Where branched thoughts, new grown with pleasant pain,
   Instead of pines shall murmur in the wind:
Far, far around shall those dark-cluster'd trees
   Fledge the wild-ridged mountains steep by steep;
And there by zephyrs, streams, and birds, and bees,
   The moss-lain Dryads shall be lull'd to sleep;
And in the midst of this wide quietness
A rosy sanctuary will I dress
With the wreath'd trellis of a working brain,     60
   With buds, and bells, and stars without a name,
With all the gardener Fancy e'er could feign,
   Who breeding flowers, will never breed the same:
And there shall be for thee all soft delight
   That shadowy thought can win,
A bright torch, and a casement ope at night,
   To let the warm Love in!


### FANCY

Ever let the fancy roam,
Pleasure never is at home:
At a touch sweet Pleasure melteth,
Like to bubbles when rain pelteth;

Then let winged Fancy wander
Through the thought still spread beyond her:
Open wide the mind's cage-door,
She'll dart forth, and cloudward soar.
O sweet Fancy! let her loose;
Summer's joys are spoilt by use,                    10
And the enjoying of the Spring
Fades as does its blossoming;
Autumn's red-lipp'd fruitage too,
Blushing through the mist and dew,
Cloys with tasting: What do then?
Sit thee by the ingle, when
The sear faggot blazes bright,
Spirit of a winter's night;
When the soundless earth is muffled,
And the caked snow is shuffled                      20
From the ploughboy's heavy shoon;
When the Night doth meet the Noon
In a dark conspiracy
To banish Even from her sky.
Sit thee there, and send abroad,
With a mind self-overaw'd,
Fancy, high-commission'd:—send her!
She has vassals to attend her:
She will bring, in spite of frost,
Beauties that the earth hath lost;                  30
She will bring thee, all together,
All delights of summer weather;
All the buds and bells of May,
From dewy sward or thorny spray;
All the heaped Autumn's wealth,
With a still, mysterious stealth:
She will mix these pleasures up
Like three fit wines in a cup,
And thou shalt quaff it:—thou shalt hear
Distant harvest-carols clear;                       40
Rustle of the reaped corn;
Sweet birds antheming the morn:
And, in the same moment—hark!
'Tis the early April lark,
Or the rooks, with busy caw,

Foraging for sticks and straw.
Thou shalt, at one glance, behold
The daisy and the marigold;
White-plum'd lillies, and the first
Hedge-grown primrose that hath burst;      50
Shaded hyacinth, alway
Sapphire queen of the mid-May;
And every leaf, and every flower
Pearled with the self-same shower.
Thou shalt see the field-mouse peep
Meagre from its celled sleep;
And the snake all winter-thin
Cast on sunny bank its skin;
Freckled nest-eggs thou shalt see
Hatching in the hawthorn-tree,      60
When the hen-bird's wing doth rest
Quiet on her mossy nest;
Then the hurry and alarm
When the bee-hive casts its swarm;
Acorns ripe down-pattering,
While the autumn breezes sing.

Oh, sweet Fancy! let her loose;
Every thing is spoilt by use:
Where's the cheek that doth not fade,
Too much gaz'd at? Where's the maid      70
Whose lip mature is ever new?
Where's the eye, however blue,
Doth not weary? Where's the face
One would meet in every place?
Where's the voice, however soft,
One would hear so very oft?
At a touch sweet Pleasure melteth
Like to bubbles when rain pelteth.
Let, then, winged Fancy find
Thee a mistress to thy mind:      80
Dulcet-eyed as Ceres' daughter,
Ere the God of Torment taught her
How to frown and how to chide;
With a waist and with a side
White as Hebe's, when her zone

Slipt its golden clasp, and down
Fell her kirtle to her feet,
While she held the goblet sweet,
And Jove grew languid.—Break the mesh
Of the Fancy's silken leash;                                90
Quickly break her prison-string
And such joys as these she'll bring.—
Let the winged Fancy roam,
Pleasure never is at home.


## ODE

BARDS of Passion and of Mirth,
Ye have left your souls on earth!
Have ye souls in heaven too,
Double lived in regions new?
Yes, and those of heaven commune
With the spheres of sun and moon;
With the noise of fountains wond'rous,
And the parle of voices thund'rous;
With the whisper of heaven's trees
And one another, in soft ease                                10
Seated on Elysian lawns
Brows'd by none but Dian's fawns;
Underneath large blue-bells tented,
Where the daisies are rose-scented,
And the rose herself has got
Perfume which on earth is not;
Where the nightingale doth sing
Not a senseless, tranced thing,
But divine melodious truth;
Philosophic numbers smooth;                                20
Tales and golden histories
Of heaven and its mysteries.

Thus ye live on high, and then
On the earth ye live again;
And the souls ye left behind you
Teach us, here, the way to find you,
Where your other souls are joying,
Never slumber'd, never cloying.

Here, your earth-born souls still speak
To mortals, of their little week;                    30
Of their sorrows and delights;
Of their passions and their spites;
Of their glory and their shame;
What doth strengthen and what maim.
Thus ye teach us, every day,
Wisdom, though fled far away.


Bards of Passion and of Mirth,
Ye have left your souls on earth!
Ye have souls in heaven too,
Double-lived in regions new!                         40


## LINES ON THE MERMAID TAVERN

SOULS of Poets dead and gone,
What Elysium have ye known,
Happy field or mossy cavern,
Choicer than the Mermaid Tavern?
Have ye tippled drink more fine
Than mine host's Canary wine?
Or are fruits of Paradise
Sweeter than those dainty pies
Of venison? O generous food!
Drest as though bold Robin Hood          10
Would, with his maid Marian,
Sup and bowse from horn and can.


I have heard that on a day
Mine host's sign-board flew away,
Nobody knew whither, till
An astrologer's old quill
To a sheepskin gave the story,
Said he saw you in your glory,
Underneath a new old sign
Sipping beverage divine,                             20
And pledging with contented smack
The Mermaid in the Zodiac.

Souls of Poets dead and gone,
What Elysium have ye known,
Happy field or mossy cavern,
Choicer than the Mermaid Tavern?

## ROBIN HOOD

### TO A FRIEND

No! those days are gone away,
And their hours are old and gray,
And their minutes buried all
Under the down-trodden pall
Of the leaves of many years:
Many times have winter's shears,
Frozen North, and chilling East,
Sounded tempests to the feast
Of the forest's whispering fleeces,
Since men knew nor rent nor leases.          10

No, the bugle sounds no more,
And the twanging bow no more;
Silent is the ivory shrill
Past the heath and up the hill;
There is no mid-forest laugh,
Where lone Echo gives the half
To some wight, amaz'd to hear
Jesting, deep in forest drear.

On the fairest time of June
You may go, with sun or moon,          20
Or the seven stars to light you,
Or the polar ray to right you;
But you never may behold
Little John, or Robin bold;
Never one, of all the clan,
Thrumming on an empty can
Some old hunting ditty, while
He doth his green way beguile
To fair hostess Merriment,
Down beside the pasture Trent;          30
For he left the merry tale
Messenger for spicy ale.

Gone, the merry morris din;
Gone, the song of Gamelyn;
Gone, the tough-belted outlaw
Idling in the 'grenè shawe';
All are gone away and past!
And if Robin should be cast
Sudden from his turfed grave,
And if Marian should have                    40
Once again her forest days,
She would weep, and he would craze:
He would swear, for all his oaks,
Fall'n beneath the dockyard strokes,
Have rotted on the briny seas;
She would weep that her wild bees
Sang not to her—strange! that honey
Can't be got without hard money!

So it is: yet let us sing,
Honour to the old bow-string!                50
Honour to the bugle-horn!
Honour to the woods unshorn!
Honour to the Lincoln green!
Honour to the archer keen!
Honour to tight little John,
And the horse he rode upon!
Honour to bold Robin Hood,
Sleeping in the underwood!
Honour to maid Marian,
And to all the Sherwood-clan!                60
Though their days have hurried by
Let us two a burden try.


## TO AUTUMN

### I

SEASON of mists and mellow fruitfulness,
  Close bosom-friend of the maturing sun;
Conspiring with him how to load and bless
  With fruit the vines that round the thatch-eves run;

To bend with apples the moss'd cottage-trees,
  And fill all fruit with ripeness to the core;
    To swell the gourd, and plump the hazel shells
  With a sweet kernel; to set budding more,
And still more, later flowers for the bees,
Until they think warm days will never cease,
    For Summer has o'er-brimm'd their clammy cells.

II

Who hath not seen thee oft amid thy store?
  Sometimes whoever seeks abroad may find
Thee sitting careless on a granary floor,
  Thy hair soft-lifted by the winnowing wind;
Or on a half-reap'd furrow sound asleep,
  Drows'd with the fume of poppies, while thy hook
    Spares the next swath and all its twined flowers:
And sometimes like a gleaner thou dost keep
  Steady thy laden head across a brook;
  Or by a cyder-press, with patient look,
    Thou watchest the last oozings hours by hours.

III

Where are the songs of Spring? Ay, where are they?
  Think not of them, thou hast thy music too,—
While barred clouds bloom the soft-dying day,
  And touch the stubble-plains with rosy hue;
Then in a wailful choir the small gnats mourn
  Among the river sallows, borne aloft
    Or sinking as the light wind lives or dies;
And full-grown lambs loud bleat from hilly bourn;
  Hedge-crickets sing; and now with treble soft
  The red-breast whistles from a garden-croft;
    And gathering swallows twitter in the skies.

## ODE ON MELANCHOLY

I

No, no, go not to Lethe, neither twist
  Wolf's-bane, tight-rooted, for its poisonous wine;
Nor suffer thy pale forehead to be kiss'd
  By nightshade, ruby grape of Proserpine;

Make not your rosary of yew-berries,
  Nor let the beetle, nor the death-moth be
    Your mournful Psyche, nor the downy owl
A partner in your sorrow's mysteries;
  For shade to shade will come too drowsily,
    And drown the wakeful anguish of the soul.


II

But when the melancholy fit shall fall
  Sudden from heaven like a weeping cloud,
That fosters the droop-headed flowers all,
  And hides the green hill in an April shroud;
Then glut thy sorrow on a morning rose,
  Or on the rainbow of the salt sand-wave,
    Or on the wealth of globed peonies;
Or if thy mistress some rich anger shows,
  Emprison her soft hand, and let her rave,
    And feed deep, deep upon her peerless eyes.


III

She dwells with Beauty—Beauty that must die;
  And Joy, whose hand is ever at his lips
Bidding adieu; and aching Pleasure nigh,
  Turning to Poison while the bee-mouth sips:
Ay, in the very temple of delight
  Veil'd Melancholy has her sovran shrine,
    Though seen of none save him whose strenuous **tongue**
Can burst Joy's grape against his palate fine;
His soul shall taste the sadness of her might,
    And be among her cloudy trophies hung.

# HYPERION

A FRAGMENT

## BOOK I

D EEP in the shady sadness of a vale
Far sunken from the healthy breath of morn,
Far from the fiery noon, and eve's one star,
Sat gray-hair'd Saturn, quiet as a stone,
Still as the silence round about his lair;
Forest on forest hung about his head
Like cloud on cloud. No stir of air was there,
Not so much life as on a summer's day
Robs not one light seed from the feather'd grass,
But where the dead leaf fell, there did it rest.          10
A stream went voiceless by, still deadened more
By reason of his fallen divinity
Spreading a shade: the Naiad 'mid her reeds
Press'd her cold finger closer to her lips.

Along the margin-sand large foot-marks went,
No further than to where his feet had stray'd,
And slept there since. Upon the sodden ground
His old right hand lay nerveless, listless, dead,
Unsceptred; and his realmless eyes were closed;
While his bow'd head seem'd list'ning to the Earth,     20
His ancient mother, for some comfort yet.

It seem'd no force could wake him from his place;
But there came one, who with a kindred hand
Touch'd his wide shoulders, after bending low
With reverence, though to one who knew it not.
She was a Goddess of the infant world;
By her in stature the tall Amazon
Had stood a pigmy's height: she would have ta'en
Achilles by the hair and bent his neck;
Or with a finger stay'd Ixion's wheel.                  30
Her face was large as that of Memphian sphinx,
Pedestal'd haply in a palace court,
When sages look'd to Egypt for their lore.
But oh! how unlike marble was that face:

How beautiful, if sorrow had not made
Sorrow more beautiful than Beauty's self.
There was a listening fear in her regard,
As if calamity had but begun;
As if the vanward clouds of evil days
Had spent their malice, and the sullen rear                    40
Was with its stored thunder labouring up.
One hand she press'd upon that aching spot
Where beats the human heart, as if just there,
Though an immortal, she felt cruel pain:
The other upon Saturn's bended neck
She laid, and to the level of his ear
Leaning with parted lips, some words she spake
In solemn tenour and deep organ tone:
Some mourning words, which in our feeble tongue
Would come in these like accents; O how frail                  50
To that large utterance of the early Gods!
'Saturn, look up!—though wherefore, poor old King?
'I have no comfort for thee, no not one:
'I cannot say, "O wherefore sleepest thou?"
'For heaven is parted from thee, and the earth
'Knows thee not, thus afflicted, for a God;
'And ocean too, with all its solemn noise,
'Has from thy sceptre pass'd; and all the air
'Is emptied of thine hoary majesty.
'Thy thunder, conscious of the new command,                    60
'Rumbles reluctant o'er our fallen house;
'And thy sharp lightning in unpractis'd hands
'Scorches and burns our once serene domain.
'O aching time! O moments big as years!
'All as ye pass swell out the monstrous truth,
'And press it so upon our weary griefs
'That unbelief has not a space to breathe.
'Saturn, sleep on:—O thoughtless, why did I
'Thus violate thy slumbrous solitude?
'Why should I ope thy melancholy eyes?                         70
'Saturn, sleep on! while at thy feet I weep.'

   As when, upon a tranced summer-night,
Those green-rob'd senators of mighty woods,
Tall oaks, branch-charmed by the earnest stars,

Dream, and so dream all night without a stir,
Save from one gradual solitary gust
Which comes upon the silence, and dies off,
As if the ebbing air had but one wave;
So came these words and went; the while in tears
She touch'd her fair large forehead to the ground,      80

Just where her falling hair might be outspread
A soft and silken mat for Saturn's feet.
One moon, with alteration slow, had shed
Her silver seasons four upon the night,
And still these two were postured motionless,
Like natural sculpture in cathedral cavern;
The frozen God still couchant on the earth,
And the sad Goddess weeping at his feet:
Until at length old Saturn lifted up
His faded eyes, and saw his kingdom gone,      90
And all the gloom and sorrow of the place,
And that fair kneeling Goddess; and then spake,
As with a palsied tongue, and while his beard
Shook horrid with such aspen-malady:
'O tender spouse of gold Hyperion,
'Thea, I feel thee ere I see thy face;
'Look up, and let me see our doom in it;
'Look up, and tell me if this feeble shape
'Is Saturn's; tell me, if thou hear'st the voice
'Of Saturn; tell me, if this wrinkling brow,      100
'Naked and bare of its great diadem,
'Peers like the front of Saturn. Who had power
'To make me desolate? whence came the strength?
'How was it nurtur'd to such bursting forth,
'While Fate seem'd strangled in my nervous grasp?
'But it is so; and I am smother'd up,
'And buried from all godlike exercise
'Of influence benign on planets pale,
'Of admonitions to the winds and seas,
'Of peaceful sway above man's harvesting,      110
'And all those acts which Deity supreme
'Doth ease its heart of love in.—I am gone
'Away from my own bosom: I have left
'My strong identity, my real self,

'Somewhere between the throne, and where I sit
'Here on this spot of earth. Search, Thea, search!
'Open thine eyes eterne, and sphere them round
'Upon all space: space starr'd, and lorn of light;
'Space region'd with life-air; and barren void;
'Spaces of fire, and all the yawn of hell.—                    120
'Search, Thea, search! and tell me, if thou seest
'A certain shape or shadow, making way
'With wings or chariot fierce to repossess
'A heaven he lost erewhile: it must—it must
'Be of ripe progress—Saturn must be King.
'Yes, there must be a golden victory;
'There must be Gods thrown down, and trumpets blown
'Of triumph calm, and hymns of festival
'Upon the gold clouds metropolitan,
'Voices of soft proclaim, and silver stir                     130
'Of strings in hollow shells; and there shall be
'Beautiful things made new, for the surprise
'Of the sky-children; I will give command:
'Thea! Thea! Thea! where is Saturn?'

    This passion lifted him upon his feet,
And made his hands to struggle in the air,
His Druid locks to shake and ooze with sweat,
His eyes to fever out, his voice to cease.
He stood, and heard not Thea's sobbing deep;
A little time, and then again he snatch'd               140
Utterance thus.—'But cannot I create?
'Cannot I form? Cannot I fashion forth
'Another world, another universe,
'To overbear and crumble this to naught?
'Where is another chaos? Where?'—That word
Found way unto Olympus, and made quake
The rebel three.—Thea was startled up,
And in her bearing was a sort of hope,
As thus she quick-voic'd spake, yet full of awe.
'This cheers our fallen house: come to our friends,    150
'O Saturn! come away, and give them heart;
'I know the covert, for thence came I hither.'
Thus brief; then with beseeching eyes she went
With backward footing through the shade a space:

He follow'd, and she turn'd to lead the way
Through aged boughs, that yielded like the mist
Which eagles cleave upmounting from their nest.

Meanwhile in other realms big tears were shed,
More sorrow like to this, and such like woe,
Too huge for mortal tongue or pen of scribe:          160
The Titans fierce, self-hid, or prison-bound,
Groan'd for the old allegiance once more,
And listen'd in sharp pain for Saturn's voice.
But one of the whole mammoth-brood still kept
His sov'reignty, and rule, and majesty;—
Blazing Hyperion on his orbed fire
Still sat, still snuff'd the incense, teeming up
From man to the sun's God; yet unsecure:
For as among us mortals omens drear
Fright and perplex, so also shuddered he—          170
Not at dog's howl, or gloom-bird's hated screech,
Or the familiar visiting of one
Upon the first toll of his passing-bell,
Or prophesyings of the midnight lamp;
But horrors, portion'd to a giant nerve,
Oft made Hyperion ache. His palace bright
Bastion'd with pyramids of glowing gold,
And touch'd with shade of bronzed obelisks,
Glar'd a blood-red through all its thousand courts,
Arches, and domes, and fiery galleries;          180
And all its curtains of Aurorian clouds
Flush'd angerly: while sometimes eagle's wings,
Unseen before by Gods or wondering men,
Darken'd the place; and neighing steeds were heard,
Not heard before by Gods or wondering men.
Also, when he would taste the spicy wreaths
Of incense, breath'd aloft from sacred hills,
Instead of sweets, his ample palate took
Savour of poisonous brass and metal sick:
And so, when harbour'd in the sleepy west,          190
After the full completion of fair day,—
For rest divine upon exalted couch
And slumber in the arms of melody,
He pac'd away the pleasant hours of ease

With stride colossal, on from hall to hall;
While far within each aisle and deep recess,
His winged minions in close clusters stood,
Amaz'd and full of fear; like anxious men
Who on wide plains gather in panting troops,
When earthquakes jar their battlements and towers.      200
Even now, while Saturn, rous'd from icy trance,
Went step for step with Thea through the woods,
Hyperion, leaving twilight in the rear,
Came slope upon the threshold of the west;
Then, as was wont, his palace-door flew ope
In smoothest silence, save what solemn tubes,
Blown by the serious Zephyrs, gave of sweet
And wandering sounds, slow-breathed melodies;
And like a rose in vermeil tint and shape,
In fragrance soft, and coolness to the eye,      210
That inlet to severe magnificence
Stood full blown, for the God to enter in.

   He enter'd, but he enter'd full of wrath;
His flaming robes stream'd out beyond his heels,
And gave a roar, as if of earthly fire,
That scar'd away the meek ethereal Hours
And made their dove-wings tremble. On he flared,
From stately nave to nave, from vault to vault,
Through bowers of fragrant and enwreathed light,
And diamond-paved lustrous long arcades,      220
Until he reach'd the great main cupola;
There standing fierce beneath, he stamped his foot,
And from the basement deep to the high towers
Jarr'd his own golden region; and before
The quavering thunder thereupon had ceas'd,
His voice leapt out, despite of godlike curb,
To this result: 'O dreams of day and night!
'O monstrous forms! O effigies of pain!
'O spectres busy in a cold, cold gloom!
'O lank-ear'd Phantoms of black-weeded pools!      230
'Why do I know ye? why have I seen ye? why
'Is my eternal essence thus distraught
'To see and to behold these horrors new?
'Saturn is fallen, am I too to fall?

'Am I to leave this haven of my rest,
'This cradle of my glory, this soft clime,
'This calm luxuriance of blissful light,
'These crystalline pavilions, and pure fanes,
'Of all my lucent empire? It is left
'Deserted, void, nor any haunt of mine.                240
'The blaze, the splendor, and the symmetry,
'I cannot see—but darkness, death and darkness.
'Even here, into my centre of repose,
'The shady visions come to domineer,
'Insult, and blind, and stifle up my pomp.—
'Fall!—No, by Tellus and her briny robes!
'Over the fiery frontier of my realms
'I will advance a terrible right arm
'Shall scare that infant thunderer, rebel Jove,
'And bid old Saturn take his throne again.'—             250
He spake, and ceas'd, the while a heavier threat
Held struggle with his throat but came not forth;
For as in theatres of crowded men
Hubbub increases more they call out 'Hush!'
So at Hyperion's words the Phantoms pale
Bestirr'd themselves, thrice horrible and cold;
And from the mirror'd level where he stood
A mist arose, as from a scummy marsh.
At this, through all his bulk an agony
Crept gradual, from the feet unto the crown,               260
Like a lithe serpent vast and muscular
Making slow way, with head and neck convuls'd
From over-strained might. Releas'd, he fled
To the eastern gates, and full six dewy hours
Before the dawn in season due should blush,
He breath'd fierce breath against the sleepy portals,
Clear'd them of heavy vapours, burst them wide
Suddenly on the ocean's chilly streams.
The planet orb of fire, whereon he rode
Each day from east to west the heavens through,            270
Spun round in sable curtaining of clouds;
Not therefore veiled quite, blindfold, and hid,
But ever and anon the glancing spheres,
Circles, and arcs, and broad-belting colure,
Glow'd through, and wrought upon the muffling dark

Sweet-shaped lightnings from the nadir deep
Up to the zenith,—hieroglyphics old
Which sages and keen-eyed astrologers
Then living on the earth, with labouring thought
Won from the gaze of many centuries:                    280
Now lost, save what we find on remnants huge
Of stone, or marble swart; their import gone,.
Their wisdom long since fled.—Two wings this orb
Possess'd for glory, two fair argent wings,
Ever exalted at the God's approach:
And now, from forth the gloom their plumes immense
Rose, one by one, till all outspreaded were;
While still the dazzling globe maintain'd eclipse,
Awaiting for Hyperion's command.
Fain would he have commanded, fain took throne         290
And bid the day begin, if but for change.
He might not:—No, though a primeval God:
The sacred seasons might not be disturb'd.
Therefore the operations of the dawn
Stay'd in their birth, even as here 'tis told.
Those silver wings expanded sisterly,
Eager to sail their orb; the porches wide
Open'd upon the dusk demesnes of night;
And the bright Titan, phrenzied with new woes,
Unus'd to bend, by hard compulsion bent                300
His spirit to the sorrow of the time;
And all along a dismal rack of clouds,
Upon the boundaries of day and night,
He stretch'd himself in grief and radiance faint.
There as he lay, the Heaven with its stars
Look'd down on him with pity, and the voice
Of Cœlus, from the universal space,
Thus whisper'd low and solemn in his ear.
'O brightest of my children dear, earth-born
'And sky-engendered, Son of Mysteries                  310
'All unrevealed even to the powers
'Which met at thy creating; at whose joys
'And palpitations sweet, and pleasures soft,
'I, Cœlus, wonder, how they came and whence;
'And at the fruits thereof what shapes they be,
'Distinct, and visible; symbols divine,

'Manifestations of that beauteous life
'Diffus'd unseen throughout eternal space:
'Of these new-form'd art thou, oh brightest child!
'Of these, thy brethren and the Goddesses!     320
'There is sad feud among ye, and rebellion
'Of son against his sire. I saw him fall,
'I saw my first-born tumbled from his throne!
'To me his arms were spread, to me his voice
'Found way from forth the thunders round his head!
'Pale wox I, and in vapours hid my face.
'Art thou, too, near such doom? vague fear there is:
'For I have seen my sons most unlike Gods.
'Divine ye were created, and divine
'In sad demeanour, solemn, undisturb'd,     330
'Unruffled, like high Gods, ye liv'd and ruled:
'Now I behold in you fear, hope, and wrath;
'Actions of rage and passion; even as
'I see them, on the mortal world beneath,
'In men who die.—This is the grief, O Son!
'Sad sign of ruin, sudden dismay, and fall!
'Yet do thou strive; as thou art capable,
'As thou canst move about, an evident God;
'And canst oppose to each malignant hour
'Ethereal presence:—I am but a voice;     340
'My life is but the life of winds and tides,
'No more than winds and tides can I avail:—
'But thou canst.—Be thou therefore in the van
'Of circumstance; yea, seize the arrow's barb
'Before the tense string murmur.—To the earth!
'For there thou wilt find Saturn, and his woes.
'Meantime I will keep watch on thy bright sun,
'And of thy seasons be a careful nurse.'—
Ere half this region-whisper had come down,
Hyperion arose, and on the stars     350
Lifted his curved lids, and kept them wide
Until it ceas'd; and still he kept them wide:
And still they were the same bright, patient stars.
Then with a slow incline of his broad breast,
Like to a diver in the pearly seas,
Forward he stoop'd over the airy shore,
And plung'd all noiseless into the deep night.

## BOOK II

Just at the self-same beat of Time's wide wings
Hyperion slid into the rustled air,
And Saturn gain'd with Thea that sad place
Where Cybele and the bruised Titans mourn'd.
It was a den where no insulting light
Could glimmer on their tears; where their own groans
They felt, but heard not, for the solid roar
Of thunderous waterfalls and torrents hoarse,
Pouring a constant bulk, uncertain where.
Crag jutting forth to crag, and rocks that seem'd          10
Ever as if just rising from a sleep,
Forehead to forehead held their monstrous horns;
And thus in thousand hugest phantasies
Made a fit roofing to this nest of woe.
Instead of thrones, hard flint they sat upon,
Couches of rugged stone, and slaty ridge
Stubborn'd with iron. All were not assembled:
Some chain'd in torture, and some wandering.
Cœus, and Gyges, and Briareüs,
Typhon, and Dolor, and Porphyrion,                          20
With many more, the brawniest in assault,
Were pent in regions of laborious breath;
Dungeon'd in opaque element, to keep
Their clenched teeth still clench'd, and all their limbs
Lock'd up like veins of metal, crampt and screw'd;
Without a motion, save of their big hearts
Heaving in pain, and horribly convuls'd
With sanguine feverous boiling gurge of pulse.
Mnemosyne was straying in the world;
Far from her moon had Phoebe wandered;                      30
And many else were free to roam abroad,
But for the main, here found they covert drear.
Scarce images of life, one here, one there,
Lay vast and edgeways; like a dismal cirque
Of Druid stones, upon a forlorn moor,
When the chill rain begins at shut of eve,
In dull November, and their chancel vault,
The Heaven itself, is blinded throughout night.
Each one kept shroud, nor to his neighbour gave

Or word, or look, or action of despair.          40
Creüs was one; his ponderous iron mace
Lay by him, and a shatter'd rib of rock
Told of his rage, ere he thus sank and pined.
Iäpetus another; in his grasp,
A serpent's plashy neck; its barbed tongue
Squeez'd from the gorge, and all its uncurl'd length
Dead; and because the creature could not spit
Its poison in the eyes of conquering Jove.
Next Cottus: prone he lay, chin uppermost,
As though in pain; for still upon the flint          50
He ground severe his skull, with open mouth
And eyes at horrid working. Nearest him
Asia, born of most enormous Caf,
Who cost her mother Tellus keener pangs,
Though feminine, than any of her sons:
More thought than woe was in her dusky face,
For she was prophesying of her glory;
And in her wide imagination stood
Palm-shaded temples, and high rival fanes,
By Oxus or in Ganges' sacred isles.          60
Even as Hope upon her anchor leans,
So leant she, not so fair, upon a tusk
Shed from the broadest of her elephants.
Above her, on a crag's uneasy shelve,
Upon his elbow rais'd, all prostrate else,
Shadow'd Enceladus; once tame and mild
As grazing ox unworried in the meads;
Now tiger-passion'd, lion-thoughted, wroth,
He meditated, plotted, and even now
Was hurling mountains in that second war,          70
Not long delay'd, that scar'd the younger Gods
To hide themselves in forms of beast and bird.
Not far hence Atlas; and beside him prone
Phorcus, the sire of Gorgons. Neighbour'd close
Oceanus, and Tethys, in whose lap
Sobb'd Clymene among her tangled hair.
In midst of all lay Themis, at the feet
Of Ops the queen all clouded round from sight;
No shape distinguishable, more than when
Thick night confounds the pine-tops with the clouds:          80

And many else whose names may not be told.
For when the Muse's wings are air-ward spread,
Who shall delay her flight? And she must chaunt
Of Saturn, and his guide, who now had climb'd
With damp and slippery footing from a depth
More horrid still. Above a sombre cliff
Their heads appear'd, and up their stature grew
Till on the level height their steps found ease:
Then Thea spread abroad her trembling arms
Upon the precincts of this nest of pain,                          90
And sidelong fix'd her eye on Saturn's face:
There saw she direst strife; the supreme God
At war with all the frailty of grief,
Of rage, of fear, anxiety, revenge,
Remorse, spleen, hope, but most of all despair.
Against these plagues he strove in vain; for Fate
Had pour'd a mortal oil upon his head,
A disanointing poison: so that Thea,
Affrighted, kept her still, and let him pass
First onwards in, among the fallen tribe.                        100

    As with us mortal men, the laden heart
Is persecuted more, and fever'd more,
When it is nighing to the mournful house
Where other hearts are sick of the same bruise;
So Saturn, as he walk'd into the midst,
Felt faint, and would have sunk among the rest,
But that he met Enceladus's eye,
Whose mightiness, and awe of him, at once
Came like an inspiration; and he shouted,
'Titans, behold your God!' at which some groan'd;              110
Some started on their feet; some also shouted;
Some wept, some wail'd, all bow'd with reverence;
And Ops, uplifting her black folded veil,
Show'd her pale cheeks, and all her forehead wan,
Her eye-brows thin and jet, and hollow eyes.
There is a roaring in the bleak-grown pines
When Winter lifts his voice; there is a noise
Among immortals when a God gives sign,
With hushing finger, how he means to load
His tongue with the full weight of utterless thought,          120

With thunder, and with music, and with pomp:
Such noise is like the roar of bleak-grown pines:
Which, when it ceases in this mountain'd world,
No other sound succeeds; but ceasing here,
Among these fallen, Saturn's voice therefrom
Grew up like organ, that begins anew
Its strain, when other harmonies, stopt short,
Leave the dinn'd air vibrating silverly.
Thus grew it up—'Not in my own sad breast,
'Which is its own great judge and searcher out,            130
'Can I find reason why ye should be thus:
'Not in the legends of the first of days,
'Studied from that old spirit-leaved book
'Which starry Uranus with finger bright
'Sav'd from the shores of darkness, when the waves
'Low-ebb'd still hid it up in shallow gloom;—
'And the which book ye know I ever kept
'For my firm-based footstool:—Ah, infirm!
'Not there, nor in sign, symbol, or portent
'Of element, earth, water, air, and fire,—                140
'At war, at peace, or inter-quarreling
'One against one, or two, or three, or all
'Each several one against the other three,
'As fire with air loud warring when rain-floods
'Drown both, and press them both against earth's face,
'Where, finding sulphur, a quadruple wrath
'Unhinges the poor world;—not in that strife,
'Wherefrom I take strange lore, and read it deep,
'Can I find reason why ye should be thus:
'No, no-where can unriddle, though I search,             150
'And pore on Nature's universal scroll
'Even to swooning, why ye, Divinities,
'The first-born of all shap'd and palpable Gods,
'Should cower beneath what, in comparison,
'Is untremendous might. Yet ye are here,
'O'erwhelm'd, and spurn'd, and batter'd, ye are here!
'O Titans, shall I say, "Arise!"—Ye groan:
'Shall I say "Crouch!"—Ye groan. What can I then?
'O Heaven wide! O unseen parent dear!
'What can I? Tell me, all ye brethren Gods,               160
'How we can war, how engine our great wrath!

'O speak your counsel now, for Saturn's ear
'Is all a-hunger'd. Thou, Oceanus,
'Ponderest high and deep; and in thy face
'I see, astonied, that severe content
'Which comes of thought and musing: give us help!'

   So ended Saturn; and the God of the Sea,
Sophist and sage, from no Athenian grove,
But cogitation in his watery shades,
Arose, with locks not oozy, and began,         170
In murmurs, which his first-endeavouring tongue
Caught infant-like from the far-foamed sands.
'O ye, whom wrath consumes! who, passion-stung,
'Writhe at defeat, and nurse your agonies!
'Shut up your senses, stifle up your ears,
'My voice is not a bellows unto ire.
'Yet listen, ye who will, whilst I bring proof
'How ye, perforce, must be content to stoop:
'And in the proof much comfort will I give,
'If ye will take that comfort in its truth.      180
'We fall by course of Nature's law, not force
'Of thunder, or of Jove. Great Saturn, thou
'Hast sifted well the atom-universe;
'But for this reason, that thou art the King,
'And only blind from sheer supremacy,
'One avenue was shaded from thine eyes,
'Through which I wandered to eternal truth.
'And first, as thou wast not the first of powers,
'So art thou not the last; it cannot be:
'Thou art not the beginning nor the end.      190
'From chaos and parental darkness came
'Light, the first fruits of that intestine broil,
'That sullen ferment, which for wondrous ends
'Was ripening in itself. The ripe hour came,
'And with it light, and light, engendering
'Upon its own producer, forthwith touch'd
'The whole enormous matter into life.
'Upon that very hour, our parentage,
'The Heavens, and the Earth, were manifest:
'Then thou first born, and we the giant race,      200
'Found ourselves ruling new and beauteous realms.

'Now comes the pain of truth, to whom 'tis pain;
'O folly! for to bear all naked truths,
'And to envisage circumstance, all calm,
'That is the top of sovereignty. Mark well!
'As Heaven and Earth are fairer, fairer far
'Than Chaos and blank Darkness, though once chiefs;
'And as we show beyond that Heaven and Earth
'In form and shape compact and beautiful,
'In will, in action free, companionship,                    210
'And thousand other signs of purer life;
'So on our heels a fresh perfection treads,
'A power more strong in beauty, born of us
'And fated to excel us, as we pass
'In glory that old Darkness: nor are we
'Thereby more conquer'd, than by us the rule
'Of shapeless Chaos. Say, doth the dull soil
'Quarrel with the proud forests it hath fed,
'And feedeth still, more comely than itself?
'Can it deny the chiefdom of green groves?            220
'Or shall the tree be envious of the dove
'Because it cooeth, and hath snowy wings
'To wander wherewithal and find its joys?
'We are such forest-trees, and our fair boughs
'Have bred forth, not pale solitary doves,
'But eagles golden-feather'd, who do tower
'Above us in their beauty, and must reign
'In right thereof; for 'tis the eternal law
'That first in beauty should be first in might:
'Yea, by that law, another race may drive              230
'Our conquerors to mourn as we do now.
'Have ye beheld the young God of the Seas,
'My dispossessor? Have ye seen his face?
'Have ye beheld his chariot, foam'd along
'By noble winged creatures he hath made?
'I saw him on the calmed waters scud,
'With such a glow of beauty in his eyes,
'That it enforc'd me to bid sad farewell
'To all my empire: farewell sad I took,
'And hither came, to see how dolorous fate            240
'Had wrought upon ye; and how I might best
'Give consolation in this woe extreme.

'Receive the truth, and let it be your balm.'

 Whether through poz'd conviction, or disdain,
They guarded silence, when Oceanus
Left murmuring, what deepest thought can tell?
But so it was, none answer'd for a space,
Save one whom none regarded, Clymene;
And yet she answer'd not, only complain'd,
With hectic lips, and eyes up-looking mild,   250
Thus wording timidly among the fierce:
'O Father, I am here the simplest voice,
'And all my knowledge is that joy is gone,
'And this thing woe crept in among our hearts,
'There to remain for ever, as I fear:
'I would not bode of evil, if I thought
'So weak a creature could turn off the help
'Which by just right should come of mighty Gods;
'Yet let me tell my sorrow, let me tell
'Of what I heard, and how it made me weep,   260
'And know that we had parted from all hope.
'I stood upon a shore, a pleasant shore,
'Where a sweet clime was breathed from a land
'Of fragrance, quietness, and trees, and flowers
'Full of calm joy it was, as I of grief;
'Too full of joy and soft delicious warmth;
'So that I felt a movement in my heart
'To chide, and to reproach that solitude
'With songs of misery, music of our woes;
'And sat me down, and took a mouthed shell   270
'And murmur'd into it, and made melody—
'O melody no more! for while I sang,
'And with poor skill let pass into the breeze
'The dull shell's echo, from a bowery strand
'Just opposite, an island of the sea,
'There came enchantment with the shifting wind,
'That did both drown and keep alive my ears.
'I threw my shell away upon the sand,
'And a wave fill'd it, as my sense was fill'd
'With that new blissful golden melody.   280
'A living death was in each gush of sounds,
'Each family of rapturous hurried notes,

'That fell, one after one, yet all at once,
'Like pearl beads dropping sudden from their string:
'And then another, then another strain,
'Each like a dove leaving its olive perch,
'With music wing'd instead of silent plumes,
'To hover round my head, and make me sick
'Of joy and grief at once. Grief overcame,
'And I was stopping up my frantic ears,                    290
'When, past all hindrance of my trembling hands,
'A voice came sweeter, sweeter than all tune,
'And still it cried, "Apollo! young Apollo!
' "The morning-bright Apollo! young Apollo!"
'I fled, it follow'd me, and cried "Apollo!"
'O Father, and O Brethren, had ye felt
'Those pains of mine; O Saturn, hadst thou felt,
'Ye would not call this too indulged tongue
'Presumptuous, in thus venturing to be heard.'

   So far her voice flow'd on, like timorous brook          300
That, lingering along a pebbled coast,
Doth fear to meet the sea: but sea it met,
And shudder'd; for the overwhelming voice
Of huge Enceladus swallow'd it in wrath:
The ponderous syllables, like sullen waves
In the half-glutted hollows of reef-rocks,
Came booming thus, while still upon his arm
He lean'd; not rising, from supreme contempt.
'Or shall we listen to the over-wise,
'Or to the over-foolish, Giant-Gods?                       310
'Not thunderbolt on thunderbolt, till all
'That rebel Jove's whole armoury were spent,
'Not world on world upon these shoulders piled,
'Could agonize me more than baby-words
'In midst of this dethronement horrible.
'Speak! roar! shout! yell! ye sleepy Titans all.
'Do ye forget the blows, the buffets vile?
'Are ye not smitten by a youngling arm?
'Dost thou forget, sham Monarch of the Waves,
'Thy scalding in the seas? What, have I rous'd             320
'Your spleens with so few simple words as these?
'O joy! for now I see ye are not lost:

'O joy! for now I see a thousand eyes
'Wide-glaring for revenge!'—As this he said,
He lifted up his stature vast, and stood,
Still without intermission speaking thus:
'Now ye are flames, I'll tell you how to burn,
'And purge the ether of our enemies;
'How to feed fierce the crooked stings of fire,
'And singe away the swollen clouds of Jove,                    330
'Stifling that puny essence in its tent.
'O let him feel the evil he hath done;
'For though I scorn Oceanus's lore,
'Much pain have I for more than loss of realms:
'The days of peace and slumberous calm are fled;
'Those days, all innocent of scathing war,
'When all the fair Existences of heaven
'Came open-eyed to guess what we would speak:—
'That was before our brows were taught to frown,
'Before our lips knew else but solemn sounds;                  340
'That was before we knew the winged thing,
'Victory, might be lost, or might be won.
'And be ye mindful that Hyperion,
'Our brightest brother, still is undisgraced—
'Hyperion, lo! his radiance is here!'

     All eyes were on Enceladus's face,
And they beheld, while still Hyperion's name
Flew from his lips up to the vaulted rocks,
A pallid gleam across his features stern:
Not savage, for he saw full many a God                         350
Wroth as himself. He look'd upon them all,
And in each face he saw a gleam of light,
But splendider in Saturn's, whose hoar locks
Shone like the bubbling foam about a keel
When the prow sweeps into a midnight cove.
In pale and silver silence they remain'd,
Till suddenly a splendour, like the morn,
Pervaded all the beetling gloomy steeps,
All the sad spaces of oblivion,
And every gulf, and every chasm old,                           360
And every height, and every sullen depth,
Voiceless, or hoarse with loud tormented streams:

And all the everlasting cataracts,
And all the headlong torrents far and near,
Mantled before in darkness and huge shade,
Now saw the light and made it terrible.
It was Hyperion:—a granite peak
His bright feet touch'd, and there he stay'd to view
The misery his brilliance had betray'd
To the most hateful seeing of itself.                    370
Golden his hair of short Numidian curl,
Regal his shape majestic, a vast shade
In midst of his own brightness, like the bulk
Of Memnon's image at the set of sun
To one who travels from the dusking East:
Sighs, too, as mournful as that Memnon's harp
He utter'd, while his hands contemplative
He press'd together, and in silence stood.
Despondence seiz'd again the fallen Gods
At sight of the dejected King of Day,                    380
And many hid their faces from the light:
But fierce Enceladus sent forth his eyes
Among the brotherhood; and, at their glare,
Uprose Ïapetus, and Creüs too,
And Phorcus, sea-born, and together strode
To where he towered on his eminence.
There those four shouted forth old Saturn's name;
Hyperion from the peak loud answered, 'Saturn!'
Saturn sat near the Mother of the Gods,
In whose face was no joy, though all the Gods           390
Gave from their hollow throats the name of 'Saturn!'

## BOOK III

THUS in alternate uproar and sad peace,
Amazed were those Titans utterly.
O leave them, Muse! O leave them to their woes;
For thou art weak to sing such tumults dire:
A solitary sorrow best befits
Thy lips, and antheming a lonely grief.
Leave them, O Muse! for thou anon wilt find
Many a fallen old Divinity
Wandering in vain about bewildered shores.

Meantime touch piously the Delphic harp,                    10
And not a wind of heaven but will breathe
In aid soft warble from the Dorian flute;
For lo! 'tis for the Father of all verse.
Flush every thing that hath a vermeil hue,
Let the rose glow intense and warm the air,
And let the clouds of even and of morn
Float in voluptuous fleeces o'er the hills;
Let the red wine within the goblet boil,
Cold as a bubbling well; let faint-lipp'd shells,
On sands, or in great deeps, vermilion turn                 20
Through all their labyrinths; and let the maid
Blush keenly, as with some warm kiss surpris'd.
Chief isle of the embowered Cyclades,
Rejoice, O Delos, with thine olives green,
And poplars, and lawn-shading palms, and beech,
In which the Zephyr breathes the loudest song,
And hazels thick, dark-stemm'd beneath the shade:
Apollo is once more the golden theme!
Where was he, when the Giant of the Sun
Stood bright, amid the sorrow of his peers?                 30
Together had he left his mother fair
And his twin-sister sleeping in their bower,
And in the morning twilight wandered forth
Beside the osiers of a rivulet,
Full ankle-deep in lillies of the vale.
The nightingale had ceas'd, and a few stars
Were lingering in the heavens, while the thrush
Began calm-throated. Throughout all the isle
There was no covert, no retired cave
Unhaunted by the murmurous noise of waves,                  40
Though scarcely heard in many a green recess.
He listen'd, and he wept, and his bright tears
Went trickling down the golden bow he held.
Thus with half-shut suffused eyes he stood,
While from beneath some cumbrous boughs hard by
With solemn step an awful Goddess came,
And there was purport in her looks for him,
Which he with eager guess began to read
Perplex'd, the while melodiously he said:
'How cam'st thou over the unfooted sea?                     50

'Or hath that antique mien and robed form
'Mov'd in these vales invisible till now?
'Sure I have heard those vestments sweeping o'er
'The fallen leaves, when I have sat alone
'In cool mid-forest. Surely I have traced
'The rustle of those ample skirts about
'These grassy solitudes, and seen the flowers
'Lift up their heads, as still the whisper pass'd.
'Goddess! I have beheld those eyes before,
'And their eternal calm, and all that face,          60
'Or I have dream'd.'—'Yes,' said the supreme shape,
'Thou hast dream'd of me; and awaking up
'Didst find a lyre all golden by thy side,
'Whose strings touch'd by thy fingers, all the vast
'Unwearied ear of the whole universe
'Listen'd in pain and pleasure at the birth
'Of such new tuneful wonder. Is't not strange
'That thou shouldst weep, so gifted? Tell me, youth,
'What sorrow thou canst feel; for I am sad
'When thou dost shed a tear: explain thy griefs          70
'To one who in this lonely isle hath been
'The watcher of thy sleep and hours of life,
'From the young day when first thy infant hand
'Pluck'd witless the weak flowers, till thine arm
'Could bend that bow heroic to all times.
'Show thy heart's secret to an ancient Power
'Who hath forsaken old and sacred thrones
'For prophecies of thee, and for the sake
'Of loveliness new born.'—Apollo then,
With sudden scrutiny and gloomless eyes,          80
Thus answer'd, while his white melodious throat
Throbb'd with the syllables.—'Mnemosyne!
'Thy name is on my tongue, I know not how;
'Why should I tell thee what thou so well seest?
'Why should I strive to show what from thy lips
'Would come no mystery? For me, dark, dark,
'And painful vile oblivion seals my eyes:
'I strive to search wherefore I am so sad,
'Until a melancholy numbs my limbs;
'And then upon the grass I sit, and moan,          90
'Like one who once had wings.—O why should I

'Feel curs'd and thwarted, when the liegeless air
'Yields to my step aspirant? why should I
'Spurn the green turf as hateful to my feet?
'Goddess benign, point forth some unknown thing:
'Are there not other regions than this isle?
'What are the stars? There is the sun, the sun!
'And the most patient brilliance of the moon!
'And stars by thousands!  Point me out the way
'To any one particular beauteous star,                      100
'And I will flit into it with my lyre
'And make its silvery splendour pant with bliss.
'I have heard the cloudy thunder: Where is power?
'Whose hand, whose essence, what divinity
'Makes this alarum in the elements,
'While I here idle listen on the shores
'In fearless yet in aching ignorance?
'O tell me, lonely Goddess, by thy harp,
'That waileth every morn and eventide,
'Tell me why thus I rave, about these groves!              110
'Mute thou remainest—mute! yet I can read
'A wondrous lesson in thy silent face:
'Knowledge enormous makes a God of me.
'Names, deeds, grey legends, dire events, rebellions,
'Majesties, sovran voices, agonies,
'Creations and destroyings, all at once
'Pour into the wide hollows of my brain,
'And deify me, as if some blithe wine
'Or bright elixir peerless I had drunk,
'And so become immortal.'—Thus the God,                    120
While his enkindled eyes, with level glance
Beneath his white soft temples, stedfast kept
Trembling with light upon Mnemosyne.
Soon wild commotions shook him, and made flush
All the immortal fairness of his limbs;
Most like the struggle at the gate of death;
Or liker still to one who should take leave
Of pale immortal death, and with a pang
As hot as death's is chill, with fierce convulse
Die into life: so young Apollo anguish'd:                  130
His very hair, his golden tresses famed
Kept undulation round his eager neck.

During the pain Mnemosyne upheld
Her arms as one who prophesied.—At length
Apollo shriek'd;—and lo! from all his limbs
Celestial    *    *    *    *    *    *    *
*    *    *    *    *    *    *    *    *

**THE END**

# POEMS FROM

## *LITERARY REMAINS*

1848

# OTHO THE GREAT

## A TRAGEDY
## IN FIVE ACTS

# DRAMATIS PERSONÆ

OTHO THE GREAT, *Emperor of Germany.*
LUDOLPH, *his son.*
CONRAD, *Duke of Franconia.*
ALBERT, *a Knight, favoured by Otho.*
SIGIFRED, *an Officer friend of Ludolph.*
THEODORE,  } *Officers.*
GONFRED,
ETHELBERT, *an Abbot.*
GERSA, *Prince of Hungary.*
*An Hungarian Captain.*
*Physician.*
*Page.*
*Nobles, Knights, Attendants, and Soldiers.*
ERMINIA, *Niece of Otho.*
AURANTHE, *Conrad's Sister.*
*Ladies and Attendants.*

SCENE. *The Castle of Friedburg, its vicinity,
    and the Hungarian Camp.*

TIME. *One Day.*

# OTHO THE GREAT

## ACT I

CONRAD. So, I am safe emerged from these broils!
  Amid the wreck of thousands I am whole;
  For every crime I have a laurel-wreath,
  For every lie a lordship. Nor yet has
  My ship of fortune furl'd her silken sails,—
  Let her glide on! This danger'd neck is saved,
  By dexterous policy, from the rebel's axe;
  And of my ducal palace not one stone
  Is bruised by the Hungarian petards.
  Toil hard, ye slaves, and from the miser-earth      10
  Bring forth once more my bullion, treasured deep,
  With all my jewel'd salvers, silver and gold,
  And precious goblets that make rich the wine.
  But why do I stand babbling to myself?
  Where is Auranthe? I have news for her
  Shall—

*Enter* AURANTHE.

AURANTHE. Conrad! what tidings? Good, if I may guess
  From your alert eyes and high-lifted brows.
  What tidings of the battle? Albert? Ludolph? Otho?
CONRAD. You guess aright. And, sister, slurring o'er
  Our by-gone quarrels, I confess my heart      20
  Is beating with a child's anxiety,
  To make our golden fortune known to you.
AURANTHE. So serious?
CONRAD.                 Yes, so serious, that before
  I utter even the shadow of a hint
  Concerning what will make that sin-worn cheek
  Blush joyous blood through every lineament,
  You must make here a solemn vow to me.
AURANTHE. I prythee, Conrad, do not overact
  The hypocrite—what vow would you impose?

CONRAD. Trust me for once,—that you may be assur'd    30
   'Tis not confiding in a broken reed,
   A poor Court-bankrupt, outwitted and lost,
   Revolve these facts in your acutest mood,
   In such a mood as now you listen to me:—
   A few days since, I was an open rebel
   Against the Emperor, had suborn'd his son,
   Drawn off his nobles to revolt, and shown
   Contented fools causes for discontent
   Fresh hatch'd in my ambition's eagle nest—
   So thriv'd I as a rebel, and behold    40
   Now I am Otho's favourite, his dear friend,
   His right hand, his brave Conrad.
AURANTHE.                            I confess
   You have intrigued with these unsteady times
   To admiration; but to be a favourite—
CONRAD. I saw my moment. The Hungarians,
   Collected silently in holes and corners,
   Appear'd, a sudden host, in the open day.
   I should have perish'd in our empire's wreck,
   But, calling interest loyalty, swore faith
   To most believing Otho; and so help'd    50
   His blood-stain'd ensigns to the victory
   In yesterday's hard fight, that it has turn'd
   The edge of his sharp wrath to eager kindness.
AURANTHE. So far yourself. But what is this to me
   More than that I am glad? I gratulate you.
CONRAD. Yes, sister, but it does regard you greatly,
   Nearly, momentously,—aye, painfully!
   Make me this vow—
AURANTHE.              Concerning whom or what?
CONRAD. Albert!
AURANTHE.      I would inquire somewhat of him:
   You had a letter from me touching him?    60
   No treason 'gainst his head in deed or word!
   Surely you spar'd him at my earnest prayer?
   Give me the letter—it should not exist!
CONRAD. At one pernicious charge of the enemy,
   I, for a moment-whiles, was prisoner ta'en
   And rifled,—stuff! the horses' hoofs have minc'd it!
AURANTHE. He is alive?

CONRAD.                He is! but here make oath
  To alienate him from your scheming brain,
  Divorce him from your solitary thoughts,
  And cloud him in such utter banishment,                70
  That when his person meets again your eye,
  Your vision shall quite lose its memory,
  And wander past him as through vacancy.
AURANTHE. I'll not be perjured.
CONRAD.                No, nor great, nor mighty;
  You would not wear a crown, or rule a kingdom.
  To you it is indifferent.
AURANTHE.            What means this?
CONRAD. You'll not be perjured! Go to Albert then,
  That camp-mushroom—dishonour of our house.
  Go, page his dusty heels upon a march,
  Furbish his jingling baldric while he sleeps,        80
  And share his mouldy ratio in a siege.
  Yet stay,—perhaps a charm may call you back,
  And make the widening circlets of your eyes
  Sparkle with healthy fevers.—The Emperor
  Hath given consent that you should marry Ludolph!
AURANTHE. Can it be, brother? For a golden crown
  With a queen's awful lips I doubly thank you!
  This is to wake in Paradise! Farewell
  Thou clod of yesterday—'twas not myself!
  Not till this moment did I ever feel                90
  My spirit's faculties! I'll flatter you
  For this, and be you ever proud of it;
  Thou, Jove-like, struck'dst thy forehead,
  And from the teeming marrow of thy brain
  I spring complete Minerva! But the prince—
  His highness Ludolph—where is he?
CONRAD.                        I know not:
  When, lackeying my counsel at a beck,
  The rebel lords, on bended knees, received
  The Emperor's pardon, Ludolph kept aloof,
  Sole, in a stiff, fool-hardy, sulky pride;          100
  Yet, for all this, I never saw a father
  In such a sickly longing for his son.
  We shall soon see him, for the Emperor
  He will be here this morning.

AURANTHE.                    That I heard
Among the midnight rumours from the camp.
CONRAD. You give up Albert to me?
AURANTHE.                    Harm him not!
E'en for his highness Ludolph's sceptry hand,
I would not Albert suffer any wrong.
CONRAD. Have I not laboured, plotted—?
AURANTHE.                    See you spare him:
Nor be pathetic, my kind benefactor,                    110
On all the many bounties of your hand,—
'Twas for yourself you laboured—not for me!
Do you not count, when I am queen, to take
Advantage of your chance discoveries
Of my poor secrets, and so hold a rod
Over my life?
CONRAD.        Let not this slave—this villain—
Be cause of feud between us. See! he comes!
Look, woman, look, your Albert is quite safe!
In haste it seems. Now shall I be in the way,
And wish'd with silent curses in my grave,                    120
Or side by side with 'whelmed mariners.

*Enter* ALBERT.

ALBERT. Fair on your graces fall this early morrow!
So it is like to do, without my prayers,
For your right noble names, like favourite tunes,
Have fall'n full frequent from our Emperor's lips,
High commented with smiles.
AURANTHE.                    Noble Albert!
CONRAD (*aside*).                    Noble!
AURANTHE. Such salutation argues a glad heart
In our prosperity. We thank you, sir.
ALBERT. Lady! O, would to Heaven your poor servant
Could do you better service than mere words!                    130
But I have other greeting than mine own,
From no less man than Otho, who has sent
This ring as pledge of dearest amity;
'Tis chosen I hear from Hymen's jewel'ry,
And you will prize it, lady, I doubt not,
Before all pleasures past, and all to come.
To you great duke—

CONRAD. To me! What of me, ha?

ALBERT. What pleas'd your grace to say?

CONRAD. Your message, sir!

ALBERT. You mean not this to me?

CONRAD. Sister, this way;
  For there shall be no 'gentle Alberts' now,     [*Aside.*
  No 'sweet Auranthes!'     141
        [*Exeunt* CONRAD *and* AURANTHE.

ALBERT (*solus*). The duke is out of temper; if he knows
  More than a brother of a sister ought,
  I should not quarrel with his peevishness.
  Auranthe—Heaven preserve her always fair!—
  Is in the heady, proud, ambitious vein;
  I bicker not with her,—bid her farewell!
  She has taken flight from me, then let her soar,—
  He is a fool who stands at pining gaze!
  But for poor Ludolph, he is food for sorrow:     150
  No levelling bluster of my licens'd thoughts,
  No military swagger of my mind,
  Can smother from myself the wrong I've done him,—
  Without design, indeed,—yet it is so,—
  And opiate for the conscience have I none!     [*Exit.*

SCENE II. *The Court-yard of the Castle.*

*Martial Music. Enter, from the outer gate,* OTHO, *Nobles, Knights, and Attendants. The Soldiers halt at the gate, with Banners in sight.*

OTHO. Where is my noble herald?

*Enter* CONRAD, *from the Castle, attended by two Knights and Servants.* ALBERT *following.*
  Well, hast told
  Auranthe our intent imperial?
  Lest our rent banners, too o' the sudden shown,
  Should fright her silken casements, and dismay
  Her household to our lack of entertainment.
  A victory!

CONRAD. God save imperial Otho!

OTHO. Aye, Conrad, it will pluck out all grey hairs;
  It is the best physician for the spleen;
  The courtliest inviter to a feast;

The subtlest excuser of small faults;                              10
And a nice judge in the age and smack of wine.

*Enter, from the Castle,* AURANTHE, *followed by Pages holding
up her robes, and a train of Women. She kneels.*

Hail my sweet hostess! I do thank the stars,
Or my good soldiers, or their ladies' eyes,
That, after such a merry battle fought,
I can, all safe in body and in soul,
Kiss your fair hand and lady fortune's too.
My ring! now, on my life, it doth rejoice
These lips to feel't on this soft ivory!
Keep it, my brightest daughter; it may prove
The little prologue to a line of kings.                            20
I strove against thee and my hot-blood son,
Dull blockhead that I was to be so blind,
But now my sight is clear; forgive me, lady.
AURANTHE. My lord, I was a vassal to your frown,
And now your favour makes me but more humble;
In wintry winds the simple snow is safe,
But fadeth at the greeting of the sun:
Unto thine anger I might well have spoken,
Taking on me a woman's privilege,
But this so sudden kindness makes me dumb.                         30
OTHO. What need of this? Enough, if you will be
A potent tutoress to my wayward boy,
And teach him, what it seems his nurse could not,
To say, for once, I thank you. Sigifred!
ALBERT. He has not yet return'd, my gracious liege.
OTHO. What then! No tidings of my friendly Arab?
CONRAD. None, mighty Otho.
                          [*To one of his Knights, who goes out.*
                          Send forth instantly
An hundred horsemen from my honoured gates,
To scour the plains and search the cottages.
Cry a reward, to him who shall first bring                         40
News of that vanished Arabian,
A full-heap'd helmet of the purest gold.
OTHO. More thanks, good Conrad; for, except my son's,
There is no face I rather would behold
Than that same quick-eyed pagan's. By the saints,

This coming night of banquets must not light
Her dazzling torches; nor the music breathe
Smooth, without clashing cymbal, tones of peace
And in-door melodies; nor the ruddy wine
Ebb spouting to the lees; if I pledge not,                    50
In my first cup, that Arab!

ALBERT.                              Mighty Caesar,
I wonder not this stranger's victor-deeds
So hang upon your spirit. Twice in the fight
It was my chance to meet his olive brow,
Triumphant in the enemy's shatter'd rhomb;
And, to say truth, in any Christian arm
I never saw such prowess.

OTHO.                              Did you ever?
O, 'tis a noble boy!—tut!—what do I say?
I mean a triple Saladin, whose eyes,
When in the glorious scuffle they met mine,                   60
Seem'd to say—'Sleep, old man, in safety sleep;
I am the victory!'

CONRAD.                    Pity he's not here.

OTHO. And my son too, pity he is not here.
Lady Auranthe, I would not make you blush,
But can you give a guess where Ludolph is?
Know you not of him?

AURANTHE.              Indeed, my liege, no secret—

OTHO. Nay, nay, without more words, dost know of him?

AURANTHE. I would I were so over-fortunate,
Both for his sake and mine, and to make glad
A father's ears with tidings of his son.                      70

OTHO. I see 'tis like to be a tedious day.
Were Theodore and Gonfred and the rest
Sent forth with my commands?

ALBERT.                            Aye, my lord.

OTHO. And no news! No news! 'Faith! 'tis very strange
He thus avoids us. Lady, is't not strange?
Will he be truant to you too? It is a shame.

CONRAD. Will't please your highness enter, and accept
The unworthy welcome of your servant's house?
Leaving your cares to one whose diligence
May in few hours make pleasures of them all.                  80

OTHO. Not so tedious, Conrad. No, no, no, no,—

I must see Ludolph or the— What's that shout!
VOICES WITHOUT. Huzza! huzza! Long live the Emperor!
OTHER VOICES. Fall back! Away there!
OTHO.                                 Say, what noise is that?

[ALBERT *advancing from the back of the Stage, whither he had
              hastened on hearing the cheers of the soldiery.*
ALBERT. It is young Gersa, the Hungarian prince,
    Pick'd like a red stag from the fallow herd
    Of prisoners. Poor prince, forlorn he steps,
    Slow, in the demure proudness of despair.
    If I may judge by his so tragic bearing,
    His eye not downcast, and his folded arm,                    90
    He doth this moment wish himself asleep
    Among his fallen captains on yon plains.

              *Enter* GERSA, *in chains, and guarded.*
OTHO. Well said, Sir Albert.
GERSA.                         Not a word of greeting,
    No welcome to a princely visitor,
    Most mighty Otho? Will not my great host
    Vouchsafe a syllable, before he bids
    His gentlemen conduct me with all care
    To some securest lodging?—cold perhaps!
OTHO. What mood is this? Hath fortune touch'd thy brain?
GERSA. O kings and princes of this fev'rous world,        100
    What abject things, what mockeries must ye be,
    What nerveless minions of safe palaces!
    When here, a monarch, whose proud foot is used
    To fallen princes' necks, as to his stirrup,
    Must needs exclaim that I am mad forsooth,
    Because I cannot flatter with bent knees
    My conqueror!
OTHO.             Gersa, I think you wrong me:
    I think I have a better fame abroad.
GERSA. I prythee mock me not with gentle speech,
    But, as a favour, bid me from thy presence;             110
    Let me no longer be the wondering food
    Of all these eyes; prythee command me hence!
OTHO. Do not mistake me, Gersa. That you may not,
    Come, fair Auranthe, try if your soft hands
    Can manage those hard rivets to set free

So brave a prince and soldier.
AURANTHE (*sets him free*).     Welcome task!
GERSA. I am wound up in deep astonishment!
　Thank you, fair lady. Otho! emperor!
　You rob me of myself; my dignity
　Is now your infant; I am a weak child.                120
OTHO. Give me your hand, and let this kindly grasp
　Live in our memories.
GERSA.                    In mine it will.
　I blush to think of my unchasten'd tongue;
　But I was haunted by the monstrous ghost
　Of all our slain battalions. Sire, reflect,
　And pardon you will grant, that, at this hour,
　The bruised remnants of our stricken camp
　Are huddling undistinguish'd my dear friends,
　With common thousands, into shallow graves.
OTHO. Enough, most noble Gersa. You are free      130
　To cheer the brave remainder of your host
　By your own healing presence, and that too,
　Not as their leader merely, but their king;
　For, as I hear, your wily enemy,
　Who eas'd the crownet from your infant brows,
　Bloody Taraxa, is among the dead.
GERSA. Then I retire, so generous Caesar please,
　Bearing with me a weight of benefits
　Too heavy to be borne.
OTHO.                     It is not so;
　Still understand me, King of Hungary,            140
　Nor judge my open purposes awry.
　Though I did hold you high in my esteem
　For your self's sake, I do not personate
　The stage-play emperor to entrap applause,
　To set the silly sort o' the world agape,
　And make the politic smile; no, I have heard
　How in the Council you condemn'd this war,
　Urging the perfidy of broken faith,—
　For that I am your friend.
GERSA.                    If ever, sire,
　You are my enemy, I dare here swear            150
　'Twill not be Gersa's fault. Otho, farewell!
OTHO. Will you return, Prince, to our banqueting?

GERSA. As to my father's board I will return.
OTHO. Conrad, with all due ceremony, give
   The prince a regal escort to his camp;
   Albert, go thou and bear him company.
   Gersa, farewell!
GERSA.            All happiness attend you!
OTHO. Return with what good speed you may; for soon
   We must consult upon our terms of peace.
                    [*Exeunt* GERSA *and* ALBERT *with others.*

   And thus a marble column do I build                160
   To prop my empire's dome. Conrad, in thee
   I have another stedfast one, to uphold
   The portals of my state; and, for my own
   Pre-eminence and safety, I will strive
   To keep thy strength upon its pedestal.
   For, without thee, this day I might have been
   A show-monster about the streets of Prague,
   In chains, as just now stood that noble prince:
   And then to me no mercy had been shown,
   For when the conquer'd lion is once dungeon'd,    170
   Who lets him forth again? or dares to give
   An old lion sugar-cates of mild reprieve?
   Not to thine ear alone I make confession,
   But to all here, as, by experience,
   I know how the great basement of all power
   Is frankness, and a true tongue to the world;
   And how intriguing secrecy is proof
   Of fear and weakness, and a hollow state.
   Conrad, I owe thee much.
CONRAD.                To [kneel and] kiss that hand,
   My emperor, is ample recompense,                  180
   For a mere act of duty.
OTHO.                Thou art wrong;
   For what can any man on earth do more?
   We will make trial of your house's welcome,
   My bright Auranthe!
CONRAD.                How is Friedburg honoured!

       *Enter* ETHELBERT *and six Monks.*

ETHELBERT. The benison of heaven on your head,
   Imperial Otho!

OTHO.                 Who stays me? Speak! Quick!
ETHELBERT. Pause but one moment, mighty conqueror
  Upon the threshold of this house of joy.
OTHO. Pray, do not prose, good Ethelbert, but speak
  What is your purpose.                                    190
ETHELBERT. The restoration of some captive maids,
  Devoted to Heaven's pious ministries,
  Who, driven forth from their religious cells,
  And kept in thraldom by our enemy,
  When late this province was a lawless spoil,
  Still weep amid the wild Hungarian camp,
  Though hemm'd around by thy victorious arms.
OTHO. Demand the holy sisterhood in our name
  From Gersa's tents. Farewell, old Ethelbert.             199
ETHELBERT. The saints will bless you for this pious care.
OTHO. Daughter, your hand; Ludolph's would fit it best.
CONRAD. Ho! let the music sound!

[*Music.* ETHELBERT *raises his hands, as in benediction of* OTHO.
            *Exeunt severally. The scene closes on them.*


SCENE III. *The Country, with the Castle in the distance.*

*Enter* LUDOLPH *and* SIGIFRED.

LUDOLPH. You have my secret; let it not be breath'd.
SIGIFRED. Still give me leave to wonder that my Prince
  Ludolph and the swift Arab are the same;
  Still to rejoice that 'twas a German arm
  Death doing in a turban's masquerade.
LUDOLPH. The Emperor must not know it, Sigifred.
SIGIFRED. I prythee, why? What happier hour of time
  Could thy pleas'd star point down upon from heaven
  With silver index, bidding thee make peace?
LUDOLPH. Still it must not be known, good Sigifred;       10
  The star may point oblique.
SIGIFRED.                      If Otho knew
  His son to be that unknown Mussulman
  After whose spurring heels he sent me forth,
  With one of his well-pleas'd Olympian oaths,
  The charters of man's greatness, at this hour
  He would be watching round the castle walls,

And, like an anxious warder, strain his sight
For the first glimpse of such a son return'd—
Ludolph, that blast of the Hungarians,
That Saracenic meteor of the fight,                              20
That silent fury, whose fell scymitar
Kept danger all aloof from Otho's head,
And left him space for wonder.

LUDOLPH.                                    Say no more.
Not as a swordsman would I pardon claim,
But as a son. The bronz'd centurion,
Long toil'd in foreign wars, and whose high deeds
Are shaded in a forest of tall spears,
Known only to his troop, hath greater plea
Of favour with my sire than I can have.

SIGIFRED. My lord, forgive me that I cannot see            30
How this proud temper with clear reason squares.
What made you then, with such an anxious love,
Hover around that life, whose bitter days
You vext with bad revolt? Was't opium,
Or the mad-fumed wine? Nay, do not frown,
I rather would grieve with you than upbraid.

LUDOLPH. I do believe you. No, 'twas not to make
A father his son's debtor, or to heal
His deep heart-sickness for a rebel child.
'Twas done in memory of my boyish days,                     40
Poor cancel for his kindness to my youth,
For all his calming of my childish griefs,
And all his smiles upon my merriment.
No, not a thousand foughten fields could sponge
Those days paternal from my memory,
Though now upon my head he heaps disgrace.

SIGIFRED. My Prince, you think too harshly—

LUDOLPH.                                         Can I so?
Hath he not gall'd my spirit to the quick?
And with a sullen rigour obstinate
Pour'd out a phial of wrath upon my faults?                 50
Hunted me as a Tartar does the boar,
Driven me to the very edge o' the world,
And almost put a price upon my head?

SIGIFRED. Remember how he spar'd the rebel lords

LUDOLPH. Yes, yes, I know he hath a noble nature

That cannot trample on the fallen. But his
Is not the only proud heart in his realm.
He hath wrong'd me, and I have done him wrong;
He hath lov'd me, and I have shown him kindness;
We should be almost equal.
SIGIFRED.                          Yet, for all this,          60
I would you had appear'd among those lords,
And ta'en his favour.
LUDOLPH.                       Ha! till now I thought
My friend had held poor Ludolph's honour dear.
What! would you have me sue before his throne
And kiss the courtier's missal, its silk steps?
Or hug the golden housings of his steed,
Amid a camp, whose steeled swarms I dar'd
But yesterday? And, at the trumpet sound,
Bow like some unknown mercenary's flag,
And lick the soiled grass? No, no, my friend,        70
I would not, I, be pardon'd in the heap,
And bless indemnity with all that scum,—
Those men I mean, who on my shoulders propp'd
Their weak rebellion, winning me with lies,
And pitying forsooth my many wrongs;
Poor self-deceived wretches, who must think
Each one himself a king in embryo,
Because some dozen vassals cry'd—my lord!
Cowards, who never knew their little hearts,
Till flurried danger held the mirror up,        80
And then they own'd themselves without a blush,
Curling, like spaniels, round my father's feet.
Such things deserted me and are forgiven,
While I, least guilty, am an outcast still,
And will be, for I love such fair disgrace.
SIGIFRED. I know the clear truth; so would Otho see,
For he is just and noble. Fain would I
Be pleader for you—
LUDOLPH.                       He'll hear none of it;
You know his temper, hot, proud, obstinate;
Endanger not yourself so uselessly.        90
I will encounter his thwart spleen myself,
To-day, at the Duke Conrad's, where he keeps
His crowded state after the victory.

There will I be, a most unwelcome guest,
And parley with him, as a son should do,
Who doubly loathes a father's tyranny;
Tell him how feeble is that tyranny;
How the relationship of father and son
Is no more valid than a silken leash
Where lions tug adverse, if love grow not          100
From interchanged love through many years.
Aye, and those turreted Franconian walls,
Like to a jealous casket, hold my pearl—
My fair Auranthe! Yes, I will be there.

SIGIFRED. Be not so rash; wait till his wrath shall pass,
Until his royal spirit softly ebbs
Self-influenced; then, in his morning dreams
He will forgive thee, and awake in grief
To have not thy good morrow.

LUDOLPH.                              Yes, to-day
I must be there, while her young pulses beat          110
Among the new-plum'd minions of the war.
Have you seen her of late? No? Auranthe,
Franconia's fair sister, 'tis I mean.
She should be paler for my troublous days—
And there it is—my father's iron lips
Have sworn divorcement 'twixt me and my right.

SIGIFRED [*aside*]. Auranthe! I had hop'd this whim had
     pass'd.

LUDOLPH. And, Sigifred, with all his love of justice,
When will he take that grandchild in his arms,
That, by my love I swear, shall soon be his?          120
This reconcilement is impossible,
For see—but who are these?

SIGIFRED.                              They are messengers
From our great emperor; to you, I doubt not,
For couriers are abroad to seek you out.

*Enter* THEODORE *and* GONFRED.

THEODORE. Seeing so many vigilant eyes explore
The province to invite your highness back
To your high dignities, we are too happy.

GONFRED. We have no eloquence to colour justly
The emperor's anxious wishes.

LUDOLPH.                    Go. I follow you.

*[Exeunt* THEODORE *and* GONFRED.

I play the prude: it is but venturing—                    130
Why should he be so earnest? Come, my friend,
Let us to Friedburg castle.


# ACT II

SCENE I. *An Ante-chamber in the Castle.*

*Enter* LUDOLPH *and* SIGIFRED.

LUDOLPH. No more advices, no more cautioning:
  I leave it all to fate—to any thing!
  I cannot square my conduct to time, place,
  Or circumstance; to me 'tis all a mist!
SIGIFRED. I say no more.
LUDOLPH.                    It seems I am to wait
  Here in the ante-room;—that may be a trifle.
  You see now how I dance attendance here,
  Without that tyrant temper, you so blame,
  Snapping the rein. You have medicin'd me
  With good advices; and I here remain,                    10
  In this most honourable ante-room,
  Your patient scholar.
SIGIFRED.                    Do not wrong me, Prince.
  By Heavens, I'd rather kiss Duke Conrad's slipper,
  When in the morning he doth yawn with pride,
  Than see you humbled but a half-degree!
  Truth is, the Emperor would fain dismiss
  The nobles ere he sees you.

*Enter* GONFRED, *from the Council-room.*

LUDOLPH.                    Well, sir! what?
GONFRED. Great honour to the Prince! The Emperor,
  Hearing that his brave son had re-appeared,
  Instant dismiss'd the Council from his sight,                    20
  As Jove fans off the clouds. Even now they pass.

*[Exit.*

*Enter the Nobles from the Council-room. They cross the stage, bowing with respect to* LUDOLPH, *he frowning on them.* CONRAD *follows. Exeunt Nobles.*

LUDOLPH. Not the discoloured poisons of a fen,
   Which he who breathes feels warning of his death,
   Could taste so nauseous in the bodily sense,
   As these prodigious sycophants disgust
   The soul's fine palate.
CONRAD.               Princely Ludolph, hail!
   Welcome, thou younger sceptre to the realm!
   Strength to thy virgin crownet's golden buds,
   That they, against the winter of thy sire,
   May burst, and swell, and flourish round thy brows,    30
   Maturing to a weighty diadem!
   Yet be that hour far off; and may he live,
   Who waits for thee, as the chapp'd earth for rain.
   Set my life's star! I have lived long enough,
   Since under my glad roof, propitiously,
   Father and son each other re-possess.
LUDOLPH. Fine wording, Duke! but words could never yet
   Forestall the fates; have you not learnt that yet?
   Let me look well: your features are the same;
   Your gait the same; your hair of the same shade;    40
   As one I knew some passed weeks ago,
   Who sung far different notes into mine ears.
   I have mine own particular comments on 't;
   You have your own, perhaps.
CONRAD.              My gracious Prince,
   All men may err. In truth I was deceived
   In your great father's nature, as you were.
   Had I known that of him I have since known,
   And what you soon will learn, I would have turn'd
   My sword to my own throat, rather than held
   Its threatening edge against a good King's quiet:    50
   Or with one word fever'd you, gentle Prince,
   Who seem'd to me, as rugged times then went,
   Indeed too much oppress'd. May I be bold
   To tell the Emperor you will haste to him?
LUDOLPH. Your Dukedom's privilege will grant so much.
                              [*Exit* CONRAD.

He's very close to Otho, Sigifred.
Your hand—I go. Ha! here the thunder comes
Sullen against the wind! If in two angry brows
My safety lies, then Sigifred, I'm safe.

*Enter* OTHO *and* CONRAD.

OTHO. Will you make Titan play the lackey-page          60
    To chattering pigmies? I would have you know
    That such neglect of our high Majesty
    Annuls all feel of kindred. What is son,—
    Or friend,—or brother,—or all ties of blood,—
    When the whole kingdom, centred in ourself,
    Is rudely slighted? Who am I to wait?
    By Peter's chair! I have upon my tongue
    A word to fright the proudest spirit here!—
    Death!—and slow tortures to the hardy fool,
    Who dares take such large charter from our smiles!      70
    Conrad, we would be private. Sigifred!
    Off! And none pass this way on pain of death!

                    [*Exeunt* CONRAD *and* SIGIFRED.

LUDOLPH. This was but half expected, my good sire,
    Yet I am griev'd at it, to the full height,
    As though my hopes of favour had been whole.
OTHO. How you indulge yourself! What can you hope for?
LUDOLPH. Nothing, my liege; I have to hope for nothing.
    I come to greet you as a loving son,
    And then depart, if I may be so free,
    Seeing that blood of yours in my warm veins          80
    Has not yet mitigated into milk.
OTHO. What would you, sir?
LUDOLPH.                    A lenient banishment;
    So please you let me unmolested pass
    This Conrad's gates, to the wide air again.
    I want no more. A rebel wants no more.
OTHO. And shall I let a rebel loose again
    To muster kites and eagles 'gainst my head?
    No, obstinate boy, you shall be kept cag'd up,
    Serv'd with harsh food, with scum for Sunday-drink.
LUDOLPH. Indeed!
OTHO.                    And chains too heavy for your life:      90

I'll choose a gaoler, whose swart monstrous face
Shall be a hell to look upon, and she—

LUDOLPH.                                    Ha!

OTHO. Shall be your fair Auranthe

LUDOLPH.                          Amaze! Amaze!

OTHO. To-day you marry her.

LUDOLPH.                      This is a sharp jest!

OTHO. No. None at all. When have I said a lie?

LUDOLPH. If I sleep not, I am a waking wretch.

OTHO. Not a word more. Let me embrace my child.

LUDOLPH. I dare not. 'Twould pollute so good a father!
   O heavy crime! that your son's blinded eyes
   Could not see all his parent's love aright,          100
   As now I see it. Be not kind to me—
   Punish me not with favour.

OTHO.                          Are you sure,
   Ludolph, you have no saving plea in store?

LUDOLPH. My father, none!

OTHO.                      Then you astonish me.

LUDOLPH. No, I have no plea. Disobedience,
   Rebellion, obstinacy, blasphemy,
   Are all my counsellors. If they can make
   My crooked deed show good and plausible,
   Then grant me loving pardon, but not else,
   Good Gods! not else, in any way, my liege!          110

OTHO. You are a most perplexing, noble boy.

LUDOLPH. You not less a perplexing noble father.

OTHO. Well, you shall have free passport through the gates.
   Farewell!

LUDOLPH. Farewell! and by these tears believe,
   And still remember, I repent in pain
   All my misdeeds!

OTHO.              Ludolph, I will! I will!
   But, Ludolph, ere you go, I would enquire
   If you, in all your wandering, ever met
   A certain Arab haunting in these parts.

LUDOLPH. No, my good lord, I cannot say I did.          120

OTHO. Make not your father blind before his time;
   Nor let these arms paternal hunger more
   For an embrace, to dull the appetite
   Of my great love for thee, my supreme child!

Come near, and let me breathe into thine ear.
I knew you through disguise. You are the Arab!
You can't deny it.                    [*Embracing him.*
LUDOLPH.          Happiest of days!
OTHO. We'll make it so.
LUDOLPH.                  'Stead of one fatted calf
  Ten hecatombs shall bellow out their last,
  Smote 'twixt the horns by the death-stunning mace     130
  Of Mars, and all the soldiery shall feast
  Nobly as Nimrod's masons, when the towers
  Of Nineveh new kiss'd the parted clouds!
OTHO. Large as a God speak out, where all is thine.
LUDOLPH. Aye, father, but the fire in my sad breast
  Is quench'd with inward tears! I must rejoice
  For you, whose wings so shadow over me
  In tender victory, but for myself
  I still must mourn. The fair Auranthe mine!
  Too great a boon! I prythee let me ask         140
  What more than I know of could so have changed
  Your purpose touching her?
OTHO.                    At a word, this:
  In no deed did you give me more offence
  Than your rejection of Erminia.
  To my appalling, I saw too good proof
  Of your keen-eyed suspicion,—she is naught!
LUDOLPH. You are convinc'd?
OTHO.                    Aye, spite of her sweet looks.
  O, that my brother's daughter should so fall!
  Her fame has pass'd into the grosser lips
  Of soldiers in their cups.
LUDOLPH.              'Tis very sad.         150
OTHO. No more of her. Auranthe—Ludolph, come!
  This marriage be the bond of endless peace!    [*Exeunt.*


SCENE II. *The Entrance of* GERSA'S *Tent in the Hungarian
            Camp.*

*Enter* ERMINIA.

ERMINIA. Where! where! where shall I find a messenger?
  A trusty soul? A good man in the camp?

Shall I go myself? Monstrous wickedness!
O cursed Conrad! devilish Auranthe!
Here is proof palpable as the bright sun!
O for a voice to reach the Emperor's ears!
                                    [*Shouts in the Camp.*

*Enter an* HUNGARIAN CAPTAIN.

CAPTAIN. Fair prisoner, hear you those joyous shouts?
    The king—aye, now our king,—but still your slave,
    Young Gersa, from a short captivity
    Has just return'd. He bids me say, bright Dame,        10
    That even the homage of his ranged chiefs
    Cures not his hot impatience to behold
    Such beauty once again. What ails you, lady?
ERMINIA. Say, is not that a German, yonder? There!
CAPTAIN. Methinks by his stout bearing he should be—
    Yes—'tis one Albert; a brave German knight,
    And much in the emperor's favour.
ERMINIA.                                I would fain
    Enquire of friends and kinsfolk; how they fared
    In these rough times. Brave soldier, as you pass
    To royal Gersa with my humble thanks,                  20
    Will you send yonder knight to me?
CAPTAIN.                                I will.        [*Exit.*
ERMINIA. Yes, he was ever known to be a man
    Frank, open, generous; Albert I may trust.
    O proof! proof! proof! Albert's an honest man;
    Not Ethelbert the monk, if he were here,
    Would I hold more trustworthy. Now!

*Enter* ALBERT.

ALBERT.                                Good Gods!
    Lady Erminia! are you prisoner
    In this beleaguer'd camp? Or are you here
    Of your own will? You pleas'd to send for me.
    By Venus, 'tis a pity I knew not                       30
    Your plight before, and, by her Son, I swear
    To do you every service you can ask.
    What would the fairest—?
ERMINIA.                        Albert, will you swear?
ALBERT. I have. Well?

ERMINIA.                Albert, you have fame to lose.
  If men, in court and camp, lie not outright,
  You should be, from a thousand, chosen forth
  To do an honest deed. Shall I confide—?
ALBERT. Aye, anything to me, fair creature. Do;
  Dictate my task. Sweet woman,—
ERMINIA.                        Truce with that.
  You understand me not; and, in your speech,          40
  I see how far the slander is abroad.
  Without proof could you think me innocent?
ALBERT. Lady, I should rejoice to know you so.
ERMINIA. If you have any pity for a maid,
  Suffering a daily death from evil tongues;
  Any compassion for that Emperor's niece,
  Who, for your bright sword and clear honesty,
  Lifted you from the crowd of common men
  Into the lap of honour;—save me, knight!
ALBERT. How? Make it clear; if it be possible,          50
  I, by the banner of Saint Maurice, swear
  To right you.
ERMINIA.            Possible!—Easy. O my heart!
  This letter's not so soil'd but you may read it:—
  Possible! There—that letter! Read—read it.
                              [*Gives him a letter.*
ALBERT (*reading*). 'To the Duke Conrad.—Forget the threat
  you made at parting, and I will forget to send the Emperor
  letters and papers of your's I have become possessed of.
  His life is no trifle to me; his death you shall find none to
  yourself.' [*Speaks to himself:*] 'Tis me—my life that's
  pleaded for! [*Reads*] 'He, for his own sake, will be dumb as
  the grave. Erminia has my shame fix'd upon her, sure as a
  wen. We are safe.   AURANTHE.'
  A she-devil! A dragon! I her imp!
  Fire of Hell! Auranthe—lewd demon!
  Where got you this? Where? When?
ERMINIA. I found it in the tent, among some spoils
  Which, being noble, fell to Gersa's lot.
  Come in, and see.              [*They go in and return.*
ALBERT.              Villainy! Villainy!
  Conrad's sword, his corslet, and his helm,
  And his letter. Caitiff, he shall feel—

ERMINIA. I see you are thunderstruck. Haste, haste away!

ALBERT. O I am tortured by this villainy.

ERMINIA. You needs must be. Carry it swift to Otho;
Tell him, moreover, I am prisoner
Here in this camp, where all the sisterhood,
Forc'd from their quiet cells, are parcell'd out
For slaves among these Huns. Away! Away!

ALBERT. I am gone.

ERMINIA.                 Swift be your steed! Within this hour
The Emperor will see it.

ALBERT.                 Ere I sleep:
That I can swear.                          [*Hurries out*.

GERSA [*without*]. Brave captains! thanks. Enough          80
Of loyal homage now!

*Enter* GERSA.

ERMINIA.                 Hail, royal Hun!

GERSA. What means this, fair one? Why in such alarm?
Who was it hurried by me so distract?
It seem'd you were in deep discourse together;
Your doctrine has not been so harsh to him
As to my poor deserts. Come, come, be plain.
I am no jealous fool to kill you both,
Or, for such trifles, rob the adorned world
Of such a beauteous vestal.

ERMINIA.                 I grieve, my Lord,
To hear you condescend to ribald phrase.                   90

GERSA. This is too much! Hearken, my lady pure!

ERMINIA. Silence! and hear the magic of a name—
Erminia! I am she,—the Emperor's niece!
Prais'd be the Heavens, I now dare own myself!

GERSA. Erminia! Indeed! I've heard of her.
Prythee, fair lady, what chance brought you here?

ERMINIA. Ask your own soldiers.

GERSA.                 And you dare own your name.
For loveliness you may—and for the rest
My vein is not censorious.

ERMINIA.                 Alas! poor me!
'Tis false indeed.

GERSA.                 Indeed you are too fair:          100
The swan, soft leaning on her fledgy breast,

When to the stream she launches, looks not back
With such a tender grace; nor are her wings
So white as your soul is, if that but be
Twin-picture to your face. Erminia!
To-day, for the first day, I am a king,
Yet would I give my unworn crown away
To know you spotless.

ERMINIA.                    Trust me one day more,
Generously, without more certain guarantee,
Than this poor face you deign to praise so much;          110
After that, say and do whate'er you please.
If I have any knowledge of you, sir,
I think, nay I am sure, you will grieve much
To hear my story. O be gentle to me,
For I am sick and faint with many wrongs,
Tir'd out, and weary-worn with contumelies.

GERSA. Poor lady!

*Enter* ETHELBERT.

ERMINIA.              Gentle Prince, 'tis false indeed.
Good morrow, holy father! I have had
Your prayers, though I look'd for you in vain.           119

ETHELBERT. Blessings upon you, daughter! Sure you look
Too cheerful for these foul pernicious days.
Young man, you heard this virgin say 'twas false,—
'Tis false, I say. What! can you not employ
Your temper elsewhere, 'mong these burly tents,
But you must taunt this dove, for she hath lost
The Eagle Otho to beat off assault?
Fie! fie! But I will be her guard myself;
In the Emperor's name. I here demand of you
Herself, and all her sisterhood. She false!

GERSA. Peace! peace, old man! I cannot think she is.     130

ETHELBERT. Whom I have known from her first infancy,
Baptiz'd her in the bosom of the Church,
Watch'd her, as anxious husbandmen the grain,
From the first shoot till the unripe mid-May,
Then to the tender ear of her June days,
Which, lifting sweet abroad its timid green,
Is blighted by the touch of calumny;
You cannot credit such a monstrous tale.

GERSA. I cannot. Take her. Fair Erminia,
   I follow you to Friedburg,—is't not so?                    140
ERMINIA. Aye, so we purpose.
ETHELBERT.                     Daughter, do you so?
   How's this? I marvel! Yet you look not mad.
ERMINIA. I have good news to tell you, Ethelbert.
GERSA. Ho! ho, there! Guards!
   Your blessing, father! Sweet Erminia,
   Believe me, I am well nigh sure—
ERMINIA.                          Farewell!
   Short time will show.              [*Enter Chiefs.*
                        Yes, father Ethelbert,
   I have news precious as we pass along.
ETHELBERT. Dear daughter, you shall guide me.
ERMINIA.                                To no ill.
GERSA. Command an escort to the Friedburg lines.   150
                                   [*Exeunt Chiefs.*

   Pray let me lead. Fair lady, forget not
   Gersa, how he believ'd you innocent.
   I follow you to Friedburg with all speed.      [*Exeunt.*


## ACT III

### SCENE I. *The Country.*

#### *Enter* ALBERT.

ALBERT. O that the earth were empty, as when Cain
   Had no perplexity to hide his head!
   Or that the sword of some brave enemy
   Had put a sudden stop to my hot breath,
   And hurl'd me down the illimitable gulph
   Of times past, unremember'd! Better so
   Than thus fast-limed in a cursed snare,
   The limbo of a wanton. This the end
   Of an aspiring life! My boyhood past
   In feud with wolves and bears, when no eye saw    10
   The solitary warfare, fought for love
   Of honour 'mid the growling wilderness.
   My sturdier youth, maturing to the sword,
   Won by the syren-trumpets, and the ring

Of shields upon the pavement, when bright-mail'd
Henry the Fowler pass'd the streets of Prague.
Was't to this end I louted and became
The menial of Mars, and held a spear
Sway'd by command, as corn is by the wind?
Is it for this, I now am lifted up                          20
By a well-judging Emperor, to see
My honour be my executioner,—
My love of fame, my prided honesty
Put to the torture for confessional?
Then the damn'd crime of blurting to the world
A woman's secret—though a fiend she be,
Too tender of my ignominious life;
But then to wrong the generous Emperor
In such a searching point, were to give up
My soul for foot-ball at Hell's holiday!                    30
I must confess,—and cut my throat,—to-day?
To-morrow? Ho! some wine!

*Enter* SIGIFRED.

SIGIFRED.                          A fine humour—
ALBERT. Who goes there? Count Sigifred? Ha! Ha!
SIGIFRED. What, man, do you mistake the hollow sky
   For a throng'd tavern,—and these stubbed trees
   For old serge hangings,—me, your humble friend,
   For a poor waiter? Why, man, how you stare!
   What gipsies have you been carousing with?
   No, no more wine; methinks you've had enough.
ALBERT. You well may laugh and banter. What a fool    40
   An injury may make of a staid man!
   You shall know all anon.
SIGIFRED.                      Some tavern brawl?
ALBERT. 'Twas with some people out of common reach;
   Revenge is difficult.
SIGIFRED.                   I am your friend;
   We meet again to-day, and can confer
   Upon it. For the present I'm in haste.
ALBERT. Whither?
SIGIFRED.           To fetch King Gersa to the feast.
   The Emperor on this marriage is so hot,
   Pray Heaven it end not in apoplexy!

The very porters, as I pass'd the doors,                    50
Heard his loud laugh, and answer'd in full choir.
I marvel, Albert, you delay so long
From those bright revelries; go, show yourself,
You may be made a duke.

ALBERT.                          Aye, very like:
Pray, what day has his Highness fix'd upon?

SIGIFRED. For what?

ALBERT.                    The marriage. What else can I mean?

SIGIFRED. To-day! O, I forgot, you could not know;
The news is scarce a minute old with me.

ALBERT. Married to-day! To-day! You did not say so?

SIGIFRED. Now, while I speak to you, their comely heads 60
Are bow'd before the mitre.

ALBERT.                          O! monstrous!

SIGIFRED. What is this?

ALBERT.                    Nothing, Sigifred. Farewell!
We'll meet upon our subject. Farewell, count!
                                              [*Exit.*

SIGIFRED. Is this clear-headed Albert? He brain-turn'd!
'Tis as portentous as a meteor.              [*Exit.*


SCENE II. *An Apartment in the Castle.*

*Enter, as from Marriage,* OTHO, LUDOLPH, AURANTHE,
    CONRAD, *Nobles, Knights, Ladies, &c. &c. &c. Music.*

OTHO. Now, Ludolph! Now, Auranthe! Daughter fair!
What can I find to grace your nuptial day
More than my love, and these wide realms in fee?

LUDOLPH. I have too much.

AURANTHE.                    And I, my liege, by far.

LUDOLPH. Auranthe! I have! O, my bride, my love!
Not all the gaze upon us can restrain
My eyes, too long poor exiles from thy face,
From adoration, and my foolish tongue
From uttering soft responses to the love
I see in thy mute beauty beaming forth!            10
Fair creature, bless me with a single word!
All mine!

AURANTHE. Spare, spare me, my Lord; I swoon else.

LUDOLPH. Soft beauty! by to-morrow I should die,
    Wert thou not mine.                  [*They talk apart.*
FIRST LADY.        How deep she has bewitch'd him!
FIRST KNIGHT. Ask you for her recipe for love philtres.
SECOND LADY. They hold the Emperor in admiration.
OTHO. If ever king was happy, that am I!
    What are the cities 'yond the Alps to me,
    The provinces about the Danube's mouth,
    The promise of fair soil beyond the Rhone;       20
    Or routing out of Hyperborean hordes,
    To these fair children, stars of a new age?
    Unless perchance I might rejoice to win
    This little ball of earth, and chuck it them
    To play with!
AURANTHE. Nay, my Lord, I do not know.
LUDOLPH. Let me not famish.
OTHO (*to Conrad*).        Good Franconia,
    You heard what oath I sware, as the sun rose,
    That unless Heaven would send me back my son,
    My Arab,—no soft music should enrich
    The cool wine, kiss'd off with a soldier's smack;    30
    Now all my empire, barter'd for one feast,
    Seems poverty.
CONRAD.        Upon the neighbour-plain
    The heralds have prepar'd a royal lists;
    Your knights, found war-proof in the bloody field,
    Speed to the game.
OTHO.        Well, Ludolph, what say you?
LUDOLPH. My lord!
OTHO.        A tourney?
CONRAD.        Or, if 't please you best—
LUDOLPH. I want no more!
FIRST LADY.        He soars!
SECOND LADY.        Past all reason.
LUDOLPH. Though heaven's choir
    Should in a vast circumference descend
    And sing for my delight, I'd stop my ears!    40
    Though bright Apollo's car stood burning here,
    And he put out an arm to bid me mount,
    His touch an immortality, not I!
    This earth, this palace, this room, Auranthe!

OTHO. This is a little painful; just too much.
   Conrad, if he flames longer in this wise,
   I shall believe in wizard-woven loves
   And old romances; but I'll break the spell.
   Ludolph!
CONRAD.  He will be calm, anon.
LUDOLPH.                    You call'd?
OTHO. Come, come, a little sober sense, Ludolph.      49a
LUDOLPH. Yes, yes, yes, I offend. You must forgive me;  50
   Not being quite recover'd from the stun
   Of your large bounties. A tourney, is it not?

                                [*A senet heard faintly.*

CONRAD. The trumpets reach us.
ETHELBERT [*without*].          On your peril, sirs,
   Detain us!
FIRST VOICE [*without*]. Let not the abbot pass.
SECOND VOICE [*without*].                    No,
   On your lives!
FIRST VOICE [*without*]. Holy father, you must not.
ETHELBERT [*without*]. Otho!
OTHO.                 Who calls on Otho?
ETHELBERT [*without*].                    Ethelbert!
OTHO. Let him come in.

        *Enter* ETHELBERT *leading in* ERMINIA.

                    Thou cursed abbot, why
   Hast brought pollution to our holy rites?
   Hast thou no fear of hangman, or the faggot?
   Mad Churchman, would'st thou be impaled alive?    59a
LUDOLPH. What portent—what strange prodigy is this?  60
CONRAD. Away!
ETHELBERT.      You, Duke?
ERMINIA.                Albert has surely fail'd me!
   Look at the Emperor's brow upon me bent!
ETHELBERT. A sad delay!
CONRAD.                Away, thou guilty thing!
ETHELBERT. You again, Duke? Justice, most mighty Otho!
   You—go to your sister there and plot again,
   A quick plot, swift as thought to save your heads;
   For lo! the toils are spread around your den,

The world is all agape to see dragg'd forth
Two ugly monsters.
LUDOLPH.                    What means he, my lord?
CONRAD. I cannot guess.
ETHELBERT.              Best ask your lady sister,        70
Whether the riddle puzzles her beyond
The power of utterance.
CONRAD.                    Foul barbarian, cease:
The Princess faints!
LUDOLPH.              Stab him! O, sweetest wife!

*[Attendants bear off* AURANTHE.

ERMINIA. Alas!
ETHELBERT.   Your wife?
LUDOLPH.                    Aye, Satan! does that yerk ye?
ETHELBERT. Wife! so soon!
LUDOLPH.                    Aye, wife! Oh, impudence!
Thou bitter mischief! Venomous mad priest!
How dar'st thou lift those beetle brows at me?
Me—the prince Ludolph, in this presence here,
Upon my marriage-day, and scandalize
My joys with such opprobrious surprise?        80
Wife! Why dost linger on that syllable,
As if it were some demon's name pronounc'd
To summon harmful lightning, and make roar
The sleepy thunder? Hast no sense of fear?
No ounce of man in thy mortality?
Tremble! for, at my nod, the sharpen'd axe
Will make thy bold tongue quiver to the roots,
Those grey lids wink, and thou not know it more!
ETHELBERT. O, poor deceived Prince! I pity thee!
Great Otho! I claim justice—
LUDOLPH.                    Thou shalt have 't!        90
Thine arms from forth a pulpit of hot fire
Shall sprawl distracted! O that that dull cowl
Were some most sensitive portion of thy life,
That I might give it to my hounds to tear!
Thy girdle some fine zealous-pained nerve
To girth my saddle! And those devil's beads
Each one a life, that I might, every day,
Crush one with Vulcan's hammer!

OTHO.                                    Peace, my son;
  You far outstrip my spleen in this affair.
  Let us be calm, and hear the abbot's plea            100
  For this intrusion.
LUDOLPH.            I am silent, sire.
OTHO. Conrad, see all depart not wanted here.
                 [*Exeunt Knights, Ladies, &c.*
  Ludolph, be calm. Ethelbert, peace awhile.
  This mystery demands an audience
  Of a just judge, and that will Otho be.
LUDOLPH. Why has he time to breathe another word?
OTHO. Ludolph, old Ethelbert, be sure, comes not
  To beard us for no cause; he's not the man
  To cry himself up an ambassador
  Without credentials.
LUDOLPH.               I'll chain up myself.           110
OTHO. Old Abbot, stand here forth. Lady Erminia,
  Sit. And now, Abbot! what have you to say?
  Our ear is open. First we here denounce
  Hard penalties against thee, if 't be found
  The cause for which you have disturb'd us here,
  Making our bright hours muddy, be a thing
  Of little moment.
ETHELBERT.          See this innocent!
  Otho! thou father of the people call'd,
  Is her life nothing? Her fair honour nothing?
  Her tears from matins until even-song            120
  Nothing? Her burst heart nothing? Emperor!
  Is this your gentle niece—the simplest flower
  Of the world's herbal—this fair lilly blanch'd
  Still with the dews of piety, this meek lady
  Here sitting like an angel newly-shent,
  Who veils its snowy wings and grows all pale,—
  Is she nothing?
OTHO.              What more to the purpose, abbot?
LUDOLPH. Whither is he winding?
CONRAD.                          No clue yet!
ETHELBERT. You have heard, my Liege, and so, no doubt,
    all here,
  Foul, poisonous, malignant whisperings;            130
  Nay open speech, rude mockery grown common,

Against the spotless nature and clear fame
Of the princess Erminia, your niece.
I have intruded here thus suddenly,
Because I hold those base weeds, with tight hand,
Which now disfigure her fair growing stem,
Waiting but for your sign to pull them up
By the dark roots, and leave her palpable,
To all men's sight, a Lady, innocent.
The ignominy of that whisper'd tale                       140
About a midnight gallant, seen to climb
A window to her chamber neighbour'd near,
I will from her turn off, and put the load
On the right shoulders; on that wretch's head,
Who, by close stratagems, did save herself,
Chiefly by shifting to this lady's room
A rope-ladder for false witness.

LUDOLPH.                        Most atrocious!

OTHO. Ethelbert, proceed.

ETHELBERT.                With sad lips I shall:
For, in the healing of one wound, I fear
To make a greater. His young highness here              150
To-day was married.

LUDOLPH.           Good.

ETHELBERT.                    Would it were good!
Yet why do I delay to spread abroad
The names of those two vipers, from whose jaws
A deadly breath went forth to taint and blast
This guileless lady?

OTHO.               Abbot, speak their names.

ETHELBERT. A minute first. It cannot be—but may
I ask, great judge, if you to-day have put
A letter by unread?

OTHO.               Does 't end in this?

CONRAD. Out with their names!

ETHELBERT.                  Bold sinner, say you so?

LUDOLPH. Out, tedious monk!

OTHO.                      Confess, or by the wheel— 160

ETHELBERT. My evidence cannot be far away;
And, though it never come, be on my head
The crime of passing an attaint upon
The slanderers of this virgin.

LUDOLPH.                              Speak aloud!

ETHELBERT. Auranthe, and her brother there.

CONRAD.                                          Amaze!

LUDOLPH. Throw them from the windows!

OTHO. Do what you will!

LUDOLPH.                     What shall I do with them?
　Something of quick dispatch, for should she hear,
　My soft Auranthe, her sweet mercy would
　Prevail against my fury. Damned priest!                170
　What swift death wilt thou die? As to the lady
　I touch her not.

ETHELBERT.            Illustrious Otho, stay!
　An ample store of misery thou hast,
　Choak not the granary of thy noble mind
　With more bad bitter grain, too difficult
　A cud for the repentance of a man
　Grey-growing. To thee only I appeal,
　Not to thy noble son, whose yeasting youth
　Will clear itself, and crystal turn again.
　A young man's heart, by Heaven's blessing, is          180
　A wide world, where a thousand new-born hopes
　Empurple fresh the melancholy blood:
　But an old man's is narrow, tenantless
　Of hopes, and stuff'd with many memories,
　Which, being pleasant, ease the heavy pulse—
　Painful, clog up and stagnate. Weigh this matter
　Even as a miser balances his coin;
　And, in the name of mercy, give command
　That your knight Albert be brought here before you.
　He will expound this riddle; he will show              190
　A noon-day proof of bad Auranthe's guilt.

OTHO. Let Albert straight be summon'd.

                                    [*Exit one of the Nobles.*

LUDOLPH.                                Impossible!
　I cannot doubt—I will not—no—to doubt
　Is to be ashes!—wither'd up to death!

OTHO. My gentle Ludolph, harbour not a fear;
　You do yourself much wrong.

LUDOLPH.                        O, wretched dolt!
　Now, when my foot is almost on thy neck,
　Wilt thou infuriate me? Proof! Thou fool!

Why wilt thou teaze impossibility
With such a thick-skull'd persevering suit?                    200
Fanatic obstinacy! Prodigy!
Monster of folly! Ghost of a turn'd brain!
You puzzle me,—you haunt me,—when I dream
Of you my brain will split! Bald sorcerer!
Juggler! May I come near you? On my soul
I know not whether to pity, curse, or laugh.

*Enter* ALBERT, *and the Nobleman.*

Here, Albert, this old phantom wants a proof!
Give him his proof! A camel's load of proofs!
OTHO. Albert, I speak to you as to a man
Whose words once utter'd pass like current gold;              210
And therefore fit to calmly put a close
To this brief tempest. Do you stand possess'd
Of any proof against the honourableness
Of Lady Auranthe, our new-spoused daughter?
ALBERT. You chill me with astonishment. How's this?
My Liege, what proof should I have 'gainst a fame
Impossible of slur?                      [OTHO *rises.*
ERMINIA.            O wickedness!
ETHELBERT. Deluded monarch, 'tis a cruel lie.
OTHO. Peace, rebel-priest!
CONRAD.               Insult beyond credence!
ERMINIA. Almost a dream!
LUDOLPH.               We have awaken'd from          220
A foolish dream that from my brow hath wrung
A wrathful dew. O folly! why did I
So act the lion with this silly gnat?
Let them depart. Lady Erminia!
I ever griev'd for you, as who did not?
But now you have, with such a brazen front,
So most maliciously, so madly striven
To dazzle the soft moon, when tenderest clouds
Should be unloop'd around to curtain her;
I leave you to the desert of the world                        230
Almost with pleasure. Let them be set free
For me! I take no personal revenge
More than against a nightmare, which a man
Forgets in the new dawn.           [*Exit* LUDOLPH.

OTHO. Still in extremes! No, they must not be loose.

ETHELBERT. Albert, I must suspect thee of a crime
So fiendish—

OTHO.          Fear'st thou not my fury, monk?
Conrad, be they in your sure custody
Till we determine some fit punishment.
It is so mad a deed, I must reflect                           240
And question them in private; for perhaps,
By patient scrutiny, we may discover
Whether they merit death, or should be placed
In care of the physicians.

          [*Exeunt* OTHO *and Nobles,* ALBERT *following.*

CONRAD. My guards, ho!

ERMINIA.                    Albert, wilt thou follow there?
Wilt thou creep dastardly behind his back,
And slink away from a weak woman's eye?
Turn, thou court-Janus! thou forget'st thyself;
Here is the Duke, waiting with open arms,

          [*Enter Guards.*

To thank thee; here congratulate each other;           250
Wring hands; embrace; and swear how lucky 'twas
That I, by happy chance, hit the right man
Of all the world to trust in.

ALBERT.                    Trust! to me!

CONRAD [*aside*]. He is the sole one in this mystery.

ERMINIA. Well, I give up, and save my prayers for Heaven!
You, who could do this deed, would ne'er relent,
Though, at my words, the hollow prison-vaults
Would groan for pity.

CONRAD.                    Manacle them both!

ETHELBERT. I know it—it must be—I see it all!
Albert, thou art the minion!

ERMINIA.                    Ah! too plain—           260

CONRAD. Silence! Gag up their mouths! I cannot bear
More of this brawling. That the Emperor
Had plac'd you in some other custody!
Bring them away.                    [*Exeunt all but* ALBERT.

ALBERT. Though my name perish from the book of honour,
Almost before the recent ink is dry,
And be no more remember'd after death,
Than any drummer's in the muster-roll;
Yet shall I season high my sudden fall

With triumph o'er that evil-witted duke!  270
He shall feel what it is to have the hand
Of a man drowning, on his hateful throat.

*Enter* GERSA *and* SIGIFRED.

GERSA. What discord is at ferment in this house?
SIGIFRED. We are without conjecture; not a soul
    We met could answer any certainty.
GERSA. Young Ludolph, like a fiery arrow, shot
    By us.
SIGIFRED. The Emperor, with cross'd arms, in thought.
GERSA. In one room music, in another sadness,
    Perplexity every where!
ALBERT.                    A trifle mere!
    Follow; your presences will much avail  280
    To tune our jarred spirits. I'll explain.      [*Exeunt.*

## ACT IV

### SCENE I. AURANTHE'S *Apartment.*

AURANTHE *and* CONRAD *discovered.*

CONRAD. Well, well, I know what ugly jeopardy       "
    We are cag'd in; you need not pester that
    Into my ears. Prythee, let me be spared
    A foolish tongue, that I may bethink me
    Of remedies with some deliberation.
    You cannot doubt but 'tis in Albert's power
    To crush or save us?
AURANTHE.               No, I cannot doubt.
    He has, assure yourself, by some strange means,
    My secret; which I ever hid from him,
    Knowing his mawkish honesty.
CONRAD.                         Curs'd slave!       10
AURANTHE. Ay, I could almost curse him now myself.
    Wretched impediment! Evil genius!
    A glue upon my wings, that cannot spread,
    When they should span the provinces! A snake,
    A scorpion, sprawling on the first gold step,
    Conducting to the throne, high canopied.
CONRAD. You would not hear my counsel, when his life

Might have been trodden out, all sure and hush'd;
Now the dull animal forsooth must be
Intreated, managed! When can you contrive          20
The interview he demands?

AURANTHE.                    As speedily
It must be done as my brib'd woman can
Unseen conduct him to me; but I fear
'Twill be impossible, while the broad day
Comes through the panes with persecuting glare.
Methinks, if 't now were night I could intrigue
With darkness, bring the stars to second me,
And settle all this trouble.

CONRAD.                    Nonsense! Child!
See him immediately; why not now?

AURANTHE.  Do you forget that even the senseless door-
     posts                                          30
Are on the watch and gape through all the house?
How many whisperers there are about,
Hungry for evidence to ruin me;
Men I have spurn'd, and women I have taunted?
Besides, the foolish prince sends, minute whiles,
His pages—so they tell me—to enquire
After my health, entreating, if I please,
To see me.

CONRAD.        Well, suppose this Albert here;
What is your power with him?

AURANTHE.                    He should be
My echo, my taught parrot! but I fear             40
He will be cur enough to bark at me;
Have his own say; read me some silly creed
'Bout shame and pity.

CONRAD.                What will you do then?

AURANTHE. What I shall do, I know not: what I would
Cannot be done; for see, this chamber-floor
Will not yield to the pick-axe and the spade,—
Here is no quiet depth of hollow ground.

CONRAD. Sister, you have grown sensible and wise,
Seconding, ere I speak it, what is now,
I hope, resolv'd between us.

AURANTHE.            Say, what is 't?          50

CONRAD. You need not be his sexton too: a man

May carry that with him shall make him die
Elsewhere,—give that to him; pretend the while
You will to-morrow succumb to his wishes,
Be what they may, and send him from the Castle
On some fool's errand; let his latest groan
Frighten the wolves!

AURANTHE.              Alas! he must not die!

CONRAD. Would you were both hears'd up in stifling lead!
    Detested—

AURANTHE. Conrad, hold! I would not bear
    The little thunder of your fretful tongue,                60
    Tho' I alone were taken in these toils,
    And you could free me; but remember, sir,
    You live alone in my security:
    So keep your wits at work, for your own sake,
    Not mine, and be more mannerly.

CONRAD.                        Thou wasp!
    If my domains were emptied of these folk,
    And I had thee to starve—

AURANTHE.                    O, marvellous!
    But Conrad, now be gone; the Host is look'd for;
    Cringe to the Emperor, entertain the nobles.
    And, do ye mind, above all things, proclaim          70
    My sickness, with a brother's sadden'd eye,
    Condoling with Prince Ludolph. In fit time
    Return to me.

CONRAD.        I leave you to your thoughts.        [Exit.

AURANTHE (sola). Down, down, proud temper! down,
        Auranthe's pride!
    Why do I anger him when I should kneel?
    Conrad! Albert! help! help! What can I do?
    O wretched woman! lost, wreck'd, swallow'd up,
    Accursed, blasted! O, thou golden Crown,
    Orbing along the serene firmament
    Of a wide empire, like a glowing moon;              80
    And thou, bright sceptre! lustrous in my eyes,—
    There—as the fabled fair Hesperian tree,
    Bearing a fruit more precious! graceful thing,
    Delicate, godlike, magic! must I leave
    Thee to melt in the visionary air,
    Ere, by one grasp, this common hand is made

Imperial? I do not know the time
When I have wept for sorrow; but methinks
I could now sit upon the ground, and shed
Tears, tears of misery. O, the heavy day!            90
How shall I bear my life till Albert comes?
Ludolph! Erminia! Proofs! O heavy day!
Bring me some mourning weeds, that I may 'tire
Myself, as fits one wailing her own death:
Cut off these curls, and brand this lilly hand,
And throw these jewels from my loathing sight,—
Fetch me a missal, and a string of beads,—
A cup of bitter'd water, and a crust,—
I will confess, O holy father!—How!
What is this? Auranthe! thou fool, dolt,            100
Whimpering idiot! up! up! act and quell!
I am safe! Coward! why am I in fear?
Albert! he cannot stickle, chew the cud
In such a fine extreme,—impossible!
Who knocks?        [*Goes to the Door, listens, and opens it.*

*Enter* ALBERT.

Albert, I have been waiting for you here
With such an aching heart, such swooning throbs
On my poor brain, such cruel—cruel sorrow,
That I should claim your pity! Art not well?
ALBERT. Yes, lady, well.
AURANTHE.              You look not so, alas!      110
But pale, as if you brought some heavy news.
ALBERT. You know full well what makes me look so pale.
AURANTHE. No! Do I? Surely I am still to learn
Some horror; all I know, this present, is
I am near hustled to a dangerous gulph,
Which you can save me from,—and therefore safe,
So trusting in thy love; that should not make
Thee pale, my Albert.
ALBERT.              It does make me freeze.
AURANTHE. Why should it, love?
ALBERT.              You should not ask me that,
But make your own heart monitor, and save        120
Me the great pain of telling. You must know.

AURANTHE. Something has vext you, Albert. There are times
    When simplest things put on a sombre cast;
    A melancholy mood will haunt a man,
    Until most easy matters take the shape
    Of unachievable tasks; small rivulets
    Then seem impassable.
ALBERT.                    Do not cheat yourself
    With hope that gloss of words, or suppliant action,
    Or tears, or ravings, or self-threaten'd death,
    Can alter my resolve.
AURANTHE.              You make me tremble;          130
    Not so much at your threats, as at your voice,
    Untun'd, and harsh, and barren of all love.
ALBERT. You suffocate me! Stop this devil's parley,
    And listen to me; know me once for all.
AURANTHE. I thought I did. Alas! I am deceiv'd.
ALBERT. No, you are not deceiv'd. You took me for
    A man detesting all inhuman crime;
    And therefore kept from me your demon's plot
    Against Erminia. Silent? Be so still;
    For ever! Speak no more; but hear my words,          140
    Thy fate. Your safety I have bought to-day
    By blazoning a lie, which in the dawn
    I'll expiate with truth.
AURANTHE.            O cruel traitor!
ALBERT. For I would not set eyes upon thy shame;
    I would not see thee dragg'd to death by the hair,
    Penanc'd, and taunted on a scaffolding!
    To-night, upon the skirts of the blind wood
    That blackens northward of these horrid towers,
    I wait for you with horses. Choose your fate.
    Farewell.
AURANTHE. Albert, you jest; I'm sure you must.          150
    You, an ambitious Soldier! I, a Queen,
    One who could say,—Here, rule these Provinces!
    Take tribute from those cities for thyself!
    Empty these armouries, these treasuries,
    Muster thy warlike thousands at a nod!
    Go! conquer Italy!
ALBERT.            Auranthe, you have made
    The whole world chaff to me. Your doom is fix'd.

AURANTHE. Out, villain! dastard!

ALBERT. Look there to the door!
Who is it?

AURANTHE. Conrad, traitor!

ALBERT. Let him in.

[*Enter* CONRAD.

Do not affect amazement, hypocrite,   160
At seeing me in this chamber.

CONRAD. Auranthe?

ALBERT. Talk not with eyes, but speak your curses out
Against me, who would sooner crush and grind
A brace of toads, than league with them to oppress
An innocent lady, gull an Emperor,
More generous to me than autumn's sun
To ripening harvests.

AURANTHE. No more insult, sir!

ALBERT. Aye, clutch your scabbard; but, for prudence
sake,
Draw not the sword; 'twould make an uproar, Duke,
You would not hear the end of. At nightfall   170
Your lady sister, if I guess aright,
Will leave this busy castle. You had best
Take farewell too of worldly vanities.

CONRAD. Vassal!

ALBERT. To-morrow, when the Emperor sends
For loving Conrad, see you fawn on him.
Good even!

AURANTHE. You'll be seen!

ALBERT. See the coast clear then.

AURANTHE [*as he goes*]. Remorseless Albert! Cruel, cruel,
wretch! [*She lets him out.*

CONRAD. So, we must lick the dust?

AURANTHE. I follow him.

CONRAD. How? Where? The plan of your escape?

AURANTHE. He waits
For me with horses by the forest-side,   180
Northward.

CONRAD. Good, good! he dies. You go, say you?

AURANTHE. Perforce.

CONRAD. Be speedy, darkness! Till that comes,
Fiends keep you company! [*Exit.*

AURANTHE.                    And you! And you!
  And all men! Vanish! Oh! Oh! Oh!
                              [*Retires to an inner apartment.*


### SCENE II. *An Apartment in the Castle.*

*Enter* LUDOLPH *and* PAGE.

PAGE. Still very sick, my Lord; but now I went
  Knowing my duty to so good a Prince;
  And there her women in a mournful throng
  Stood in the passage whispering: if any
  Mov'd 'twas with careful steps and hush'd as death;
  They bid me stop.
LUDOLPH.               Good fellow, once again
  Make soft enquiry; prythee be not stay'd
  By any hindrance, but with gentlest force
  Break through her weeping servants, till thou com'st
  E'en to her chamber door, and there, fair boy,        10
  If with thy mother's milk thou hast suck'd in
  Any diviner eloquence; woo her ears
  With plaints for me more tender than the voice
  Of dying Echo, echoed.
PAGE.                    Kindest master!
  To know thee sad thus, will unloose my tongue
  In mournful syllables. Let but my words reach
  Her ears and she shall take them coupled with
  Moans from my heart and sighs not counterfeit.
  May I speed better!                  [*Exit* PAGE.
LUDOLPH.           Auranthe! My Life!
  Long have I lov'd thee, yet till now not lov'd:        20
  Remembering, as I do, hard-hearted times
  When I had heard even of thy death perhaps,
  And thoughtless—suffered thee to pass alone
  Into Elysium! now I follow thee
  A substance or a shadow, wheresoe'er
  Thou leadest me,—whether thy white feet press,
  With pleasant weight, the amorous-aching earth
  Or thro' the air thou pioneerest me,
  A shade! Yet sadly I predestinate!
  O unbenignest Love, why wilt thou let        30

Darkness steal out upon the sleepy world
So wearily; as if night's chariot wheels
Were clog'd in some thick cloud. O, changeful Love,
Let not her steeds with drowsy-footed pace
Pass the high stars, before sweet embassage
Comes from the pillow'd beauty of that fair
Completion of all delicate nature's wit.
Pout her faint lips anew with rubious health
And with thine infant fingers lift the fringe
Of her sick eyelids; that those eyes may glow          40
With wooing light upon me, ere the Morn
Peers with disrelish, grey, barren, and cold.

*Enter* GERSA *and Courtiers.*

Otho calls me his Lion—should I blush
To be so tam'd, so——
GERSA.                    Do me the courtesy
  Gentlemen to pass on.
COURTIER.           We are your servants.
                                [*Exeunt Courtiers.*
LUDOLPH. It seems then, Sir, you have found out the man
  You would confer with; me?
GERSA.                    If I break not
  Too much upon your thoughtful mood, I will
  Claim a brief while your patience.
LUDOLPH.                    For what cause
  Soe'er I shall be honour'd.
GERSA.                    I not less.          50
LUDOLPH. What may it be? No trifle can take place
  Of such deliberate prologue, serious 'haviour.
  But be it what it may I cannot fail
  To listen with no common interest—
  For though so new your presence is to me,
  I have a soldier's friendship for your fame—
  Please you explain.
GERSA.           As thus—for, pardon me,
  I cannot in plain terms grossly assault
  A noble nature; and would faintly sketch
  What your quick apprehension will fill up          60
  So finely I esteem you.
LUDOLPH.           I attend—

GERSA. Your generous Father, most illustrious Otho,
  Sits in the Banquet room among his chiefs—
  His wine is bitter, for you are not there—
  His eyes are fix'd still on the open doors,
  And every passer in he frowns upon
  Seeing no Ludolph comes.
LUDOLPH.                 I do neglect—
GERSA. And for your absence, may I guess the cause?
LUDOLPH. Stay there! no—guess? more princely you must be—
  Than to make guesses at me. 'Tis enough,            70
  I'm sorry I can hear no more.
GERSA.                     And I
  As griev'd to force it on you so abrupt;
  Yet one day you must know a grief whose sting
  Will sharpen more the longer 'tis conceal'd.
LUDOLPH. Say it at once, sir, dead, dead, is she dead?
GERSA. Mine is a cruel task: she is not dead—
  And would for your sake she were innocent—
LUDOLPH. Hungarian! thou amazest me beyond
  All scope of thought; convulsest my heart's blood
  To deadly churning—Gersa, you are young            80
  As I am; let me observe you face to face;
  Not grey-brow'd like the poisonous Ethelbert,
  No rheumed eyes, no furrowing of age,
  No wrinkles where all vices nestle in
  Like crannied vermin—no, but fresh and young
  And hopeful featur'd. Ha! by heaven you weep
  Tears, human tears—Do you repent you then
  Of a curs'd torturer's office! Why shouldst join—
  Tell me, the league of Devils? Confess—confess
  The Lie.—
GERSA. Lie!—but begone all ceremonious points          90
  Of honour battailous. I could not turn
  My wrath against thee for the orbed world.
LUDOLPH. Your wrath, weak boy? Tremble at mine unless
  Retraction follow close upon the heels
  Of that late stounding insult: why has my sword
  Not done already a sheer judgment on thee?
  Despair, or eat thy words. Why, thou wast nigh
  Whimpering away my reason: hark ye, Sir,
  It is no secret;—that Erminia,

Erminia, Sir, was hidden in your tent;    100
O bless'd asylum! comfortable home!
Begone, I pity thee, thou art a Gull—
Erminia's fresh puppet—
GERSA.                              Furious fire!
Thou mak'st me boil as hot as thou canst flame!
And in thy teeth I give thee back the lie!
Thou liest! Thou, Auranthe's fool, a wittol——-
LUDOLPH. Look! look at this bright sword;
There is no part of it to the very hilt
But shall indulge itself about thine heart—
Draw—but remember thou must cower thy plumes,    110
As yesterday the Arab made thee stoop—
GERSA. Patience! not here, I would not spill thy blood
Here underneath this roof where Otho breathes,
Thy father—almost mine—
LUDOLPH.                              O faltering coward!

*Re-enter* PAGE.

Stay, stay, here is one I have half a word with—
Well—What ails thee, child?
PAGE.                              My lord,
LUDOLPH.                              What would'st say?
PAGE. They are fled!
LUDOLPH.              They—who?
PAGE.                              When anxiously
I hasten'd back, your grieving messenger,
I found the stairs all dark, the lamps extinct,
And not a foot or whisper to be heard.    120
I thought her dead, and on the lowest step
Sat listening; when presently came by
Two muffled up,—one sighing heavily,
The other cursing low, whose voice I knew
For the Duke Conrad's. Close I follow'd them
Thro' the dark ways they chose to the open air;
And, as I follow'd, heard my lady speak.
LUDOLPH. Thy life answers the truth!
PAGE.                              The chamber's empty!
LUDOLPH. As I will be of mercy! So, at last,
This nail is in my temples!
GERSA.                         Be calm in this.    130

LUDOLPH. I am.

GERSA.            And Albert too has disappear'd;
  Ere I met you, I sought him everywhere;
  You would not hearken.

LUDOLPH.                    Which way went they, boy?

GERSA. I'll hunt with you.

LUDOLPH.                   No, no, no. My senses are
  Still whole. I have surviv'd. My arm is strong—
  My appetite sharp—for revenge! I'll no sharer
  In my feast; my injury is all my own,
  And so is my revenge, my lawful chattels!
  Jackall, lead on: the lion preys tonight,            138a
  Terrier, ferret them out! Burn—burn the witch!
  Trace me their footsteps! Away!                      140

                                    ⌜*Exeunt.*

ACT V

SCENE I. *A part of the Forest.*

*Enter* CONRAD *and* AURANTHE.

AURANTHE. Go no further; not a step more; thou art
  A master-plague in the midst of miseries.
  Go—I fear thee. I tremble every limb,
  Who never shook before. There's moody death
  In thy resolved looks—Yes, I could kneel
  To pray thee far away. Conrad, go, go—
  There! yonder underneath the boughs I see
  Our horses!

CONRAD. Aye, and the man.

AURANTHE.                   Yes, he is there.
  Go, go,—no blood, no blood; go, gentle Conrad!

CONRAD. Farewell!

AURANTHE.          Farewell, for this Heaven pardon you. 10
                                ⌜*Exit* AURANTHE.

CONRAD. If he escape me, may I die the death
  In unimagined tortures—or breathe through
  A long life in the foulest sink of the world!
  He dies—'tis well she do not advertise
  The caitiff of the cold steel at his back.

                            ⌜*Exit* CONRAD.

*Enter* LUDOLPH *and* PAGE.

LUDOLPH. Miss'd the way, boy, say not that on your peril!
PAGE. Indeed, indeed I cannot trace them further.
LUDOLPH. Must I stop here? Here solitary die?
  Stifled beneath the thick oppressive shade
  Of these dull boughs,—this oven of dark thickets,—    20
  Silent,—without revenge?—pshaw!—bitter end,—
  A bitter death,—a suffocating death,—
  A gnawing—silent—deadly, quiet death!
  Escap'd?—fled?—vanish'd? melted into air?
  She's gone! I cannot clutch her! no revenge!
  A muffled death, ensnar'd in horrid silence!
  Suck'd to my grave amid a dreamy calm!
  O, where is that illustrious noise of war,
  To smother up this sound of labouring breath,
  This rustle of the trees!
                        [AURANTHE *shrieks at a distance.*
PAGE.              My Lord, a noise!    30
  This way—hark!
LUDOLPH.         Yes, yes! A hope! A music!
  A glorious clamour! Now I live again!    [*Exeunt.*

SCENE II. *Another part of the Forest.*

*Enter* ALBERT (*wounded*).

ALBERT. O for enough life to support me on
  To Otho's feet—

*Enter* LUDOLPH.

LUDOLPH.        Thrice villainous, stay there!
  Tell me where that detested woman is
  Or this is through thee!
ALBERT.            My good Prince, with me
  The sword has done its worst; not without worst
  Done to another—Conrad has it home—
  I see you know it all—
LUDOLPH.          Where is his sister?

AURANTHE *rushes in.*

AURANTHE.                 Albert!

LUDOLPH. Ha! There! there!—He is the paramour!—
  There—hug him—dying! O, thou innocence,
  Shrine him and comfort him at his last gasp,                    10
  Kiss down his eyelids! Was he not thy love?
  Wilt thou forsake him at his latest hour?
  Keep fearful and aloof from his last gaze,
  His most uneasy moments, when cold death
  Stands with the door ajar to let him in?
ALBERT. O that that door with hollow slam would close
  Upon me sudden, for I cannot meet,
  In all the unknown chambers of the dead,
  Such horrors——
LUDOLPH.          Auranthe! what can he mean?
  What horrors? Is it not a joyous time?                          20
  Am I not married to a paragon
  'Of personal beauty and untainted soul?'
  A blushing fair-eyed Purity! A Sylph,
  Whose snowy timid hand has never sin'd
  Beyond a flower pluck'd, white as itself?
  Albert, you do insult my Bride—your Mistress—
  To talk of horrors on our wedding night.
ALBERT. Alas! poor Prince, I would you knew my heart.
  'Tis not so guilty—
LUDOLPH.          Hear you he pleads not guilty—
  You are not? or if so what matters it?                          30
  You have escap'd me,—free as the dusk air—
  Hid in the forest—safe from my revenge;
  I cannot catch you—You should laugh at me,
  Poor cheated Ludolph,—make the forest hiss
  With jeers at me—You tremble; faint at once,
  You will come to again. O Cockatrice,
  I have you. Whither wander those fair eyes
  To entice the Devil to your help, that he
  May change you to a Spider, so to crawl
  Into some cranny to escape my wrath?                            40
ALBERT. Sometimes the counsel of a dying man
  Doth operate quietly when his breath is gone—
  Disjoin those hands—part—part, do not destroy
  Each other—forget her—our miseries
  Are equal shar'd, and mercy is—
LUDOLPH.                    A boon

When one can compass it. Auranthe, try
Your oratory—your breath is not so hitch'd—
Aye, stare for help—            [ALBERT *groans and dies.*
                    There goes a spotted soul
Howling in vain along the hollow night—
Hear him—he calls you—Sweet Auranthe, come!      50
AURANTHE. Kill me.
LUDOLPH.            No! What? upon our marriage-night!
The earth would shudder at so foul a deed—
A fair Bride, a sweet Bride, an innocent Bride!
No, we must revel it, as 'tis in use
In times of delicate brilliant ceremony:
Come, let me lead you to our halls again—
Nay, linger not—make no resistance, sweet—
Will you—Ah wretch, thou canst not, for I have
The strength of twenty lions 'gainst a lamb—
Now one adieu for Albert—come away.—      60
                    [*Exeunt.*


SCENE III. *An inner Court of the Castle.*

*Enter* SIGIFRED, GONFRED, *and* THEODORE *meeting.*

THEODORE. Was ever such a night?
SIGIFRED.                    What horrors more?
Things unbeliev'd one hour, so strange they are,
The next hour stamps with credit.
THEODORE.                    Your last news?
GONFRED. After the Page's story of the death
Of Albert and Duke Conrad?
SIGIFRED.                    And the return
Of Ludolph with the Princess.
GONFRED.                    No more, save
Prince Gersa's freeing Abbot Ethelbert,
And the sweet lady, fair Erminia,
From prison.
THEODORE.    Where are they now? hast yet heard?
GONFRED. With the sad Emperor they are closeted;      10
I saw the three pass slowly up the stairs,
The lady weeping, the old Abbot cowl'd.
SIGIFRED. What next?
THEODORE.            I ache to think on't.

GONFRED.                              'Tis with fate.
THEODORE. One while these proud towers are hush'd as death.
GONFRED. The next our poor Prince fills the arched rooms
    With ghastly ravings.
SIGIFRED.                     I do fear his brain.
GONFRED. I will see more. Bear you so stout a heart?
                                    [*Exeunt into the Castle.*

SCENE IV. *A Cabinet, opening towards a Terrace.*

OTHO, ERMINIA, ETHELBERT, *and a Physician, discovered.*

OTHO. O, my poor Boy! my Son! my Son! my Ludolph!
    Have ye no comfort for me, ye Physicians
    Of the weak Body and Soul?
ETHELBERT.                   'Tis not the Medicine,
    Either of heaven or earth can cure unless
    Fit time be chosen to administer—
OTHO. A kind forbearance, holy Abbot—come
    Erminia, here sit by me, gentle Girl;
    Give me thy hand—hast thou forgiven me?
ERMINIA. Would I were with the saints to pray for you!
OTHO. Why will ye keep me from my darling child?        10
PHYSICIAN. Forgive me, but he must not see thy face—
OTHO. Is then a father's countenance a Gorgon?
    Hath it not comfort in it? Would it not
    Console my poor Boy, cheer him, heal his spirits?
    Let me embrace him, let me speak to him—
    I will—who hinders me? Who's Emperor?
PHYSICIAN. You may not, Sire—'twould overwhelm him quite,
    He is so full of grief and passionate wrath,
    Too heavy a sigh would kill him—or do worse.
    He must be sav'd by fine contrivances—           20
    And most especially we must keep clear
    Out of his sight a Father whom he loves—
    His heart is full, it can contain no more,
    And do its ruddy office.
ETHELBERT.                  Sage advice;
    We must endeavour how to ease and slacken
    The tight-wound energies of his despair,
    Not make them tenser—

OTHO.                          Enough! I hear, I hear.
  Yet you were about to advise more——I listen.
ETHELBERT. This learned doctor will agree with me,
  That not in the smallest point should he be thwarted    30
  Or gainsaid by one word——his very motions,
  Nods, becks and hints, should be obey'd with care,
  Even on the moment: so his troubled mind
  May cure itself——
PHYSICIAN.         There is no other means.
OTHO. Open the door: let's hear if all is quiet——
PHYSICIAN. Beseech you, Sire, forbear.
ERMINIA.                          Do, do.
OTHO.                                 I command!
  Open it straight——Sh!——quiet——my lost Boy!
  My miserable Child!
LUDOLPH (*indistinctly without*). Fill, full,——
  My goblet——here's a health!
ERMINIA.                    O, close the door!
OTHO. Let, let me hear his voice; this cannot last——    40
  And fain would I catch up his dying words
  Though my own knell they be——this cannot last——
  O let me catch his voice——for lo! I hear
  This silence whisper me that he is dead!
  It is so. Gersa?


*Enter* GERSA.

PHYSICIAN.      Say, how fares the prince?
GERSA. More calm——his features are less wild and flush'd——
  Once he complain'd of weariness——
PHYSICIAN.                          Indeed!
  'Tis good——'tis good——let him but fall asleep,
  That saves him.
OTHO.            Gersa, watch him like a child——
  Ward him from harm——and bring me better news——    50
PHYSICIAN. Humour him to the height. I fear to go;
  For should he catch a glimpse of my dull garb,
  It might affright him——fill him with suspicion
  That we believe him sick, which must not be——
GERSA. I will invent what soothing means I can.
                              [*Exit* GERSA.

PHYSICIAN. This should cheer up your Highness—weariness
  Is a good symptom, and most favourable—
  It gives me pleasant hopes. Please you walk forth
  Onto the Terrace; the refreshing air
  Will blow one half of your sad doubts away.        60
                                        [*Exeunt.*


SCENE V. *A Banqueting Hall, brilliantly illuminated, and set
  forth with all costly magnificence, with Supper-tables, laden
  with services of Gold and Silver. A door in the back scene,
  guarded by two Soldiers. Lords, Ladies, Knights, Gentlemen,
  &c. whispering sadly, and ranging themselves; part entering
  and part discovered.*

FIRST KNIGHT. Grievously are we tantaliz'd, one and all—
  Sway'd here and there, commanded to and fro
  As though we were the shadows of a dream
  And link'd to a sleeping fancy. What do we here?
GONFRED. I am no Seer—you know we must obey
  The prince from A to Z—though it should be
  To set the place in flames. I pray hast heard
  Where the most wicked Princess is?
FIRST KNIGHT.                           There, Sir,
  In the next room—have you remark'd those two
  Stout soldiers posted at the door?
GONFRED.                          For what?        10
                                        [*They whisper.*

FIRST LADY. How ghast a train!
SECOND LADY. Sure this should be some splendid burial.
FIRST LADY. What fearful whispering! See, see,—Gersa
  there!


                    *Enter* GERSA.

GERSA. Put on your brightest looks; smile if you can;
  Behave as all were happy; keep your eyes
  From the least watch upon him; if he speaks
  To any one, answer collectedly,
  Without surprise, his questions, howe'er strange.
  Do this to the utmost,—though, alas! with me
  The remedy grows hopeless! Here he comes,—        20
  Observe what I have said,—show no surprise.

*Enter* LUDOLPH, *followed by* SIGIFRED *and* PAGE.

LUDOLPH. A splendid company! rare beauties here!
  I should have Orphean lips, and Plato's fancy,
  Amphion's utterance, toned with his lyre,
  Or the deep key of Jove's sonorous mouth,
  To give fit salutation. Methought I heard,
  As I came in, some whispers,—what of that?
  'Tis natural men should whisper; at the kiss
  Of Psyche given by Love, there was a buzz
  Among the gods!—and silence is as natural.     30
  These draperies are fine, and, being a mortal,
  I should desire no better; yet, in truth,
  There must be some superior costliness,
  Some wider-domed high magnificence!
  I would have, as a mortal I may not,
  Hanging of heaven's clouds, purple and gold,
  Slung from the spheres; gauzes of silver mist,
  Loop'd up with cords of twisted wreathed light,
  And tassell'd round with weeping meteors!
  These pendent lamps and chandeliers are bright     40
  As earthly fires from dull dross can be cleansed;
  Yet could my eyes drink up intenser beams
  Undazzled,—this is darkness,—when I close
  These lids, I see far fiercer brilliances,—
  Skies full of splendid moons, and shooting stars,
  And spouting exhalations, diamond fires,
  And panting fountains quivering with deep glows!
  Yes—this is dark—is it not dark?
SIGIFRED.                   My Lord,
  'Tis late; the lights of festival are ever
  Quench'd in the morn.
LUDOLPH.            'Tis not to-morrow then?     50
SIGIFRED. 'Tis early dawn.
GERSA.              Indeed full time we slept;
  Say you so, Prince?
LUDOLPH.         I say I quarrell'd with you;
  We did not tilt each other,—that's a blessing,—
  Good gods! no innocent blood upon my head!
SIGIFRED. Retire, Gersa!
LUDOLPH.          There should be three more here:

For two of them, they stay away perhaps,
Being gloomy-minded, haters of fair revels,—
They know their own thoughts best.
                                    As for the third,
Deep blue eyes—semi-shaded in white lids,
Finish'd with lashes fine for more soft shade,                   60
Completed by her twin-arch'd ebon brows—
White temples of exactest elegance,
Of even mould felicitous and smooth—
Cheeks fashion'd tenderly on either side,
So perfect, so divine that our poor eyes
Are dazzled with the sweet proportioning,
And wonder that 'tis so,—the magic chance!
Her nostrils, small, fragrant, faery-delicate;
Her lips—I swear no human bones e'er wore
So taking a disguise—you shall behold her!                       70
We'll have her presently; aye, you shall see her,
And wonder at her, friends, she is so fair—
She is the world's chief Jewel, and by heaven
She's mine by right of marriage—she is mine!
Patience, good people, in fit time I send
A Summoner—she will obey my call,
Being a wife most mild and dutiful.
First I would hear what music is prepared
To herald and receive her—let me hear!
SIGIFRED. Bid the musicians soothe him tenderly.                 80
                              [*A soft strain of Music.*
LUDOLPH. Ye have none better—no—I am content;
'Tis a rich sobbing melody, with reliefs
Full and majestic; it is well enough,
And will be sweeter, when ye see her pace
Sweeping into this presence, glisten'd o'er
With emptied caskets, and her train upheld
By ladies, habited in robes of lawn,
Sprinkled with golden crescents; (others bright
In silks, with spangles shower'd,) and bow'd to
By Duchesses and pearled Margravines—                            90
Sad, that the fairest creature of the earth—
.I pray you mind me not—'tis sad, I say,
That the extremest beauty of the world
Should so entrench herself away from me,

Behind a barrier of engender'd guilt!

SECOND LADY. Ah! what a moan!

FIRST KNIGHT.                    Most piteous indeed!

LUDOLPH. She shall be brought before this company,
    And then—then—

FIRST LADY.          He muses.

GERSA.                    O, Fortune, where will this end?

SIGIFRED. I guess his purpose! Indeed he must not have
    That pestilence brought in,—that cannot be,                    100
    There we must stop him.

GERSA.                    I am lost! Hush, hush!
    He is about to rave again.

LUDOLPH. A barrier of guilt! I was the fool.
    She was the cheater! Who's the cheater now,
    And who the fool? The entrapp'd, the caged fool,
    The bird-lim'd raven? She shall croak to death
    Secure! Methinks I have her in my fist,
    To crush her with my heel! Wait, wait! I marvel
    My father keeps away: good friend, ah! Sigifred!
    Do bring him to me—and Erminia                    110
    I fain would see before I sleep—and [holy] Ethelbert,
    That he may bless me, as I know he will
    Though I have curs'd him.

SIGIFRED.                    Rather suffer me
    To lead you to them—

LUDOLPH.                    No, excuse me, no—
    The day is not quite done—go bring them hither.

                    [*Exit* SIGIFRED.

    Certes, a father's smile should, like sun light,
    Slant on my sheafed harvest of ripe bliss—
    Besides, I thirst to pledge my lovely Bride
    In a deep goblet: let me see—what wine?
    The strong Iberian juice, or mellow Greek?                    120
    Or pale Calabrian? Or the Tuscan grape?
    Or of old Ætna's pulpy wine presses,
    Black stain'd with the fat vintage, as it were
    The purple slaughter-house, where Bacchus' self
    Prick'd his own swollen veins? Where is my Page?

PAGE.                    Here, here!

LUDOLPH. Be ready to obey me; anon thou shalt
    Bear a soft message for me—for the hour

Draws near when I must make a winding up
Of bridal Mysteries—a fine-spun vengeance!
Carve it on my Tomb, that when I rest beneath          130
Men shall confess—This Prince was gull'd and cheated,
But from the ashes of disgrace he rose
More than a fiery Dragon—and did burn
His ignominy up in purging fires—
Did I not send, Sir, but a moment past,
For my Father?
GERSA.          You did.
LUDOLPH.                Perhaps 'twould be
    Much better he came not.
GERSA.                        He enters now!


*Enter* OTHO, ERMINIA, ETHELBERT, SIGIFRED, *and*
                    *Physician.*

LUDOLPH. O thou good Man, against whose sacred head
    I was a mad conspirator, chiefly too
    For the sake of my fair newly wedded wife,          140
    Now to be punish'd, do not look so sad!
    Those charitable eyes will thaw my heart,
    Those tears will wash away a just resolve,
    A verdict ten times sworn! Awake—awake—
    Put on a judge's brow, and use a tongue
    Made iron-stern by habit! Thou shalt see
    A deed to be applauded, 'scribed in gold!
    Join a loud voice to mine, and so denounce
    What I alone will execute!
OTHO.                      Dear son,
    What is it? By your father's love, I sue          150
    That it be nothing merciless!
LUDOLPH.                      To that demon?
    Not so! No! She is in temple-stall
    Being garnish'd for the sacrifice, and I,
    The Priest of Justice, will immolate her
    Upon the altar of wrath! She stings me through!—
    Even as the worm doth feed upon the nut,
    So she, a scorpion, preys upon my brain!
    I feel her gnawing here! Let her but vanish,
    Then, father, I will lead your legions forth,

Compact in steeled squares, and speared files,                    160
And bid our trumpets speak a fell rebuke
To nations drows'd in peace!

OTHO.                                    To-morrow, Son,
Be your word law—forget to-day—

LUDOLPH.                                    I will
When I have finish'd it—now! now! I'm pight,
Tight-footed for the deed!

ERMINIA.                              Alas! Alas!

LUDOLPH. What Angel's voice is that? Erminia!
Ah! gentlest creature, whose sweet innocence
Was almost murder'd; I am penitent,
Wilt thou forgive me? And thou, holy Man,
Good Ethelbert, shall I die in peace with you?              170

ERMINIA. Die, my lord!

LUDOLPH.                    I feel it possible.

OTHO.                                    Physician?

PHYSICIAN. I fear me he is past my skill.

OTHO.                                    Not so!

LUDOLPH. I see it, I see it—I have been wandering—
Half-mad—not right here—I forget my purpose.
Bestir, bestir, Auranthe! ha! ha! ha!
Youngster! Page! go bid them drag her to me!
Obey! This shall finish it!            [*Draws a dagger*

OTHO.                    O my Son! my Son!

SIGIFRED. This must not be—stop there!

LUDOLPH.                              Am I obey'd?
A little talk with her—no harm—haste! haste!
                                        [*Exit Page.*
Set her before me—never fear I can strike.              180

SEVERAL VOICES. My Lord! My Lord!

GERSA.                              Good Prince!

LUDOLPH. Why do ye trouble me? out—out—out away!
There she is! take that! and that! no, no—
That's not well done—Where is she?

> [*The doors open. Enter* PAGE. *Several women are seen
> grouped about* AURANTHE *in the inner room*

PAGE. Alas! My Lord, my Lord! they cannot move her!
Her arms are stiff,—her fingers clench'd and cold—

LUDOLPH. She's dead!    [*Staggers and falls into their arms.*

ETHELBERT.            Take away the dagger.

GERSA.                                    Softly; so!

OTHO. Thank God for that!

SIGIFRED.                   I fear it could not harm him.

GERSA. No!—brief be his anguish!

LUDOLPH.  She's  gone—I  am  content—Nobles,  good
    night!                                              190
  We are all weary—faint—set ope the doors—
  I will to bed!—To-morrow—                          [*Dies.*

THE  CURTAIN  FALLS

# KING STEPHEN

## A DRAMATIC FRAGMENT

# KING STEPHEN:

## A DRAMATIC FRAGMENT

### ACT I

SCENE I. *Field of Battle.*

*Alarum. Enter King* STEPHEN, *Knights, and Soldiers.*

STEPHEN. If shame can on a soldier's vein-swoll'n front
  Spread deeper crimson than the battle's toil,
  Blush in your casing helmets! for see, see!
  Yonder my chivalry, my pride of war,
  Wrench'd with an iron hand from firm array,
  Are routed loose about the plashy meads,
  Of honour forfeit. O that my known voice
  Could reach your dastard ears, and fright you more!
  Fly, cowards, fly! Glocester is at your backs!
  Throw your slack bridles o'er the flurried manes,     10
  Ply well the rowel with faint trembling heels,
  Scampering to death at last!
FIRST KNIGHT.            The enemy
  Bears his flaunt standard close upon their rear.
SECOND KNIGHT. Sure of a bloody prey, seeing the fens
  Will swamp them girth-deep.
STEPHEN.              Over head and ears,
  No matter! 'Tis a gallant enemy;
  How like a comet he goes streaming on.
  But we must plague him in the flank,—hey, friends.
  We are well breathed,—follow!

*Enter Earl* BALDWIN *and Soldiers, as defeated.*

STEPHEN.             De Redvers!
  What is the monstrous bugbear that can fright     20
  Baldwin?
BALDWIN. No scare-crow, but the fortunate star
  Of boisterous Chester, whose fell truncheon now
  Points level to the goal of victory.
  This way he comes, and if you would maintain

Your person unaffronted by vile odds,
Take horse, my Lord.
STEPHEN.                    And which way spur for life?
Now I thank Heaven I am in the toils,
That soldiers may bear witness how my arm
Can burst the meshes. Not the eagle more
Loves to beat up against a tyrannous blast,              30
Than I to meet the torrent of my foes.
This is a brag,—be't so,—but if I fall,
Carve it upon my 'scutcheon'd sepulchre.
On, fellow soldiers! Earl of Redvers, back!
Not twenty Earls of Chester shall brow-beat
The diadem.                              [*Exeunt. Alarum*

SCENE II. *Another part of the Field.*

*Trumpets sounding a Victory. Enter* GLOCESTER,
*Knights, and Forces.*

GLOCESTER. Now may we lift our bruised vizors up,
And take the flattering freshness of the air,
While the wide din of battle dies away
Into times past, yet to be echoed sure
In the silent pages of our chroniclers.
FIRST KNIGHT. Will Stephen's death be mark'd there, my
    good Lord,
Or that we gave him lodging in yon towers?
GLOCESTER. Fain would I know the great usurper's fate.

*Enter two Captains severally.*

FIRST CAPTAIN. My Lord!
SECOND CAPTAIN.                    Most noble Earl!
FIRST CAPTAIN.                                        The King—
SECOND CAPTAIN. The Empress greets—                    10
GLOCESTER. What of the King?
FIRST CAPTAIN.                        He sole and lone maintains
A hopeless bustle mid our swarming arms,
And with a nimble savageness attacks,
Escapes, makes fiercer onset, then anew
Eludes death, giving death to most that dare
Trespass within the circuit of his sword!

He must by this have fallen. Baldwin is taken;
And for the Duke of Bretagne, like a stag
He flies, for the Welsh beagles to hunt down.
God save the Empress!
GLOCESTER.        Now our dreaded Queen:     20
What message from her Highness?
SECOND CAPTAIN.       Royal Maud
From the throng'd towers of Lincoln hath look'd down,
Like Pallas from the walls of Ilion,
And seen her enemies havock'd at her feet.
She greets most noble Glocester from her heart,
Intreating him, his captains, and brave knights,
To grace a banquet. The high city gates
Are envious which shall see your triumph pass;
The streets are full of music.

*Enter* SECOND KNIGHT.

GLOCESTER.       Whence come you?
SECOND KNIGHT. From Stephen, my good Prince,—
Stephen! Stephen!     30
GLOCESTER. Why do you make such echoing of his name?
SECOND KNIGHT. Because I think, my lord, he is no man,
But a fierce demon, 'nointed safe from wounds,
And misbaptized with a Christian name.
GLOCESTER. A mighty soldier!—Does he still hold out?
SECOND KNIGHT. He shames our victory. His valour still
Keeps elbow-room amid our eager swords,
And holds our bladed falchions all aloof—
His gleaming battle-axe being slaughter-sick,
Smote on the morion of a Flemish knight,     40
Broke short in his hand; upon the which he flung
The heft away with such a vengeful force,
It paunch'd the Earl of Chester's horse, who then
Spleen-hearted came in full career at him.
GLOCESTER. Did no one take him at a vantage then?
SECOND KNIGHT. Three then with tiger leap upon him flew,
Whom, with his sword swift-drawn and nimbly held,
He stung away again, and stood to breathe,
Smiling. Anon upon him rush'd once more
A throng of foes, and in this renew'd strife,     50
My sword met his and snapp'd off at the hilts.

GLOCESTER. Come, lead me to this Mars—and let us move
  In silence, not insulting his sad doom
  With clamorous trumpets. To the Empress bear
  My salutation as befits the time.
                    [*Exeunt* GLOCESTER *and Forces.*

SCENE III. *The Field of Battle. Enter* STEPHEN *unarmed.*

STEPHEN. Another sword! And what if I could seize
  One from Bellona's gleaming armoury,
  Or choose the fairest of her sheaved spears!
  Where are my enemies? Here, close at hand,
  Here come the testy brood. O for a sword!
  I'm faint—a biting sword! A noble sword!
  A hedge-stake—or a ponderous stone to hurl
  With brawny vengeance, like the labourer Cain.
  Come on! Farewell my kingdom, and all hail
  Thou superb, plumb'd, and helmeted renown,            10
  All hail—I would not truck this brilliant day
  To rule in Pylos with a Nestor's beard—
  Come on!

              *Enter* DE KAIMS *and Knights, &c.*

DE KAIMS. Is't madness, or a hunger after death,
  That makes thee thus unarm'd throw taunts at us?
  Yield, Stephen, or my sword's point dip in
  The gloomy current of a traitor's heart.
STEPHEN. Do it, De Kaims, I will not budge an inch.
DE KAIMS. Yes, of thy madness thou shalt take the meed.
STEPHEN. Darest thou?
DE KAIMS.              How dare, against a man disarm'd?
STEPHEN. What weapons has the lion but himself?        20
  Come not near me, De Kaims, for by the price
  Of all the glory I have won this day,
  Being a king, I will not yield alive
  To any but the second man of the realm,
  Robert of Glocester.
DE KAIMS.            Thou shalt vail to me.
STEPHEN. Shall I, when I have sworn against it, sir?
  Thou think'st it brave to take a breathing king,
  That, on a court-day bow'd to haughty Maud
  The awed presence-chamber may be bold

To whisper, there's the man who took alive            30
Stephen—me—prisoner. Certes, De Kaims,
The ambition is a noble one.
DE KAIMS.                              'Tis true,
And, Stephen, I must compass it.
STEPHEN.                               No, no,
Do not tempt me to throttle you on the gorge,
Or with my gauntlet crush your hollow breast,
Just when your knighthood is grown ripe and full
For lordship.
A SOLDIER. Is an honest yeoman's spear
Of no use at a need? Take that.
STEPHEN.                           Ah, dastard!
DE KAIMS. What, you are vulnerable! my prisoner!
STEPHEN. No, not yet. I disclaim it, and demand     40
Death as a sovereign right unto a king
Who 'sdains to yield to any but his peer,
If not in title, yet in noble deeds,
The Earl of Glocester. Stab to the hilts, De Kaims,
For I will never by mean hands be led
From this so famous field. Do ye hear! Be quick!
   *Trumpets. Enter the Earl of* CHESTER *and Knights.*


SCENE IV. *A Presence Chamber. Queen* MAUD *in a Chair of
State, the Earls of* GLOCESTER *and* CHESTER, *Lords,
Attendants.*

MAUD. Glocester, no more: I will behold that Boulogne:
Set him before me. Not for the poor sake
Of regal pomp and a vain-glorious hour,
As thou with wary speech, yet near enough,
Hast hinted.
GLOCESTER. Faithful counsel have I given;
If wary, for your Highness' benefit.
MAUD. The Heavens forbid that I should not think so.
For by thy valour have I won this realm,
Which by thy wisdom I will ever keep
To sage advisers let me ever bend                   10
A meek attentive ear, so that they treat
Of the wide kingdom's rule and government,
Not trenching on our actions personal.

Advis'd, not school'd, I would be; and henceforth
Spoken to in clear, plain, and open terms,
Not side-ways sermon'd at.
GLOCESTER.                    Then, in plain terms,
Once more for the fallen king—
MAUD.                         Your pardon, Brother,
I would no more of that; for, as I said,
'Tis not for worldly pomp I wish to see
The rebel, but as dooming judge to give                      20
A sentence something worthy of his guilt.
GLOCESTER. If 't must be so, I'll bring him to your presence.
                              [*Exit* GLOCESTER.
MAUD. A meaner summoner might do as well—
My Lord of Chester, is't true what I hear
Of Stephen of Boulogne, our prisoner,
That he, as a fit penance for his crimes,
Eats wholesome, sweet, and palatable food
Off Glocester's golden dishes—drinks pure wine,
Lodges soft?
CHESTER.    More than that, my gracious Queen,
Has anger'd me. The noble Earl, methinks,                    30
Full soldier as he is, and without peer
In counsel, dreams too much among his books.
It may read well, but sure 'tis out of date
To play the Alexander with Darius.
MAUD. Truth! I think so. By Heavens it shall not last!
CHESTER. It would amaze your Highness now to mark
How Glocester overstrains his courtesy
To that crime-loving rebel, that Boulogne—
MAUD. That ingrate!
CHESTER.            For whose vast ingratitude
To our late sovereign lord, your noble sire,                 40
The generous Earl condoles in his mishaps,
And with a sort of lackeying friendliness,
Talks off the mighty frowning from his brow,
Woos him to hold a duet in a smile,
Or, if it please him, play an hour at chess—
MAUD. A perjured slave!
CHESTER.               And for his perjury,
Glocester has fit rewards—nay, I believe,
He sets his bustling household's wits at work

For flatteries to ease this Stephen's hours,
And make a heaven of his purgatory;                    50
Adorning bondage with the pleasant gloss
Of feasts and music, and all idle shows
Of indoor pageantry; while syren whispers,
Predestin'd for his ear, 'scape as half-check'd
From lips the courtliest and the rubiest
Of all the realm, admiring of his deeds.

MAUD. A frost upon his summer!

CHESTER.                          A queen's nod
Can make his June December. Here he comes.

# THE CAP AND BELLS;

## OR, THE JEALOUSIES

A FAËRY TALE. UNFINISHED

I

In midmost Ind, beside Hydaspes cool,
There stood, or hover'd, tremulous in the air,
A faery city, 'neath the potent rule
Of Emperor Elfinan; fam'd ev'rywhere
For love of mortal women, maidens fair,
Whose lips were solid, whose soft hands were made
Of a fit mould and beauty, ripe and rare,
To pamper his slight wooing, warm yet staid:
He lov'd girls smooth as shades, but hated a mere shade.

II

This was a crime forbidden by the law;
And all the priesthood of his city wept,
For ruin and dismay they well foresaw,
If impious prince no bound or limit kept,
And faery Zendervester overstept;
They wept, he sin'd, and still he would sin on,
They dreamt of sin, and he sin'd while they slept;
In vain the pulpit thunder'd at the throne,
Caricature was vain, and vain the tart lampoon.

III

Which seeing, his high court of parliament
Laid a remonstrance at his Highness' feet,
Praying his royal senses to content
Themselves with what in faery land was sweet,
Befitting best that shade with shade should meet:
Whereat, to calm their fears, he promis'd soon
From mortal tempters all to make retreat,—
Aye, even on the first of the new moon,
An immaterial wife to espouse as heaven's boon.

### IV

Meantime he sent a fluttering embassy
To Pigmio, of Imaus sovereign,
To half beg, and half demand, respectfully,
The hand of his fair daughter Bellanaine;
An audience had, and speeching done, they gain
Their point, and bring the weeping bride away;
Whom, with but one attendant, safely lain
Upon their wings, they bore in bright array,
While little harps were touch'd by many a lyric fay.

### V

As in old pictures tender cherubim
A child's soul thro' the sapphir'd canvas bear,
So, thro' a real heaven, on they swim
With the sweet princess on her plumag'd lair,
Speed giving to the winds her lustrous hair;
And so she journey'd, sleeping or awake,
Save when, for healthful exercise and air,
She chose to *promener à l'aile*, or take
A pigeon's somerset, for sport or change's sake.

### VI

'Dear Princess, do not whisper me so loud,'
Quoth Corallina, nurse and confidant,
'Do not you see there, lurking in a cloud,
Close at your back, that sly old Crafticant?
He hears a whisper plainer than a rant:
Dry up your tears, and do not look so blue;
He's Elfinan's great state-spy militant,
His running, lying, flying foot-man too,—
Dear mistress, let him have no handle against you!

### VII

'Show him a mouse's tail, and he will guess,
With metaphysic swiftness, at the mouse;
Show him a garden, and with speed no less,
He'll surmise sagely of a dwelling house,
And plot, in the same minute, how to chouse

The owner out of it; show him a'— 'Peace!
Peace! nor contrive thy mistress' ire to rouse!'
Return'd the Princess, 'my tongue shall not cease
Till from this hated match I get a free release.

### VIII

'Ah, beauteous mortal!' 'Hush!' quoth Coralline,
'Really you must not talk of him, indeed.'
'You hush!' replied the mistress, with a shine
Of anger in her eyes, enough to breed
In stouter hearts than nurse's fear and dread:
'Twas not the glance itself made Nursey flinch,
But of its threat she took the utmost heed;
Not liking in her heart an hour-long pinch,
Or a sharp needle run into her back an inch.

### IX

So she was silenc'd, and fair Bellanaine,
Writhing her little body with ennui,
Continued to lament and to complain,
That Fate, cross-purposing, should let her be
Ravish'd away far from her dear countree;
That all her feelings should be set at naught,
In trumping up this match so hastily,
With lowland blood; and lowland blood she thought
Poison, as every staunch true-born Imaian ought.

### X

Sorely she griev'd, and wetted three or four
White Provence rose-leaves with her faery tears,
But not for this cause;—alas! she had more
Bad reasons for her sorrow, as appears
In the fam'd memoirs of a thousand years,
Written by Crafticant, and published
By Parpaglion and Co., (those sly compeers
Who rak'd up ev'ry fact against the dead,)
In Scarab Street, Panthea, at the Jubal's Head.

### XI

Where, after a long hypercritic howl
Against the vicious manners of the age
He goes on to expose, with heart and soul,
What vice in this or that year was the rage,
Backbiting all the world in every page;

With special strictures on the horrid crime,
(Section'd and subsection'd with learning sage,)
Of faeries stooping on their wings sublime
To kiss a mortal's lips, when such were in their prime.

XII

Turn to the copious index, you will find
Somewhere in the column, headed letter B,
The name of Bellanaine, if you're not blind;
Then pray refer to the text, and you will see
An article made up of calumny
Against this highland princess, rating her
For giving way, so over fashionably,
To this new-fangled vice, which seems a burr
Stuck in his moral throat, no coughing e'er could stir.

XIII

There he says plainly that she lov'd a man!
That she around him flutter'd, flirted, toy'd,
Before her marriage with great Elfinan;
That after marriage too, she never joy'd
In husband's company, but still employ'd
Her wits to 'scape away to Angle-land;
Where liv'd the youth, who worried and annoy'd
Her tender heart, and its warm ardours fann'd
To such a dreadful blaze, her side would scorch her hand.

XIV

But let us leave this idle tittle-tattle
To waiting-maids, and bed-room coteries,
Nor till fit time against her fame wage battle.
Poor Elfinan is very ill at ease,
Let us resume his subject if you please:
For it may comfort and console him much
To rhyme and syllable his miseries;
Poor Elfinan! whose cruel fate was such,
He sat and curs'd a bride he knew he could not touch.

XV

Soon as (according to his promises)
The bridal embassy had taken wing,
And vanish'd, bird-like, o'er the suburb trees,
The Emperor, empierc'd with the sharp sting
Of love, retired, vex'd and murmuring

Like any drone shut from the fair bee-queen,
Into his cabinet, and there did fling
His limbs upon a sofa, full of spleen,
And damn'd his House of Commons, in complete chagrin.

### XVI

'I'll trounce some of the members,' cried the Prince,
'I'll put a mark against some rebel names,
I'll make the Opposition-benches wince,
I'll show them very soon, to all their shames,
What 'tis to smother up a Prince's flames;
That ministers should join in it, I own,
Surprises me!—they too at these high games!
Am I an Emperor? Do I wear a crown?
Imperial Elfinan, go hang thyself or drown!

### XVII

'I'll trounce 'em!—there's the square-cut chancellor,
His son shall never touch that bishopric;
And for the nephew of old Palfior,
I'll show him that his speech has made me sick,
And give the colonelcy to Phalaric;
The tiptoe marquis, moral and gallant,
Shall lodge in shabby taverns upon tick;
And for the Speaker's second cousin's aunt,
She sha'n't be maid of honour,—by heaven that she sha'n't!

### XVIII

'I'll shirk the Duke of A.; I'll cut his brother;
I'll give no garter to his eldest son;
I won't speak to his sister or his mother!
The Viscount B. shall live at cut-and-run;
But how in the world can I contrive to stun
That fellow's voice, which plagues me worse than any,
That stubborn fool, that impudent state-dun,
Who sets down ev'ry sovereign as a zany,—
That vulgar commoner, Esquire Biancopany?

### XIX

'Monstrous affair! Pshaw! pah! what ugly minx
Will they fetch from Imaus for my bride?
Alas! my wearied heart within me sinks,
To think that I must be so near allied
To a cold dullard fay,—ah, woe betide!

Ah, fairest of all human loveliness!
Sweet Bertha! what crime can it be to glide
About the fragrant pleatings of thy dress,
Or kiss thine eyes, or count thy locks, tress after tress?'

### XX

So said, one minute's while his eyes remain'd
Half lidded, piteous, languid, innocent;
But, in a wink, their splendour they regain'd,
Sparkling revenge with amorous fury blent.
Love thwarted in bad temper oft has vent:
He rose, he stampt his foot, he rang the bell,
And order'd some death-warrants to be sent
For signature:—somewhere the tempest fell,
As many a poor felon does not live to tell.

### XXI

'At the same time Eban,'—(this was his page,
A fay of colour, slave from top to toe,
Sent as a present, while yet under age,
From the Viceroy of Zanguebar,—wise, slow,
His speech, his only words were 'yes' and 'no,'
But swift of look, and foot, and wing was he,—)
'At the same time, Eban, this instant go
To Hum the soothsayer, whose name I see
Among the fresh arrivals in our empery.

### XXII

'Bring Hum to me! But stay—here, take my ring,
The pledge of favour, that he not suspect
Any foul play, or awkward murdering,
Tho' I have bowstrung many of his sect;
Throw in a hint, that if he should neglect
One hour, the next shall see him in my grasp,
And the next after that shall see him neck'd,
Or swallow'd by my hunger-starved asp,—
And mention ('tis as well) the torture of the wasp.'

### XXIII

These orders given, the Prince, in half a pet,
Let o'er the silk his propping elbow slide,
Caught up his little legs, and, in a fret,
Fell on the sofa on his royal side.
The slave retreated backwards, humble-eyed,

And with a slave-like silence clos'd the door,
And to old Hum thro' street and alley hied;
He 'knew the city,' as we say, of yore,
And for short cuts and turns, was nobody knew more.

### XXIV

It was the time when wholesale houses close
Their shutters with a moody sense of wealth,
But retail dealers, diligent, let loose
The gas (objected to on score of health),
Convey'd in little solder'd pipes by stealth,
And make it flare in many a brilliant form,
That all the powers of darkness it repell'th,
Which to the oil-trade doth great scaith and harm,
And supersedeth quite the use of the glow-worm.

### XXV

Eban, untempted by the pastry-cooks,
(Of pastry he got store within the palace,)
With hasty steps, wrapp'd cloak, and solemn looks,
Incognito upon his errand sallies,
His smelling-bottle ready for the allies;
He pass'd the Hurdy-gurdies with disdain,
Vowing he'd have them sent aboard the gallies;
Just as he made his vow, it 'gan to rain,
Therefore he call'd a coach, and bade it drive amain.

### XXVI

'I'll pull the string,' said he, and further said,
'Polluted Jarvey! Ah, thou filthy hack!
Whose springs of life are all dried up and dead,
Whose linsey-woolsey lining hangs all slack,
Whose rug is straw, whose wholeness is a crack;
And evermore thy steps go clatter-clitter;
Whose glass once up can never be got back,
Who prov'st, with jolting arguments and bitter,
That 'tis of modern use to travel in a litter.

### XXVII

'Thou inconvenience! thou hungry crop
For all corn! thou snail-creeper to and fro,
Who while thou goest ever seem'st to stop,
And fiddle-faddle standest while you go;
I' the morning, freighted with a weight of woe,

Unto some lazar-house thou journeyest,
And in the evening tak'st a double row
Of dowdies, for some dance or party drest,
Besides the goods meanwhile thou movest east and west.

### XXVIII

'By thy ungallant bearing and sad mien,
An inch appears the utmost thou couldst budge;
Yet at the slightest nod, or hint, or sign,
Round to the curb-stone patient dost thou trudge,
School'd in a beckon, learned in a nudge,
A dull-eyed Argus watching for a fare;
Quiet and plodding, thou dost bear no grudge
To whisking Tilburies, or Phaetons rare,
Curricles, or Mail-coaches, swift beyond compare.'

### XXIX

Philosophizing thus, he pull'd the check,
And bade the Coachman wheel to such a street,
Who, turning much his body, more his neck,
Louted full low, and hoarsely did him greet:
'Certes, Monsieur were best take to his feet,
Seeing his servant can no further drive
For press of coaches, that to-night here meet
Many as bees about a straw-capp'd hive,
When first for April honey into faint flowers they dive.'

### XXX

Eban then paid his fare, and tiptoe went
To Hum's hotel; and, as he on did pass
With head inclin'd, each dusky lineament
Show'd in the pearl-pav'd street, as in a glass;
His purple vest, that ever peeping was
Rich from the fluttering crimson of his cloak,
His silvery trowsers, and his silken sash
Tied in a burnish'd knot, their semblance took
Upon the mirror'd walls, wherever he might look.

### XXXI

He smil'd at self, and, smiling, show'd his teeth,
And seeing his white teeth, he smil'd the more;
Lifted his eye-brows, spurn'd the path beneath,
Show'd teeth again, and smil'd as heretofore,
Until he knock'd at the magician's door;

Where, till the porter answer'd, might be seen,
In the clear panel more he could adore,—
His turban wreath'd of gold, and white, and green,
Mustachios, ear-ring, nose-ring, and his sabre keen.

### XXXII

'Does not your master give a rout to-night?'
Quoth the dark page. 'Oh, no!' return'd the Swiss,
'Next door but one to us, upon the right,
The *Magazin des Modes* now open is
Against the Emperor's wedding;—and, sir, this
My master finds a monstrous horrid bore;
As he retir'd, an hour ago I wis,
With his best beard and brimstone, to explore
And cast a quiet figure in his second floor.

### XXXIII

'Gad! he's oblig'd to stick to business!
For chalk, I hear, stands at a pretty price;
And as for aqua vitæ—there's a mess!
The *dentes sapientiæ* of mice,
Our barber tells me too, are on the rise,—
Tinder's a lighter article,—nitre pure
Goes off like lightning,—grains of Paradise
At an enormous figure!—stars not sure!—
Zodiac will not move without a sly douceur!

### XXXIV

'Venus won't stir a peg without a fee,
And master is too partial, *entre nous*,
To'— 'Hush—hush!' cried Eban, 'sure that is he
Coming down stairs,—by St. Bartholomew!
As backwards as he can,—is't something new?
Or is't his custom, in the name of fun?'
'He always comes down backward, with one shoe'—
Return'd the porter—'off, and one shoe on,
Like, saving shoe for sock or stocking, my man John!'

### XXXV

It was indeed the great Magician,
Feeling, with careful toe, for every stair,
And retrograding careful as he can,
Backwards and downwards from his own two pair:
'Salpietro!' exclaim'd Hum, 'is the dog there?

He's always in my way upon the mat!'
'He's in the kitchen, or the Lord knows where,'—
Replied the Swiss,—'the nasty, yelping brat!'
'Don't beat him!' return'd Hum, and on the floor came pat.

XXXVI

Then facing right about, he saw the Page,
And said: 'Don't tell me what you want, Eban;
The Emperor is now in a huge rage,—
'Tis nine to one he'll give you the rattan!
Let us away!' Away together ran
The plain-dress'd sage and spangled blackamoor,
Nor rested till they stood to cool, and fan,
And breathe themselves at the Emperor's chamber door,
When Eban thought he heard a soft imperial snore.

XXXVII

'I thought you guess'd, foretold, or prophesied,
That's Majesty was in a raving fit?'
'He dreams,' said Hum, 'or I have ever lied,
That he is tearing you, sir, bit by bit.'
'He's not asleep, and you have little wit,'
Replied the page: 'that little buzzing noise,
Whate'er your palmistry may make of it,
Comes from a play-thing of the Emperor's choice,
From a Man-Tiger-Organ, prettiest of his toys.'

XXXVIII

Eban then usher'd in the learned Seer:
Elfinan's back was turn'd, but, ne'ertheless,
Both, prostrate on the carpet, ear by ear,
Crept silently, and waited in distress,
Knowing the Emperor's moody bitterness;
Eban especially, who on the floor 'gan
Tremble and quake to death,—he feared less
A dose of senna-tea or nightmare Gorgon
Than the Emperor when he play'd on his Man-Tiger-Organ.

XXXIX

They kiss'd nine times the carpet's velvet face
Of glossy silk, soft, smooth, and meadow-green,
Where the close eye in deep rich fur might trace
A silver tissue, scantly to be seen,
As daisies lurk'd in June-grass, buds in treen;

Sudden the music ceased, sudden the hand
Of majesty, by dint of passion keen,
Doubled into a common fist, went grand,
And knock'd down three cut glasses, and his best inkstand.

### X L

Then turning round, he saw those trembling two:
'Eban,' said he, 'as slaves should taste the fruits
Of diligence, I shall remember you
To-morrow, or the next day, as time suits,
In a finger conversation with my mutes,—
Begone!—for you, Chaldean! here remain!
Fear not, quake not, and as good wine recruits
A conjurer's spirits, what cup will you drain?
Sherry in silver, hock in gold, or glass'd champagne?'

### X L I

'Commander of the Faithful!' answer'd Hum,
'In preference to these, I'll merely taste
A thimble-full of old Jamaica rum.'
'A simple boon!' said Elfinan; 'thou may'st
Have Nantz, with which my morning-coffee's lac'd.'
'I'll have a glass of Nantz, then,'—said the Seer,—
'Made racy—(sure my boldness is misplac'd!)—
With the third part—(yet that is drinking dear!)—
Of the least drop of *crème de citron*, crystal clear.'

### X L I I

'I pledge you, Hum! and pledge my dearest love,
My Bertha!' 'Bertha! Bertha!' cried the sage,
'I know a many Berthas!' 'Mine's above
All Berthas!' sighed the Emperor. 'I engage,'
Said Hum, 'in duty, and in vassalage,
To mention all the Berthas in the Earth;—
There's Bertha Watson,—and Miss Bertha Page,—
This fam'd for languid eyes, and that for mirth,—
There's Bertha Blount of York,—and Bertha Knox of Perth.'

### X L I I I

'You seem to know'—'I do know,' answer'd Hum,
'Your Majesty's in love with some fine girl
Named Bertha; but her surname will not come,
Without a little conjuring.' ''Tis Pearl,
'Tis Bertha Pearl that makes my brains so whirl;

And she is softer, fairer than her name!'
'Where does she live?' ask'd Hum. 'Her fair locks curl
So brightly, they put all our fays to shame!—
Live?—O! at Canterbury, with her old grand-dame.'

XLIV

'Good! good!' cried Hum, 'I've known her from a child!
She is a changeling of my management;
She was born at midnight in an Indian wild;
Her mother's screams with the striped tiger's blent,
While the torch-bearing slaves a halloo sent
Into the jungles; and her palanquin,
Rested amid the desert's dreariment,
Shook with her agony, till fair were seen
The little Bertha's eyes oped on the stars serene.'

XLV

'I can't say,' said the monarch; 'that may be
Just as it happen'd, true or else a bam!
Drink up your brandy, and sit down by me,
Feel, feel my pulse, how much in love I am;
And if your science is not all a sham,
Tell me some means to get the lady here.'
'Upon my honour!' said the son of Cham,
'She is my dainty changeling, near and dear,
Although her story sounds at first a little queer.'

XLVI

'Convey her to me, Hum, or by my crown,
My sceptre, and my cross-surmounted globe,
I'll knock you'—'Does your majesty mean—*down?*
No, no, you never could my feelings probe
To such a depth!' The Emperor took his robe,
And wept upon its purple palatine,
While Hum continued, shamming half a sob,—
'In Canterbury doth your lady shine?
But let me cool your brandy with a little wine.'

XLVII

Whereat a narrow Flemish glass he took,
That once belong'd to Admiral de Witt,
Admir'd it with a connoisseuring look,
And with the ripest claret crowned it,
And, ere one lively bead could burst and flit,

He turn'd it quickly, nimbly upside down,
His mouth being held conveniently fit
To catch the treasure: 'Best in all the town!'
He said, smack'd his moist lips, and gave a pleasant frown.

### XLVIII

'Ah! good my Prince, weep not!' And then again
He fill'd a bumper. 'Great Sire, do not weep!
Your pulse is shocking, but I'll ease your pain.'
'Fetch me that Ottoman, and prithee keep
Your voice low,' said the Emperor; 'and steep
Some lady's-fingers nice in Candy wine;
And prithee, Hum, behind the screen do peep
For the rose-water vase, magician mine!
And sponge my forehead,—so my love doth make me pine.

### XLIX

'Ah, cursed Bellanaine!' 'Don't think of her,'
Rejoin'd the Mago, 'but on Bertha muse;
For, by my choicest best barometer,
You shall not throttled be in marriage noose;
I've said it, Sire; you only have to choose
Bertha or Bellanaine.' So saying, he drew
From the left pocket of his threadbare hose,
A sampler hoarded slyly, good as new,
Holding it by his thumb and finger full in view.

### L

'Sire, this is Bertha Pearl's neat handy-work,
Her *name*, see here, *Midsummer, ninety-one.*'
Elfinan snatch'd it with a sudden jerk,
And wept as if he never would have done,
Honouring with royal tears the poor homespun;
Whereon were broider'd tigers with black eyes,
And long-tail'd pheasants, and a rising sun,
Plenty of posies, great stags, butterflies
Bigger than stags,—a moon,—with other mysteries.

### LI

The monarch handled o'er and o'er again
These day-school hieroglyphics with a sigh;
Somewhat in sadness, but pleas'd in the main,
Till this oracular couplet met his eye
Astounded—*Cupid I, do thee defy!*

It was too much. He shrunk back in his chair,
Grew pale as death, and fainted—very nigh!
'Pho! nonsense!' exclaim'd Hum, 'now don't despair;
She does not mean it really. Cheer up hearty there!

### LII

'And listen to my words. You say you won't,
On any terms, marry Miss Bellanaine;
It goes against your conscience—good! Well, don't.
You say you love a mortal. I would fain
Persuade your honour's highness to refrain
From peccadilloes. But, Sire, as I say,
What good would that do? And, to be more plain,
You would do me a mischief some odd day,
Cut off my ears and hands, or head too, by my fay!

### LIII

'Besides, manners forbid that I should pass any
Vile strictures on the conduct of a prince
Who should indulge his genius, if he has any,
Not, like a subject, foolish matters mince.
Now I think on't, perhaps I could convince
Your Majesty there is no crime at all
In loving pretty little Bertha, since
She's very delicate,—not over tall,—
A fairy's hand, and in the waist, why—very small.'

### LIV

'Ring the repeater, gentle Hum!' ''Tis five,'
Said gentle Hum; 'the nights draw in apace;
The little birds I hear are all alive;
I see the dawning touch'd upon your face;
Shall I put out the candles, please your Grace?'
'Do put them out, and, without more ado,
Tell me how I may that sweet girl embrace,—
How you can bring her to me.' 'That's for you,
Great Emperor! to adventure, like a lover true.'

### LV

'I fetch her!'—'Yes, an't like your Majesty;
And as she would be frighten'd wide awake
To travel such a distance through the sky,
Use of some soft manœuvre you must make,
For your convenience, and her dear nerves' sake;

Nice way would be to bring her in a swoon,
Anon, I'll tell what course were best to take;
You must away this morning.' 'Hum! so soon?'
'Sire, you must be in Kent by twelve o'clock at noon.'

### LVI

At this great Cæsar started on his feet,
Lifted his wings, and stood attentive-wise.
'Those wings to Canterbury you must beat,
If you hold Bertha as a worthy prize.
Look in the Almanack—*Moore* never lies—
April the twenty-fourth,—this coming day,
Now breathing its new bloom upon the skies,
Will end in St. Mark's Eve;—you must away,
For on that eve alone can you the maid convey.'

### LVII

Then the magician solemnly 'gan frown,
So that his frost-white eyebrows, beetling low,
Shaded his deep-green eyes, and wrinkles brown
Plaited upon his furnace-scorched brow:
Forth from the hood that hung his neck below,
He lifted a bright casket of pure gold,
Touch'd a spring-lock, and there in wool, or snow
Charm'd into ever-freezing, lay an old
And legend-leaved book, mysterious to behold.

### LVIII

'Take this same book,—it will not bite you, Sire;
There, put it underneath your royal arm;
Though it's a pretty weight it will not tire,
But rather on your journey keep you warm:
This is the magic, this the potent charm,
That shall drive Bertha to a fainting fit!
When the time comes, don't feel the least alarm,
Uplift her from the ground, and swiftly flit
Back to your palace, where I wait for guerdon fit.'

### LIX

'What shall I do with this same book?' 'Why merely
Lay it on Bertha's table, close beside
Her work-box, and 'twill help your purpose dearly;
I say no more.' 'Or good or ill betide,
Through the wide air to Kent this morn I glide!'

Exclaim'd the Emperor. 'When I return,
Ask what you will,—I'll give you my new bride!
And take some more wine, Hum;—O Heavens! I burn
To be upon the wing! Now, now, that minx I spurn!'

LX

'Leave her to me,' rejoin'd the magian:
'But how shall I account, illustrious fay!
For thine imperial absence? Pho! I can
Say you are very sick, and bar the way
To your so loving courtiers for one day;
If either of their two archbishops' graces
Should talk of extreme unction, I shall say
You do not like cold pig with Latin phrases,
Which never should be used but in alarming cases.'

LXI

'Open the window, Hum; I'm ready now!'
'Zooks!' exclaim'd Hum, as up the sash he drew,
'Behold, your Majesty, upon the brow
Of yonder hill, what crowds of people!' 'Whew!
The monster's always after something new,'
Return'd his Highness, 'they are piping hot
To see my pigsny Bellanaine. Hum! do
Tighten my belt a little,—so, so,—not
Too tight,—the book!—my wand!—so, nothing is forgot.'

LXII

'Wounds! how they shout!' said Hum, 'and there,—see, see!
The Ambassadors return'd from Pigmio!
The morning's very fine,—uncommonly!
See, past the skirts of yon white cloud they go,
Tinging it with soft crimsons! Now below
The sable-pointed heads of firs and pines
They dip, move on, and with them moves a glow
Along the forest side! Now amber lines
Reach the hill top, and now throughout the valley shines.'

LXIII

'Why, Hum, you're getting quite poetical!
Those *nows* you managed in a special style.'
'If ever you have leisure, Sire, you shall
See scraps of mine will make it worth your while,
Tit-bits for Phœbus!—yes, you well may smile.

Hark! Hah! the bells!' 'A little further yet,
Good Hum, and let me view this mighty coil.'
Then the great Emperor full graceful set
His elbow for a prop, and snuff'd his mignonnette.

### LXIV

The morn is full of holiday; loud bells
With rival clamours ring from every spire;
Cunningly-station'd music dies and swells
In echoing places; when the winds respire,
Light flags stream out like gauzy tongues of fire;
A metropolitan murmur, lifeful, warm,
Comes from the northern suburbs; rich attire
Freckles with red and gold the moving swarm;
While here and there clear trumpets blow a keen alarm.

### LXV

And now the fairy escort was seen clear,
Like the old pageant of Aurora's train,
Above a pearl-built minster, hovering near;
First wily Crafticant, the chamberlain,
Balanc'd upon his grey-grown pinions twain,
His slender wand officially reveal'd;
Then black gnomes scattering sixpences like rain;
Then pages three and three; and next, slave-held,
The Imaian 'scutcheon bright,—one mouse in argent field.

### LXVI

Gentlemen pensioners next; and after them,
A troop of winged Janizaries flew;
Then Slaves, as presents bearing many a gem;
Then twelve physicians fluttering two and two;
And next a chaplain in a cassock new;
Then Lords in waiting; then (what head not reels
For pleasure?)—the fair Princess in full view,
Borne upon wings,—and very pleas'd she feels
To have such splendour dance attendance at her heels.

### LXVII

For there was more magnificence behind:
She wav'd her handkerchief. 'Ah, very grand!'
Cried Elfinan, and clos'd the window-blind;
'And, Hum, we must not shilly-shally stand,—
Adieu! adieu! I'm off for Angle-land!

I say, old Hocus, have you such a thing
About you,—feel your pockets, I command,—
I want, this instant, an invisible ring,—
Thank you, old mummy!—now securely I take wing.'

### LXVIII

Then Elfinan swift vaulted from the floor,
And lighted graceful on the window-sill;
Under one arm the magic book he bore,
The other he could wave about at will;
Pale was his face, he still look'd very ill:
He bow'd at Bellanaine, and said—'Poor Bell!
Farewell! farewell! and if for ever! still
For ever fare thee well!'—and then he fell
A laughing!—snapp'd his fingers!—shame it is to tell!

### LXIX

'By'r Lady! he is gone!' cries Hum, 'and I—
(I own it)—have made too free with his wine;
Old Crafticant will smoke me. By the bye—
This room is full of jewels as a mine,—
Dear valuable creatures, how ye shine!
Sometime to-day I must contrive a minute,
If Mercury propitiously incline,
To examine his scrutoire, and see what's in it,
For of superfluous diamonds I as well may thin it.

### LXX

'The Emperor's horrid bad; yes, that's my cue!'
Some histories say that this was Hum's last speech;
That, being fuddled, he went reeling through
The corridor, and scarce upright could reach
The stair-head; that being glutted as a leech,
And us'd, as we ourselves have just now said,
To manage stairs reversely, like a peach
Too ripe, he fell, being puzzled in his head
With liquor and the staircase: verdict—*found stone dead.*

### LXXI

This as a falsehood Crafticanto treats;
And as his style is of strange elegance,
Gentle and tender, full of soft conceits,
(Much like our Boswell's,) we will take a glance
At his sweet prose, and, if we can, make dance

His woven periods into careless rhyme;
O, little faery Pegasus! rear—prance—
Trot round the quarto—ordinary time!
March, little Pegasus, with pawing hoof sublime!

### LXXII

Well, let us see,—*tenth book and chapter nine,*—
Thus Crafticant pursues his diary:—
"Twas twelve o'clock at night, the weather fine,
Latitude thirty-six; our scouts descry
A flight of starlings making rapidly
Towards Thibet. Mem.:—birds fly in the night;
From twelve to half-past—wings not fit to fly
For a thick fog—the Princess sulky quite
Call'd for an extra shawl, and gave her nurse a bite.

### LXXIII

'Five minutes before one—brought down a moth
With my new double-barrel—stew'd the thighs
And made a very tolerable broth—
Princess turn'd dainty;—to our great surprise,
Alter'd her mind, and thought it very nice:
Seeing her pleasant, tried her with a pun,
She frown'd; a monstrous owl across us flies
About this time,—a sad old figure of fun;
Bad omen—this new match can't be a happy one.

### LXXIV

'From two till half-past, dusky way we made,
Above the plains of Gobi,—desert, bleak;
Beheld afar off, in the hooded shade
Of darkness, a great mountain (strange to speak),
Spitting, from forth its sulphur-baken peak,
A fan-shap'd burst of blood-red, arrowy fire,
Turban'd with smoke, which still away did reek,
Solid and black from that eternal pyre,
Upon the laden wind that scantly could respire.

### LXXV

'Just upon three o'clock a falling star
Created an alarm among our troop,
Kill'd a man-cook, a page, and broke a jar,
A tureen, and three dishes, at one swoop,
Then passing by the Princess, singed her hoop:

Could not conceive what Coralline was at,
She clapp'd her hands three times and cried out "Whoop!"
Some strange Imaian custom. A large bat
Came sudden 'fore my face, and brush'd against my hat.

LXXVI

'Five minutes thirteen seconds after three,
Far in the west a mighty fire broke out,
Conjectur'd, on the instant, it might be
The city of Balk—'twas Balk beyond all doubt:
A Griffin, wheeling here and there about,
Kept reconnoitring us—doubled our guard—
Lighted our torches, and kept up a shout,
Till he sheer'd off—the Princess very scar'd—
And many on their marrow-bones for death prepar'd.

LXXVII

'At half-past three arose the cheerful moon—
Bivouack'd for four minutes on a cloud—
Where from the earth we heard a lively tune
Of tambourines and pipes, serene and loud,
While on a flowery lawn a brilliant crowd
Cinque-parted danc'd, some half asleep reposed
Beneath the green-fan'd cedars, some did shroud
In silken tents, and 'mid light fragrance dozed,
Or on the open turf their soothed eyelids closed.

LXXVIII

'Dropp'd my gold watch, and kill'd a kettledrum—
It went for apoplexy—foolish folks!—
Left it to pay the piper—a good sum—
(I've got a conscience, maugre people's jokes;)
To scrape a little favour 'gan to coax
Her Highness' pug-dog—got a sharp rebuff—
She wish'd a game at whist—made three revokes—
Turn'd from myself, her partner, in a huff;
His majesty will know her temper time enough.

LXXIX

'She cried for chess—I play'd a game with her—
Castled her king with such a vixen look,
It bodes ill to his Majesty—(refer
To the second chapter of my fortieth book,
And see what hoity-toity airs she took).

At half-past four the morn essay'd to beam—
Saluted, as we pass'd, an early rook—
The Princess fell asleep, and, in her dream,
Talk'd of one Master Hubert, deep in her esteem.

### LXXX

'About this time,—making delightful way,—
Shed a quill-feather from my larboard wing—
Wish'd, trusted, hop'd 'twas no sign of decay—
Thank heaven, I'm hearty yet!—'twas no such thing:—
At five the golden light began to spring,
With fiery shudder through the bloomed east;
At six we heard Panthea's churches ring—
The city all her unhiv'd swarms had cast,
To watch our grand approach, and hail us as we pass'd.

### LXXXI

'As flowers turn their faces to the sun,
So on our flight with hungry eyes they gaze,
And, as we shap'd our course, this, that way run,
With mad-cap pleasure, or hand-clasp'd amaze;
Sweet in the air a mild-ton'd music plays,
And progresses through its own labyrinth;
Buds gather'd from the green spring's middle-days,
They scatter'd,—daisy, primrose, hyacinth,—
Or round white columns wreath'd from capital to plinth.

### LXXXII

'Onward we floated o'er the panting streets,
That seem'd throughout with upheld faces paved;
Look where we will, our bird's-eye vision meets
Legions of holiday; bright standards waved,
And fluttering ensigns emulously craved
Our minute's glance; a busy thunderous roar,
From square to square, among the buildings raved,
As when the sea, at flow, gluts up once more
The craggy hollowness of a wild reefed shore.

### LXXXIII

'And "Bellanaine for ever!" shouted they,
While that fair Princess, from her winged chair,
Bow'd low with high demeanour, and, to pay
Their new-blown loyalty with guerdon fair,
Still emptied, at meet distance, here and there,

A plenty horn of jewels. And here I
(Who wish to give the devil her due) declare
Against that ugly piece of calumny,
Which calls them Highland pebble-stones not worth a fly.

### LXXXIV

'Still "Bellanaine!" they shouted, while we glide
"Slant to a light Ionic portico,
The city's delicacy, and the pride
Of our Imperial Basilic; a row
Of lords and ladies, on each hand, make show
Submissive of knee-bent obeisance,
All down the steps; and, as we enter'd, lo!
The strangest sight—the most unlook'd-for chance—
All things turn'd topsy-turvy in a devil's dance.

### LXXXV

"Stead of his anxious Majesty and court
At the open doors, with wide saluting eyes,
*Congées* and scape-graces of every sort,
And all the smooth routine of gallantries,
Was seen, to our immoderate surprise,
A motley crowd thick gather'd in the hall,
Lords, scullions, deputy-scullions, with wild cries
Stunning the vestibule from wall to wall,
Where the Chief Justice on his knees and hands doth crawl.

### LXXXVI

'Counts of the palace, and the state purveyor
Of moth's-down, to make soft the royal beds,
The Common Council and my fool Lord Mayor
Marching a-row, each other slipshod treads;
Powder'd bag-wigs and ruffy-tuffy heads
Of cinder wenches meet and soil each other;
Toe crush'd with heel ill-natur'd fighting breeds,
Frill-rumpling elbows brew up many a bother,
And fists in the short ribs keep up the yell and pother.

### LXXXVII

'A Poet, mounted on the Court-Clown's back,
Rode to the Princess swift with spurring heels,
And close into her face, with rhyming clack,
Began a Prothalamion;—she reels,
She falls, she faints! while laughter peals

Over her woman's weakness. "Where!" cried I,
"Where is his Majesty?" No person feels
Inclin'd to answer; wherefore instantly
I plung'd into the crowd to find him or to die.

LXXXVIII

'Jostling my way I gain'd the stairs, and ran
To the first landing, where, incredible!
I met, far gone in liquor, that old man,
That vile impostor Hum,——'

So far so well,—
For we have prov'd the Mago never fell
Down stairs on Crafticanto's evidence;
And therefore duly shall proceed to tell,
Plain in our own original mood and tense,
The sequel of this day, though labour 'tis immense!

LXXXIX

Now Hum, new fledg'd with high Authority,
Came forth to quell the Hubbub in the Hall.

\*    \*    \*    \*    \*    \*

# SHORTER POEMS

FROM

## *LITERARY REMAINS*

1848

# ODE TO APOLLO

I N thy western halls of gold
    When thou sittest in thy state,
Bards, that erst sublimely told
    Heroic deeds, and sang of fate,
With fervour seize their adamantine lyres,
Whose chords are solid rays, and twinkle radiant fires.

Here Homer with his nervous arms
    Strikes the twanging harp of war,
And even the western splendour warms,
    While the trumpets sound afar:          10
But, what creates the most intense surprise,
His soul looks out through renovated eyes.

Then, through thy Temple wide, melodious swells
    The sweet majestic tone of Maro's lyre:
The soul delighted on each accent dwells,—
    Enraptur'd dwells,—not daring to respire,
The while he tells of grief around a funeral pyre.

'Tis awful silence then again;
    Expectant stand the spheres;
    Breathless the laurell'd peers,          20
Nor move, till ends the lofty strain,
Nor move till Milton's tuneful thunders cease,
And leave once more the ravish'd heavens in peace.

Thou biddest Shakspeare wave his hand,
    And quickly forward spring
The Passions—a terrific band—
    And each vibrates the string
That with its tyrant temper best accords,
While from their Master's lips pour forth the inspiring words.

A silver trumpet Spenser blows,          30
    And, as its martial notes to silence flee,
From a virgin chorus flows
    A hymn in praise of spotless Chastity.
'Tis still! Wild warblings from the Æolian lyre
Enchantment softly breathe, and tremblingly expire.

Next thy Tasso's ardent numbers
 Float along the pleased air,
Calling youth from idle slumbers,
 Rousing them from Pleasure's lair:—
Then o'er the strings his fingers gently move,   40
And melt the soul to pity and to love.

But when *Thou* joinest with the Nine,
And all the powers of song combine,
 We listen here on earth:
The dying tones that fill the air,
And charm the ear of evening fair,
From thee, great God of Bards, receive their heavenly birth.


## HYMN TO APOLLO

GOD of the golden bow,
 And of the golden lyre,
And of the golden hair,
 And of the golden fire,
  Charioteer
  Of the patient year,
  Where—where slept thine ire,
When like a blank idiot I put on thy wreath,
 Thy laurel, thy glory,
 The light of thy story,   10
Or was I a worm—too low crawling, for death?
 O Delphic Apollo!

The Thunderer grasp'd and grasp'd,
 The Thunderer frown'd and frown'd;
The eagle's feathery mane
 For wrath became stiffen'd—the sound
  Of breeding thunder
  Went drowsily under,
  Muttering to be unbound.
O why didst thou pity, and for a worm   20
 Why touch thy soft lute
 Till the thunder was mute,
Why was not I crush'd—such a pitiful germ?
 O Delphic Apollo!

The Pleiades were up,
    Watching the silent air;
The seeds and roots in the Earth
    Were swelling for summer fare:
      The Ocean, its neighbour,
      Was at its old labour,          30
    When, who—who did dare
To tie, like a madman, thy plant round his brow,
    And grin and look proudly,
    And blaspheme so loudly,
And live for that honour, to stoop to thee now?
    O Delphic Apollo!

## TO —

Think not of it, sweet one, so;—
    Give it not a tear;
Sigh thou mayst, and bid it go
    Any, any where.

Do not look so sad, sweet one,—
    Sad and fadingly;
Shed one drop, then it is gone,
    Oh 'twas born to die.

Still so pale? then, dearest, weep;
    Weep, I'll count the tears,          10
And each one shall be a bliss
    For thee in after years.

Brighter has it left thine eyes
    Than a sunny rill;
And thy whispering melodies
    Are tenderer still.

Yet—as all things mourn awhile
    At fleeting blisses,
E'en let us too! but be our dirge
    A dirge of kisses.          20

## LINES

I

UNFELT, unheard, unseen,
I've left my little queen,
Her languid arms in silver slumber lying:
Ah! through their nestling touch,
Who—who could tell how much
There is for madness—cruel, or complying?

II

Those faery lids how sleek!
Those lips how moist!—they speak,
In ripest quiet, shadows of sweet sounds:
Into my fancy's ear
Melting a burden dear,
How 'Love doth know no fullness nor no bounds.'

III

True!—tender monitors!
I bend unto your laws:
This sweetest day for dalliance was born!
So, without more ado,
I'll feel my heaven anew,
For all the blushing of the hasty morn.


## SONG

I

HUSH, hush! tread softly! hush, hush my dear!
All the house is asleep, but we know very well
That the jealous, the jealous old bald-pate may hear,
Tho' you've padded his night-cap—O sweet Isabel!
Tho' your feet are more light than a Fairy's feet,
Who dances on bubbles where brooklets meet,—
Hush, hush! soft tiptoe! hush, hush my dear!
For less than a nothing the jealous can hear.

II

No leaf doth tremble, no ripple is there
On the river,—all's still, and the night's sleepy eye
Closes up, and forgets all its Lethean care,
Charm'd to death by the drone of the humming Mayfly;

And the Moon, whether prudish or complaisant,
Has fled to her bower, well knowing I want
No light in the dusk, no torch in the gloom,
But my Isabel's eyes, and her lips pulp'd with bloom.


### III

Lift the latch! ah gently! ah tenderly—sweet!
    We are dead if that latchet gives one little clink!
Well done—now those lips, and a flowery seat—
    The old man may sleep, and the planets may wink;
        The shut rose shall dream of our loves, and awake
        Full blown, and such warmth for the morning's take,
The stock-dove shall hatch her soft brace and shall coo,
While I kiss to the melody, aching all through!


## SONG

I HAD a dove and the sweet dove died;
    And I have thought it died of grieving:
O, what could it grieve for? Its feet were tied,
    With a silken thread of my own hand's weaving;
Sweet little red feet! why should you die—
Why should you leave me, sweet dove! why?
You liv'd alone on the forest-tree,
Why, pretty thing! could you not live with me?
I kiss'd you oft and gave you white peas;
Why not live sweetly, as in the green trees?                10


## FAIRY'S SONG

SHED no tear—O shed no tear!
The flower will bloom another year.
Weep no more—O weep no more!
Young buds sleep in the root's white core.
Dry your eyes—O dry your eyes,
For I was taught in Paradise
To ease my breast of melodies—
            Shed no tear.

Overhead—look overhead
'Mong the blossoms white and red—                    10
Look up, look up—I flutter now
On this flush pomegranate bough—
See me—'tis this silvery bill
Ever cures the good man's ill—
Shed no tear—O shed no tear!
The flower will bloom another year.
Adieu—Adieu—I fly, adieu,
I vanish in the heaven's blue—
              Adieu, Adieu!


## SONG

I

SPIRIT here that reignest!
Spirit here that painest!
Spirit here that burnest!
Spirit here that mournest!
    Spirit, I bow
    My forehead low,
  Enshaded with thy pinions.
    Spirit, I look
    All passion-struck
  Into thy pale dominions.

II

Spirit here that laughest!
Spirit here that quaffest!
Spirit here that dancest!
Noble soul that prancest!
    Spirit, with thee
    I join in the glee
  A-nudging the elbow of Momus.
    Spirit, I flush
    With a Bacchanal blush
  Just fresh from the Banquet of Comus.

# FAERY SONG

A<small>H</small>! woe is me! poor silver-wing!
  That I must chant thy lady's dirge,
And death to this fair haunt of spring,
  Of melody, and streams of flowery verge,—
Poor silver-wing! ah! woe is me!
      That I must see
These blossoms snow upon thy lady's pall!
  Go, pretty page! and in her ear
  Whisper that the hour is near!
  Softly tell her not to fear         10
Such calm favonian burial!
  Go, pretty page! and soothly tell,—
  The blossoms hang by a melting spell,
And fall they must, ere a star wink thrice
      Upon her closed eyes,
That now in vain are weeping their last tears,
  At sweet life leaving, and these arbours green,—
Rich dowry from the Spirit of the Spheres,—
      Alas! poor Queen!

# EXTRACTS FROM AN OPERA

O! <small>WERE</small> I one of the Olympian twelve,
Their godships should pass this into a law—
That when a man doth set himself in toil
After some beauty veiled far away,
Each step he took should make his lady's hand
More soft, more white, and her fair cheek more fair;
And for each briar-berry he might eat,
A kiss should bud upon the tree of love,
And pulp and ripen richer every hour,
To melt away upon the traveller's lips.     10

    *    *    *    *    *    *

### DAISY'S SONG

I

  T<small>HE</small> sun, with his great eye,
  Sees not so much as I;
  And the moon, all silver-proud,
  Might as well be in a cloud.

II

And O the spring—the spring!
I lead the life of a king!
Couch'd in the teeming grass,
I spy each pretty lass.

III

I look where no one dares,
And I stare where no one stares,
And when the night is nigh,
Lambs bleat my lullaby.

\*      \*      \*      \*      \*      \*

FOLLY'S SONG

WHEN wedding fiddles are a-playing,
            Huzza for folly O!
And when maidens go a-maying,
            Huzza, &c.
When a milk-pail is upset,
            Huzza, &c.
And the clothes left in the wet,
            Huzza, &c.
When the barrel's set abroach,
            Huzza, &c.                          10
When Kate Eyebrow keeps a coach,
            Huzza, &c.
When the pig is over-roasted,
            Huzza, &c.
And the cheese is over-toasted,
            Huzza, &c.
When Sir Snap is with his lawyer,
            Huzza, &c.
And Miss Chip has kiss'd the sawyer,
            Huzza, &c.                          20

\*      \*      \*      \*      \*      \*

OH, I am frighten'd with most hateful thoughts!
Perhaps her voice is not a nightingale's,
Perhaps her teeth are not the fairest pearl;
Her eye-lashes may be, for aught I know,
Not longer than the May-fly's small fan-horns;

There may not be one dimple on her hand;
And freckles many; ah! a careless nurse,
In haste to teach the little thing to walk,
May have crumpt up a pair of Dian's legs
And warpt the ivory of a Juno's neck.

\*　　\*　　\*　　\*　　\*　　\*

SONG

I

THE stranger lighted from his steed,
　　And ere he spake a word,
He seiz'd my lady's lilly hand,
　　And kiss'd it all unheard.

II

The stranger walk'd into the hall,
　　And ere he spake a word,
He kiss'd my lady's cherry lips,
　　And kiss'd 'em all unheard.

III

The stranger walk'd into the bower,—
　　But my lady first did go,—
Aye hand in hand into the bower,
　　Where my lord's roses blow.

IV

My lady's maid had a silken scarf,
　　And a golden ring had she,
And a kiss from the stranger, as off he went
　　Again on his fair palfrey.

\*　　\*　　\*　　\*　　\*　　✿

ASLEEP! O sleep a little while, white pearl!
And let me kneel, and let me pray to thee,
And let me call Heaven's blessing on thine eyes,
And let me breathe into the happy air,
That doth enfold and touch thee all about,
Vows of my slavery, my giving up,
My sudden adoration, my great love!

# LA BELLE DAME SANS MERCI

### A BALLAD

#### I

O, what can ail thee, knight-at-arms,
  Alone and palely loitering?
The sedge has wither'd from the lake,
  And no birds sing.

#### II

O, what can ail thee, knight-at-arms,
  So haggard and so woe-begone?
The squirrel's granary is full,
  And the harvest's done.

#### III

I see a lilly on thy brow,
  With anguish moist and fever dew;
And on thy cheeks a fading rose
  Fast withereth too.

#### IV

I met a lady in the meads,
  Full beautiful—a faery's child,
Her hair was long, her foot was light,
  And her eyes were wild.

#### V

I made a garland for her head,
  And bracelets too, and fragrant zone;
She look'd at me as she did love,
  And made sweet moan.

#### VI

I set her on my pacing steed,
  And nothing else saw all day long;
For sidelong would she bend, and sing
  A faery's song.

### VII

She found me roots of relish sweet,
   And honey wild, and manna dew,
And sure in language strange she said—
   'I love thee true'.

### VIII

She took me to her elfin grot,
   And there she wept and sigh'd full sore,
And there I shut her wild wild eyes
   With kisses four.

### IX

And there she lulled me asleep
   And there I dream'd—Ah! woe betide!
The latest dream I ever dream'd
   On the cold hill side.

### X

I saw pale kings and princes too,
   Pale warriors, death-pale were they all;
They cried—'La Belle Dame sans Merci
   Hath thee in thrall!'

### XI

I saw their starved lips in the gloam,
   With horrid warning gaped wide,
And I awoke and found me here,
   On the cold hill's side.

### XII

And this is why I sojourn here
   Alone and palely loitering,
Though the sedge has wither'd from the lake,
   And no birds sing.

## SONG OF FOUR FAIRIES

### FIRE, AIR, EARTH, AND WATER

### SALAMANDER, ZEPHYR, DUSKETHA, AND BREAMA

#### SALAMANDER

HAPPY, happy glowing fire!

ZEPHYR

Fragrant air! delicious light!


DUSKETHA

Let me to my glooms retire!


BREAMA

I to green-weed rivers bright!


SALAMANDER

Happy, happy glowing fire!
Dazzling bowers of soft retire,
Ever let my nourish'd wing,
Like a bat's, still wandering,
Faintly fan your fiery spaces,
Spirit sole in deadly places.                    10
In unhaunted roar and blaze,
Open eyes that never daze,
Let me see the myriad shapes
Of men, and beasts, and fish, and apes,
Portray'd in many a fiery den,
And wrought by spumy bitumen.
On the deep intenser roof,
Arched every way aloof,
Let me breathe upon their skies,
And anger their live tapestries;                 20
Free from cold, and every care,
Of chilly rain, and shivering air.


ZEPHYR

Spirit of Fire! away! away!
Or your very roundelay
Will sear my plumage newly budded
From its quilled sheath, all studded
With the self-same dews that fell
On the May-grown Asphodel.
Spirit of Fire—away! away!

### BREAMA

Spirit of Fire—away! away!                    30
Zephyr, blue-eyed Faery, turn,
And see my cool sedge-bury'd urn,
Where it rests its mossy brim
'Mid water-mint and cresses dim;
And the flowers, in sweet troubles
Lift their eyes above the bubbles,
Like our Queen, when she would please
To sleep, and Oberon *will* teaze.
Love me, blue-eyed Faery, true!
Soothly I am sick for you.                     40

### ZEPHYR

Gentle Breama! by the first
Violet young nature nurst,
I will bathe myself with thee,
So you sometimes follow me
To my home, far, far, in west,
Beyond the nimble-wheeled quest
Of the golden-presenc'd sun:
Come with me, o'er tops of trees.
To my fragrant palaces,
Where they ever floating are                   50
Beneath the cherish of a star
Call'd Vesper, who with silver veil
Ever hides his brilliance pale,
Ever gently-drows'd doth keep
Twilight for the Fayes to sleep.
Fear not that your watery hair
Will thirst in drouthy ringlets there:
Clouds of stored summer rains
Thou shalt taste, before the stains
Of the mountain soil they take,               60
And too unlucent for thee make.
I love thee, crystal Faery, true!
Sooth I am as sick for you!

### SALAMANDER

Out, ye aguish Faeries, out!
Chilly lovers, what a rout

Keep ye with your frozen breath,
Colder than the mortal death.
Adder-eyed Dusketha, speak,
Shall we leave these, and go seek
In the earth's wide entrails old                    70
Couches warm as their's are cold?
O for a fiery gloom and thee,
Dusketha, so enchantingly
Freckle-wing'd and lizard-sided!

#### DUSKETHA

By thee, Sprite, will I be guided!
I care not for cold or heat;
Frost and flame, or sparks, or sleet,
To my essence are the same;—
But I honour more the flame.
Sprite of Fire, I follow thee                       80
Wheresoever it may be,
To the torrid spouts and fountains,
Underneath earth-quaked mountains;
Or, at thy supreme desire,
Touch the very pulse of fire
With my bare unlidded eyes.

#### SALAMANDER

Sweet Dusketha! paradise!
Off, ye icy Spirits, fly!
Frosty creatures of the sky!

#### DUSKETHA

Breathe upon them, fiery sprite!                    90

#### ZEPHYR AND BREAMA

Away! away to our delight!

#### SALAMANDER

Go, feed on icicles, while we
Bedded in tongue-flames will be.

DUSKETHA

Lead me to those feverous glooms,
Sprite of Fire!


BREAMA

Me to the blooms,
Blue-eyed Zephyr, of those flowers
Far in the west where the May-cloud lowers;
And the beams of still Vesper, when winds are all wist,
Are shed thro' the rain and the milder mist,
And twilight your floating bowers          100


## ODE ON INDOLENCE

'They toil not, neither do they spin.'

I

ONE morn before me were three figures seen,
   With bowed necks, and joined hands, side-faced;
And one behind the other stepp'd serene,
   In placid sandals, and in white robes graced;
They pass'd, like figures on a marble urn,
   When shifted round to see the other side;
      They came again; as when the urn once more
Is shifted round, the first seen shades return;
   And they were strange to me, as may betide
      With vases, to one deep in Phidian lore.          10


II

How is it, Shadows! that I knew ye not?
   How came ye muffled in so hush a mask?
Was it a silent deep-disguised plot
   To steal away, and leave without a task
My idle days? Ripe was the drowsy hour;
   The blissful cloud of summer-indolence
      Benumb'd my eyes; my pulse grew less and less;
Pain had no sting, and pleasure's wreath no flower:
   O, why did ye not melt, and leave my sense
      Unhaunted quite of all but—nothingness?          20

### III

A third time came they by;—alas! wherefore?
  My sleep had been embroider'd with dim dreams;
My soul had been a lawn besprinkled o'er
  With flowers, and stirring shades, and baffled beams.
The morn was clouded, but no shower fell,
    Tho' in her lids hung the sweet tears of May;
      The open casement press'd a new-leav'd vine,
    Let in the budding warmth and throstle's lay;
O Shadows! 'twas a time to bid farewell!
    Upon your skirts had fallen no tears of mine.    30

### IV

A third time pass'd they by, and, passing, turn'd
  Each one the face a moment whiles to me;
Then faded, and to follow them I burn'd
  And ach'd for wings because I knew the three;
The first was a fair Maid, and Love her name;
    The second was Ambition, pale of cheek,
      And ever watchful with fatigued eye;
The last, whom I love more, the more of blame
    Is heap'd upon her, maiden most unmeek,—
    I knew to be my demon Poesy.    40

### V

They faded, and, forsooth! I wanted wings:
  O folly! What is love! and where is it?
And for that poor Ambition! it springs
  From a man's little heart's short fever-fit;
For Poesy!—no,—she has not a joy,—
    At least for me,—so sweet as drowsy noons,
      And evenings steep'd in honied indolence;
O, for an age so shelter'd from annoy,
    That I may never know how change the moons,
    Or hear the voice of busy common-sense!    50

### VI

So, ye Three Ghosts, adieu! Ye cannot raise
  My head cool-bedded in the flowery grass;
For I would not be dieted with praise,
  A pet-lamb in a sentimental farce!

Fade softly from my eyes, and be once more
  In masque-like figures on the dreamy urn;
    Farewell! I yet have visions for the night,
And for the day faint visions there is store;
    Vanish, ye Phantoms! from my idle spright,
  Into the clouds, and never more return!          60

## THE EVE OF SAINT MARK

Upon a Sabbath-day it fell;
Twice holy was the Sabbath-bell,
That call'd the folk to evening prayer;
The city streets were clean and fair
From wholesome drench of April rains;
And, on the western window panes,
The chilly sunset faintly told
Of unmatur'd green vallies cold,
Of the green thorny bloomless hedge,
Of rivers new with spring-tide sedge,          10
Of primroses by shelter'd rills,
And daisies on the aguish hills.
Twice holy was the Sabbath-bell:
The silent streets were crowded well
With staid and pious companies,
Warm from their fire-side orat'ries;
And moving, with demurest air,
To even-song, and vesper prayer.
Each arched porch, and entry low,
Was fill'd with patient folk and slow,          20
With whispers hush, and shuffling feet,
While play'd the organ loud and sweet.

The bells had ceas'd, the prayers begun,
And Bertha had not yet half done
A curious volume, patch'd and torn,
That all day long, from earliest morn,
Had taken captive her two eyes,
Among its golden broideries;
Perplex'd her with a thousand things,—
The stars of Heaven, and angels' wings,          30
Martyrs in a fiery blaze,
Azure saints in silver rays,

Moses' breastplate, and the seven
Candlesticks John saw in Heaven,
The winged Lion of Saint Mark,
And the Covenantal Ark,
With its many mysteries,
Cherubim and golden mice.

Bertha was a maiden fair,
Dwelling in the old Minster-square;    40
From her fire-side she could see,
Sidelong, its rich antiquity,
Far as the Bishop's garden-wall;
Where sycamores and elm-trees tall,
Full-leav'd, the forest had outstript,
By no sharp north-wind ever nipt,
So shelter'd by the mighty pile.
Bertha arose, and read awhile,
With forehead 'gainst the window-pane.
Again she try'd, and then again,    50
Until the dusk eve left her dark
Upon the legend of St. Mark.
From plaited lawn-frill, fine and thin,
She lifted up her soft warm chin,
With aching neck and swimming eyes,
And daz'd with saintly imageries.

All was gloom, and silent all,
Save now and then the still foot-fall
Of one returning homewards late,
Past the echoing minster-gate.    60

The clamorous daws, that all the day
Above tree-tops and towers play,
Pair by pair had gone to rest,
Each in its ancient belfry-nest,
Where asleep they fall betimes,
To music of the drowsy chimes.

All was silent, all was gloom,
Abroad and in the homely room:

Down she sat, poor cheated soul!
And struck a lamp from the dismal coal;     70
Lean'd forward, with bright drooping hair
And slant book, full against the glare.
Her shadow, in uneasy guise,
Hover'd about, a giant size,
On ceiling-beam and old oak chair,
The parrot's cage, and panel square;
And the warm angled winter screen,
On which were many monsters seen,
Call'd doves of Siam, Lima mice,
And legless birds of Paradise,     80
Macaw, and tender Avadavat,
And silken-furr'd Angora cat.
Untir'd she read, her shadow still
Glower'd about, as it would fill
The room with wildest forms and shades,
As though some ghostly queen of spades
Had come to mock behind her back,
And dance, and ruffle her garments black.
Untir'd she read the legend page,
Of holy Mark, from youth to age,     90
On land, on sea, in pagan chains,
Rejoicing for his many pains
Sometimes the learned eremite,
With golden star, or dagger bright,
Referr'd to pious poesies
Written in smallest crow-quill size
Beneath the text; and thus the rhyme
Was parcell'd out from time to time:     98
'Gif ye wol stonden hardie wight—     98 *a*
Amiddes of the blacke night—     *b*
Righte in the churche porch, pardie     *c*
Ye wol behold a companie     *d*
Appouchen thee full dolourouse     *e*
For sooth to sain from everich house     *f*
Be it in City or village     *g*
Wol come the Phantom and image     *h*
Of ilka gent and ilka carle     *i*
Whom coldè Deathè hath in parle     *j*
And wol some day that very year     *k*

Touchen with foulè venìme spear     98 *l*
And sadly do them all to die—      *m*
Hem all shalt thou see verilie—     *n*
And everichon shall by the[e] pass   *o*
All who must die that year Alas     *p*
——Als writith he of swevenis,
Men han beforne they wake in bliss,    100
Whanne that hir friendes thinke hem bound
In crimped shroude farre under grounde;
And how a litling child mote be
A saint er its nativitie,
Gif that the modre (God her blesse!)
Kepen in solitarinesse,
And kissen devoute the holy croce.
Of Goddes love, and Sathan's force,—
He writith; and thinges many mo:
Of swiche thinges I may not show.    110
Bot I must tellen verilie
Somdel of Saintè Cicilie,
And chieflie what he auctorethe
Of Saintè Markis life and dethe:'


At length her constant eyelids come
Upon the fervent martyrdom;
Then lastly to his holy shrine,
Exalt amid the tapers' shine
At Venice,—


# ODE TO FANNY

### I

PHYSICIAN Nature! let my spirit blood!
  O ease my heart of verse and let me rest;
Throw me upon thy Tripod, till the flood
  Of stifling numbers ebbs from my full breast.
A theme! a theme! great nature! give a theme;
    Let me begin my dream.
I come—I see thee, as thou standest there,
Beckon me not into the wintry air.

II

Ah! dearest love, sweet home of all my fears,
  And hopes, and joys, and panting miseries,—
To-night, if I may guess, thy beauty wears
      A smile of such delight,
      As brilliant and as bright,
  As when with ravished, aching, vassal eyes,
      Lost in soft amaze,
      I gaze, I gaze!


III

Who now, with greedy looks, eats up my feast?
  What stare outfaces now my silver moon!
Ah! keep that hand unravish'd at the least;
      Let, let, the amorous burn—
      But, pr'ythee, do not turn
  The current of your heart from me so soon.
      O! save, in charity,
      The quickest pulse for me.


IV

Save it for me, sweet love! though music breathe
  Voluptuous visions into the warm air;
Though swimming through the dance's dangerous wreath,
      Be like an April day,
      Smiling and cold and gay,
  A temperate lilly, temperate as fair;
      Then, Heaven! there will be
      A warmer June for me.


V

Why, this—you'll say, my Fanny! is not true:
  Put your soft hand upon your snowy side,
Where the heart beats: confess—'tis nothing new—
      Must not a woman be
      A feather on the sea,
  Sway'd to and fro by every wind and tide?
      Of as uncertain speed
      As blow-ball from the mead?

VI

I know it—and to know it is despair
  To one who loves you as I love, sweet Fanny!
Whose heart goes fluttering for you every where,
      Nor, when away you roam,
      Dare keep its wretched home,
  Love, love alone, has pains severe and many:
      Then, loveliest! keep me free
      From torturing jealousy.


VII

Ah! if you prize my subdued soul above
  The poor, the fading, brief, pride of an hour;
Let none profane my Holy See of love,
      Or with a rude hand break
      The sacramental cake:
  Let none else touch the just new-budded flower;
      If not—may my eyes close,
      Love! on their last repose.

# SONNETS

## I

OH how I love, on a fair summer's eve,
   When streams of light pour down the golden west,
   And on the balmy zephyrs tranquil rest
The silver clouds, far—far away to leave
All meaner thoughts, and take a sweet reprieve
   From little cares; to find, with easy quest,
   A fragrant wild, with Nature's beauty drest,
And there into delight my soul deceive.
There warm my breast with patriotic lore,
   Musing on Milton's fate—on Sydney's bier—     10
   Till their stern forms before my mind arise:
Perhaps on wing of Poesy upsoar,
   Full often dropping a delicious tear,
     When some melodious sorrow spells mine eyes.

## II

### TO A YOUNG LADY WHO SENT ME
### A LAUREL CROWN

FRESH morning gusts have blown away all fear
   From my glad bosom,—now from gloominess
   I mount for ever—not an atom less
Than the proud laurel shall content my bier.
No! by the eternal stars! or why sit here
   In the Sun's eye, and 'gainst my temples press
   Apollo's very leaves, woven to bless
By thy white fingers and thy spirit clear.
Lo! who dares say, 'Do this'? Who dares call down
   My will from its high purpose? Who say, 'Stand,'   10
Or 'Go'? This mighty moment I would frown
   On abject Cæsars—not the stoutest band
Of mailed heroes should tear off my crown:
   Yet would I kneel and kiss thy gentle hand!

### III

AFTER dark vapours have oppress'd our plains
   For a long dreary season, comes a day
   Born of the gentle South, and clears away
From the sick heavens all unseemly stains.
The anxious month, relieved of its pains,
   Takes as a long-lost right the feel of May;
   The eyelids with the passing coolness play
Like rose leaves with the drip of Summer rains.
The calmest thoughts come round us; as of leaves
   Budding—fruit ripening in stillness—Autumn suns   10
Smiling at eve upon the quiet sheaves—
Sweet Sappho's cheek—a smiling infant's breath—
   The gradual sand that through an hour-glass runs—
A woodland rivulet—a Poet's death.

### IV

*[Written at the end of Chaucer's tale*
*'The Floure and the Lefe']*

THIS pleasant tale is like a little copse:
   The honied lines do freshly interlace
   To keep the reader in so sweet a place,
So that he here and there full-hearted stops;
And oftentimes he feels the dewy drops
   Come cool and suddenly against his face,
   And by the wandering melody may trace
Which way the tender-legged linnet hops.
Oh! what a power hath white Simplicity!
   What mighty power has this gentle story!   10
   I that for ever feel athirst for glory
Could at this moment be content to lie
   Meekly upon the grass, as those whose sobbings
   Were heard of none beside the mournful robins.

## V

## ON THE SEA

I T keeps eternal whisperings around
   Desolate shores, and with its mighty swell
   Gluts twice ten thousand Caverns, till the spell
Of Hecate leaves them their old shadowy sound.
Often 'tis in such gentle temper found,
   That scarcely will the very smallest shell
   Be mov'd for days from where it sometime fell,
When last the winds of Heaven were unbound.
Oh ye! who have your eye-balls vex'd and tir'd,
   Feast them upon the wideness of the Sea;     10
      Oh ye! whose ears are dinn'd with uproar rude,
   Or fed too much with cloying melody—
      Sit ye near some old Cavern's Mouth and brood,
Until ye start, as if the sea-nymphs quir'd!

## VI

## ON LEIGH HUNT'S POEM 'THE STORY
## OF RIMINI'

W H O loves to peer up at the morning sun,
   With half-shut eyes and comfortable cheek,
   Let him, with this sweet tale, full often seek
For meadows where the little rivers run;
Who loves to linger with that brightest one
   Of Heaven—Hesperus—let him lowly speak
   These numbers to the night, and starlight meek,
Or moon, if that her hunting be begun.
He who knows these delights, and too is prone
   To moralize upon a smile or tear,     10
Will find at once a region of his own,
   A bower for his spirit, and will steer
To alleys where the fir-tree drops its cone,
   Where robins hop, and fallen leaves are sear.

## VII

WHEN I have fears that I may cease to be
  Before my pen has glean'd my teeming brain,
Before high-piled books, in charactery,
  Hold like rich garners the full ripen'd grain;
When I behold, upon the night's starr'd face,
  Huge cloudy symbols of a high romance,
And think that I may never live to trace
  Their shadows, with the magic hand of chance;
And when I feel, fair creature of an hour,
  That I shall never look upon thee more,          10
Never have relish in the faery power
  Of unreflecting love;—then on the shore
Of the wide world I stand alone, and think
Till love and fame to nothingness do sink.

## VIII

### TO HOMER

STANDING aloof in giant ignorance,
  Of thee I hear and of the Cyclades,
As one who sits ashore and longs perchance
  To visit dolphin-coral in deep seas.
So thou wast blind;—but then the veil was rent,
  For Jove uncurtain'd Heaven to let thee live,
And Neptune made for thee a spumy tent,
  And Pan made sing for thee his forest-hive;
Aye on the shores of darkness there is light,
  And precipices show untrodden green,          10
There is a budding morrow in midnight,
  There is a triple sight in blindness keen;
Such seeing hadst thou, as it once befel
To Dian, Queen of Earth, and Heaven, and Hell.

IX

# WRITTEN IN ANSWER TO A SONNET
## ENDING THUS:

**Dark eyes are dearer far
Than those that mock the hyacinthine bell—**

By J. H. REYNOLDS

BLUE! 'Tis the life of heaven,—the domain
 Of Cynthia,—the wide palace of the sun —
The tent of Hesperus, and all his train,—
 The bosomer of clouds, gold, grey and dun.
Blue! 'Tis the life of waters:—Ocean
 And all its vassal streams, pools numberless,
May rage, and foam, and fret, but never can
 Subside, if not to dark blue nativeness.
Blue! Gentle cousin of the forest-green,
 Married to green in all the sweetest flowers,—     10
Forget-me-not,—the Blue bell,—and, that Queen
 Of secrecy, the Violet: what strange powers
Hast thou, as a mere shadow! But how great,
When in an Eye thou art, alive with fate!


X

## TO J. R.

O THAT a week could be an age, and we
 Felt parting and warm meeting every week,
Then one poor year a thousand years would be,
 The flush of welcome ever on the cheek:
So could we live long life in little space,
 So time itself would be annihilate,
So a day's journey in oblivious haze
 To serve our joys would lengthen and dilate.
O to arrive each Monday morn from Ind!
 To land each Tuesday from the rich Levant!     10
In little time a host of joys to bind,
 And keep our souls in one eternal pant!
This morn, my friend, and yester-evening taught
Me how to harbour such a happy thought.

XI

## TO —

Time's sea hath been five years at its slow ebb,
    Long hours have to and fro let creep the sand,
Since I was tangled in thy beauty's web,
    And snared by the ungloving of thine hand.
And yet I never look on midnight sky,
    But I behold thine eyes' well memory'd light;
I cannot look upon the rose's dye,
    But to thy cheek my soul doth take its flight.
I cannot look on any budding flower,
    But my fond ear, in fancy at thy lips         10
And hearkening for a love-sound, doth devour
    Its sweets in the wrong sense:—Thou dost eclipse
Every delight with sweet remembering,
And grief unto my darling joys dost bring.

XII

## TO SLEEP

O soft embalmer of the still midnight,
    Shutting, with careful fingers and benign,
Our gloom-pleas'd eyes, embower'd from the light,
    Enshaded in forgetfulness divine:
O soothest Sleep! if so it please thee, close
    In midst of this thine hymn my willing eyes,
Or wait the amen, ere thy poppy throws
    Around my bed its lulling charities.
Then save me, or the passed day will shine
Upon my pillow, breeding many woes,—         10
    Save me from curious Conscience, that still lords
Its strength for darkness, burrowing like a mole;
    Turn the key deftly in the oiled wards,
And seal the hushed Casket of my Soul.

## XIII

## ON FAME

FAME, like a wayward Girl, will still be coy
    To those who woo her with too slavish knees,
But makes surrender to some thoughtless Boy,
    And dotes the more upon a heart at ease;
She is a Gipsey, will not speak to those
    Who have not learnt to be content without her;
A Jilt, whose ear was never whisper'd close,
    Who thinks they scandal her who talk about her;
A very Gipsey is she, Nilus-born,
    Sister-in-law to jealous Potiphar;        10
Ye love-sick Bards, repay her scorn for scorn,
    Ye Artists lovelorn, madmen that ye are!
Make your best bow to her and bid adieu,
Then, if she likes it, she will follow you.

## XIV

## ON FAME

'You cannot eat your cake and have it too.'—*Proverb.*

How fever'd is the man, who cannot look
    Upon his mortal days with temperate blood,
Who vexes all the leaves of his life's book,
    And robs his fair name of its maidenhood;
It is as if the rose should pluck herself,
    Or the ripe plum finger its misty bloom,
As if a Naiad, like a meddling elf,
    Should darken her pure grot with muddy gloom,
But the rose leaves herself upon the briar,
    For winds to kiss and grateful bees to feed,     10
And the ripe plum still wears its dim attire,
    The undisturbed lake has crystal space,
      Why then should man, teasing the world for grace,
    Spoil his salvation for a fierce miscreed?

## XV

WHY did I laugh to-night? No voice will tell:
  No God, no Demon of severe response,
Deigns to reply from Heaven or from Hell.
  Then to my human heart I turn at once.
Heart! Thou and I are here sad and alone;
  I say, why did I laugh! O mortal pain!
O Darkness! Darkness! ever must I moan,
  To question Heaven and Hell and Heart in vain.
Why did I laugh? I know this Being's lease,
  My fancy to its utmost blisses spreads;                    10
Yet would I on this very midnight cease,
  And the world's gaudy ensigns see in shreds;
Verse, Fame, and Beauty are intense indeed,
But Death intenser—Death is Life's high meed.

## XVI

## A DREAM,
## AFTER READING DANTE'S EPISODE
## OF PAOLO AND FRANCESCA

As Hermes once took to his feathers light,
  When lulled Argus, baffled, swoon'd and slept,
So on a Delphic reed, my idle spright
  So play'd, so charm'd, so conquer'd, so bereft
The dragon-world of all its hundred eyes;
  And, seeing it asleep, so fled away—
Not to pure Ida with its snow-cold skies,
  Nor unto Tempe where Jove griev'd a day;
But to that second circle of sad hell,
  Where 'mid the gust, the whirlwind, and the flaw      10
Of rain and hail-stones, lovers need not tell
  Their sorrows. Pale were the sweet lips I saw,
Pale were the lips I kiss'd, and fair the form
I floated with, about that melancholy storm.

## XVII

I F by dull rhymes our English must be chain'd,
And, like Andromeda, the Sonnet sweet
Fetter'd, in spite of pained loveliness,
Let us find out, if we must be constrain'd,
Sandals more interwoven and complete
To fit the naked foot of Poesy:
Let us inspect the Lyre, and weigh the stress
Of every chord, and see what may be gain'd
By ear industrious, and attention meet;
Misers of sound and syllable, no less                    10
Than Midas of his coinage, let us be
Jealous of dead leaves in the bay wreath crown;
So, if we may not let the Muse be free,
She will be bound with garlands of her own.

## XVIII

T H E day is gone, and all its sweets are gone!
   Sweet voice, sweet lips, soft hand, and softer breast,
Warm breath, light whisper, tender semi-tone,
   Bright eyes, accomplish'd shape, and lang'rous waist!
Faded the flower and all its budded charms,
   Faded the sight of beauty from my eyes,
Faded the shape of beauty from my arms,
   Faded the voice, warmth, whiteness, paradise—
Vanish'd unseasonably at shut of eve,
   When the dusk holiday—or holinight                    10
Of fragrant-curtain'd love begins to weave
   The woof of darkness thick, for hid delight;
But, as I've read love's missal through to-day,
He'll let me sleep, seeing I fast and pray.

## XIX

I C R Y your mercy—pity—love!—aye, love!
   Merciful love that tantalizes not,
One-thoughted, never-wandering, guileless love,
   Unmask'd, and being seen—without a blot!
O! let me have thee whole,—all—all—be mine!
   That shape, that fairness, that sweet minor zest
Of love, your kiss,—those hands, those eyes divine,
   That warm, white, lucent, million-pleasured breast,—

Yourself—your soul—in pity give me all,
  Withhold no atom's atom or I die,          10
Or living on perhaps, your wretched thrall,
  Forget, in the mist of idle misery,
Life's purposes,—the palate of my mind
Losing its gust, and my ambition blind!


XX.

*[Written on a Blank Page in Shakespeare's Poems,*
*facing 'A Lover's Complaint']*

BRIGHT star, would I were stedfast as thou art—
  Not in lone splendour hung aloft the night
And watching, with eternal lids apart,
  Like nature's patient, sleepless Eremite,
The moving waters at their priestlike task
  Of pure ablution round earth's human shores,
Or gazing on the new soft-fallen mask
  Of snow upon the mountains and the moors—
No—yet still stedfast, still unchangeable,
  Pillow'd upon my fair love's ripening breast,    10
To feel for ever its soft fall and swell,
  Awake for ever in a sweet unrest,
Still, still to hear her tender-taken breath,
And so live ever—or else swoon to death.

SHORTER POEMS FROM THE
MEMOIR IN *LIFE, LETTERS,*
*AND LITERARY REMAINS*

SPENSER! a jealous honourer of thine,
    A forester deep in thy midmost trees,
Did last eve ask my promise to refine
    Some English that might strive thine ear to please.
But Elfin Poet 'tis impossible
    For an inhabitant of wintry earth
To rise like Phœbus with a golden quell
    Fire-wing'd and make a morning in his mirth.
It is impossible to escape from toil
    O' the sudden and receive thy spiriting:          10
The flower must drink the nature of the soil
    Before it can put forth its blossoming:
Be with me in the summer days and I
Will for thine honour and his pleasure try.


## TO CHATTERTON

O CHATTERTON! how very sad thy fate!
    Dear child of sorrow—son of misery!
    How soon the film of death obscur'd that eye,
Whence Genius mildly flash'd, and high debate.
How soon that voice, majestic and elate,
    Melted in dying numbers! Oh! how nigh
    Was night to thy fair morning. Thou didst die
A half-blown flow'ret which cold blasts amate.
But this is past: thou art among the stars
    Of highest Heaven: to the rolling spheres          10
Thou sweetly singest: naught thy hymning mars,
    Above the ingrate world and human fears.
On earth the good man base detraction bars
    From thy fair name, and waters it with tears.

## TO BYRON

BYRON! how sweetly sad thy melody!
   Attuning still the soul to tenderness,
   As if soft Pity, with unusual stress,
Had touch'd her plaintive lute, and thou, being by,
Hadst caught the tones, nor suffer'd them to die.
   O'ershading sorrow doth not make thee less
   Delightful: thou thy griefs dost dress
With a bright halo, shining beamily,
As when a cloud the golden moon doth veil,
   Its sides are ting'd with a resplendent glow,    10
Through the dark robe oft amber rays prevail,
   And like fair veins in sable marble flow;
Still warble, dying swan! still tell the tale,
   The enchanting tale, the tale of pleasing woe.

## ON SEEING THE ELGIN MARBLES

MY spirit is too weak—mortality
   Weighs heavily on me like unwilling sleep,
   And each imagin'd pinnacle and steep
Of godlike hardship, tells me I must die
Like a sick Eagle looking at the sky.
   Yet 'tis a gentle luxury to weep
   That I have not the cloudy winds to keep,
Fresh for the opening of the morning's eye.
Such dim-conceived glories of the brain
   Bring round the heart an undescribable feud;    10
So do these wonders a most dizzy pain,
   That mingles Grecian grandeur with the rude
Wasting of old Time—with a billowy main—
   A sun—a shadow of a magnitude.

## TO B. R. HAYDON

HAYDON! forgive me that I cannot speak
  Definitively on these mighty things;
  Forgive me that I have not Eagle's wings—
That what I want I know not where to seek:
And think that I would not be over meek
  In rolling out upfollow'd thunderings,
  Even to the steep of Heliconian springs,
Were I of ample strength for such a freak—
Think too, that all those numbers should be thine;
  Whose else? In this who touch thy vesture's hem? 10
For when men star'd at what was most divine
  With browless idiotism—o'erwise phlegm—
Thou hadst beheld the Hesperean shine
  Of their star in the East, and gone to worship them.

## ON SEEING A LOCK OF MILTON'S HAIR

    CHIEF of organic numbers!
      Old Scholar of the Spheres!
    Thy spirit never slumbers,
      But rolls about our ears,
    For ever, and for ever!
    O what a mad endeavour
      Worketh he,
Who to thy sacred and ennobled hearse
Would offer a burnt sacrifice of verse
      And melody.           10

    How heavenward thou soundest,
      Live Temple of sweet noise,
    And Discord unconfoundest,
      Giving Delight new joys,
    And Pleasure nobler pinions!
    O, where are thy dominions?
      Lend thine ear
To a young Delian oath,—aye, by thy soul,
By all that from thy mortal lips did roll,
And by the kernel of thine earthly love,     20
Beauty, in things on earth, and things above
      I swear!

When every childish fashion
    Has vanish'd from my rhyme,
Will I, grey-gone in passion,
    Leave to an after-time
        Hymning and harmony
Of thee, and of thy works, and of thy life;
But vain is now the burning and the strife,
Pangs are in vain, until I grow high-rife                    30
        With old Philosophy,
And mad with glimpses of futurity!

For many years my offerings must be hush'd;
    When I do speak, I'll think upon this hour,
Because I feel my forehead hot and flush'd,
    Even at the simplest vassal of thy power,—
        A lock of thy bright hair,—
        Sudden it came,
And I was startled, when I caught thy name
        Coupled so unaware;                                  40
Yet, at the moment, temperate was my blood.
I thought I had beheld it from the flood.


SONG

Hence Burgundy, Claret, and Port,
    Away with old Hock and Madeira,
Too earthly ye are for my sport;
    There's a beverage brighter and clearer.
Instead of a pitiful rummer,
My wine overbrims a whole summer;
    My bowl is the sky,
    And I drink at my eye,
    Till I feel in the brain
    A Delphian pain—                                        10
Then follow, my Caius! then follow:
    On the green of the hill
    We will drink our fill
    Of golden sunshine,
    Till our brains intertwine
With the glory and grace of Apollo!

# GOD OF THE MERIDIAN

God of the Meridian,
    And of the East and West,
To thee my soul is flown,
    And my body is earthward press'd.—
It is an awful mission,
A terrible division:
And leaves a gulph austere
To be fill'd with worldly fear.
Aye, when the soul is fled
To high above our head,          10
Affrighted do we gaze
After its airy maze,
As doth a mother wild,
When her young infant child
Is in an eagle's claws—
And is not this the cause
Of madness?—God of Song,
Thou bearest me along
Through sights I scarce can bear:
O let me, let me share          20
With the hot lyre and thee,
The staid Philosophy.
Temper my lonely hours,
And let me see thy bowers
More unalarm'd!

# O THOU WHOSE FACE HATH FELT

O thou whose face hath felt the Winter's wind,
    Whose eye has seen the snow-clouds hung in mist,
    And the black elm tops 'mong the freezing stars,
    To thee the spring will be a harvest-time.
O thou, whose only book has been the light
    Of supreme darkness which thou feddest on
    Night after night when Phœbus was away,
    To thee the Spring shall be a triple morn.

O fret not after knowledge—I have none,
  And yet my song comes native with the warmth.    10
O fret not after knowledge—I have none,
  And yet the Evening listens. He who saddens
At thought of idleness cannot be idle,
And he's awake who thinks himself asleep.


## ON SITTING DOWN TO READ
## KING LEAR ONCE AGAIN

O GOLDEN tongued Romance, with serene lute!
  Fair plumed Syren, Queen of far-away!
  Leave melodizing on this wintry day,
Shut up thine olden pages, and be mute:
Adieu! for, once again, the fierce dispute
  Betwixt damnation and impassion'd clay
  Must I burn through; once more humbly assay
The bitter-sweet of this Shakespearian fruit:
Chief Poet! and ye clouds of Albion,
  Begetters of our deep eternal theme!    10
When through the old oak Forest I am gone,
  Let me not wander in a barren dream,
But, when I am consumed in the fire,
Give me new Phœnix wings to fly at my desire.


## TO THE NILE

Son of the old moon-mountains African!
  Chief of the Pyramid and Crocodile!
  We call thee fruitful, and, that very while,
A desert fills our seeing's inward span;
Nurse of swart nations since the world began,
  Art thou so fruitful? or dost thou beguile
  Such men to honour thee, who, worn with toil,
Rest for a space 'twixt Cairo and Decan?
O may dark fancies err! they surely do;
  'Tis ignorance that makes a barren waste    10
Of all beyond itself, thou dost bedew
  Green rushes like our rivers, and dost taste
The pleasant sun-rise, green isles hast thou too,
  And to the sea as happily dost haste.

## TO J. H. REYNOLDS ESQ.

DEAR Reynolds! as last night I lay in bed,
There came before my eyes that wonted thread
Of shapes, and shadows, and remembrances,
That every other minute vex and please:
Things all disjointed come from north and south,—
Two Witch's eyes above a Cherub's mouth,
Voltaire with casque and shield and habergeon,
And Alexander with his nightcap on;
Old Socrates a-tying his cravat,
And Hazlitt playing with Miss Edgeworth's cat;          10
And Junius Brutus, pretty well so so,
Making the best of's way towards Soho.

Few are there who escape these visitings,—
Perhaps one or two whose lives have patent wings,
And thro' whose curtains peeps no hellish nose,
No wild-boar tushes, and no Mermaid's toes;
But flowers bursting out with lusty pride,
And young Æolian harps personified;
Some Titian colours touch'd into real life,—
The sacrifice goes on; the pontiff knife          20
Gleams in the Sun, the milk-white heifer lows,
The pipes go shrilly, the libation flows:
A white sail shows above the green-head cliff,
Moves round the point, and throws her anchor stiff;
The mariners join hymn with those on land.

You know the Enchanted Castle,—it doth stand
Upon a rock, on the border of a Lake,
Nested in trees, which all do seem to shake
From some old magic-like Urganda's Sword.
O Phœbus! that I had thy sacred word          30
To show this Castle, in fair dreaming wise,
Unto my friend, while sick and ill he lies!

You know it well enough, where it doth seem
A mossy place, a Merlin's Hall, a dream;
You know the clear Lake, and the little Isles,
The mountains blue, and cold near neighbour rills,

All which elsewhere are but half animate;
There do they look alive to love and hate,
To smiles and frowns; they seem a lifted mound
Above some giant, pulsing underground.                    40

Part of the Building was a chosen See,
Built by a banish'd Santon of Chaldee;
The other part, two thousand years from him,
Was built by Cuthbert de Saint Aldebrim;
Then there's a little wing, far from the Sun,
Built by a Lapland Witch turn'd maudlin Nun;
And many other juts of aged stone
Founded with many a mason-devil's groan.

The doors all look as if they op'd themselves,
The windows as if latch'd by Fays and Elves,          50
And from them comes a silver flash of light,
As from the westward of a Summer's night;
Or like a beauteous woman's large blue eyes
Gone mad thro' olden songs and poesies.

See! what is coming from the distance dim!
A golden Galley all in silken trim!
Three rows of oars are lightening, moment whiles,
Into the verd'rous bosoms of those isles;
Towards the shade, under the Castle wall,
It comes in silence,—now 'tis hidden all.             60
The Clarion sounds, and from a Postern-gate
An echo of sweet music doth create
A fear in the poor Herdsman, who doth bring
His beasts to trouble the enchanted spring,—
He tells of the sweet music, and the spot,
To all his friends, and they believe him not.

O that our dreamings all, of sleep or wake,
Would all their colours from the sunset take:
From something of material sublime,
Rather than shadow our own soul's day-time             70
In the dark void of night. For in the world
We jostle,—but my flag is not unfurl'd
On the Admiral-staff,—and so philosophize
I dare not yet! Oh, never will the prize,

High reason, and the lore of good and ill,
Be my award! Things cannot to the will
Be settled, but they tease us out of thought;
Or is it that imagination brought
Beyond its proper bound, yet still confin'd,
Lost in a sort of Purgatory blind, 80
Cannot refer to any standard law
Of either earth or heaven? It is a flaw
In happiness, to see beyond our bourn,—
It forces us in summer skies to mourn,
It spoils the singing of the Nightingale.

    Dear Reynolds! I have a mysterious tale,
And cannot speak it: the first page I read
Upon a Lampit rock of green sea-weed
Among the breakers; 'twas a quiet eve,
The rocks were silent, the wide sea did weave 90
An untumultuous fringe of silver foam
Along the flat brown sand; I was at home
And should have been most happy,—but I saw
Too far into the sea, where every maw
The greater on the less feeds evermore.—
But I saw too distinct into the core
Of an eternal fierce destruction,
And so from happiness I far was gone.
Still am I sick of it, and tho', to-day,
I've gather'd young spring-leaves, and flowers gay 100
Of periwinkle and wild strawberry,
Still do I that most fierce destruction see,—
The Shark at savage prey,—the Hawk at pounce,—
The gentle Robin, like a Pard or Ounce,
Ravening a worm,—Away, ye horrid moods!
Moods of one's mind! You know I hate them well.
You know I'd sooner be a clapping Bell
To some Kamtschatcan Missionary Church,
Than with these horrid moods be left i' the lurch.

OVER the hill and over the dale,
And over the bourn to Dawlish—
Where Gingerbread Wives have a scanty sale
And gingerbre[a]d nuts are smallish.

Rantipole Betty she ran down a hill
And ki[c]ked up her pettic[o]ats fairly
Says I I'll be Jack if you will be Gill.
So she sat on the Grass debonnairly.

Here's somebody coming, here's somebody coming!
  Says I 'tis the Wind at a parley         10
So without any fuss any hawing and humming
  She lay on the grass debonnai[r]ly.

Here's somebody here and here's somebody there!
  Says I hold your tongue you young Gipsey.
So she held her tongue and lay plump and fair
  And dead as a venus tipsy.

O who wouldn't hie to Dawlish fair
  O who wouldn't stop in a Meadow
O [who] would not rumple the daisies there
  And make the wild fern for a bed do.        20

## ODE TO MAY. FRAGMENT

MOTHER of Hermes! and still youthful Maia!
    May I sing to thee
As thou wast hymned on the shores of Baiæ?
    Or may I woo thee
In earlier Sicilian? or thy smiles
Seek as they once were sought, in Grecian isles,
By bards who died content on pleasant sward,
  Leaving great verse unto a little clan?
O, give me their old vigour, and unheard
  Save of the quiet Primrose, and the span    10
    Of heaven and few ears,
Rounded by thee, my song should die away
    Content as theirs,
Rich in the simple worship of a day.

## ON VISITING THE TOMB OF BURNS

THE town, the churchyard, and the setting sun,
  The clouds, the trees, the rounded hills all seem,
  Though beautiful, cold—strange—as in a dream,
I dreamed long ago, now new begun.
The short-liv'd, paly Summer is but won
  From Winter's ague, for one hour's gleam;
  Though sapphire-warm, their stars do never beam:
All is cold Beauty; pain is never done:
For who has mind to relish, Minos-wise,
  The Real of Beauty, free from that dead hue          10
    Sickly imagination and sick pride
  Cast wan upon it! Burns! with honour due
    I oft have honour'd thee. Great shadow, hide
Thy face; I sin against thy native skies.

## SONNET WRITTEN IN THE COTTAGE
## WHERE BURNS WAS BORN

THIS mortal body of a thousand days
  Now fills, O Burns, a space in thine own room,
Where thou didst dream alone on budded bays,
  Happy and thoughtless of thy day of doom!
My pulse is warm with thine own Barley-bree,
  My head is light with pledging a great soul,
My eyes are wandering, and I cannot see,
  Fancy is dead and drunken at its goal;
Yet can I stamp my foot upon thy floor,
  Yet can I ope thy window-sash to find          10
The meadow thou hast tramped o'er and o'er,—
  Yet can I think of thee till thought is blind,—
Yet can I gulp a bumper to thy name,—
O smile among the shades, for this is fame!

## OLD MEG

OLD MEG she was a Gipsy,
  And liv'd upon the Moors:
Her bed it was the brown heath turf,
  And her house was out of doors.

Her apples were swart blackberries,
  Her currants pods o' broom;
Her wine was dew of the wild white rose,
  Her book a churchyard tomb.

Her Brothers were the craggy hills,
  Her Sisters larchen trees—      10
Alone with her great family
  She liv'd as she did please.

No breakfast had she many a morn,
  No dinner many a noon,
And 'stead of supper she would stare
  Full hard against the Moon.

But every morn of woodbine fresh
  She made her garlanding,
And every night the dark glen Yew
  She wove, and she would sing.      20

And with her fingers old and brown
  She plaited Mats o' Rushes,
And gave them to the Cottagers
  She met among the Bushes.

Old Meg was brave as Margaret Queen
  And tall as Amazon:
And old red blanket cloak she wore;
  A chip hat had she on.
God rest her aged bones somewhere—
  She died full long agone!      30

## TO AILSA ROCK

Hearken, thou craggy ocean pyramid!
  Give answer from thy voice, the sea-fowls' screams!
  When were thy shoulders mantled in huge streams?
When, from the sun, was thy broad forehead hid?
How long is't since the mighty power bid
  Thee heave to airy sleep from fathom dreams?
  Sleep in the lap of thunder or sunbeams,
Or when grey clouds are thy cold coverlid?

Thou answer'st not; for thou art dead asleep;
   Thy life is but two dead eternities—                    10
The last in air, the former in the deep;
   First with the whales, last with the eagle-skies—
Drown'd wast thou till an earthquake made thee steep,
   Another cannot wake thy giant size.


## LINES WRITTEN IN THE HIGHLANDS
## AFTER A VISIT TO BURNS'S COUNTRY

THERE is a charm in footing slow across a silent plain,
Where patriot battle has been fought, where glory had the
      gain;
There is a pleasure on the heath where Druids old have been,
Where mantles grey have rustled by and swept the nettles
      green;
There is a joy in every spot made known by times of old,
New to the feet, although each tale a hundred times be told;
There is a deeper joy than all, more solemn in the heart,
More parching to the tongue than all, of more divine a smart,
When weary steps forget themselves upon a pleasant turf,
Upon hot sand, or flinty road, or sea-shore iron scurf,    10
Toward the castle or the cot, where long ago was born
One who was great through mortal days, and died of fame
      unshorn!
Light heather-bells may tremble then, but they are far away;
Wood-lark may sing from sandy fern,—the Sun may hear his
      lay;
Runnels may kiss the grass on shelves and shallows clear,
But their low voices are not heard, though come on travels
      drear;
Blood-red the Sun may set behind black mountain peaks;
Blue tides may sluice and drench their time in caves and
      weedy creeks;
Eagles may seem to sleep wing-wide upon the air;
Ring-doves may fly convuls'd across to some high-cedar'd
      lair;                                                 20
But the forgotten eye is still fast lidded to the ground,
As Palmer's, that with weariness, mid-desert shrine hath
      found.

At such a time the soul's a child, in childhood is the brain;
Forgotten is the worldly heart—alone, it beats in vain.—
Aye, if a madman could have leave to pass a healthful day
To tell his forehead's swoon and faint when first began decay,
He might make tremble many a one whose spirit had gone
    forth
To find a Bard's low cradle-place about the silent North!
Scanty the hour and few the steps beyond the bourn of care,
Beyond the sweet and bitter world,—beyond it unaware!  30
Scanty the hour and few the steps, because a longer stay
Would bar return, and make a man forget his mortal way:
O horrible! to lose the sight of well remember'd face,
Of Brother's eyes, of Sister's brow—constant to every place;
Filling the air, as on we move, with portraiture intense;
More warm than those heroic tints that pain a painter's
    sense,
When shapes of old come striding by, and visages of old,
Locks shining black, hair scanty grey, and passions manifold.
No, no, that horror cannot be, for at the cable's length
Man feels the gentle anchor pull and gladdens in its
    strength:—                                            40
One hour, half-idiot, he stands by mossy waterfall,
But in the very next he reads his soul's memorial:—
He reads it on the mountain's height, where chance he may sit
    down
Upon rough marble diadem—that hill's eternal crown.
Yet be his anchor e'er so fast, room is there for a prayer
That man may never lose his mind on mountains black and
    bare;
That he may stray league after league some great birth-place
    to find
And keep his vision clear from speck, his inward sight
    unblind.


## ON VISITING STAFFA

> Not Aladdin magian
> Ever such a work began;
> Not the wizard of the Dee
> Ever such a dream could see;

Not St. John, in Patmos' Isle,
In the passion of his toil,
When he saw the churches seven,
Golden aisl'd, built up in heaven,
Gaz'd at such a rugged wonder.
As I stood its roofing under,                    10
Lo! I saw one sleeping there,
On the marble cold and bare.
While the surges wash'd his feet,
And his garments white did beat
Drench'd about the sombre rocks,
On his neck his well-grown locks,
Lifted dry above the main,
Were upon the curl again.
'What is this? and what art thou?'
Whisper'd I, and touch'd his brow;               20
'What art thou? and what is this?'
Whisper'd I, and strove to kiss
The spirit's hand, to wake his eyes;
Up he started in a trice:
'I am Lycidas,' said he,
'Fam'd in funeral minstrelsy!
This was architected thus
By the great Oceanus!—
Here his mighty waters play
Hollow organs all the day;                       30
Here by turns his dolphins all,
Finny palmers great and small,
Come to pay devotion due—
Each a mouth of pearls must strew.
Many a mortal of these days,
Dares to pass our sacred ways,
Dares to touch audaciously
This Cathedral of the Sea!
I have been the pontiff-priest
Where the waters never rest,                     40
Where a fledgy sea-bird choir
Soars for ever; holy fire
I have hid from mortal man;
Proteus is my Sacristan.
But the stupid eye of mortal

Hath pass'd beyond the rocky portal;
So for ever will I leave
Such a taint, and soon unweave
All the magic of the place.'                          49
'Tis now free to stupid face,               49 *a*
To cutters, and to Fashion boats,            *b*
To cravats and to petticoats:—              *c*
The great sea shall war it down,             *d*
For its fame shall not be blown              *e*
At each farthing Quadrille dance.            *f*
So saying, with a Spirit's glance                     50
He dived!


READ me a lesson, Muse, and speak it loud
    Upon the top of Nevis, blind in mist!
I look into the chasms, and a shroud
    Vapourous doth hide them,—just so much I wist
Mankind do know of hell; I look o'erhead,
    And there is sullen mist,—even so much
Mankind can tell of heaven; mist is spread
    Before the earth, beneath me,—even such,
Even so vague is man's sight of himself!
    Here are the craggy stones beneath my feet,—      10
Thus much I know that, a poor witless elf,
    I tread on them,—that all my eye doth meet
Is mist and crag, not only on this height,
But in the world of thought and mental might!


'TIS the witching hour of night,
Orbed is the moon and bright,
And the stars they glisten, glisten,
Seeming with bright eyes to listen—
    For what listen they?
For a song and for a charm,
See they glisten in alarm,
And the moon is waxing warm
    To hear what I shall say.
Moon! keep wide thy golden ears—                      10
Hearken, stars! and hearken, spheres!—

Hearken, thou eternal sky!
I sing an infant's lullaby,
    A pretty lullaby.
Listen, listen, listen, listen,
Glisten, glisten, glisten, glisten,
    And hear my lullaby!
Though the rushes that will make
Its cradle still are in the lake—
Though the linen that will be                    20
Its swathe, in on the cotton tree—
Though the woollen that will keep
It warm, is on the silly sheep—
Listen, starlight, listen, listen,
Glisten, glisten, glisten, glisten,
    And hear my lullaby!
Child, I see thee! Child, I've found thee
Midst of the quiet all around thee!
Child, I see thee! Child, I spy thee!
And thy mother sweet is nigh thee!               30
Child, I know thee! Child no more,
But a Poet evermore!
See, see, the lyre, the lyre,
In a flame of fire,
Upon the little cradle's top
Flaring, flaring, flaring,
Past the eyesight's bearing.
Awake it from its sleep,
And see if it can keep
Its eyes upon the blaze—                          40
    Amaze, amaze!
It stares, it stares, it stares,
It dares what no one dares!
It lifts its little hand into the flame
Unharm'd, and on the strings
Paddles a little tune, and sings,
With dumb endeavour sweetly—
Bard art thou completely!
    Little child
        O' th' western wild,                     50
Bard art thou completely!
Sweetly with dumb endeavour,

A Poet now or never,
    Little child
    O' th' western wild,
A Poet now or never!


## TRANSLATED FROM RONSARD

NATURE withheld Cassandra in the skies,
    For more adornment, a full thousand years;
She took their cream of Beauty's fairest dyes,
    And shap'd and tinted her above all Peers:
Meanwhile Love kept her dearly with his wings,
    And underneath their shadow fill'd her eyes
With such a richness that the cloudy Kings
    Of high Olympus utter'd slavish sighs.
When from the Heavens I saw her first descend,
    My heart took fire, and only burning pains,        10
They were my pleasures—they my Life's sad end;
    Love pour'd her beauty into my warm veins . . .

    *     *     *     *     *     *
    *     *     *     *     *     *


## CHARACTER OF CHARLES BROWN

### I

HE is to weet a melancholy carle:
Thin in the waist, with bushy head of hair,
As hath the seeded thistle when in parle
It holds the Zephyr, ere it sendeth fair
Its light balloons into the summer air;
Therto his beard had not begun to bloom,
No brush had touch'd his chin or razor sheer;
No care had touch'd his cheek with mortal doom,
But new he was and bright as scarf from Persian loom.


### II

Ne cared he for wine, or half-and-half
Ne cared he for fish or flesh or fowl,
And sauces held he worthless as the chaff;
He 'sdeigned the swine-head at the wassail-bowl;

Ne with lewd ribbalds sat he cheek by jowl;
Ne with sly Lemans in the scorner's chair;
But after water-brooks this Pilgrim's soul
Panted, and all his food was woodland air
Though he would oft-times feast on gilliflowers rare.

### III

The slang of cities in no wise he knew,
*Tipping the wink* to him was heathen Greek;
He sipp'd no olden Tom or ruin blue,
Or nantz or cherry-brandy drank full meek
By many a damsel hoarse and rouge of cheek;
Nor did he know each aged watchman's beat,
Nor in obscured purlieus would he seek
For curled Jewesses, with ankles neat,
Who as they walk abroad make tinkling with their feet.

[*Written at the close of Canto II, Book V, of 'The Faerie Queene'.*]

IN after-time, a sage of mickle lore
Yclep'd Typographus, the Giant took,
And did refit his limbs as heretofore,
And made him read in many a learned book,
And into many a lively legend look;
Thereby in goodly themes so training him,
That all his brutishness he quite forsook,
When, meeting Artegall and Talus grim,
The one he struck stone-blind, the other's eyes wox dim.

## THE POET

#### A FRAGMENT

WHERE'S the Poet? show him! show him,
Muses nine! that I may know him!
'Tis the man who with a man
   Is an equal, be he King,
Or poorest of the beggar-clan,
   Or any other wondrous thing

A man may be 'twixt ape and Plato;
  'Tis the man who with a bird,
Wren or Eagle, finds his way to
  All its instincts; he hath heard        10
The Lion's roaring, and can tell
  What his horny throat expresseth,
And to him the Tiger's yell
  Comes articulate and presseth
On his ear like mother-tongue.


## MODERN LOVE

AND what is love? It is a doll dress'd up
For idleness to cosset, nurse, and dandle;
A thing of soft misnomers, so divine
That silly youth doth think to make itself
Divine by loving, and so goes on
Yawning and doting a whole summer long,
Till Miss's comb is made a pearl tiara,
And common Wellingtons turn Romeo boots;
Then Cleopatra lives at number seven,
And Antony resides in Brunswick Square.    10
Fools! if some passions high have warm'd the world,
If Queens and Soldiers have play'd deep for hearts,
It is no reason why such agonies
Should be more common than the growth of weeds.
Fools! make me whole again that weighty pearl
The Queen of Egypt melted, and I'll say
That ye may love in spite of beaver hats.


## FRAGMENT OF THE 'CASTLE BUILDER'

### CASTLE BUILDER

❋    ❋    ❋    ❋    ❋    ❋

IN short, convince you that however wise
You may have grown from Convent libraries,
I have, by many yards at least, been carding
A longer skein of wit in Convent garden.

### BERNARDINE

A very Eden that same place must be!
Pray what demesne? Whose Lordship's legacy?
What, have you convents in that Gothic Isle?
Pray pardon me, I cannot help but smile.

\*   \*   \*   \*   \*   \*

### CASTLE BUILDER

Sir, Convent Garden is a monstrous beast
From morning, four o'clock, to twelve at noon,          10
It swallows cabbages without a spoon,
And then, from twelve till two, this Eden made is
A promenade for cooks and ancient ladies;
And then for supper, 'stead of soup and poaches,
It swallows chairmen, damns, and Hackney coaches.
In short, Sir, 'tis a very place for monks,
For it containeth twenty thousand punks,
Which any man may number for his sport,
By following fat elbows up a court.

\*   \*   \*   \*   \*   \*

In such like nonsense would I pass an hour          20
With random Friar, or Rake upon his tour,
Or one of few of that imperial host
Who came unmaimed from the Russian frost.
To-night I'll have my friar—let me think
About my room,—I'll have it in the pink;
It should be rich and sombre, and the moon,
Just in its mid-life in the midst of June,
Should look thro' four large windows and display
Clear, but for gold-fish vases in the way,
Their glassy diamonding on Turkish floor;          30
The tapers keep aside, an hour and more,
To see what else the moon alone can show;
While the night-breeze doth softly let us know
My terrace is well bower'd with oranges.
Upon the floor the dullest spirit sees
A guitar-ribband and a lady's glove
Beside a crumple-leaved tale of love;

A tambour-frame, with Venus sleeping there,
All finish'd but some ringlets of her hair;
A viol, bowstrings torn, cross-wise upon                40
A glorious folio of Anacreon;
A skull upon a mat of roses lying,
Ink'd purple with a song concerning dying;
An hour-glass on the turn, amid the trails
Of passion-flower;—just in time there sails
A cloud across the moon,—the lights bring in!
And see what more my phantasy can win.
It is a gorgeous room, but somewhat sad;
The draperies are so, as tho' they had
Been made for Cleopatra's winding-sheet;                50
And opposite the stedfast eye doth meet
A spacious looking-glass, upon whose face,
In letters raven-sombre, you may trace
Old 'Mene, Mene, Tekel, Upharsin.'
Greek busts and statuary have ever been
Held, by the finest spirits, fitter far
Than vase grotesque and Siamesian jar;
Therefore 'tis sure a want of Attic taste
That I should rather love a Gothic waste
Of eyesight on cinque-coloured potter's clay,          60
Than on the marble fairness of old Greece.
My table-coverlits of Jason's fleece
And black Numidian sheep-wool should be wrought,
Gold, black, and heavy, from the Lama brought.
My ebon sofas should delicious be
With down from Leda's cygnet progeny.
My pictures all Salvator's, save a few
Of Titian's portraiture, and one, though new,
Of Haydon's in its fresh magnificence.
My wine—O good! 'tis here at my desire,                70
And I must sit to supper with my friar.

\*    \*    \*    \*    \*    \*

# FRAGMENT

'Under the flag
Of each his faction, they to battle bring
Their embryon atoms.' MILTON

WELCOME joy, and welcome sorrow,
  Lethe's weed and Hermes' feather;
Come to-day, and come to-morrow,
  I do love you both together!
  I love to mark sad faces in fair weather;
And hear a merry laugh amid the thunder;
  Fair and foul I love together.
Meadows sweet where flames are under,
And a giggle at a wonder;
Visage sage at pantomime;                                    10
Funeral, and steeple-chime;
Infant playing with a skull;
Morning fair, and shipwreck'd hull;
Nightshade with the woodbine kissing:
Serpents in red roses hissing;
Cleopatra regal-dress'd
With the aspic at her breast;
Dancing music, music sad,
Both together, sane and mad;
Muses bright and muses pale;                                 20
Sombre Saturn, Momus hale;—
Laugh and sigh, and laugh again;
Oh the sweetness of the pain!
Muses bright, and muses pale,
Bare your faces of the veil;
Let me see; and let me write
Of the day, and of the night—
Both together:—let me slake
All my thirst for sweet heart-ache!
Let my bower be of yew,                                      30
Interwreath'd with myrtles new;
Pines and lime-trees full in bloom,
And my couch a low grass tomb.

## CANCELLED STANZA OF THE ODE
## ON MELANCHOLY

THOUGH you should build a bark of dead men's bones,
    And rear a phantom gibbet for a mast,
Stitch shrouds together for a sail, with groans
    To fill it out, blood-stained and aghast;
Although your rudder be a dragon's tail
    Long sever'd, yet still hard with agony,
      Your cordage large uprootings from the skull
Of bald Medusa, certes you would fail
      To find the Melancholy—whether she
      Dreameth in any isle of Lethe dull.


## TO —

WHAT can I do to drive away
Remembrance from my eyes? for they have seen,
Aye, an hour ago, my brilliant Queen!
Touch has a memory. O say, love, say,
What can I do to kill it and be free
In my old liberty?
When every fair one that I saw was fair,
Enough to catch me in but half a snare,
Not keep me there:
When, howe'er poor or particolour'd things,      10
My muse had wings,
And ever ready was to take her course
Whither I bent her force,
Unintellectual, yet divine to me;—
Divine, I say!—What sea-bird o'er the sea
Is a philosopher the while he goes
Winging along where the great water throes?

How shall I do
To get anew
Those moulted feathers, and so mount once more      20
    Above, above
    The reach of fluttering Love,
And make him cower lowly while I soar?

Shall I gulp wine? No, that is vulgarism,
A heresy and schism,
   Foisted into the canon law of love;—
No,—wine is only sweet to happy men;
   More dismal cares
   Seize on me unawares,—
Where shall I learn to get my peace again?     30
To banish thoughts of that most hateful land,
Dungeoner of my friends, that wicked strand
Where they were wreck'd and live a wrecked life;
That monstrous region, whose dull rivers pour,
Ever from their sordid urns unto the shore,
Unown'd of any weedy-haired gods;
Whose winds, all zephyrless, hold scourging rods,
Iced in the great lakes, to afflict mankind;
Whose rank-grown forests, frosted, black, and blind,
Would fright a Dryad; whose harsh herbag'd meads 40
Make lean and lank the starv'd ox while he feeds;
There flowers have no scent, birds no sweet song,
And great unerring Nature once seems wrong.

O, for some sunny spell
To dissipate the shadows of this hell!
Say they are gone,—with the new dawning light
Steps forth my lady bright!
O, let me once more rest
My soul upon that dazzling breast!
Let once again these aching arms be plac'd,    50
The tender gaolers of thy waist!
And let me feel that warm breath here and there
To spread a rapture in my very hair,—
O, the sweetness of the pain!
Give me those lips again!
Enough! Enough! it is enough for me
To dream of thee!

# THE FALL OF HYPERION

## A DREAM

### AN ATTEMPT MADE AT THE END OF 1819 TO RECONSTRUCT THE POEM

# THE FALL OF HYPERION

## A DREAM

### [CANTO I]

FANATICS have their dreams, wherewith they weave
A paradise for a sect; the savage too
From forth the loftiest fashion of his sleep
Guesses at Heaven; pity these have not
Trac'd upon vellum or wild Indian leaf
The shadows of melodious utterance.
But bare of laurel they live, dream, and die;
For Poesy alone can tell her dreams,
With the fine spell of words alone can save
Imagination from the sable charm          10
And dumb enchantment. Who alive can say,
'Thou art no Poet—may'st not tell thy dreams?'
Since every man whose soul is not a clod
Hath visions, and would speak, if he had loved,
And been well nurtured in his mother tongue.
Whether the dream now purpos'd to rehearse
Be poet's or fanatic's will be known
When this warm scribe my hand is in the grave.

    Methought I stood where trees of every clime,
Palm, myrtle, oak, and sycamore, and beech,          20
With plantain, and spice-blossoms, made a screen;
In neighbourhood of fountains (by the noise
Soft-showering in my ears), and, (by the touch
Of scent,) not far from roses. Turning round
I saw an arbour with a drooping roof
Of trellis vines, and bells, and larger blooms,
Like floral censers, swinging light in air;
Before its wreathed doorway, on a mound
Of moss, was spread a feast of summer fruits,
Which, nearer seen, seem'd refuse of a meal          30
By angel tasted or our Mother Eve;
For empty shells were scattered on the grass,
And grape-stalks but half bare, and remnants more,

Sweet-smelling, whose pure kinds I could not know.
Still was more plenty than the fabled horn
Thrice emptied could pour forth, at banqueting
For Proserpine return'd to her own fields,
Where the white heifers low. And appetite
More yearning than on Earth I ever felt
Growing within, I ate deliciously;                              40
And, after not long, thirsted, for thereby
Stood a cool vessel of transparent juice
Sipp'd by the wander'd bee, the which I took,
And, pledging all the mortals of the world,
And all the dead whose names are in our lips,
Drank. That full draught is parent of my theme.
No Asian poppy nor elixir fine
Of the soon-fading jealous Caliphat;
No poison gender'd in close monkish cell,
To thin the scarlet conclave of old men,                        50
Could so have rapt unwilling life away.
Among the fragrant husks and berries crush'd,
Upon the grass I struggled hard against
The domineering potion; but in vain:
The cloudy swoon came on, and down I sank,
Like a Silenus on an antique vase.
How long I slumber'd 'tis a chance to guess.
When sense of life return'd, I started up
As if with wings; but the fair trees were gone,
The mossy mound and arbour were no more:                        60
I look'd around upon the carved sides
Of an old sanctuary with roof august,
Builded so high, it seem'd that filmed clouds
Might spread beneath, as o'er the stars of heaven;
So old the place was, I remember'd none
The like upon the Earth: what I had seen
Of grey cathedrals, buttress'd walls, rent towers,
The superannuations of sunk realms,
Or Nature's rocks toil'd hard in waves and winds,
Seem'd but the faulture of decrepit things                      70
To that eternal domed Monument.—
Upon the marble at my feet there lay
Store of strange vessels and large draperies,
Which needs had been of dyed asbestos wove,

Or in that place the moth could not corrupt,
So white the linen, so, in some, distinct
Ran imageries from a sombre loom.
All in a mingled heap confus'd there lay
Robes, golden tongs, censer and chafing-dish,
Girdles, and chains, and holy jewelries.              80

Turning from these with awe, once more I rais'd
My eyes to fathom the space every way;
The embossed roof, the silent massy range
Of columns north and south, ending in mist
Of nothing, then to eastward, where black gates
Were shut against the sunrise evermore.—
Then to the west I look'd, and saw far off
An image, huge of feature as a cloud,
At level of whose feet an altar slept,
To be approach'd on either side by steps,            90
And marble balustrade, and patient travail
To count with toil the innumerable degrees.
Towards the altar sober-paced I went,
Repressing haste, as too unholy there;
And, coming nearer, saw beside the shrine
One minist'ring; and there arose a flame.—
When in mid-May the sickening East wind
Shifts sudden to the south, the small warm rain
Melts out the frozen incense from all flowers,
And fills the air with so much pleasant health       100
That even the dying man forgets his shroud;—
Even so that lofty sacrificial fire,
Sending forth Maian incense, spread around
Forgetfulness of everything but bliss,
And clouded all the altar with soft smoke;
From whose white fragrant curtains thus I heard
Language pronounc'd: 'If thou canst not ascend
'These steps, die on that marble where thou art.
'Thy flesh, near cousin to the common dust,
'Will parch for lack of nutriment—thy bones          110
'Will wither in few years, and vanish so
'That not the quickest eye could find a grain
'Of what thou now art on that pavement cold.
'The sands of thy short life are spent this hour,

'And no hand in the universe can turn
'Thy hourglass, if these gummed leaves be burnt
'Ere thou canst mount up these immortal steps.'
I heard, I look'd: two senses both at once,
So fine, so subtle, felt the tyranny
Of that fierce threat and the hard task proposed.     120
Prodigious seem'd the toil; the leaves were yet
Burning—when suddenly a palsied chill
Struck from the paved level up my limbs,
And was ascending quick to put cold grasp
Upon those streams that pulse beside the throat:
I shriek'd, and the sharp anguish of my shriek
Stung my own ears—I strove hard to escape
The numbness; strove to gain the lowest step.
Slow, heavy, deadly was my pace: the cold
Grew stifling, suffocating, at the heart;     130
And when I clasp'd my hands I felt them not.
One minute before death, my iced foot touch'd
The lowest stair; and as it touch'd, life seem'd
To pour in at the toes: I mounted up,
As once fair angels on a ladder flew
From the green turf to Heaven—'Holy Power,'
Cried I, approaching near the horned shrine,
'What am I that should so be saved from death?
'What am I that another death come not
'To choke my utterance sacrilegious, here?'     140
Then said the veiled shadow—'Thou hast felt
'What 'tis to die and live again before
'Thy fated hour, that thou hadst power to do so
'Is thy own safety; thou hast dated on
Thy doom.'—'High Prophetess,' said I, 'purge off,
Benign, if so it please thee, my mind's film.'—
'None can usurp this height,' return'd that shade,
'But those to whom the miseries of the world
'Are misery, and will not let them rest.
'All else who find a haven in the world,     150
'Where they may thoughtless sleep away their days,
'If by a chance into this fane they come,
'Rot on the pavement where thou rottedst half.'—
'Are there not thousands in the world,' said I,
Encourag'd by the sooth voice of the shade,

'Who love their fellows even to the death,
'Who feel the giant agony of the world,
'And more, like slaves to poor humanity,
'Labour for mortal good? I sure should see
'Other men here; but I am here alone.'                    160
'Those whom thou spak'st of are no vision'ries,'
Rejoin'd that voice—'They are no dreamers weak,
'They seek no wonder but the human face;
'No music but a happy-noted voice—
'They come not here, they have no thought to come—
'And thou art here, for thou art less than they—
'What benefit canst thou, or all thy tribe,
'To the great world? Thou art a dreaming thing,
'A fever of thyself—think of the Earth;
'What bliss even in hope is there for thee?            170
'What haven? every creature hath its home;
'Every sole man hath days of joy and pain,
'Whether his labours be sublime or low—
'The pain alone; the joy alone; distinct:
'Only the dreamer venoms all his days,
'Bearing more woe than all his sins deserve.
'Therefore, that happiness be somewhat shar'd,
'Such things as thou art are admitted oft
'Into like gardens thou didst pass erewhile,
'And suffer'd in these temples: for that cause         180
'Thou standest safe beneath this statue's knees.'
'That I am favour'd for unworthiness,
'By such propitious parley medicin'd
'In sickness not ignoble, I rejoice,
'Aye, and could weep for love of such award.'
So answer'd I, continuing, 'If it please,
'Majestic shadow, tell me: sure not all
'Those melodies sung into the World's ear
'Are useless: sure a poet is a sage;
'A humanist, physician to all men.                     190
'That I am none I feel, as vultures feel
'They are no birds when eagles are abroad.
'What am I then: Thou spakest of my tribe:
'What tribe?' The tall shade veil'd in drooping white
Then spake, so much more earnest, that the breath
Moved the thin linen folds that drooping hung

About a golden censer from the hand
Pendent—'Art thou not of the dreamer tribe?
'The poet and the dreamer are distinct,
'Diverse, sheer opposite, antipodes.                              200
'The one pours out a balm upon the World,
'The other vexes it.' Then shouted I
Spite of myself, and with a Pythia's spleen,
'Apollo! faded! O far flown Apollo!
'Where is thy misty pestilence to creep
'Into the dwellings, through the door crannies
'Of all mock lyrists, large self worshipers
'And careless Hectorers in proud bad verse.
'Though I breathe death with them it will be life
'To see them sprawl before me into graves.                        210
'Majestic shadow, tell me where I am,
'Whose altar this; for whom this incense curls;
'What image this whose face I cannot see,
'For the broad marble knees; and who thou art,
'Of accent feminine so courteous?'

       Then the tall shade, in drooping linens veil'd,
Spoke out, so much more earnest, that her breath
Stirr'd the thin folds of gauze that drooping hung
About a golden censer from her hand
Pendent; and by her voice I knew she shed                         220
Long-treasured tears. 'This temple, sad and lone,
'Is all spar'd from the thunder of a war
'Foughten long since by giant hierarchy
'Against rebellion: this old image here,
'Whose carved features wrinkled as he fell,
'Is Saturn's; I Moneta, left supreme
'Sole Priestess of this desolation,'—
I had no words to answer, for my tongue,
Useless, could find about its roofed home
No syllable of a fit majesty                                      230
To make rejoinder to Moneta's mourn.
There was a silence, while the altar's blaze
Was fainting for sweet food: I look'd thereon,
And on the paved floor, where nigh were piled
Faggots of cinnamon, and many heaps
Of other crisped spice-wood—then again

I look'd upon the altar, and its horns
Whiten'd with ashes, and its lang'rous flame,
And then upon the offerings again;
And so by turns—till sad Moneta cried,          240
'The sacrifice is done, but not the less
'Will I be kind to thee for thy good will.
'My power, which to me is still a curse,
'Shall be to thee a wonder; for the scenes
'Still swooning vivid through my globed brain,
'With an electral changing misery,
'Thou shalt with those dull mortal eyes behold,
'Free from all pain, if wonder pain thee not.'
As near as an immortal's sphered words
Could to a mother's soften, were these last:       250
And yet I had a terror of her robes,
And chiefly of the veils, that from her brow
Hung pale, and curtain'd her in mysteries,
That made my heart too small to hold its blood.
This saw that Goddess, and with sacred hand
Parted the veils. Then saw I a wan face,
Not pin'd by human sorrows, but bright-blanch'd
By an immortal sickness which kills not;
It works a constant change, which happy death
Can put no end to; deathwards progressing        260
To no death was that visage; it had past
The lilly and the snow; and beyond these
I must not think now, though I saw that face—
But for her eyes I should have fled away.
They held me back, with a benignant light,
Soft mitigated by divinest lids
Half-closed, and visionless entire they seem'd
Of all external things;—they saw me not,
But in blank splendor, beam'd like the mild moon,
Who comforts those she sees not, who knows not    270
What eyes are upward cast. As I had found
A grain of gold upon a mountain side,
And twing'd with avarice strain'd out my eyes
To search its sullen entrails rich with ore,
So at the view of sad Moneta's brow,
I ach'd to see what things the hollow brain
Behind enwombed: what high tragedy

In the dark secret chambers of her skull
Was acting, that could give so dread a stress
To her cold lips, and fill with such a light          280
Her planetary eyes; and touch her voice
With such a sorrow—'Shade of Memory!'—
Cried I, with act adorant at her feet,
'By all the gloom hung round thy fallen house,
'By this last temple, by the golden age,
'By great Apollo, thy dear Foster Child,
'And by thyself, forlorn divinity,
'The pale Omega of a withered race,
'Let me behold, according as thou saidst,
'What in thy brain so ferments to and fro!'          290
No sooner had this conjuration pass'd
My devout lips, than side by side we stood
(Like a stunt bramble by a solemn pine)
Deep in the shady sadness of a vale,
Far sunken from the healthy breath of morn,
Far from the fiery noon and eve's one star.
Onward I look'd beneath the gloomy boughs,
And saw, what first I thought an image huge,
Like to the image pedestal'd so high
In Saturn's temple. Then Moneta's voice          300
Came brief upon mine ear—'So Saturn sat
When he had lost his Realms—' whereon there grew
A power within me of enormous ken
To see as a god sees, and take the depth
Of things as nimbly as the outward eye
Can size and shape pervade. The lofty theme
At those few words hung vast before my mind,
With half-unravel'd web. I set myself
Upon an eagle's watch, that I might see,
And seeing ne'er forget. No stir of life          310
Was in this shrouded vale, not so much air
As in the zoning of a summer's day
Robs not one light seed from the feather'd grass,
But where the dead leaf fell there did it rest:
A stream went voiceless by, still deaden'd more
By reason of the fallen divinity
Spreading more shade; the Naiad 'mid her reeds
Prest her cold finger closer to her lips.

Along the margin-sand large footmarks went
No farther than to where old Saturn's feet                320
Had rested, and there slept, how long a sleep!
Degraded, cold, upon the sodden ground
His old right hand lay nerveless, listless, dead,
Unsceptred; and his realmless eyes were clos'd,
While his bow'd head seem'd listening to the Earth,
His ancient mother, for some comfort yet.

It seem'd no force could wake him from his place;
But there came one who, with a kindred hand
Touch'd his wide shoulders after bending low
With reverence, though to one who knew it not.       330
Then came the griev'd voice of Mnemosyne,
And griev'd I hearken'd. 'That divinity
'Whom thou saw'st step from yon forlornest wood,
'And with slow pace approach our fallen King,
'Is Thea, softest-natur'd of our Brood.'
I mark'd the Goddess in fair statuary
Surpassing wan Moneta by the head,
And in her sorrow nearer woman's tears.
There was a listening fear in her regard,
As if calamity had but begun;                        340
As if the vanward clouds of evil days
Had spent their malice, and the sullen rear
Was with its stored thunder labouring up.
One hand she press'd upon that aching spot
Where beats the human heart, as if just there,
Though an immortal, she felt cruel pain;
The other upon Saturn's bended neck
She laid, and to the level of his hollow ear
Leaning with parted lips, some words she spake
In solemn tenor and deep organ tune;                 350
Some mourning words, which in our feeble tongue
Would come in this-like accenting; how frail
To that large utterance of the early Gods!

'Saturn! look up—and for what, poor lost King?
'I have no comfort for thee; no not one;
'I cannot cry, wherefore thus sleepest thou?
'For Heaven is parted from thee, and the Earth

'Knows thee not, so afflicted, for a God;
'And Ocean too, with all its solemn noise,
'Has from thy sceptre pass'd, and all the air          360
'Is emptied of thine hoary majesty:
'Thy thunder, captious at the new command,
'Rumbles reluctant o'er our fallen house;
'And thy sharp lightning, in unpracticed hands,
'Scorches and burns our once serene domain.
'With such remorseless speed still come new woes,
'That unbelief has not a space to breathe.
'Saturn! sleep on:—Me thoughtless, why should I
'Thus violate thy slumbrous solitude?
'Why should I ope thy melancholy eyes?                 370
'Saturn, sleep on, while at thy feet I weep.'

      As when upon a tranced summer-night
Forests, branch-charmed by the earnest stars,
Dream, and so dream all night without a noise,
Save from one gradual solitary gust,
Swelling upon the silence; dying off;
As if the ebbing air had but one wave;
So came these words, and went; the while in tears
She prest her fair large forehead to the earth,
Just where her fallen hair might spread in curls,     380
A soft and silken mat for Saturn's feet.
Long, long those two were postured motionless,
Like sculpture builded-up upon the grave
Of their own power. A long awful time
I look'd upon them: still they were the same;
The frozen God still bending to the earth,
And the sad Goddess weeping at his feet,
Moneta silent. Without stay or prop,
But my own weak mortality, I bore
The load of this eternal quietude,                     390
The unchanging gloom, and the three fixed shapes
Ponderous upon my senses, a whole moon.
For by my burning brain I measured sure
Her silver seasons shedded on the night,
And ever day by day methought I grew
More gaunt and ghostly.—Oftentimes I pray'd
Intense, that Death would take me from the Vale

And all its burthens—gasping with despair
Of change, hour after hour I curs'd myself;
Until old Saturn rais'd his faded eyes,                    400
And look'd around and saw his kingdom gone,
And all the gloom and sorrow of the place,
And that fair kneeling Goddess at his feet.
As the moist scent of flowers, and grass, and leaves,
Fills forest dells with a pervading air,
Known to the woodland nostril, so the words
Of Saturn fill'd the mossy glooms around,
Even to the hollows of time-eaten oaks,
And to the windings of the foxes' hole,
With sad low tones, while thus he spake, and sent    410
Strange musings to the solitary Pan.
'Moan, brethren, moan; for we are swallow'd up
'And buried from all Godlike exercise
'Of influence benign on planets pale,
'And peaceful sway above man's harvesting,
'And all those acts which Deity supreme
'Doth ease its heart of love in. Moan and wail,
'Moan, brethren, moan; for lo, the rebel spheres
'Spin round, the stars their ancient courses keep,
'Clouds still with shadowy moisture haunt the earth,    420
'Still suck their fill of light from sun and moon;
'Still buds the tree, and still the sea-shores murmur;
'There is no death in all the Universe,
'No smell of death—there shall be death—Moan, moan,
'Moan, Cybele, moan; for thy pernicious Babes
'Have changed a god into a shaking Palsy.
'Moan, brethren, moan, for I have no strength left,
'Weak as the reed—weak—feeble as my voice—
'O, O, the pain, the pain of feebleness.
'Moan, moan, for still I thaw—or give me help;    430
'Throw down those imps, and give me victory.
'Let me hear other groans, and trumpets blown
'Of triumph calm, and hymns of festival,
'From the gold peaks of Heaven's high-piled clouds;
'Voices of soft proclaim, and silver stir
'Of strings in hollow shells; and let there be
'Beautiful things made new for the surprise
'Of the sky-children.' So he feebly ceas'd,

With such a poor and sickly sounding pause,
Methought I heard some old man of the earth       440
Bewailing earthly loss; nor could my eyes
And ears act with that pleasant unison of sense
Which marries sweet sound with the grace of form,
And dolorous accent from a tragic harp
With large-limb'd visions.—More I scrutinized:
Still fix'd he sat beneath the sable trees,
Whose arms spread straggling in wild serpent forms,
With leaves all hush'd; his awful presence there
(Now all was silent) gave a deadly lie
To what I erewhile heard—only his lips       450
Trembled amid the white curls of his beard.
They told the truth, though, round, the snowy locks
Hung nobly, as upon the face of heaven
A mid-day fleece of clouds. Thea arose,
And stretched her white arm through the hollow dark,
Pointing some whither: whereat he too rose
Like a vast giant, seen by men at sea
To grow pale from the waves at dull midnight.
They melted from my sight into the woods;
Ere I could turn, Moneta cried, 'These twain       460
'Are speeding to the families of grief,
'Where roof'd in by black rocks they waste, in pain
'And darkness, for no hope.'—And she spake on,
As ye may read who can unwearied pass
Onward from the Antichamber of this dream,
Where even at the open doors awhile
I must delay, and glean my memory
Of her high phrase:—perhaps no further dare.

END OF CANTO I

## CANTO II

'MORTAL, that thou may'st understand aright,
'I humanize my sayings to thine ear,
'Making comparisons of earthly things;
'Or thou might'st better listen to the wind,
'Whose language is to thee a barren noise,
'Though it blows legend-laden thro' the trees.—

'In melancholy realms big tears are shed,
'More sorrow like to this, and such like woe,
'Too huge for mortal tongue, or pen of scribe.
'The Titans fierce, self hid or prison bound,                10
'Groan for the old allegiance once more,
'Listening in their doom for Saturn's voice.
'But one of our whole eagle-brood still keeps
'His sov'reignty, and rule, and majesty;
'Blazing Hyperion on his orbed fire
'Still sits, still snuffs the incense teeming up
'From Man to the Sun's God: yet unsecure.
'For as upon the earth dire prodigies
'Fright and perplex, so also shudders he:
'Nor at dog's howl or gloom-bird's Even screech,            20
'Or the familiar visitings of one
'Upon the first toll of his passing bell:
'But horrors, portioned to a giant nerve,
'Make great Hyperion ache. His palace bright,
'Bastion'd with pyramids of glowing gold,
'And touch'd with shade of bronzed obelisks,
'Glares a blood-red thro' all the thousand courts,
'Arches, and domes, and fiery galleries:
'And all its curtains of Aurorian clouds
'Flush angerly; when he would taste the wreaths            30
'Of incense breathed aloft from sacred hills,
'Instead of sweets, his ample palate takes
'Savour of poisonous brass and metals sick.
'Wherefore when harbour'd in the sleepy West,
'After the full completion of fair day,
'For rest divine upon exalted couch
'And slumber in the arms of melody,
'He paces through the pleasant hours of ease
'With strides colossal, on from hall to hall;
'While far within each aisle and deep recess               40
'His winged minions in close clusters stand
'Amaz'd, and full of fear; like anxious men,
'Who on a wide plain gather in sad troops,
'When earthquakes jar their battlements and towers.
'Even now, while Saturn, roused from icy trance,
'Goes, step for step, with Thea from yon woods,
'Hyperion, leaving twilight in the rear,

'Is sloping to the threshold of the West.—
'Thither we tend.'—Now in clear light I stood,
Reliev'd from the dusk vale. Mnemosyne                    50
Was sitting on a square-edg'd polish'd stone,
That in its lucid depth reflected pure
Her priestess-garments.—My quick eyes ran on
From stately nave to nave, from vault to vault,
Through bow'rs of fragrant and enwreathed light
And diamond-paved lustrous long arcades.
Anon rush'd by the bright Hyperion;
His flaming robes stream'd out beyond his heels,
And gave a roar, as if of earthly fire,
That scared away the meek ethereal hours,                60
And made their dove-wings tremble. On he flared.

# POSTHUMOUS AND FUGITIVE
# PIECES

NOT INCLUDED IN
*LIFE, LETTERS, AND LITERARY
REMAINS,* 1848

# SONNETS

## ON PEACE

O PEACE! and dost thou with thy presence bless
 The dwellings of this war-surrounded Isle;
Soothing with placid brow our late distress,
 Making the triple kingdom brightly smile?
Joyful I hail thy presence; and I hail
 The sweet companions that await on thee;
Complete my joy—let not my first wish fail,
 Let the sweet mountain nymph thy favourite be,
With England's happiness proclaim Europa's Liberty.
O Europe! let not sceptred tyrants see    10
 That thou must shelter in thy former state;
Keep thy chains burst, and boldly say thou art free;
 Give thy kings law—leave not uncurbed the great;
 So with the horrors past thou'lt win thy happier fate!

## THE POET

AT morn, at noon, at Eve, and Middle Night
 He passes forth into the charmed air,
 With talisman to call up spirits rare
From plant, cave, rock, and fountain.—To his sight
The husk of natural objects opens quite
 To the core; and every secret essence there
 Reveals the elements of good and fair;
Making him see, where Learning hath no light.
Sometimes above the gross and palpable things
 Of this diurnal sphere, his spirit flies    10
 On awful wing; and with its destined skies
Holds premature and mystic communings;
 Till such unearthly intercourses shed
 A visible halo round his mortal head.

## ON RECEIVING A LAUREL CROWN
## FROM LEIGH HUNT

MINUTES are flying swiftly, and as yet
  Nothing unearthly has enticed my brain
  Into a delphic Labyrinth—I would fain
Catch an unmortal thought to pay the debt
I owe to the kind Poet who has set
  Upon my ambitious head a glorious gain.
  Two bending laurel Sprigs—'tis nearly pain
To be conscious of such a Coronet.
Still time is fleeting, and no dream arises
  Gorgeous as I would have it—only I see    10
A Trampling down of what the world most prizes
  Turbans and Crowns, and blank regality:
And then I run into most wild surmises
  Of all the many glories that may be.


## TO THE LADIES WHO SAW ME
## CROWN'D

WHAT is there in the universal Earth
  More lovely than a Wreath from the bay tree?
  Haply a Halo round the Moon—a glee
Circling from three sweet pair of Lips in Mirth;
And haply you will say the dewy birth
  Of morning Roses—riplings tenderly
  Spread by the Halcyon's breast upon the Sea—
But these Comparisons are nothing worth—
Then is there nothing in the world so fair?
  The silvery tears of April?—Youth of May?    10
Or June that breaths out life for butterflies?
  No—none of these can from my favourite bear
Away the Palm—yet shall it ever pay
  Due Reverence to your most sovereign eyes.

As from the darkening gloom a silver dove
   Upsoars, and darts into the Eastern light,
   On pinions that naught moves but pure delight,
So fled thy soul into the realms above,
Regions of peace and everlasting love;
   Where happy spirits, crown'd with circlets bright
   Of starry beam, and gloriously bedight,
Taste the high joy none but the blest can prove.
There thou or joinest the immortal quire
   In melodies that even Heaven fair            10
Fill with superior bliss, or, at desire
   Of the omnipotent Father, cleavest the air
On holy message sent—What pleasures higher?
   Wherefore does any grief our joy impair?


## WRITTEN IN DISGUST OF VULGAR
## SUPERSTITION

THE church bells toll a melancholy round,
   Calling the people to some other prayers,
   Some other gloominess, more dreadful cares,
More hearkening to the sermon's horrid sound.
Surely the mind of man is closely bound
   In some black spell; seeing that each one tears
   Himself from fireside joys, and Lydian airs,
And converse high of those with glory crown'd.
Still, still they toll, and I should feel a damp,—
   A chill as from a tomb, did I not know           10
That they are dying like an outburnt lamp;
   That 'tis their sighing, wailing ere they go
   Into oblivion;—that fresh flowers will grow,
And many glories of immortal stamp.

## NEBUCHADNEZZAR'S DREAM

BEFORE he went to feed with owls and bats
 Nebuchadnezzar had an ugly dream,
 Worse than an Hus'if's when she thinks her cream
Made a Naumachia for mice and rats.
So scared, he sent for that 'Good King of Cats'
 Young Daniel, who soon did pluck the beam
 From out his eye, and said 'I do not deem
Your sceptre worth a straw—your Cushions old door-mats'.
A horrid nightmare similar somewhat
 Of late has haunted a most valiant crew                    10
  Of loggerheads and Chapmen—we are told
That any Daniel though he be a sot
 Can make their lying lips turn pale of hue
  By drawling out 'ye are that head of Gold.'

## ON MRS. REYNOLDS'S CAT

CAT! who hast pass'd thy grand climacteric,
 How many mice and rats hast in thy days
 Destroy'd?—How many tit bits stolen? Gaze
With those bright languid segments green, and prick
Those velvet ears—but pr'ythee do not stick
 Thy latent talons in me—and upraise
 Thy gentle mew—and tell me all thy frays
Of fish and mice, and rats and tender chick.
Nay, look not down, nor lick thy dainty wrists—
 For all the wheezy asthma,—and for all          10
Thy tail's tip is nick'd off—and though the fists
 Of many a maid have given thee many a maul,
Still is that fur as soft as when the lists
 In youth thou enter'dst on glass-bottled wall.

## ON A LEANDER WHICH MISS REYNOLDS
## MY KIND FRIEND GAVE ME

COME hither all sweet maidens soberly,
  Down-looking—, and with a chasten'd light,
  Hid in the fringes of your eyelids white,
And meekly let your fair hands joined be,
As if so gentle that ye could not see,
  Untouch'd, a victim of your beauty bright,
  Sinking away to his young spirit's night,—
Sinking bewilder'd 'mid the dreary sea:
'Tis young Leander toiling to his death;
  Nigh swooning, he doth purse his weary lips      10
    For Hero's cheek, and smiles against her smile.
  O horrid dream! see how his body dips
    Dead-heavy; arms and shoulders gleam awhile:
He's gone: up bubbles all his amorous breath!

FOUR seasons fill the measure of the year;
  There are four seasons in the mind of man:
He has his lusty Spring, when fancy clear
  Takes in all beauty with an easy span:
He has his Summer, when luxuriously
  Spring's honey'd cud of youthful thought he loves
To ruminate, and by such dreaming high
  Is nearest unto heaven: quiet coves
His soul has in its Autumn, when his wings
  He furleth close; contented so to look      10
On mists in idleness—to let fair things
  Pass by unheeded as a threshold brook.
He has his Winter too of pale misfeature,
Or else he would forego his mortal nature.

OF late two dainties were before me plac'd
　Sweet, holy, pure, sacred and innocent,
　From the ninth sphere to me benignly sent
That Gods might know my own particular taste.
First the soft Bag-pipe mourn'd with zealous haste,
　The Stranger next with head on bosom bent
　Sigh'd; rueful again the piteous Bag-pipe went,
Again the Stranger sighings fresh did waste.
O Bag-pipe thou didst steal my heart away—
　O Stranger thou my nerves from Pipe didst charm—   10
O Bag-pipe thou didst re-assert thy sway—
　Again thou Stranger gav'st me fresh alarm—
Alas! I could not choose. Ah! my poor heart,
Mum chance art thou with both oblig'd to part.


THE House of Mourning written by Mr. Scott,—
　A sermon at the Magdalen—a tear
　Dropt on a greasy novel,—want of cheer
After a walk up hill to a friend's cot,—
Tea with a Maiden Lady—a curs'd lot
　Of worthy poems with the Author near,—
　A patron lord—a drunkenness from beer,—
Haydon's great picture,—a cold coffee pot
At midnight when the Muse is ripe for labour,—
　The voice of Mr. Coleridge,—a french Bonnet   10
Before you in the pit,—a pipe and tabour,—
A damn'd inseparable flute and neighbour,—
　All these are vile,—but viler Wordsworth's Sonnet
On Dover:—Dover!—who *could* write upon it?

## TO A. G. S.

ON READING HIS ADMIRABLE VERSES WRITTEN IN
THIS [MISS REYNOLDS'S] ALBUM, ON EITHER SIDE OF
THE FOLLOWING ATTEMPT TO PAY SMALL TRIBUTE
THERETO

WHERE didst thou find, young Bard, thy sounding lyre?
  Where the bland accent, and the tender tone?
A-sitting snugly by thy Parlour fire?
  Or didst thou with Apollo pick a bone?
The Muse will have a crow to pick with me
  For thus assaying in thy brightening path:
Who, that with his own brace of eyes can see,
  Unthunderstruck beholds thy gentle wrath?
Who from a pot of stout e'er blew the froth
Into the bosom of the wandering wind,                    10
  Light as the Powder on the back of Moth,
But drank thy muses with a grateful mind?
  Yea, unto thee Beldams drink metheglin
  And annisies, and carraway, and gin.

# POEMS OTHER THAN SONNETS

See, the ship in the Bay is riding,
Dearest Ellen, I go from thee;
Boldly go, in thy love confiding,
Over the deep and trackless sea:—
When thy dear form no longer is near me,
This soothing thought shall at midnight chear me;
'My love is breathing a prayer for me'.—

When the thunder of war is roaring,
When the bullets around me fly,
When the rage of the tempest pouring            10
Bends the billowy sea and sky,
Yet shall my heart, to fear a stranger,
Cherish its fondest hopes for thee:—
This dear reflection disarming danger,
'My love is breathing a prayer for me'.


## ON DEATH

### I

Can death be sleep, when life is but a dream,
    And scenes of bliss pass as a phantom by?
The transient pleasures as a vision seem,
    And yet we think the greatest pain's to die.


### II

How strange it is that man on earth should roam,
    And lead a life of woe, but not forsake
His rugged path; nor dare he view alone
    His future doom which is but to awake.

## WRITTEN ON 29 MAY

### THE ANNIVERSARY OF THE RESTORATION OF CHARLES THE 2ND

INFATUATE Britons, will you still proclaim
His memory, your direst, foulest shame?
    Nor patriots revere?

Ah! while I hear each traitorous lying bell,
'Tis gallant Sydney's, Russel's, Vane's sad knell,
    That pains my wounded ear.


FILL for me a brimming bowl
And let me in it drown my soul:
But put therein some drug, designed
To Banish Women from my mind:
For I want not the stream inspiring
That fills the mind with—fond desiring,
But I want as deep a draught
As e'er from Lethe's wave was quaff'd;
From my despairing heart to charm
The Image of the fairest form          10
That e'er my reveling eyes beheld,
That e'er my wandering fancy spell'd.
In vain! away I cannot chace
The melting softness of that face,
The beaminess of those bright eyes,
That breast—earth's only Paradise.
My sight will never more be blest;
For all I see has lost its zest:
Nor with delight can I explore
The Classic page, or Muse's lore.        20
Had she but known how beat my heart,
And with one smile reliev'd its smart,
I should have felt a sweet relief,
I should have felt 'the joy of grief'.
Yet as the Tuscan mid the snow
Of Lapland thinks on sweet Arno,
Even so for ever shall she be
The Halo of my Memory.

HITHER, hither, love—
    'Tis a shady mead—
Hither, hither, love,
    Let me feed and feed.

Hither, hither, sweet—
    'Tis a cowslip bed—
Hither, hither, sweet!
    'Tis with dew bespread!

Hither, hither, dear,
    By the breath of life,                           10
Hither, hither, dear!
    Be the summer's wife!

Though one moment's pleasure
    In one moment flies,
Though the passion's treasure
    In one moment dies;

Yet it has not passed—
    Think how near, how near!—
And while it doth last,
    Think how dear, how dear!                        20

Hither, hither, hither,
    Love this boon hath sent—
If I die and wither
    I shall die content.


## TO EMMA

O COME, dearest Emma, the rose is full blown,
The riches of Flora are lavishly strown,
The air is all softness, and crystal the streams,
The West is resplendently clothed in beams.

O come! let us haste to the freshening shades,
The quaintly carv'd seats, and the opening glades;
Where the faeries are chanting their evening hymns,
And in the last sun-beam the sylph lightly swims.

And when thou art weary I'll find thee a bed,
Of mosses and flowers to pillow thy head:                                    10
There, beauteous Emma, I'll sit at thy feet,
While my story of love I enraptur'd repeat.

So fondly I'll breathe, and so softly I'll sigh,
Thou wilt think that some amorous Zephyr is nigh:
Yet no—as I breathe I will press thy fair knee,
And then thou wilt know that the sigh comes from me.

Then why dearest girl should we lose all these blisses?
That mortal's a fool who such happiness misses:
So smile acquiescence, and give me thy hand,
With love-looking eyes, and with voice sweetly bland.  20

## SONG

TUNE —'*Julia to the Wood-Robin*'

STAY, ruby-breasted warbler, stay,
    And let me see thy sparkling eye,
Oh brush not yet the pearl-strung spray
    Nor bow thy pretty head to fly.

Stay while I tell thee, fluttering thing,
    That thou of love an emblem art,
Yes! patient plume thy little wing,
    Whilst I my thoughts to thee impart.

When summer nights the dews bestow,
    And summer suns enrich the day,                                            10
Thy notes the blossoms charm to blow,
    Each opes delighted at thy lay.

So when in youth the eye's dark glance
    Speaks pleasure from its circle bright,
The tones of love our joys enhance
    And make superior each delight.

And when bleak storms resistless rove,
    And every rural bliss destroy,
Nought comforts then the leafless grove
    But thy soft note—its only joy—                                           20

E'en so the words of love beguile
When Pleasure's tree no flower bears,
And draw a soft endearing smile
Amid the gloom of grief and tears.

## SONG

### I

O BLUSH not so! O blush not so!
Or I shall think you knowing;
And if you smile the blushing while,
Then maidenheads are going.

### II

There's a blush for won't, and a blush for shan't,
And a blush for having done it:
There's a blush for thought and a blush for naught,
And a blush for just begun it.

### III

O sigh not so! O sigh not so!
For it sounds of Eve's sweet pippin;
By these loosen'd lips you have tasted the pips
And fought in an amorous nipping.

### IV

Will you play once more at nice-cut-core,
For it only will last our youth out,
And we have the prime of the kissing time,
We have not one sweet tooth out.

### V

There's a sigh for yes, and a sigh for no,
And a sigh for I can't bear it!
O what can be done, shall we stay or run?
O cut the sweet apple and share it!

## APOLLO TO THE GRACES

*Written to the tune of the air in 'Don Giovanni'*

APOLLO

WHICH of the fairest three
Today will ride with me?
My Steeds are all pawing on the thresholds of Morn:
  Which of the fairest three
  Today will ride with me
Across the gold Autumn's whole Kingdom of corn?

THE GRACES *all answer*

I will, I— I— I—
O young Apollo let me fly along with thee,
I will—I, I, I,
  The many wonders see                          10
  I— I— I— I—
And thy lyre shall never have a slackened string:
  I, I, I, I,
Thro' the whole golden day will sing.

## STANZAS

I

Y ou say you love; but with a voice
  Chaster than a nun's, who singeth
The soft Vespers to herself
  While the chime-bell ringeth—
    O love me truly!

II

You say you love; but with a smile
  Cold as sunrise in September,
As you were Saint Cupid's nun,
  And kept his weeks of Ember.
    O love me truly!

III

You say you love—but then your lips
  Coral tinted teach no blisses.
More than coral in the sea—
  They never pout for kisses—
    O love me truly!

IV

You say you love; but then your hand
  No soft squeeze for squeeze returneth,
It is like a statue's, dead,—
  While mine to passion burneth—
    O love me truly!


V

O breathe a word or two of fire!
  Smile, as if those words should burn me,
Squeeze as lovers should—O kiss
  And in thy heart inurn me!
    O love me truly!


I

WHERE be ye going, you Devon Maid?
  And what have ye there in the Basket?
Ye tight little fairy just fresh from the dairy,
  Will ye give me some cream if I ask it?


II

I love your Meads, and I love your flowers,
  And I love your junkets mainly,
But 'hind the door I love kissing more,
  O look not so disdainly.


III

I love your hills, and I love your dales,
  And I love your flocks a-bleating—
But O, on the heather to lie together,
  With both our hearts a-beating!


IV

I'll put your Basket all safe in a nook,
  Your shawl I hang up on the willow,
And we will sigh in the daisy's eye
And kiss on a grass green pillow.

Sweet, sweet is the greeting of eyes,
And sweet is the voice in its greeting,
When Adieux have grown old and goodbyes
Fade away where old Time is retreating.

Warm the nerve of a welcoming hand,
And earnest a Kiss on the Brow,
When we meet over sea and o'er Land
Where Furrows are new to the Plough.


## STANZAS ON SOME SKULLS

### IN BEAULEY ABBEY, NEAR INVERNESS

[*Only the lines printed in italics are by Keats; the rest was written
by Brown*]

I

*In silent barren Synod met*
*Within those roofless walls*, where yet
The shafted arch and carved fret
      Cling to the Ruin,
The Brethren's Skulls mourn, dewy wet,
      Their Creed's undoing.

II

The mitred ones of Nice and Trent
Were not so tongue-tied,—no, they went
Hot to their Councils, scarce content
      With Orthodoxy;
But ye, poor tongueless things, were meant
      To speak by proxy.

III

Your chronicles no more exist,
Since Knox, the Revolutionist,
Destroy'd the work of every fist
      That scrawl'd black letter;
Well! I'm a Craniologist
      And may do better.

IV

The skull-cap wore the cowl from sloth
Or discontent, perhaps from both,
And yet one day, against his oath,
                He tried escaping,
For men, tho' idle, may be loth
                To live on gaping.


V

A Toper this! he plied his glass
More strictly than he said the Mass,
And lov'd to see a tempting Lass
                Come to Confession,
Letting his absolution pass
                O'er first transgression.


VI

This crawl'd thro' life in feebleness,
Boasting he never knew excess,
Cursing those crimes he scarce could guess,
                Or feel but faintly,
With prayers that Heaven would come to bless
                Men so unsaintly.


VII

Here's a true Churchman! he'd affect
Much charity, and ne'er neglect
To pray for mercy on th' elect,
                But thought no evil
In sending Heathen, Turk and Sect
                All to the Devil!


VIII

*Poor Skull, thy fingers set ablaze,*
*With silver Saint in golden rays,*
*The holy Missal, thou did'st craze*
                *'Mid bead and spangle,*
*While others pass'd their idle days*
                *In coil and wrangle.*

### IX

Long time this sconce a helmet wore,
But sickness smites the conscience sore;
He broke his sword, and hither bore
        His gear and plunder,
Took to the cowl,—then rav'd and swore
        At his damn'd blunder!

### X

*This lily-colour'd skull, with all*
*The teeth complete, so white and small,*
*Belong'd to one whose early pall*
        *A lover shaded;*
*He died ere Superstition's gall*
        *His heart invaded.*

### XI

Ha! here is 'undivulged crime!'
Despair forbad his soul to climb
Beyond this world, this mortal time
        Of fevered sadness,
Until this Monkish Pantomime
        Dazzled his madness!

### XII

A younger brother this! a man
Aspiring as a Tartar Khan,
But, curb'd and baffled, he began
        The trade of frightening;
It smack'd of power!—and here he ran
        To deal Heaven's lightening.

### XIII

This ideot-skull belong'd to one,
A buried Miser's only son,
Who, penitent, ere he'd begun
        To taste of pleasure,
And hoping Heaven's dread wrath to shun,
        Gave Hell his treasure.

XIV

Here is the forehead of an Ape,
A robber's mask,—and near the nape
That bone, fie on't, bears just the shape
        Of carnal passion;
Ah! he was one for theft and rape,
        In Monkish fashion!


XV

This was the Porter!—he could ring,
Or dance, or play, do anything,
And what the Friars bade him bring,
        They ne'er were balk'd of;
Matters not worth remembering
        And seldom talk'd of.


XVI

Enough! why need I further pore?
This corner holds at least a score,
And yonder twice as many more
        Of Reverend Brothers;
'Tis the same story o'er and o'er,—
        They're like the others!


## STANZAS

I

In drear-nighted December,
    Too happy, happy tree,
Thy Branches ne'er remember
    Their green felicity:
The north cannot undo them,
    With a sleety whistle through them;
Nor frozen thawings glue them
    From budding at the prime.


II

In drear-nighted December,
    Too happy, happy Brook,
Thy bubblings ne'er remember
    Apollo's summer look;

But with a sweet forgetting,
They stay their crystal fretting,
Never, never petting
       About the frozen time.


III

Ah! would 'twere so with many
       A gentle girl and boy!
But were there ever any
       Writh'd not of passed joy?
The feel of not to feel it,
When there is none to heal it,
Nor numbed sense to steel it,
       Was never said in rhyme.


AH! ken ye what I met the day
       Out oure the Mountains
A coming down by craggies grey
       An mossie fountains—
Ah goud hair'd Marie yeve I pray
       Ane minute's guessing—
For that I met upon the way
       Is past expressing.
As I stood where a rocky brig
       A torrent crosses                          10
I spied upon a misty rig
       A troup o' Horses—
And as they trotted down the glen
       I sped to meet them
To see if I might know the Men
       To stop and greet them.
First Willie on his sleek mare came
       At canting gallop
His long hair rustled like a flame
       On board a shallop.                        20
Then came his brother Rab and then
       Young Peggy's Mither
And Peggy too—adown the glen
       They went togither—

I saw her wrappit in her hood
    Fra wind and raining—
Her cheek was flush wi' timid blood
    Twixt growth and waning—
She turn'd her dazed head full oft
    For there her Brithers
Came riding with her Bridegroom soft    30
    And mony ithers.
Young Tam came up an' eyed me quick
    With reddened cheek—
Braw Tam was daffed like a chick—
    He coud na speak—
Ah Marie they are all gane hame
    Through blustering weather
An' every heart is full on flame
    An' light as feather.    40
Ah! Marie they are all gone hame
    Fra happy wedding,
Whilst I—Ah is it not a shame?
    Sad tears am shedding.


THIS living hand, now warm and capable
Of earnest grasping, would, if it were cold
And in the icy silence of the tomb,
So haunt thy days and chill thy dreaming nights
That thou wouldst wish thine own heart dry of blood
So in my veins red life might stream again,
And thou be conscience-calm'd—see here it is—
I hold it towards you.

# TRIVIA

## WOMEN, WINE, AND SNUFF

GIVE me women, wine and snuff
Until I cry out 'hold, enough!'
You may do so sans objection
Till the day of resurrection;
For bless my beard they aye shall be
My beloved Trinity.


THEY weren fully glad of their gude hap
And tasten all the pleasaunces of joy.


## LINES RHYMED IN A LETTER RECEIVED
### (By J. H. R.) FROM OXFORD

I

THE Gothic looks solemn,
The plain Doric column
Supports an old Bishop and Crosier;
The mouldering arch,
Shaded o'er by a larch
Stands next door to Wilson the Hosier.

II

Vicè—that is, by turns,—
O'er pale faces mourns
The black tassell'd trencher and common hat;
The Chantry boy sings,
The Steeple-bell rings,
And as for the Chancellor—*dominat.*

III

There are plenty of trees,
And plenty of ease,
And plenty of fat deer for Parsons;
And when it is venison,
Short is the benison,—
Then each on a leg or thigh fastens.

## TEIGNMOUTH

['*Some Doggerel*' *sent in a Letter to B. R. Haydon*]

'HERE ALL THE SUMMER COULD I STAY'

I

For there's Bishop's teign
And King's teign
And Coomb at the clear teign head—
Where close by the stream
You may have your cream
All spread upon barley bread.

II

There's arch Brook
And there's larch Brook
Both turning many a mill;
And cooling the drouth
Of the salmon's mouth,
And fattening his silver gill.

III

There is Wild wood,
A Mild hood
To the sheep on the lea o' the down,
Where the golden furze,
With its green, thin spurs,
Doth catch at the maiden's gown.

IV

There is Newton marsh
With its spear grass harsh—
A pleasant summer level
Where the maidens sweet
Of the Market Street,
Do meet in the dusk to revel.

### V

There's the Barton rich
With dyke and ditch
And hedge for the thrush to live in
And the hollow tree
For the buzzing bee
And a bank for the wasp to hive in.


### VI

And O, and O
The daisies blow
And the primroses are waken'd,
And violets white
Sit in silver plight,
And the green bud's as long as the spike end.


### VII

Then who would go
Into dark Soho,
And chatter with dack'd-hair'd critics,
When he can stay
For the new-mown hay,
And startle the dappled Prickets?


## A SONG ABOUT MYSELF

FROM A LETTER TO FANNY KEATS, 2 JULY 1818

### I

THERE was a naughty Boy,
A naughty boy was he,
He would not stop at home,
He could not quiet be—
He took
In his Knapsack
A Book
Full of vowels

And a shirt
With some towels—
A slight cap
For night cap—
A hair brush,
Comb ditto,
New Stockings
For old ones
Would split O!
This Knapsack
Tight at's back
He rivetted close
And followed his Nose
To the North,
To the North,
And follow'd his nose
To the North.


II

There was a naughty boy
And a naughty boy was he,
For nothing would he do
But scribble poetry—
He took
An ink stand
In his hand
And a pen
Big as ten
In the other.
And  away
In a Pother
He ran
To the mountains
And fountains
And ghostes
And Postes
And witches
And ditches
And wrote
In his coat

When the weather
Was cool,
Fear of gout,
And without
When the weather
Was warm—
Och the charm
When we choose
To follow one's nose
To the north,
To the north,
To follow one's nose
To the north!

III

There was a naughty boy
And a naughty boy was he,
He kept little fishes
In washing tubs three
In spite
Of the might
Of the Maid
Nor afraid
Of his Granny-good—
He often would
Hurly burly
Get up early
And go
By hook or crook
To the brook
And bring home
Miller's thumb,
Tittlebat
Not over fat,
Minnows small
As the stall
Of a glove,
Not above
The size
Of a nice
Little Baby's

Little fingers—
O he made
'Twas his trade
Of Fish a pretty Kettle
A Kettle—
A Kettle
Of Fish a pretty Kettle
A Kettle!

IV

There was a naughty Boy,
    And a naughty Boy was he,
He ran away to Scotland
    The people for to see—
        Then he found
        That the ground
        Was as hard,
        That a yard
        Was as long,
        That a song
        Was as merry,
        That a cherry
        Was as red—
        That lead
        Was as weighty,
        That fourscore
        Was as eighty,
        That a door
        Was as wooden
        As in England—
So he stood in his shoes
    And he wonder'd,
    He wonder'd,
He stood in his
    Shoes and he wonder'd.


ALL gentle folks who owe a grudge
    To any living thing
Open your ears and stay your trudge
    Whilst I in dudgeon sing.

The Gadfly he hath stung me sore—
  O may he ne'er sting you!
But we have many a horrid bore
  He may sting black and blue.

Has any here an old grey Mare
  With three legs all her store,                10
O put it to her Buttocks bare
  And straight she'll run on four.

Has any here a Lawyer suit
  Of Seventeen-Forty-Three,
Take Lawyer's nose and put it to 't
  And you the end will see.

Is there a Man in Parliament
  Dum[b-]founder'd in his speech,
O let his neighbour make a rent
  And put one in his breech.                    20

O Lowther how much better thou
  Hadst figur'd t'other day
When to the folks thou mad'st a bow
  And hadst no more to say

If lucky Gadfly had but ta'en
  His seat upon thine A—e
And put thee to a little pain
  To save thee from a worse.

Better than Southey it had been,
  Better than Mr. D—,                           30
Better than Wordsworth too, I ween,
  Better than Mr. V—.

Forgive me pray good people all
  For deviating so—
In spirit sure I had a call—
  And now I on will go.

Has any here a daughter fair
　　Too fond of reading novels,
Too apt to fall in love with care
　　And charming Mister Lovels,　　　　　　40

O put a Gadfly to that thing
　　She keeps so white and pert—
I mean the finger for the ring,
　　And it will breed a wort.

Has any here a pious spouse
　　Who seven times a day
Scolds as King David pray'd, to chouse
　　And have her holy way—

O let a Gadfly's little sting
　　Persuade her sacred tongue　　　　　　50
That noises are a common thing,
　　But that her bell has rung.

And as this is the summum bo-
　　num of all conquering,
I leave withouten wordes mo
　　The Gadfly's little sting.

MRS. C.

UPON my life Sir Nevis I am pique'd
That I have so far panted tugg'd and reek'd
To do an honor to your old bald pate
And now am sitting on you just to bate,
Without your paying me one compliment.
Alas 'tis so with all, when our intent
Is plain, and in the eye of all Mankind
We fair ones show a preference, too blind!
You Gentle man immediately turn tail—
O let me then my hapless fate bewail!　　　　　10
Ungrateful Baldpate, have I not disdain'd
The pleasant Valleys—have I not, madbrain'd,
Deserted all my Pickles and preserves,
My China closet too—with wretched Nerves

To boot—say, wretched ingrate, have I not
Left my soft cushion chair and caudle pot?
'Tis true I had no corns—no! thank the fates,
My Shoemaker was always Mr. Bates.
And if not Mr. Bates why I'm not old!
Still dumb, ungrateful Nevis—still so cold!     20

Here the Lady took some more wiskey and was putting even
more to her lips when she dashed [it] to the Ground for
the Mountain began to grumble—which continued for a few
minutes before he thus began,     20 *d*

### BEN NEVIS

What whining bit of tongue and Mouth thus dares
Disturb my slumber of a thousand years?
Even so long my sleep has been secure—
And to be so awaked I'll not endure.
Oh pain—for since the Eagle's earliest scream
I've had a damn'd confounded ugly dream,
A Nightmare sure. What, Madam, was it you?
It cannot be! My old eyes are not true!
Red-Crag, my Spectacles! Now let me see!
Good Heavens, Lady, how the gemini     30
Did you get here? O I shall split my sides!
I shall earthquake——

### MRS. C.

Sweet Nevis, do not quake, for though I love
Your honest Countenance all things above,
Truly I should not like to be convey'd
So far into your Bosom—gentle Maid
Loves not too rough a treatment, gentle Sir—
Pray thee be calm and do not quake nor stir,
No not a Stone, or I shall go in fits—

### BEN NEVIS

I must—I shall—I meet not such tit bits—     40
I meet not such sweet creatures every day—
By my old night-cap, night-cap night and day,
I must have one sweet Buss—I must and shall!
Red-Crag!—What, Madam, can you then repent

**B 5432**     Q

Of all the toil and vigour you have spent
To see Ben Nevis and to touch his nose?
Red-Crag, I say! O I must have them close!
Red-Crag, there lies beneath my farthest toe
A vein of Sulphur—go dear Red-Crag, go—
And rub your flinty back against it—budge!          50
Dear Madam, I must kiss you, faith I must!
I must Embrace you with my dearest gust!
Block-head, d'ye hear—Block-head, I'll make her feel—
There lies beneath my east leg's northern heel
A cave of young earth dragons—well, my boy,
Go thither quick and (so complete my joy)
Take you a bundle of the largest pines
And when the sun on fiercest Phosphor shines
Fire them and ram them in the Dragon's nest,
Then will the dragons fry and fizz their best          60
Until ten thousand now no bigger than
Poor Al[l]igators—poor things of one span—
Will each one swell to twice ten times the size
Of northern whale—then for the tender prize—
The moment then—for then will Red-Crag rub
His flinty back—and I shall kiss and snub
And press my dainty morsel to my breast.
Block-head, make haste!
                                O Muses weep the rest—
The Lady fainted and he thought her dead
So pulled the clouds again about his head          70
And went to sleep again—soon she was rous'd
By her affrighted servants—next day hous'd
Safe on the lowly ground she bless'd her fate
That fainting fit was not delayed too late.



WHEN they were come into the Faery's Court
They rang—no one at home—all gone to sport
And dance and kiss and love as faeries do—
For Faeries be as humans, lovers true—
Amid the woods they were, so lone and wild,
Where even the Robin feels himself exil'd

And where the very brooks as if afraid
Hurry along to some less magic shade.
'No one at home!' the fretful princess cry'd
'And all for nothing such a dreary ride,                    10
And all for nothing my new diamond cross,
No one to see my Persian feathers toss,
No one to see my Ape, my Dwarf, my Fool,
Or how I pace my Otahaeitan mule.
Ape, Dwarf and Fool, why stand you gaping there?
Burst the door open, quick—or I declare
I'll switch you soundly and in pieces tear.'
The Dwarf began to tremble and the Ape
Star'd at the Fool, the Fool was all agape,
The Princess grasp'd her switch, but just in time      20
The dwarf with piteous face began to rhyme.
'O mighty Princess, did you ne'er hear tell
What your poor servants know but too too well?
Know you the three great crimes in faery land?
The first, alas! poor Dwarf, I understand—
I made a whipstock of a faery's wand—
The next is snoring in their company—
The next, the last, the direst of the three
Is making free when they are not at home.
I was a Prince—a baby prince—my doom                    30
You see, I made a whipstock of a wand—
My top has henceforth slept in faery land.
He was a Prince, the Fool, a grown up Prince,
But he has never been a King's son since
He fell a-snoring at a faery Ball—
Your poor Ape was a prince and he, poor thing,
Picklock'd a faery's boudoir—now no king,
But ape—so pray your highness stay awhile;
'Tis sooth indeed, we know it to our sorrow—
Persist and *you* may be an ape tomorrow'—          40
While the Dwarf spake the Princess all for spite
Peel'd the brown hazel twig to lilly white,
Clench'd her small teeth, and held her lips apart,
Try'd to look unconcern'd with beating heart.
They saw her highness had made up her mind
And quaver'd like the reeds before the wind,
And they had had it, but, O happy chance!

The Ape for very fear began to dance
And grin'd as all his ugliness did ache—
She staid her vixen fingers for his sake,          50
He was so very ugly: then she took
Her pocket mirror and began to look
First at herself and then at him and then
She smil'd at her own beauteous face again.
Yet for all this—for all her pretty face
She took it in her head to see the place.
Women gain little from experience
Either in Lovers, husbands or expense.
'The more the beauty, the more fortune too:
'Beauty before the wide world never knew—'          60
So each fair reasons, tho' it oft miscarries.
She thought *her* pretty face would please the faeries.
'My darling Ape I won't whip you today—
Give me the Picklock, sirrah, and go play.'
They all three wept—but counsel was as vain
As crying 'C'up, biddy' to drops of rain.
Yet lingeringly did the sad Ape forth draw
The Picklock from the Pocket in his Jaw.
The Princess took it and dismounting straight
Trip'd in blue silver'd slippers to the gate          70
And touch'd the wards, the Door full courteously
Opened—she enter'd with her servants three.
Again it clos'd and there was nothing seen
But the Mule grazing on the herbage green.

 END OF CANTO XII


Canto the xiii

The Mule no sooner saw himself alone
Than he prick'd up his Ears—and said 'well done!
At least, unhappy Prince, I may be free—
No more a Princess shall side-saddle me.
O King of Otahaietè—tho' a Mule
"Aye every inch a King"—tho' "Fortune's fool"—          80
Well done—for by what Mr. Dwarfy said
I would not give a sixpence for her head.'
Even as he spake he trotted in high glee
To the knotty side of an old Pollard tree

And rub'd his sides against the mossed bark
Till his Girths burst and left him naked stark
Except his Bridle—how get rid of that,
Buckle and tied with many a twist and plait?
At last it struck him to pretend to sleep
And then the thievish Monkeys down would creep          90
And filch the unpleasant trammels quite away.
No sooner thought of than adown he lay,
Shamm'd a good snore—the Monkey-men descended
And whom they thought to injure they befriended.
They hung his Bridle on a topmost bough
And off he went, run, trot, or anyhow.


TWO or three Posies
With two or three simples—
Two or three Noses
With two or three pimples—
Two or three wise men
And two or three ninny's—
Two or three purses
And two or three guineas—
Two or three raps
At two or three doors—          10
Two or three naps
Of two or three hours—
Two or three Cats
And two or three mice—
Two or three sprats
At a very great price—
Two or three sandies
And two or three tabbies—
Two or three dandies
And two Mrs ——          mum!          20
Two or three Smiles
And two or three frowns—
Two or three Miles
To two or three towns—

Two or three pegs
For two or three bonnets—
Two or three dove eggs
To hatch into sonnets.

## ACROSTIC

### GEORGIANA AUGUSTA KEATS

GIVE me your patience Sister while I frame
Exact in Capitals your golden name
Or sue the fair Apollo and he will
Rouse from his heavy slumber and instil
Great love in me for thee and Poesy.
Imagine not that greatest mastery
And kingdom over all the Realms of verse
Nears more to Heaven in aught than when we nurse
And surety give to love and Brotherhood.

Anthropophagi in Othello's mood;                    10
Ulysses stormed, and his enchanted belt
Glowed with the Muse, but they are never felt
Unbosom'd so and so eternal made,
Such tender incense in their Laurel shade,
To all the regent sisters of the Nine
As this poor offering to you, sister mine.

Kind sister! aye, this third name says you are;
Enchanted has it been the Lord knows where.
And may it taste to you like good old wine,
Take you to real happiness and give                    20
Sons, daughters and a home like honied hive.

PENSIVE they sit, and roll their languid eyes,
Nibble their toast and cool their tea with sighs;
Or else forget the purpose of the night,
Forget their tea, forget their appetite.
See, with cross'd arms they sit—Ah! hapless crew,

The fire is going out and no one rings
For coals, and therefore no coals Betty brings.
A fly is in the milk-pot. Must he die
Circled by a humane Society?
No, no; there, Mr. Werter takes his spoon,          10
Inverts it, dips the handle, and lo! soon
The little struggler, sav'd from perils dark,
Across the teaboard draws a long wet mark.
　Romeo! Arise! take snuffers by the handle,
There's a large cauliflower in each candle.
A winding sheet—ah, me! I must away
To No. 7, just beyond the Circus gay.
'Alas, my friend, your coat sits very well;
Where may your Tailor live?' 'I may not tell.
O pardon me—I'm absent: now and then.          20
Where *might* my Tailor live? I say again
I cannot tell, let me no more be teas'd;
He lives in Wapping, *might* live where he pleas'd.'


　　　　O GRANT that like to Peter I
　　　　May like to Peter B,
　　　　And tell me, lovely Jesus, Y
　　　　This Peter went to C.

　　　　O grant that like to Peter I
　　　　May like to Peter B,
　　　　And tell me, lovely Jesus, Y
　　　　Old Jonah went to C.


　　　　I AM as brisk
　　　　As a bottle of Wisk-
　　　　Ey and as nimble
　　　　As a Milliner's thimble.

# GRIPUS

Undated. From the Woodhouse Transcript in the Pierpont Morgan Library.

First printed by Amy Lowell, *John Keats*, ii. 535–44, 1925. [The manuscript is almost wholly wanting in punctuation. I have supplied the pointing and filled in the names of the *dramatis personae*.]

GRIPUS. And gold and silver are but filthy dross.
  Then seek not gold and silver which are dross,
  But rather lay thy treasure up in heav'n!—
SLIM. Hem!
GRIPUS. And thou hast meat & drink & lodging too
  And clothing too, what more can Man require?
  And thou art single—
  But I must lay up money for my children,
  My children's children & my great grand children;
  For, Slim! thy master will be shortly married—
SLIM. Married!
GRIPUS.          Yea! married. Wherefore dost thou stare,  10
  As thou⟨gh⟩ my words had spoke of aught impossible?
SLIM. My lord, I stare not but my ears playd false.
  Methought you had said married.
GRIPUS.                        Married, fool!
  Is't aught unlikely? I'm not very old,
  And my intended has a noble fortune.
SLIM. My lord 'tis likely.
GRIPUS.                   Haste, then, to the butchers,
  And ere thou go, tell Bridget she is wanted—
SLIM. I go—Gods! what a subject for an ode.
  With Hymen, Cupids, Venus, Loves & Graces!     [*Exit*

### Gripus *solus*

GRIPUS. This matrimony is no light affair;     20
  Tis downright venture & mere speculation.

  *Title: wanting in MS*.          15 intendended *MS*.

Less risk there is in what the merchant trusts
To winds & waves and the uncertain elements—
For he can have assurance for his goods
And put himself beyond the reach of losses—
But who can e'er ensure to me a wife
Industrious and managing and frugal,
Who will not spend far more than she has brought,
But be almost a saving to her husband?—
But none can tell—the broker cannot tell          30
He is not cheated in the wares he buys,
And to judge well of women or the seas
Wou⟨l⟩d oft surpass the wisest merchant's prudence;
For both are deep alike—capricious too—
And the worst things that money can be sunk in.
But Bridget comes—
BRIDGET.                    Your pleasure, Sir, with me?
GRIPUS. Bridget, I wish to have a little converse
Upon a matter that concerns us both
Of like importance both to thee and me.
BRIDGET [*aside*]. Of like importance and concerning both!
What can your Honour have to say to me?          41
O lord! I would give all that I am worth
To know what tis—
GRIPUS.                    Then pry'thee rein thy tongue
That ever battles with thine own impatience.
But to the point. Thou knows't, for twenty years
Together we have liv'd as man and wife,
But never hath the sanction of the Church
Stamp'd its legality upon our union.
BRIDGET. Well, what of that?
GRIPUS.                    Why, when in wiser years
Men look upon the follies of their youth,          50
They oft repent, & wish to make amends,
And seek for happier in more virtuous days.
In such a case, & such is mine I own,
'Tis Marriage offers us the readiest way
To make atonement for our former deeds.
And thus have I determin'd in my heart
To make amends—in other words to marry.

39 thee *over* [you] *MS*.

BRIDGET. O lord! how overjoy'd I am to hear it!
I vow that I have often thought myself,
What wickedness it was to live as we did!                    60
But do you joke?
GRIPUS.              Not so upon my oath.
I am resolv'd to marry and beget
A little heir to leave my little wealth to.
I am not old, my hair is hardly grey
My health is good, what hast thou to object?
BRIDGET. O dear! how close your honour puts the question!
I've said as much already as was fit
And incompatible with female modesty—
But would your honour please to name a day?
GRIPUS. To name a day! but hark! I hear a knock—        70
'Tis perhaps young Prodigal, I did expect him.
BRIDGET. But Sir—a day?
GRIPUS.                    Zounds! dost thou hear the bell?
Wilt thou not run? he was to bring me money!
                              [Exit B and returns.
BRIDGET. 'Tis he, I've shown him to the little study.
GRIPUS. Then stay thee here, and when I've settled him
I will return & hold more converse with thee.    [Exit.
BRIDGET [solus]. My head runs round! O, what a happy
    change!
Now I shall be another woman quite.
Dame Bridget, then, adieu! and don't forget
Your lady Gripus now that is to be;                          80
Great Lady Gripus—O lord!—
The Lady of the old and rich Sir Gripus!
O how will people whisper, as I pass,
'There goes my lady'—'what a handsome gownd,
All scarlet silk embroidered with gold!'
Or green & gold will perhaps become me better—
How vastly fine, how handsome I shall be
In green & gold—besides, a lady too!
I'll have a footman too, to walk behind me.
Slim is too slender to set off a livery,                      90
I must have one more lustier than him,

63 too MS.              78 [lady] woman MS.

A proper man to walk behind his lady.
O how genteel! methinks I see myself
In green and gold and carrying my fan—
*Or perhaps I'd have a redicule about me!*
The lusty footman all so spruce behind me
Walking on tiptoe in a bran new livery;
And he shall have a favour in his hat
As sure as ever I am lady Gripus!

*Enter* SLIM

SLIM. Why how now, Bridget, you're turn'd actress sure!          100
BRIDGET. An actor, fellow, no! To something better,
    To something grander and more ladylike,
    Know I am turn'd!
SLIM.                 A lunatic, 'tis plain.
    But, lovee, leave this jesting for a while,
    And hear thy servant, who thus pleads for favor.
BRIDGET. For favour Sirrah! But I must be kind,
    I will forget your insolence this once,
    And condescend to keep you in my service.
    But no! I want a much more lustier man,
    You are too slender to become my livery          110
    I must excard you, you must suit yourself!
SLIM. Why, how now, Bridget—
BRIDGET.                 You forget me, sure!
SLIM. Forget thee, Bridget? Never from my heart
    Shall thy dear image part.
        Ah! no,
        I love you so
    No language can impart!
    Alas! 'tis love that makes me thin,
    I have a fiery flame within,
    That burns and shrivels up my skin—          120
        'Tis Cupid's little dart,
        And by this kiss I swear—[*Attempts to kiss her*]
BRIDGET. Ruffin, begone, or I will tell my lord.
    Do you not care for difference of rank,
    Nor make distinction between dirt & dignity?

95 *redicule*] i.e. reticule. *The whole verse is underlined in MS.* redicule
*is the same kind of error as* allegolly *in* 132.
99 ever *added above MS.* [handsome] lady *MS.*

SLIM. Why, Bridget, once you did not treat me thus.
BRIDGET. No, times are alter'd, Fortune's wheel is
    turn'd,
  You still are Slim, but, tho' I once was Bridget,
  I'm Lady Gripus now that is to be.
  Did not his Honour tell you he should marry?      130
SLIM. Yea, to a lady of an ample fortune.
BRIDGET. Why, that, you fool, he said in allegolly.
  A virtuous woman, is she not a crown,
  A crown of gold and glory to her husband?
SLIM. Heav'n is it possible? I pray forgive me
  That I could doubt a moment of that fortune
  Which is but due to your assembled merits.
BRIDGET. Well, Slim, I do not wish to harbour malice,
  But while you show a proper due respect
  You may be certain of my condescension.          140
  But hark! I hear his lordship on the stairs,
  And we must have some privacy together.    [*Exit* SLIM.
  O lord, how overjoy'd I am your honour—
GRIPUS. Bridget, I thank thee for thy friendly zeal,
  That seems to glory in thy Master's bliss;
  And much it grieves me that I can't requite it
  Except by mere reciprocal good-wishes.
  For as a change in my domestic government
  Will make thy place in future but a sinecure,
  It grieves me much that I must warn you thus     150
  To seek and get a situation elsewhere.
BRIDGET. O dear! O lord! O what a shock! O lord!   [*Faints*]
GRIPUS. Ho! Slim—the devil's in the fool, to faint.
  Halloo!—what shall I do? halloo! halloo!
  Ho! Slim, I say—run, Sirrah, for the brandy!
SLIM. The brandy, Sir? there is none in the house!
GRIPUS. No brandy! none! what, none at all, thou
    knave?
  What, none at all? thou rascal thou hast drunk it.
  Why Bridget, Bridget—what, no brandy, knave?
  Zounds! what a fit! Where is my brandy, Wretch!   160
  Thou toping Villain, say, or I will slay thee!

        *Lets* BRIDGET *fall and collars* SLIM

        129 *omitted in Miss Lowell's transcript.*

SLIM. O lord! Forgive me, Bridget had the wind,
  And drank the brandy up to warm her stomach.
GRIPUS. A tipsy Bacchanal! then let her lie!
  I'll not be drunken out of house & home.
  Zounds! brandy for the wind—a cure indeed!
  A little water had done just as well.
  This is the way, then, when I want a drop;
  I always find my cellar is stark naked.
  But both shall go, yes, I discard ye. Thieves!                170
  Begone, ye thieves!

BRIDGET *jumps up*

BRIDGET.              No, not without my wages!
  I'll have a month's full wages or my warning!
  I'll not be left at non-plust for a place.
GRIPUS. A month's full warning! what, another month,
  To sack, to ransack, and to strip the house,
  And then depart in triumph with your booty!
  Begone, I say!
BRIDGET.          No, not without my wages!
  And I'll have damages, you cruell man!
  I will convict you of a breach of marriage!
GRIPUS. Begone, I say! Deceitful Thing! begone—         180
  Who ever dar'd to promise such a match
  But thy own fancy, & thy lying tongue?
  What, marry one as poor as a church mouse,
  And equally devoid of rank and Beauty!
  Reason would sleep and prudence would be blind,
  And Gripus then would be no longer Gripus,
  But only fitting for more sober men
  To lodge in Bedlam & to call a lunatic.                    188

184 and [money] Beauty! *MS*.
187 sober *over* [prudent].

# CRITICAL NOTES

*p. 38. On first looking into Chapman's Homer.*

Of this, perhaps the most famous of Keats's sonnets, we have two autograph copies, one in the Harvard Library, the other in the Morgan Library. Of the manuscript variants, the most interesting may be thought to be 'low-brow'd Homer', in line 6, corrected by Keats to 'deep-brow'd'. Keats probably took his 'low-brow'd' from Milton, *L'Allegro* 8 ('low-brow'd rocks'). In line 11, again, the Harvard draft has 'wond'ring eyes' for 'eagle eyes'. In line 7, both our manuscripts have 'Yet could I never judge what men could mean'; and this reading appears in the earliest printed version, the *Examiner* for 1 December 1816.

*p. 53.* The Morgan Library preserves, in Keats's autograph, a cancelled title-page, Dedication, and Preface. The title-page offered the following:

## ENDYMION

### A ROMANCE

### BY JOHN KEATS

The stretched metre of an antique song—
*Shakespeare's Sonnets.*

The cancelled Dedication offered:

### INSCRIBED,

#### WITH EVERY FEELING OF PRIDE AND REGRET
#### AND WITH 'A BOWED MIND,'
#### TO THE MEMORY OF
#### THE MOST ENGLISH OF POETS EXCEPT SHAKESPEARE,

## THOMAS CHATTERTON.

The original preface reads as follows:

ORIGINAL PREFACE REJECTED ON CONSIDERATION

IN a great nation, the work of an individual is of so little importance; his pleadings and excuses are so uninteresting; his 'way of life' such a nothing, that a Preface seems a sort of impertinent bow to strangers who care nothing about it.

A Preface, however, should be down in so many words; and such a one that by an eye-glance over the type the Reader may catch an idea of an Author's modesty, and non-opinion of himself—which I sincerely hope may be seen in the few lines I have to write, notwithstanding many proverbs of many ages old which men find a great pleasure in receiving as gospel.

About a twelvemonth since, I published a little book of verses; it was read by some dozen of my friends who lik'd it; and some dozen whom I was unacquainted with, who did not.

Now, when a dozen human beings are at words with another dozen, it becomes a matter of anxiety to side with one's friends—more especially when excited thereto by a great love of Poetry. I fought under disadvantages. Before I began I had no inward feel of being able to finish; and as I proceeded my steps were all uncertain. So this Poem must rather be considered as an endeavour than a thing accomplished; a poor prologue to what, if I live, I humbly hope to do. In duty to the Public I should have kept it back for a year or two, knowing it to be so faulty: but I really cannot do so,—by repetition my favourite passages sound vapid in my ears, and I would rather redeem myself with a new Poem should this one be found of any interest.

I have to apologize to the lovers of simplicity for touching the spell of loneliness that hung about Endymion; if any of my lines plead for me with such people I shall be proud.

It has been too much the fashion of late to consider men bigoted and addicted to every word that may chance to escape their lips; now I here declare that I have not any particular affection for any particular phrase, word, or letter in the whole affair. I have written to please myself, and in hopes to please others, and for a love of fame; if I neither please myself, nor others, nor get fame, of what consequence is Phraseology?

I would fain escape the bickerings that all Works not exactly in chime bring upon their begetters—but this is not fair to expect, there must be conversation of some sort and to object shows a man's consequence. In case of a London drizzle or a Scotch mist, the following quotation from Marston may perhaps 'stead me as an umbrella for an hour or so: 'let it be the curtesy of my peruser rather to pity my self-hindering labours than to malice me.'

One word more—for we cannot help seeing our own affairs in every point of view—should any one call my dedication to Chatterton affected I answer as followeth: 'Were I dead, sir, I should like a Book dedicated to me.'

Teignmouth, *March 19th, 1818*

*p. 55. Endymion,* i. 1.

A thing of beauty is a joy for ever⌝ Everybody knows the first line of *Endymion*. Not many people know what the first line once was. Henry Stephens, who for a while shared rooms with Keats in St. Thomas' Street, when they were both students at Guy's Hospital, recalled a cancelled first line—

A thing of beauty is a constant joy

which he called 'a fine line but wanting something'. Many years later, writing about Keats to G. F. Mathew, 'His poetry', he says, 'was not generally to my taste.' But if we may believe what he told Sir Benjamin Ward Richardson, the first line of *Endymion* would, but for his advice, have been not good but bad.

*p.* 152. *Endymion,* iv. 805.

Endymion, weep not so] Woodhouse records from Keats's autograph draft the variant 'Dear Endy, weep not so'; 'which', says Buxton Forman, 'I should not like to accept literally without seeing the original'. The 'original' has been missing since 2 July 1847, when Reynolds, to whom it belonged, sent it to Monckton Milnes. But Woodhouse was a man careful, conscientious, incapable of tampering with Keats's autograph. We may not like 'Dear Endy', but we cannot away with it.

*p.* 209. *Ode to a Nightingale,* 69–70.

Keats's autograph, once at Crewe House, now in the Fitzwilliam Museum at Cambridge, shows that Keats wrote originally:

> Char[m]'d the wide casements, opening on the foam
> Of ruthless seas in fairy lands fo[r]lorn.

In line 70 the second word has been read as 'keelless'. But Woodhouse, who made a shorthand copy of the original, read (and wrote, without query), 'ruthless'. Keats had a good reason for cancelling 'ruthless'—four lines earlier he had spoken of 'the sad heart of *Ruth*'.

*p.* 221. *Hyperion.*

Woodhouse has preserved for us the following cancelled *Advertisement* to the poem:

### ADVERTISEMENT

The Publishers think it right to state that it was not the wish of the Author that the ensuing fragment should meet the public eye. He commenced the Poem just before the publication of his Endymion; and he abandoned the intention of proceeding with it, in consequence of the reception that work experienced from some of the reviews.— The fragment remains therefore in the same state in which it was originally written; and the Author's health is not at present such as to enable him to make any corrections. The Publishers have however prevailed upon him to allow of its forming a part of this volume: and they are content to take upon themselves whatever blame may attach to its publication.

*p.* 272. *Otho,* III. i. 8.

'The limbo of a wanton. . . .'] Monckton Milnes's 1848 text offers 'The white limbs of a wanton', and this stood unquestioned in all editions of Keats previous to the Oxford English Texts edition of 1939. But there can be little doubt that 'white limbs' is a conjectural emendation made by Milnes when his 1848 text was in proof. The copy which he gave to the printer was a transcript, still extant, in the hand of Charles Brown, offering many indications of its having been used by the printers. The transcript has, for *white limbs, limbo.* The printer (and Milnes) read *limbo* as *limbs*; and Milnes stopped the metrical gap by *white.* Keats's autograph agrees with Brown's transcript, showing plainly 'limbo'. Keats, it may be added, had seen Brown's transcript, making here and there additions and corrections in it.

*p* 350. *La Belle Dame sans Merci.*

The earliest known version of this poem is to be found in an autograph letter of Keats to his brother George (Letter 123, April 1819). The manner in which it is there written out suggests recent composition—corrections are numerous. A revised version, the revision pretty certainly by Keats, was printed by Leigh Hunt in the *Indicator* on 10 May 1820. The *Indicator* version seems not to have been known either to Brown or to Woodhouse, both of whom have left us copies of the poem (Woodhouse two copies). Monckton Milnes, when he published the poem in 1848, seems to have followed Woodhouse's copy. The *Indicator* version stands alone. But that its variants go back to Keats himself, and are not the work of Hunt, seems sufficiently indicated by the fact that John Jeffry had a manuscript of the poem, in Keats's autograph, in which the first line was given as it appears in the *Indicator.*

The text here printed is that of 1848.

The *Indicator* offers the following variants:

1 knight-at-arms] wretched wight        3, 47 has] is        11 cheek
23 sideways would she lean        Stanzas v and vi are transposed in
the *Indicator*        30 gaz'd and sighed deep        31 wild sad eyes
32 So kiss'd to sleep        33 And there we slumber'd on the moss
39 They] Who        41 gloom        44 hill side

*p.* 355. *Ode on Indolence.*

The poem was first printed by Monckton Milnes in the 1848 *Life, Letters and Literary Remains of John Keats.* We know that the 'copy' was Brown's transcript, still extant ($T^2$). Any divergence from $T^2$ must be a change introduced in proof by Monckton Milnes. In stanza iii (5), 1, he seems to have emended *A third time* to *And once more.* He has also changed the order of the stanzas in $T^2$ (1, 2, 4, 6, 3, 5) to that of 1848 (1, 2, 3, 4, 5, 6). In the present text, *A third time* has been retained in stanza iii (5), 1; and to make this possible, the order of stanzas has been changed to 1, 2, 5, 3, 4, 6. In a transcript made by Woodhouse, which is a copy of $T^2$, the order of stanzas is that of 1848, but the reader is notified that the old order was 1, 2, 4, 6, 3, 5.

*p.* 359.

The sixteen lines which follow 98 are preserved in an autograph leaf once the property of Mr. Sabin, now in the Morgan Library. They are found also in a transcript of the poem made by Woodhouse, which bears a note 'copied from J. K.'s MS.' The lines were first printed in *The Bookman* for October 1906, and appeared in the same year in the Preface to the Oxford Standard Authors edition of Keats. In that Preface Buxton Forman writes of this fragment thus:

'It is of very high interest, though the sixteen lines which I think it authorizes us to add to the fragment are not of equal quality with what we had already, and may have been specially rejected, not merely dropped with the whole scheme of the unfinished poem. The newly recovered passage deals with the essential legend which Dante Gabriel Rossetti told me he was convinced that Keats was going to treat as the back-bone of the poem—the legend about the wraiths of people who were in peril of death trooping into church on St. Mark's Eve. Rossetti identified the fragment with the poetic scheme mentioned in a letter to Fanny Brawne (COMPLETE edition, Volume v, page 185), and was of opinion that Bertha in *The Eve of St. Mark* had trifled with her lover and, now that he was sick, was to go to the cathedral porch and watch the wraiths going in, with the view of ascertaining whether her lover's wraith came out again—for those who were to die that year would not come out; but those who were to get well would. Keats simplified the legend: for him, all whose wraiths went in would die.'

*p.* 368 *To Sleep.*

For this sonnet we have Keats's autograph draft, in the Hampstead Milton, dated 1819; and in Letter 123 (addressed to his brother and sister, 30 April 1819) his autograph fair copy. The draft is as follows (square brackets indicating words erased in the original):

O soft embalmer of the still Midnight
   Shutting with careful fingers and benign
Our gloom-pleas'd eyes embower'd from the light
[Of sun or teasing candles
   As wearisome]
   As wearisome as darkness is divine
O soothest sleep, if so it please thee close
   My (*made out of* Mine) willing eyes in midst of this thine hymn
Or wait the amen, ere thy poppy throws
   Its sweet-dath dews o'er every pulse and limb
Then shut the hushed Casket of my soul
   And turn the Key round in the oiled wards
And let it rest until the morn [has stole]
   Bright tressed from the gray east's shuddering bourn
(Bright tressed *add. in marg.*; grey east's *over* [wests]).

This draft that failed has no further history. The fair copy has a history of which some particulars are worth recording. Almost as soon as it was written, a transcript of it was made by Charles Brown; which Brown lent to Woodhouse. Woodhouse made two copies of it. One of them Keats saw, making in his own hand a change in line 8 ('lulling' for 'dewy'). In line 11 this copy has 'hoards' pencilled over 'lords' (but not in Keats's hand). In the other copy which he made Woodhouse has put 'hoards' into the text, in the place of 'lords'. On 11 October 1838 the poem was printed from Brown's transcript in the *Plymouth and Devonport Weekly Journal*, showing 'dewy' and 'lords'. Milnes, when he printed it in 1848, adopted Keats's 'lulling' and Woodhouse's 'hoards'. That Keats wrote 'lords' we know for certain, and that, when he found it in the copy of Woodhouse which he corrected, he allowed it to stand. That the 'hoards' of Woodhouse's other copy came into it from Keats nothing that we know indicates. In truth, it looks like editorial conjecture. No doubt, 'hoards' is easier than 'lords'. But when Keats wrote 'lords', it had a meaning for him. To get his meaning, we should compare the use of the verb 'lord' in *Endymion*, ii. 891:

And all the revels he had lorded there.

There 'lorded' means 'captained', 'marshalled', with some added suggestion of ostentation. And in our sonnet, when Keats says of Conscience that it 'lords its strength for darkness', may we not plausibly paraphrase this by saying that Conscience marshals, arrays, disposes proudly and boastfully, its power for darkness?

*p. 372. 'Bright Star . . .'.*

Of this celebrated sonnet there exist two versions. The text here printed is that of Monckton Milnes (*Life, Letters, and Literary Remains of John Keats*, 1848, ii, p. 306). Monckton Milnes printed from Keats's autograph, still extant in the Keats Museum at Hampstead, introducing three changes of spelling (*steadfast* for *stedfast* in 1, *splendour* for *splendor* in 2, *mask* for *masque* in 7) and correcting, conjecturally, *swell and fall* to *fall and swell* in 12; but otherwise not deviating from the manuscript. The autograph can be dated exactly. It is to be found on a blank leaf of a copy of Shakespeare (a royal octavo volume, Thomas Wilson, London, 1806) given to Keats by Reynolds in 1819. Keats took this volume with him to Italy in 1820. A note on the flyleaf tells us that he gave it to Severn in Rome in that year. The sonnet is written on the blank page preceding *A Lover's Complaint*. We know from Severn that it was written into the Shakespeare volume by Keats aboard the *Maria Crowther* on 29 September 1820. In later life, Severn came to believe that the poem was actually composed at this time; that it was, in fact, as Monckton Milnes entitled it in 1848, Keats's 'last sonnet'. Milnes, however, knew that there was an earlier version—in a footnote to his 1848 text he quotes the last line of it. The autograph gives us, in

other words, not Keats's 'last sonnet', but the final revision of a son-
net of which we possess a copy made by Charles Armitage Brown in
1819—at any rate, he dates his copy 1819; the original which he
copied may, conceivably, have been earlier. Brown's manuscript copy
is preserved among the Crewe papers, now in Harvard. The text is as
follows:

> BRIGHT star, would I were stedfast as thou art!
>   Not in lone splendour hung aloft the night
> Not watching, with eternal lids apart,
>   Like nature's devout sleepless eremite,
> The morning waters at their priestlike task
>   Of pure ablution round earth's human shores;
> Or, gazing on the new soft fallen mask
>   Of snow upon the mountains and the moors—
> No; yet still stedfast, still unchangeable.
>   Cheek pillow'd on my love's white ripening breast,
> To touch, for ever, its warm sink and swell,
>   Awake, for ever, in a sweet unrest,
> To hear, to feel her tender-taken breath,
> Half passionless, and so swoon on to death.

In line 5, Brown's *morning* would seem to be a mere misreading
of Keats's *moving*. Brown printed his version of the sonnet in the
*Plymouth and Devonport Weekly Journal*, 27 September 1838.

These divergent texts help us to arrive at the truth about this
sonnet. The truth about it is that the octave of it (for which our
manuscripts offer substantially the same text) is good and noble, the
sestet (which is full of textual variants) is vicious and ineffective.

The Bright Star is the North Star. When he wrote the octave,
Keats had in mind, I think, Shakespeare—first and foremost,
Sonnet cxvi:

> Let me not to the marriage of true minds
> Admit impediments. Love is not love
> Which alters when it alteration finds,
> Or bends with the remover to remove:
> O, no! it is an ever fixed mark,
> That looks on tempests and is never shaken;
> It is the star to every wandering bark . . . .

With that he recalled, I fancy, from *Julius Caesar*, III. i. 60–62, these
lines:

> But I am constant as the northern star,
> Of whose true-fix'd and resting quality
> There is no fellow in the firmament. . . .

In the octave, he prays that he may be steadfast as the North Star, only in a different fashion; a fashion not lonely, distant, priestlike; far rather a fashion (we learn from the sestet) near, vivid, sensuous. In the sestet he asks only to lie on his mistress' breast, content to feel the soft rise and fall of it, to be ever awake in a sweet unrest,

> Still, still to hear her tender-taken breath,
> And so live ever or else swoon to death.

But what has the Bright Star got to do with any of it? The poet asks of the Star only steadfastness and unchangeability. But do they really matter to him? Does the Bright Star really stand for anything in which the sonnet culminates?

*p. 393*. Spenserian Stanza. These lines are interesting as being, it seems probable, the last verses which Keats ever wrote. He wrote them into a copy of Spenser which he had in constant use, which passed into the possession of Fanny Brawne. From this volume, now lost, Charles Brown seems to have made a transcript of the verses. On 4 July 1839, they were printed in the *Plymouth and Devonport Weekly Journal*, in a leader on Reform. 'We give [the stanza]', the Editor says, 'not only on account of its intrinsic merit, but hitherto it has remained unpublished; and it is the last stanza, of any kind, that (Keats) wrote before his lamented death.' The Editor, it is pretty certain, had both the stanza and the information about it from Brown. Milnes, when he printed the verses in 1848, used, no doubt, Brown's text. A comparison of two letters of Keats, 214 and 215, makes it likely that, as Buxton Forman suggests, the stanza was composed in May 1820.

*p. 398*. Cancelled Stanza of the Ode on Melancholy] This cancelled stanza was first printed in Milnes's *Life, Letters, and Literary Remains of John Keats*, 1848, i, pp. 286–7. Milnes does not say, as Buxton Forman makes him say, that it was the 'opening' stanza. But he had before him two manuscript copies of it, the one in the hand of Brown, the other in that of Woodhouse. In both these copies it appears as Stanza i of the Ode; in Brown's copy it is struck through in pencil. It is wanting in the British Museum transcript—Keats had, presumably, cancelled it before he passed the poem to his brother. But was this stanza all that he cancelled? Or was it preceded by another cancelled stanza (or more than one)? I say this because, as we have it, the stanza does not make sense. No editor says that. But no editor (or commentator) has attempted to make sense of it. What, indeed, can we make of the last three lines?—

> certes you would fail
> To find the Melancholy—whether she
> Dreameth in any isle of Lethe dull.

Can we suppose that Keats calls Melancholy, personified, 'the

Melancholy'? And does he mean that we shall fail to find whether Melancholy dreams in some dull island of Lethe? As long ago as 1939 I suggested that, in line 9, *whether* was a mere miswriting; that Keats wrote, or intended to write, *weather*. You would fail to find the melancholy weather she dreameth in any dull isle of Lethe. But who is *she*? The answer to that is lost, I think, with the loss of some stanza, or stanzas, which once preceded our cancelled stanza. *She* might, perhaps, be the Soul; or, as I suggested in 1939, Love or Youth.

This cancelled stanza presents not merely an aesthetic problem— which was what interested Milnes—but a textual problem.

A minor textual difficulty lies in line 3. There both our manuscripts have 'Stitch creeds'. Both of them offer a pencil variant, 'shrouds', for 'creeds'. Plainly, 'creeds' has the ring of unbelief. By 'shrouds' Milnes, or someone else, saves religious propriety.

*p*. 405. *Fall of Hyperion*: i. 97.

'When in mid-May . . .'] The earliest printed edition of *The Fall of Hyperion* (1856) has 'When in midday . . . '. We do not know from what manuscript it was printed. Of Keats's autograph we have only scraps (lines 1–11 and 61–86 of Book I, and lines 1–6 of Book II). We have three manuscript copies, one made by Reynolds, one by Woodhouse, the third by Woodhouse's clerk. These manuscript copies agree in offering 'When in midway . . .'. It looks as though the *midday* of 1856 were Monckton Milnes's emendation. The emendation *mid-May* is due to A. E. Housman. A great emender of Latin texts, Housman did not often use his talent for conjecture on the English poets. I am disposed to think his *mid-May* perhaps the only certain correction that has been made in the text of Keats.

*p*. 436. 'In drear-nighted December . . .'] The text here offered is that of Keats's autograph fair copy, preserved in the Library of Bristol University. But I have supplied punctuation, which in the original is wholly wanting. The existence of this autograph fair copy first became known by a paper published in 1951 by Mr. Alvin Whitley in the *Harvard Library Bulletin* (v. i, pp. 116–22). Another autograph copy, perhaps a draft, was sold by Sotheby's to Charles Law in 1876. It was shown by the purchaser to H. Buxton Forman in that year, but has not been seen since. From the notes made of it by Buxton Forman, its text would seem to have been, in essentials, that of the Bristol manuscript and of the three transcripts made by Woodhouse. The poem was first printed in the *London Literary Gazette* of 19 September 1829. It was printed in the Galignani Keats, 1829; in the 1830 *Gem* (which appeared, in fact, in 1829), and (reprinted from the *Gem*) in the *New Monthly Magazine*, 1829. All these printed texts offer, for lines 1 and 9, 'In a drear-nighted December'; and, for line 21, 'To know the change and feel it'. Most editors have preferred the 1829 printed text to the text offered by the manuscripts. In line 21 the reading of the printed texts is added as a variant in the Bristol manuscript, but in a hand certainly not that of Keats. That Keats wrote 'the feel of not to feel it' is certain. 'To know the change and feel it' is a knowing and feeling alteration. If Keats did not make it, who did? Several names have been suggested—Hood, Reynolds, Woodhouse—but only to be ruled out. Keats himself seems more likely than any of them.

Two of our transcripts, one made by J. C. Stephens, the other once in the possession of Severn, offer 'To know the change and feel it'. But both of them, it seems likely, derive from one or other of the printed texts.

The Bristol manuscript is not, as its discoverer Mr. Whitley suggests, a draft. That Keats is copying from some other written text is shown by the fifth line of the first stanza, which appears in the manuscript as 'But w The north cannot undo them'. The 'But w' is erased, but witnesses that Keats, copying, allowed his eye to stray from the fifth line of stanza 1 to the fifth line of stanza 2, 'But with a sweet forgetting'.

*p*. 441. 'Give me women . . .'] Henry Stephens, a friend of Keats, and a fellow student with him at Guy's Hospital, in a letter to G. F. Mathew (March (?) 1847) writes of these verses as follows:

'In my Syllabus of Chemical Lectures he scribbled many lines on the paper cover. This cover has been long torn off, except one small piece on which is the following fragment of Doggrel rhyme:

> Give me wine & snuff
> Until I cry out 'hold enough'
> You may do so, sans objection
> Until the day of resurrection.

This is all that remains' (Rollins, *The Keats Circle*, ii. p. 210). The 'small piece' of his Syllabus of which Stephens speaks is preserved in Trinity College, Cambridge, with the 'Dogrell' in Keats's pencilled autograph. The text offered in this volume is that of the autograph; and it is interesting to note that, in the interests, we must suppose, of propriety, Stephens has omitted the word 'women' from line 1, and has suppressed entirely the concluding couplet.

# INDEX OF FIRST LINES

*Note. The first lines ʃ plays are not indexed*

STOCKTON-BILLINGHAM LIBRARY TECHNICAL COLLEGE

MA... all...